D1216812

Free Love in Utopia

John Humphrey Noyes's emotional intensity is suggested in this photograph from about 1850. (Courtesy of Oneida Community Mansion House)

Free Love in Utopia

JOHN HUMPHREY NOYES AND THE
ORIGIN OF THE ONEIDA COMMUNITY

Compiled by George Wallingford Noyes

Edited and with an introduction
by Lawrence Foster

UNIVERSITY OF ILLINOIS PRESS

URBANA AND CHICAGO

© 2001 by the Board of Trustees
of the University of Illinois
All rights reserved
Manufactured in the United States of America

C 5 4 3 2 1

♾ This book is printed on acid-free paper.

Library of Congress Cataloging-in-Publication Data
Free love in utopia : John Humphrey Noyes and the origin
of the Oneida community / compiled by George Wallingford Noyes ;
edited and with an introduction by Lawrence Foster.
p.   cm.
Includes bibliographical references and index.
ISBN 0-252-02670-5 (cloth : alk. paper)
1. Oneida Community.
2. Noyes, John Humphrey, 1811–1886.
I. Noyes, George Wallingford.
II. Foster, Lawrence, 1947–   .
BX8795.P4F74   2001
307.77′4′0974764—dc21   2001000199

Dedicated to all who seek a more just and humane world

Contents

Illustrations follow page lvi

Introduction:
The Roots of an Extraordinary Community

LAWRENCE FOSTER

Few communal experiments in America have attracted more attention than the "free love" Oneida Community (1848–81), founded in mid-nineteenth-century New York state by the eccentric, Vermont-born genius John Humphrey Noyes. This remarkable community was a product of the turbulent decades of the 1830s and 1840s before the Civil War, when thousands of Americans joined new religious movements that rejected existing marriage and sex-role patterns in favor of alternative life-styles. New York state, where groups such as the celibate Shakers, polygamous Mormons, and free-love Oneidans were founded or active, was, like California today, a hotbed of religious and social diversity.[1]

This pre–Civil War period, like the 1960s a century later, was one of major social transition. Antebellum Americans were caught between the earlier, more traditional, colonial life-styles and the developing Victorian emphasis on an internalized sense of self-control, which would predominate by the 1850s. Although the specific patterns introduced during those pre–Civil War years may sometimes appear idiosyncratic, Americans of that period struggled with larger issues that may help us better understand ourselves and our efforts to define new, more satisfying roles for men and women today.

No social experiments from the pre–Civil War period raise such questions more starkly than the Oneida Community. Historians, sociologists, psychologists, literary scholars, and the general public alike have continued to be fascinated by Oneida's "complex marriage" system and its implications. Both Noyes and his critics have somewhat misleadingly described this system—in which all adult members considered themselves heterosexually married to the group rather than to one monogamous partner—as a form of "free love."[2] Perhaps the journalist Charles Nordhoff most colorfully characterized complex marriage as an unprecedented "combination of polygamy and polyandry with certain religious and social restraints."[3]

Most writers have been primarily preoccupied with the sexual practices and

· ix ·

arrangements at Oneida, endlessly retelling the basic and well-known outlines of how complex marriage, "male continence," "mutual criticism," and other distinctive community institutions worked in practice.[4] Rather surprisingly, one of the most intriguing and significant questions about sexuality in the Oneida Community has never been systematically explored: How could a group of capable women and men have successfully made the difficult *transition* to such an unorthodox system of communal and sexual relations?

The successful transition to a system that lasted more than thirty years at Oneida was hardly accidental. It must have required careful planning, skillful leadership, and the ability to surmount a variety of complex interpersonal problems that neither Oneidans themselves nor present-day scholars could necessarily anticipate. Although the specific details of Oneida practice may or may not have resonance for the present, the *process* of transition and the institutionalization of such an unorthodox ideological and social system raise issues of perennial concern for those seeking to understand the ways in which radical social change occurs.

Not until recently, however, did the most critical documentary key to the early development of Oneida become available. It is an approximately 2,200-page, typed transcription of original Noyes family and Oneida Community letters, diaries, documents, and excerpts from community newspapers, interspersed with connecting commentary, that was compiled by John Humphrey Noyes's nephew, George Wallingford Noyes. That manuscript had been the basis for G. W. Noyes's two published documentary collections on his uncle's early religious experience and on the Putney Community. It was also the source for Constance Noyes Robertson's important documentary analysis of the causes of the breakup of the Oneida Community.[5]

In the mid-1940s nearly a truckload of irreplaceable Oneida diaries, journals, letters, and records, comprising the vast majority of surviving Oneida documents, was burned. Since then, the George Wallingford Noyes typescript—one copy of which is now held in the Syracuse University Library in an often barely legible final carbon version—has remained the sole source preserving excerpts from many of the primary materials on early Oneida development. Finally, in early April 1993, immediately before the first scholarly conference on Oneida ever held at the Oneida Community Mansion House, all restrictions on scholarly access to the G. W. Noyes manuscript were removed.[6]

The destruction of the Oneida documents and the near-destruction of the G. W. Noyes typescript itself is a dramatic and painful story that descendants of the Oneida Community would rather not discuss with outsiders.[7] I learned some important details, however, in telephone conversations on January 5 and 9, 2001, with P. Geoffrey Noyes. He is a great grandson of John Humphrey Noyes and lived the first nine years of his life in the same house—adjacent to the Oneida Community Mansion House—that had belonged to George Wallingford Noyes.[8]

G. W. Noyes had built into his house a large, fireproof, walk-in safe where he maintained personal control over the vast majority of surviving Oneida Community documents. He was using them to prepare his typescript compilation on John Humphrey Noyes's life and communities. The original documents and G. W. Noyes's efforts to write and publish books based on them made some senior executive officers of the Oneida Community, Ltd., company very uncomfortable.

These concerns were clearly set out in a twenty-eight-page legal brief prepared for Oneida Community, Ltd., by the Syracuse law firm of Mackenzie, Smith, Lewis and Michell under the signature of B. B. Aylesworth. It was written prior to G. W. Noyes's death in 1941, although no date is indicated on the document.[9] The burden of the brief's argument is that the company held the legal rights to the Oneida documents and that if George Wallingford Noyes—who was a director of Oneida Community, Ltd. and in its employ—attempted to publish his work, which "places undue emphasis upon certain social [i.e., sexual] practices of the Community," the company would have legal grounds to stop such publication because it would "destroy or impair the good will connected with its business."[10]

The legal brief also discusses as "facts susceptible of proof" the provenance of the documents in G. W. Noyes's safe.[11] They are described as having first come into the possession of the four original trustees of the Oneida Community. When concern developed that the documents might be seized "by certain public authorities" as part of legal action against the community after John Humphrey Noyes had fled to Canada in 1879, they were conveyed to Noyes there "by the actual custodian thereof."[12] After Noyes's death in 1886, the documents passed "to his son [presumably Theodore R. Noyes] and from said son to the present custodian, George [Wallingford] Noyes."[13]

G. W. Noyes was well-aware of the threat that the documents themselves and even his own work might be destroyed. He thus made multiple copies of his own 2,200-page typescript—including a final, very faint carbon copy, the existence of which he kept secret. Following George Wallingford Noyes's death, when no figure of comparable stature and determination would protect the documents, the company eventually secured control of them. All but a handful were taken from the vault and burned in 1947.[14]

According to Mark Weimer, long-time curator of Special Collections at the Syracuse University Library, with whom I spoke on January 5, 2001, George Wallingford Noyes had deposited the copies of his typescript with key individuals and in bank vaults as far away as Toronto.[15] Apparently, all of the copies, with the exception of the two held by his own family, were eventually retrieved by the company and destroyed. One of the surviving copies, G. W. Noyes's original typescript, is currently in the possession of his granddaughter, and the other, the secret final carbon copy, is now held by the Syracuse University Library.[16]

The most important part of that massive manuscript, a document that is published here for the first time, consists of three folders comprising some 450 double-spaced typed pages that cover the earliest development of the Oneida Community from 1848 through 1854.[17] George Wallingford Noyes had prepared those materials as a third documentary collection to follow his published compilations on John Humphrey Noyes's religious experience and the Putney Community, and they were virtually ready for publication before his death in 1941.

This document presents a riveting story, along with new information that highlights the complexity of the struggles of the Oneida Perfectionists to introduce new sexual ideals and practices and make them work in a close-knit communal setting. The account will be of much interest to individuals concerned about similar issues today, as well as to students and scholars interested in fields such as American social history, women's studies, anthropology, sociology, religious studies, and psychology.

To understand the context for the remainder of this volume, one must realize that crisis was nothing new to John Humphrey Noyes and his followers at Oneida in the late 1840s and early 1850s. Indeed, crisis had been an almost constant part of Noyes's life since his conversion in February 1834 to Perfectionism, a complex set of religious beliefs emphasizing the idea that a progressive process of achieving "perfect holiness" was possible on earth. Faced with his inability to convince others of the truth of his new convictions, Noyes in May 1834 experienced three emotionally devastating weeks in New York City, during which he fluctuated from extremes of manic euphoria to depression so severe that he felt on the verge of death.[18]

Although Noyes partially recovered from this psychic distress, he found the succeeding three years exceptionally difficult as he wandered around New York state and New England, trying with little success to convert the world to his highly unorthodox belief that perfection could be realized on earth. When his first idealized love object, Abigail Merwin, deserted him to marry another man, Noyes wrote a private letter in which he advocated sexual freedom within the holy

Christian community. The unauthorized publication of that 1837 letter in a socially and religiously radical newspaper edited by Theophilous Gates and colorfully entitled *The Battle-Axe and Weapons of War* caused Noyes temporarily to
lose virtually all remaining followers. Nevertheless, during the decade that followed the publication of his "Battle-Axe Letter" Noyes rebuilt his life and following. He married the socially and financially well-connected Harriet Holton
in 1838 under provisions that the marriage would not be an exclusive one. He
published a series of newspapers defending his views. And he established a small
core group of nearly forty followers in his home town of Putney, Vermont.[19]

The Putney Community, as the group came to be known, experienced a
modest degree of success despite continuing internal and external tensions. By
the mid-1840s, the group was moving toward communism of property—and of
persons. The first recorded practice of complex marriage on a limited scale began in 1846, when John and Harriet Noyes entered into an enlargement of their
marital relations with George and Mary Cragin. The formal announcement in
1847 of the group's sexual experimentation (even though that announcement was
couched in veiled terms) outraged some members of the association and of the
town of Putney. Noyes was indicted on two specific counts of adultery, and rather
than face a possible lynching or conviction he left the state, eventually forfeiting
half of his $2,000 bond.[20]

Early in 1848, Noyes and his Putney loyalists started over again on a farm
owned by Jonathan Burt, one of his supporters in Oneida, New York. Noyes,
optimistic about the future despite the recent setbacks, also at that time wrote
his extraordinary manifesto presenting his social and sexual theories, which was
published as part of his *First Annual Report of the Oneida Association* and sent
out to leading public figures in New York and New England.[21] Despite all the
turmoil, the community at Oneida grew rapidly. By January 1849 the original
nucleus of Putney Perfectionists had expanded to 87; by February 1850, to 172;
and by February 1851, to 205.[22]

Noyes's communal experimentation at Oneida can be viewed as an attempt
to overcome the religious and social disorder that he and his followers had experienced in the rapidly changing antebellum America of their day.[23] Noyes's underlying objectives at Oneida were to achieve, first, "right relations with God,"
a common set of religious values for himself and for his followers; second, "right
relations between the sexes" that would allow men and women to live together
harmoniously; and, third, "right economic relations" that would overcome the
disruptive "dog-eat-dog" capitalism of early-nineteenth-century America. The
achievement of these three objectives in his "enlarged family" at Oneida, Noyes
argued, was a precondition for the realization of a fourth goal, the full establish-

ment of the millennium, the literal kingdom of heaven on earth, and the elimination of "disease and death."[24]

The stages leading to that final goal were not static, but progressive and ever-changing. Perfection of spirit, the correct inner attitude demanded by God, might be basically unchanging once one had achieved "salvation from sin," but the external social arrangements necessary to implement that perfection of attitude in practice were constantly changing and would continue to change, even after the establishment of the millennium.[25]

How did Noyes hope to achieve these ambitious goals? He had two chief means. The first was to spread his ideas through the newspapers he published from 1834 until 1879, and the second was to establish his ideas in practice among a community, or communities, of followers. Although the communitarian side of Noyes's experimentation has attracted the greatest attention and is emphasized in this compilation, Noyes himself always emphasized the publication of his newspapers as a means of putting his ideas before the world. As the Oneida Community declared in its *Third Annual Report* in 1851, "The publication of truth shall be our central business object . . . around which all other industrial interests shall organize."[26] Noyes's communities were thus, in his mind, chiefly important as the vehicle by which the publication of truth as he understood it was possible. In addition, however, the communities themselves were profoundly important. They provided a laboratory in which Noyes's ideals could be realized in practice and a core group of followers who directly affirmed his key role as God's chief spokesperson on earth.[27]

Because the social practices implemented at Oneida were so controversial and demanding, a word must also be said about them in order to understand the crisis in the early community. As part of his effort to reestablish a holy community of Christians on earth, Noyes argued that such a community would eliminate exclusive sexual relations. Instead, his followers would consider themselves married to the entire group in a "complex marriage" in which love, including heterosexual love among adults, could be expressed freely among the entire community.

The specific arrangements that made possible this complex marriage system were developed gradually during the decade at Putney and only began to be fully implemented in 1847, shortly before the departure for Oneida.[28] One of the most important of these practices was the use of birth control by male continence, or coitus reservatus, in which couples were allowed to come together in intercourse but the men were not supposed to ejaculate, either during or after intercourse. (Noyes vehemently rejected coitus interruptus, in which the man ejaculates after withdrawal from the woman as a waste of a man's seed and vital powers.) Also important was a form of group control by "mutual criticism," in which all, or, more commonly, a small portion of, the larger group would meet to discuss and attempt to change the beliefs or behavior of individuals seen as failing to meet community standards. An informal status hierarchy known as "ascending and descending fellowship" was the basis for the informal governance of the group based on the leadership of Noyes and his closest male and female associates.

The effort to implement these controversial new beliefs and practices caused many difficulties. That all was not well at Putney and Oneida between 1846 and 1852 is suggested by numerous exhortations in the community newspapers during those years to unquestioning obedience, unity, love, harmony, right devotion, and the like. Psychosomatic illnesses and faith cures were frequently discussed, and several cases of temporary insanity and suicidal tendencies were mentioned.[29] In 1849, about a year after the founding of the Oneida Community, Noyes—who typically tried to absent himself from conflict situations he could not handle— moved with the nucleus of his most loyal Putney followers to a small community outpost in Brooklyn, New York. He lived there for most of the time between 1849 and 1854, when John R. Miller, Noyes's brother-in-law and primary lieutenant at Oneida, died.

During those years, particularly once he formally resumed editorship of his newspaper in 1851, Noyes wrote with a surprising degree of distance from his communal ventures. In his column "Ideas from the Communes," for instance, he seemed to write with an observer's detachment about his own "Associated Communities" at Oneida, New York, Wallingford, Connecticut, Newark, New Jersey, and Cambridge and Putney, Vermont.[30]

External pressures also contributed to communal tensions. In 1850 and 1851, grand juries in Oneida and Madison counties, on whose boundaries the community was located, heard complaints about the Perfectionists from their enemies. The exemplary deportment of community members, who answered highly personal questions freely and honestly, helped defuse hostility, and influential local power figures also interceded on their behalf.[31] The success of the community in weathering this crisis was partly attributable to its circumspection in not actively seeking new members at Oneida and thereby avoiding the explosive hostilities that the vigorous search for local members at Putney had entailed.

The exigencies of successfully establishing as difficult a system as complex marriage thus necessitated a move away from Noyes's desire to convert the entire world and toward the more restricted goal of establishing a tightly knit, internally unified community. Such an order could not be established if too many new people were continually joining or leaving the community.[32]

The peak of the early difficulties over institutionalizing complex marriage and the beginning of the resolution of those problems, presented most fully in George Wallingford Noyes's document, apparently came between March and August 1852. During those six months, complex marriage was temporarily discontinued at Oneida.[33]

The obvious external reason for this abrupt change of course was an all-out crusade launched by a New York religious newspaper, *The Observer*, and supported by other newspapers. On March 7, 1852, evidently in response to this pressure, the Oneida *Circular* made the surprise announcement that despite the community's continuing commitment to complex marriage, the practice would be temporarily discontinued until public feeling moderated. By this action, the community declared, it was graphically demonstrating that it was "not attached to forms," even its own. "To be able to conform to *any* circumstances, and *any* institutions, and still preserve spiritual freedom" was the goal of the Perfectionists. The community's new efforts would be devoted to the establishment of a free press and to what must appear a most puzzling objective indeed: the "abolition of death."[34]

What is one to make of this remarkable announcement? As I argued in an earlier essay, it seems clear from a close perusal of the community's newspapers that during the nearly six months between March 7, 1852, and the triumphant announcement of the restoration of complex marriage on August 29, 1852, the practice of Oneida's unorthodox marital arrangements was, indeed, temporarily discontinued.[35] During this period, the community focused on the difficult legal challenges that threatened its existence, as described in detail for the first time in the following pages, and on overcoming the emotional and psychological problems associated with the introduction of complex marriage. Complicating these factors were leadership conflicts between John Humphrey Noyes and George Cragin, who appears to have still chafed over Noyes's continuing affection for his wife, even after her untimely death in a boating accident on July 16, 1851 (chapter 18).[36]

Only after full communal commitment to Noyes's leadership and principles had been reestablished did the Oneida Community once again joyfully announce resumption of the practice of complex marriage on August 29, 1852.[37] The community went on to function successfully for more than a quarter of century until it officially discontinued its system of complex marriage in August 1879. On January 1, 1881, the community formally came to an end when it replaced its communistic economic arrangements with a joint-stock system that eventually achieved great success through the manufacture of Oneida silverware.[38]

Let us turn now to some of the key topics and issues that the George Wallingford Noyes document raises. Ten recurrent and interconnected issues, discussed here in roughly the order that they demand readers' attention, were associated with the early development of the Oneida experiment.

Personal Loyalty to John Humphrey Noyes

The first and one of the most important themes of the document, introduced in chapter 1, "Noyes Again at the Helm," is John Humphrey Noyes's demand for his followers' full loyalty to his ideas and leadership. This "belief in Noyes's divine commission," as George Wallingford Noyes called it, was central to Noyes's efforts throughout his life.[39] As early as 1837, John Humphrey Noyes declared, "I would never connect myself with any individual or association in religion unless I were acknowledged leader."[40]

Noyes described his ideal of the Kingdom of God, which he sought to realize at Putney and Oneida, as an "absolute monarchy," with authority coming from the top yet decisions tempered by the concerns of the membership below.[41] Noyes saw himself the supreme leader who benevolently delegated authority to loyal subordinates who would implement his ideals in practice. As G. W. Noyes observed, "The dogma of Noyes's divine commission became a touchstone in the Putney and Oneida Communities. Those who rejected it were turned away; those who accepted it were bound together in a brotherhood of self-sacrificing quest for the Kingdom of God."[42]

This demand for total loyalty to his ideas and his leadership, so characteristic of certain types of charismatic leadership and genius, as described in Len Oakes's *Prophetic Charisma: The Psychology of Revolutionary Religious Personalities,* may seem quite disturbing to some readers.[43] It certainly was disturbing to some of Noyes's capable followers who eventually broke with him during the earliest years of the Oneida Community. One of those individuals, William Gould, stated bluntly:

> After the strictest observation for three weeks at Putney, I am compelled to say that his government is an exhibition of the most absolute specimen of despotism I ever saw. The members are under his control in the most absolute sense in the matters of the least as well as most consequence. I do not think they feel the least right of control over their property, persons, time,

their wives, choice, judgment, will or affections. I heard them express not a solitary opinion in his presence until they heard his first, and then all gave in the same opinion. He treats counsel with contempt, and criticism as mutiny and treason, and all such intruders are placed under the ban of the community. And although I say it with pain and regret, yet truth compels me to say that, notwithstanding the exalted opinion I have of the privileges and advantages of Association, if I can have access to them only through worse than southern slavery, then I will face isolation with all of its evil.[44]

John Humphrey Noyes's preoccupation with his own authority certainly was a dual-edged sword and helps account for the intensity of reactions for or against him and other highly creative individuals who claim to have a unique handle on truth—to speak, in effect, "for God." What is particularly interesting in Noyes's case is how deftly he was able to temper the potential extremes of such demands for authority. He also had an eye for capable people, not just yes-men and -women, and once he had their basic loyalty he could be quite flexible in giving them their heads and letting them develop divergent ways of implementing his basic ideas.

Unlike some prophets, who may eventually come to be seen by some of their followers as "going off the deep end" and, as a result, may be deposed or killed, John Humphrey Noyes was a shrewd judge of character and typically sought the broadest possible input before making major decisions. He did not claim omniscience. Like Len Oakes's "prophetic" leaders, who demand primary loyalty to a set of ideas rather than to their person, as more explicitly "charismatic" leaders often do, Noyes eventually was willing to open himself to indirect criticism when it was judiciously couched in terms of the degree to which certain actions did or did not achieve underlying community goals based on his ideals. Furthermore, much of the success of the Oneida Community during its first difficult years was not due to Noyes himself, who retreated during much of the period to Brooklyn. Instead, much of the credit for Oneida's early success was due to such individuals as Noyes's capable lieutenant John R. Miller.

Given John Humphrey Noyes's stress on control and on loyalty to his leadership, Oneida may ultimately best be understood as the lengthened shadow of this one extraordinary man, reflecting both his great strengths and weaknesses. Unlike most individuals, who simply seek to reach an accommodation with the larger world, Noyes adopted a prophetic stance, arguing that his insights provided a universally valid model for setting the world straight. Possessed by that compelling idea, and unable or unwilling to work within what he considered an unstable and inconsistent value framework, Noyes sought "to initiate, both in

himself as well as in others, a process of moral regeneration."[45] He projected both
his ego strengths and weaknesses onto the world.

Noyes was one of those individuals about whom William James wrote in
whom a "superior intellect" and a "psychopathic temperament" coalesce, thereby
"creating the best possible condition for the kind of effective genius that gets into
biographical dictionaries. Such figures do not remain mere critics and under-
standers with their intellect. Their ideas possess them, they inflict them, for better or worse, upon their companions or their age."[46]

Noyes's Perfectionist Beliefs

A second key topic essential to understanding the venture at Oneida is the nature
and implications of the complex Perfectionist religious beliefs that underlay and
justified Noyes's communal experiments. Noyes went beyond mainstream Christian belief in the second coming of Christ and the eventual establishment of a
millennium of earthly peace and harmony to argue, most fully in his 504-page
volume *The Berean: A Manual for the Help of Those Who Seek the Faith of the
Primitive Church,* that "perfect holiness" was possible, and indeed required by
God, for all true Christians on earth right *now.*[47]

According to Noyes, the Second Coming had occurred in a spiritual sense in
A.D. 70, when the temple in Jerusalem was destroyed and the great diaspora began. At that time, a primary resurrection and judgment in the spiritual world
marked the beginning of the kingdom of God in the heavens. A second and final
resurrection judgment was now approaching: "The church on earth is now rising to meet the approaching kingdom in the heavens and to become its duplicate and representative on earth."[48]

The implications that these and Noyes's other unorthodox theological ideas
had in practice were enormous. He and his followers, as God's agents, could and
must free themselves from the sinful world and live in sinless perfection on earth.
The total perfection that God demanded of all true Christians was manifested
by a right attitude and an inner sense of assurance of salvation from sin, not by
any outward works per se. "Perfection" did not mean that one was not capable
of improvement, but simply that so long as one's attitude and motivation were
right, one's acts would follow a pattern that would be acceptable to God. Like
Martin Luther and many other great Christian reformers, Noyes was inspired by
the implicit radicalism of the Apostle Paul, who believed that the spirit not the
letter of the law—faith, not works—was the chief requirement for salvation.

In this context, Noyes argued that in trying to reestablish the faith of early

Christianity, "the primitive Christian church," he was not slavishly copying the specific practices of early Christians but trying to apply their underlying principles in his own time. The most controversial area to which Noyes applied those principles was sexual relations. He came to believe that if one had the right attitude, sexual relations, like other activities in life, would be expressed in an outward manner that would be pleasing to God. As he put it, "The outward act of sexual connection is as innocent and comely as any other act, or rather if there is any difference in the character of outward acts, . . . this is the most innocent and comely of all. . . . God tells me that he does not care so much what I do as how I do it."[49]

Such beliefs in sexual "anti-legality" could easily be misconstrued and misused, as Noyes discovered during the 1830s in dealing with other Perfectionists who now might appear analogous to the countercultural rebels of the late 1960s. It was all too easy for emotionally unstable individuals to equate legitimate freedom from external law or outmoded older standards as a license to engage in antinomian behavior, seeing themselves as free to act as they chose because God's will and their own were identical. Throughout his life, Noyes struggled to contain such extreme egotism, both in himself and his followers. At Putney and at Oneida, he sought to institutionalize a communal sense of "salvation from sin" in which freedom from legalistic adherence to specific forms of behavior would nevertheless be tempered by total submission to the will of God—of which Noyes considered himself the ultimate arbiter on earth. That effort raises larger issues for those concerned about how a balance between the individual and the community, freedom and structure, can be achieved in society.

Noyes's Sexual Control over the Community

Noyes's demand for leadership primacy and his Perfectionist beliefs were closely related to a third issue: the unorthodox sexual practices of the community. That issue is central to understanding the entire document that follows. It is most fully addressed in Noyes's "Bible Argument" in the *First Annual Report of the Oneida Association* and in chapter 33.

As part of the effort to overcome human "selfishness" by full submission to the will of God (and to himself as God's agent on earth), Noyes argued that, among fully faithful Christians, selfish, exclusive marital ties would be replaced by a "complex marriage" in which all adult believers could love each other fully and have the possibility of heterosexual relations with each other. Noyes wanted all believers to be unified and to share a perfect community of interests, to replace the "I-spirit" with the "we-spirit." If believers were fully to love each other while living in close communal association, they must be allowed to love each other fervently and physically, "not by pairs, as in the world, but *en masse.*" The necessary restrictions of the earthly period, governed by arbitrary human law, would eventually have to give way to the final heavenly free state. A perfect unity in all respects would result. Each should be married to all—heart, mind, and body—in a complex marriage.[50]

The catch was just how these "free" sexual relations were to be regulated. Here, just as in his demand for loyalty to his leadership and to his Perfectionist religious beliefs, John Humphrey Noyes was the ultimate referee. His demand for ultimate control over their sexual lives was perhaps his followers' most significant test of total loyalty, and it caused many disciples who otherwise were in accord with his Perfectionist religious principles to break away (chapter 1). As he remembered, "During the first days of my residence at Oneida, our social [sexual] theory was the subject of open and violent discussion between myself, Burt and others on one side and all the leading Perfectionists who deserted us on the other."[51]

Even those who stayed did not move immediately toward complete "communism of love." Many initial converts to Oneida, indeed, had not been previously aware of the unorthodox sexual practices there but had been attracted primarily by Noyes's religious beliefs. For example, John R. Miller apparently did not fully subscribe to the community's social theory at first.[52] After the publication in early 1849 of the *First Annual Report of the Oneida Association*—with its detailed "Bible Argument; Defining the Relations Between the Sexes in the Kingdom of Heaven"—the sexual platform was clear for all to see.[53] Even then, however, the move toward complete abolition of sexual exclusiveness did not occur immediately.

Noyes commented on August 30, 1849, "If a man comes into this Association with a wife that he has to watch and reserve from others, he has brought a cask of powder into a blacksmith's shop."[54] Rather than see the sparks cause the cask to explode, Noyes worked gradually to reeducate his followers, maintaining private marriage at first as a matter of expedience until individual exclusiveness could be voluntarily and completely broken down under proper oversight.

In addition to gradually extending his own sexual prerogatives, Noyes gradually allowed greater freedom to followers whom he thought ready for it. On June 11, 1849, a letter from Mary Cragin to her husband George, for instance, reports Noyes's suggestion that "if Mr. Bradley is in a good state . . . , he have liberty with Ellen and Philena if he wishes it. Sarah (Bradley) will no doubt be pleased to help her husband fellowship with others. . . . Also hint to those girls that they exercise some conservatism, and not allow themselves to be made too free with by all sorts."[55]

Noyes also withheld authorization for sexual relations, as Mary Cragin, in that same letter to her husband, delicately notes: "With regard to the state of things between you and me, I am well satisfied. God has our hearts in his power, and I have no complaint to make of his administration. When he thinks best he will give me that attraction which you desire; and until he does think best, as there is some excellent reason for withholding it, let us say, 'Thy will be done.'"[56]

Control over sexual freedom by means of "ascending fellowship," in which Noyes and those he authorized supervised and exercised their prerogatives with those deemed as being of lesser "spirituality," was critically important if the whole system was to be kept from degenerating into random licentiousness that would splinter the community into a thousand fragments.[57] Noyes continually stressed the necessity of absolute candor, or what he called "sincerity," in sexual discussion in the community. Although the detailed discussion of many of these sexual issues is not highlighted until later in this volume, the complex sexual undercurrents had an impact on other, more public, aspects of community life during the late 1840s and early 1850s.

A retrospective assessment that sheds great light on the dynamics of the sexual system at Oneida is found in a remarkable letter dated April 15, 1892, which Noyes's son Theodore wrote (but never sent) to a young medical student, Anita Newcomb McGee. In that letter, Theodore Noyes indicated that the power to regulate or withdraw sexual privileges, "inherent in the community at large and by common consent delegated to father and his subordinates, constituted by far the most effectual means of government."

> Father possessed in a remarkable degree the faculty of convincing people that the use of this arbitrary power was exercised for their own good, and for many years there was very little dissatisfaction and no envy of his prerogative. . . .
>
> But now to come closer, and take the bull fairly by the horns. In a society like the Community, the young and attractive women form the focus toward which all the social rays converge; and the arbiter to be truly one, must possess the confidence and to a certain extent the obedience of this circle of attractions and moreover, he must exercise his power by genuine sexual attraction to a large extent. To quite a late period father filled this situation perfectly. He was a man of quite extraordinary attractiveness to women, and he dominated them by his intellectual power and social "magnetism" superadded to intense religious convictions to which young women are very susceptible. The circle of young women he trained when he was between forty and fifty years of age, were by a large majority his devoted friends throughout the trouble which led to the dissolution [of the Oneida Community between 1879 and 1881].

... I must suppose that as he grew older he lost some of his attractiveness, and I know that he delegated the function [of initiating young women into sexual intercourse] to younger men in several cases, but you can see that this matter was of prime importance in the question of successorship and that the lack of a suitable successor obliged him to continue as the social center longer than would have otherwise been the case and so gave more occasion for dissatisfaction.[58]

Thus it is clear that Oneida throughout its existence was not only the lengthened shadow of John Humphrey Noyes in its intellectual and organizational aspects but also in the way it integrated sexual relations as a means of tightly linking the community together in the pursuit of a comprehensive set of religious and social goals. During the early years of the community, however, efforts to establish John Humphrey Noyes's sexual as well as intellectual and organizational primacy led to much tension within the group and, indirectly, with the outside world. Although the community was able to deal successfully with such tensions, many other new religious and communal groups have not been able to surmount such problems.

Early Legal Challenges to the Community

A fourth issue is introduced in chapter 2, "Settlement of the Putney Lawsuits," and reaches its climax in chapters 16, 23, 24, 27, and 28, which deal with the opposition of the Hubbard family. That issue was the continuing legal threat to the community's existence throughout the early years.

As Oneida was getting started, the numerous Putney lawsuits could easily have scuttled the efforts to set up a new community. Noyes had been arrested on October 26, 1847, on two specific charges of adultery, based on frank conversations with supporters or would-be supporters who subsequently defected. Released on $2,000 bond, he left the state a month later, ostensibly to avoid the possibility of a lynching. The bond forfeiture case was handled by Larkin Mead, Noyes's brother-in-law and a respected local lawyer, who defended the association despite his discomfort at their practices. Numerous other nuisance cases were also lodged, largely relating to young women such as the fifteen-year-old Lucinda Lamb, who, to the dismay of her parents, had been attracted to the group.

What is most interesting about these lawsuits and the later, more dangerous Hubbard suits at Oneida, was how skillfully they were handled. John R. Miller and other members of the community used every bit of persuasive ability they could muster, drawing upon the generally positive business and personal relationship of the Noyes family and their Putney followers with the townspeople. Compromise and conciliation were important, especially in nuisance cases that had little merit. As Noyes put it, "Our policy is to give the enemy a bridge of money, over which to make a decent retreat."[59] Even the $2,000 bond itself was only half forfeited after a case was made that money would come not directly from Noyes but from the trust fund he had set up for his family and from less controversial followers like John R. Miller, whose store would suffer bankruptcy if he were forced to pay the amount.

Noyes's prominent and well-connected family, even those members who thoroughly disapproved of his sexual theories and behavior, put family ties above other considerations. Influential local leaders also helped the association weather the storm. The tenuousness of its survival at Oneida in the face of ever-present challenges from outsiders or disaffected members must always be kept in mind. Opposition continued toward Noyes's supporters who remained in Putney, for example, and such opposition flared periodically (chapters 10 and 25).

Closely connected with the legal challenges at Putney and Oneida was the issue of how the community should deal with disaffected or mentally ill members and with seceders. Unless such individuals could be handled effectively, their disaffection might provide grist for other, more dangerous external attacks on the community. The most severe of such challenges came at the start of the Oneida Community, when numerous otherwise supportive individuals were unwilling to accept Noyes's full leadership and his controversial sexual ideas and practices (chapters 1 and 4). Equally revealing conflict erupted with the excommunication of Otis Miller (chapter 6), a case that was eventually resolved when Miller was reinstated after fully submitting to John Humphrey Noyes's authority.

Also problematic were cases such as the temporarily erratic behavior of Jonathan Burt (chapter 7). Burt was a key member whose farm served as the nucleus for the new Oneida Community. A conflict that led to a full secession was that of Francis Hyde, who left and subsequently barraged the community with demands (chapter 12). Eventually, he ceased harassing Oneida after being allowed to extract his ambivalent wife, Julia Dunn. Handled with less skill and tact, these or other internal and external tensions might have contributed to an early breakup of the community, as in so many other new religious and communal groups.

Daily Life in the Oneida Community

Some of the most interesting chapters in this volume focus on the structure of life in the community. Chapter 3 details the initial setting up of the community, including terms of admission. The comprehensive goals of the association, integrating religious, political, social, and physical life under a system based on "inspiration" rather than formal written compact, are stressed. Those joining the association were expected to surrender all their property, which would normally be returned (without interest or wages) in the event of withdrawal. A regular plan for the meetings each evening was set up, and arrangements were made for small groups of about twelve each to meet and engage in "mutual criticism."

Chapter 9 explains how children were reared communally in the "Children's House." Emphasis is placed on the greater difficulties encountered at both ends of the age spectrum. The problem with infants and very young children was to convince their parents to relinquish their "philoprogenitive" involvement sufficiently that the children could be reared communally under the principle "that children cease to be private property and become the property of the Association; and the true way to manage them is, as soon as nature allows, to place them under a system of general control."[60] Getting older boys and girls to accept the group's principles, including its sexual system, was very difficult. A particularly striking account describes the community's campaign against the selfishness expressed by the "doll spirit" (the children's attachment to dolls) and the decision of the eight- and nine-year-olds at Brooklyn to burn their dolls in response.[61]

Chapters 8, 31, and 37 focus on the industrial and financial life of the community. Chapter 8 describes the early dependence on the money brought in by converts and details efforts to become self-sufficient by various methods, including peddling community-produced products such as rustic seats. Noyes, however, emphasized that establishing the right spiritual basis for the community always took precedence over success in business ventures per se. Chapter 31 details the diverse and increasingly successful businesses of the community, most notably the animal traps invented by community member Sewall Newhouse. Demand for the traps developed rapidly during the early 1850s, and they were widely used across the United States and Canada. Their sale eventually provided the economic backbone for the community for more than a quarter of a century. Chapter 37, written by George Wallingford Noyes, provides a brief summary of the community's economic enterprises and how they developed.

Chapter 17 describes the burning of the Oneida printing office and store on July 5, 1851. The whole episode was curious. Almost all important items in the printing office and store were salvaged from the building, no subsequent effort was made to find out how the fire started, and Noyes seemed almost to welcome the episode. In an informal Home-Talk on July 7, he noted that the burning appeared to be a "criticism from God," directing the community to go along with plans he had laid out the very morning of the fire to move the group's printing operations from Oneida to Brooklyn. As he put it, "I have felt that inspiration was lacking in the editorial department, and only this morning had blocked out a plan for a change; yet I felt that what we really needed was a breathing-spell, that we might have time to fix our course anew. That is now done. We have a reasonable excuse for stopping the publication of the paper. I have no thought but that we shall begin again. . . . This event will naturally operate as an appeal to our friends and open their hearts and purses."[62] Under the circumstances, one can't help wondering whether the fire might have occurred with Noyes's connivance.

A discussion of how the community gradually eliminated the use of tobacco, as well as tea, coffee, and other stimulants, is presented in chapters 34 and 35. Before 1853, more than half the men in the Oneida Community smoked or chewed tobacco. In a carefully orchestrated campaign during the course of some six months in 1853, the entire community was gradually weaned from its "tobacco slavery," not by direct, legalistic suppression but by several well-organized campaigns to encourage voluntary reduction and then the complete elimination of tobacco use. Another gradual campaign that lasted nearly two years led to the elimination of coffee or tea drinking in the Brooklyn and Oneida communities. Both campaigns show how skillfully the community was able to use voluntary methods, in conjunction with subtle group pressure, to change the behavior of its members permanently. Oneida's efforts suggest insights that may be useful in handling similar problems today.

Noyes's Relationship with Mary Cragin

Some of the most striking new information presented in this volume relates to Noyes's relationship with Mary Cragin and how it may have influenced the development of Oneida's sexual system. Although the Noyes-Cragin relationship receives attention throughout the text, the full force of Noyes's passionate attraction to, and idealization of, Mary Cragin became most apparent after her death. His struggle to make sense of what he took as a crushing personal loss was associated with more than a year of subsequent instability in his community, which receives special attention in chapters 19, 20, and 22.

George Wallingford Noyes notes that following Mary Cragin's death, his uncle commented in a Home-Talk on July 27: "In the flesh the tendency of Mrs. Cragin's position has been to produce chafing between you [Mr. Cragin] and me and Mr. Smith; but now that she has passed into the spiritual world I can see how her position may be the occasion of a splendid condensation."[63] "Mrs. Cragin's death will lead me to overcome death just as Abigail Merwin's marriage stimulated me to break up the marriage system."[64] An August 1 entry in the *Oneida*

Journal notes, "Someone asked who was to fill Mrs. Cragin's place. John replied he did not know as God wanted it filled."[65] A week later, on August 8, Noyes remarked, using extravagant rhetoric, "This is a woman's dispensation, and I am thinking it possible that Mrs. Cragin's death is in this dispensation what the death of Christ was in the Jewish dispensation. Her death was more befitting a woman, and Christ's was more befitting a man."[66]

Additional effusions were presented in Noyes's Home-Talk on September 4, when he asserted, "It is well understood that God has raised me up to take the lead. But the point which has hung in suspense even in my own mind has been, who is the female correspondent?"[67] Previously he had thought that person was Abigail Merwin; now it was clear that it was Mary Cragin. Noyes continued:

> The female heads of the Primitive Church were all Marys, Mary the mother
> of Jesus, Mary Magdalene, and Mary whom Jesus loved. . . . [T]he thoughts
> I have had about Abigail Merwin have been and are being fulfilled in Mrs.
> Cragin. . . . The man and woman have come together, and the kingdom of
> heaven has commenced. . . . There was this difference between Abigail Merwin and Mrs. Cragin. Abigail Merwin drew my heart out but did not respond
> to it. Mrs. Cragin drew it out with equal if not greater power, and responded
> to it not only with love but union.[68]

And in a Home-Talk on September 7, Noyes "confessed before heaven and earth, that there was no other woman whom I loved as I did her."[69]

Previous scholarship has noted the key role that Mary Cragin played in the introduction and early development of John Humphrey Noyes's unorthodox marital theory and practice.[70] George Wallingford Noyes, however, highlights this factor more than previous analyses, vividly emphasizing the extent to which Oneida's unorthodox sexual system may have been influenced by Noyes's personal relationships with Mary Cragin and the other women in his life.[71] Chapter 13, for example, describes Noyes's continuing attraction to his first convert, Abigail Merwin, and his extraordinary efforts, via intermediaries that included Mary Cragin in 1851 (shortly before her death), to influence the now-widowed Merwin to join him at Oneida. Had Abigail Merwin married him, Noyes commented, he probably would never have had the motivation to develop his unorthodox sexual theories and practice.[72] Even more striking, the discussion of the Noyes-Cragin relationship throughout the following text strongly suggests that the development of the Oneida Community might well have been very different if Mary Cragin had lived beyond 1851.[73] This Oneida example provides a telling illustration of how seemingly idiosyncratic personal factors can sometimes influence larger social experimentation.

The Hubbard Suits

A disturbing case of personal misconduct associated with an attempt to deal with mental illness at Oneida came close to causing the community to disband in 1852. It is described for the first time in detail in this volume, especially in chapters 16, 23, and 27. The case was precipitated by a series of severe whippings by community member Henry Seymour of his mentally ill wife Tryphena. She had begun acting strangely—"crying nights, wandering about, frightening the children, and talking incoherently."[74] In response to the whippings, which had been intended to stop her behavior, an indictment on "assault and battery" charges was lodged in Utica on September 27, 1851, prompted by Tryphena's father, Noahdiah Hubbard.[75]

That indictment forced nine community members to go to Utica to testify on October 7. On November 4, Noyes cautioned the community: "Our system of criticism has generated more or less sharpness and severity of spirit which has precluded the softness and gentleness of Christ."[76] The case itself was settled on November 26, with the community agreeing to pay Tryphena's expenses at an asylum, and, after her release, $125 per year if she were well and $200 if she remained "unsound in body or mind."[77]

The Utica suit and attendant publicity probably contributed to a sharp editorial attack on January 22, 1852, in the *New York Observer* (chapter 24).[78] It made an extended—and unfavorable—comparison of Oneida sexual practices with those of the polygamous Mormons. In a Home-Talk on February 28, 1852, Noyes observed, "It is quite possible that the agitation which *The New York Observer* has stirred up may compel the authorities to prosecute the indictment."[79] In response, Noyes proposed what he called a "coup d'etat": The group would make temporary strategic concessions on its sexual arrangements while keeping all other valuable elements of the community intact.[80]

Despite the out-of-court settlement of the Hubbard case in November 1851 and the community's public commitment in March 1852 to discontinue complex marriage for the time-being, attacks had picked up again by April of that year. That was when the Hubbards began threatening to take to court ten other proposed indictments against the community.[81] In attempting to defuse the tension, Noyes told local critics that he would do everything in his power to honorably satisfy them and the authorities of the county—including, if necessary, dispersing and disbanding his community at Oneida.[82] As he reasoned, "I am satisfied that our true policy is to avoid a trial, as we did at Putney, by paying whatever is necessary. . . . A trial, if public and reported in the newspapers, converts a local difficulty into a general scandal. We are dealing with the enemy on the field of public opinion, and our hope is that we shall finally overcome prejudice by common sense, sound reasoning and good behavior."[83]

As part of their public relations campaign, the Oneidans invited eighty surrounding families, including the Hubbards, to a highly successful strawberries-and-cream party and open house attended by more than three hundred neighbors. After that gathering, the community offered to buy out the Hubbards by paying them $150 in mid-July on receipt of a certificate from Noahdiah Hubbard "honorably discharging them [the community] from further claims and expressing his wish that the indictments be dropped." There would be $150 more "if by that certificate and other influences which he and his family can command, those indictments shall be stopped so that we shall have no further trouble."[84] As Noyes observed, "It seems to me that the likeliest way to quash those indictments is to set the Hubbards to work as our attorneys, and pay them well for it."[85] Although the Hubbards ultimately extracted $350 from the community, the strategy proved successful. The group's major critics enthusiastically endorsed the Hubbard statement exonerating the community. One even declared, "The people in this vicinity will not consent to have you disperse."[86]

Tryphena Seymour eventually recovered and returned to the community and to her husband, by whom she had a child and with whom she lived until her death at age forty-nine in 1877.[87] Henry Seymour became one of the most influential and respected members of the Oneida Community, noted especially for his remarkable horticultural skills. After the breakup of the community, Seymour was one of the loyalists who followed John Humphrey Noyes to Canada, where he lived until his own death at age eighty in 1906.[88]

The Tryphena and Henry Seymour case suggests a host of issues that deserve further investigation. Just as Noyes's idiosyncratic relationship with Mary Cragin may have had a significant impact on the way in which complex marriage eventually developed, so the Tryphena Seymour assault-and-battery case suggests how factors that may have been exacerbated by the sexual arrangements of the community could have contributed to its overall tensions, internally and externally. For example, evidence in the manuscript suggests that part of Tryphena's instability may have been associated with her difficulties in accepting and adapting to Oneida complex marriage, to which she had initially been strongly opposed.[89] Moreover, the use of severe punishments such as whipping suggests that excesses may have occurred in other, less publicized cases, as well.[90]

What is most impressive about this case, however, is that the community learned rapidly from its mistakes.[91] By the mid-1850s, the excesses of the transition phase had been largely overcome, allowing for a further quarter century of successful communal living in what one community member described as "a home the like of which has not been seen since the world began."[92]

Internal Tensions and the Temporary Discontinuance of Complex Marriage in 1852

George Wallingford Noyes emphasizes the external tensions associated with the Hubbard suits as the primary factor in the tensions at Oneida that led to the temporary discontinuance of complex marriage between March and August 1852. However, other internal tensions within the community—no doubt further exacerbated by the external attacks—also appear to have contributed significantly to the crisis. In an editorial expansion of G. W. Noyes's document, I have added excerpts from the community's newspaper that highlight the internal tensions of 1852 (chapter 26). Other revealing insights into these factors are emphasized in chapter 36, "Wrestlings with Disease and Death."

A key to the internal tensions associated with the temporary discontinuance of complex marriage in 1852 is John Humphrey Noyes's enigmatic observation in the March 7 manifesto that for a time the primary efforts of the community would be devoted to "the abolition of death" rather than to marriage reform. A later article reasserts this primary concern, clearly indicating that "death" was being used in a special sense: If this attack on "death" might appear to be madness, there is a method to it.[93] In fact, when Noyes writes of trying to "abolish death," he usually is referring to his efforts to overcome sickness and ill-health, especially mental and emotional disorders. Such psychologically related ailments are the first that must be eliminated if the "King of Terrors" is eventually to lose his hold over the mind and spirit of humanity.[94]

Thus what Noyes may be saying, in coded language understood by his followers but not the outside world, is that for a time the community's severe mental and emotional problems (many of them associated with the introduction of complex marriage) were to be the primary focus of the group. This interpretation is supported by the numerous articles during this period on topics such as nervousness, faith and unbelief, insanity, spiritualist excesses, inattention, the uselessness of self-condemnation, problems of insubordination, and the like. The Oneida Community may have been deliberately retrenching, performing an internal and external penance that would prepare a solid foundation for a second and successful reintroduction of the practice of complex marriage later.

Noyes also appears to have been faced with serious problems of insubordination and even potential apostasy during this period. The difficulty of "bridling sensuality" and placing such drives at the service of the larger purposes of the community is discussed in numerous articles. Noyes himself did not always appear to be contributing to the solution of such problems when he wrote in enthusiastic terms of God being "married to matter" and the like.[95] A concrete threat of outright apostasy was highlighted in late March and early April 1852, when two articles appeared on Judas Iscariot, who "was not merely an unprincipled traitor, but a positive rival to Christ."[96] The articles make clear that a high community member was seen as playing the role of Judas.

In those articles, the community's Judas is portrayed as one whose sin is "covetousness"—not just of money but of affection. His character is contrasted with that of the Mary who impulsively anointed Christ with expensive ointment. This Mary, and her community counterpart, "had little worldly prudence. Her love exceeded her discretion. She was found at Jesus' feet, absorbed in his discoursing," abandoned "to the attractions of her heart—a dangerous susceptibility in the case of misplaced affections, but her glory as a follower of Christ. This led her, at the loss of dignity, into that wonderful gratitude and love, which Christ promised should be recorded of her as a memorial of praise of all generations" (chapter 26). But Judas, with his base, uncomprehending heart, could not appreciate Mary's "tribute of affection" and so betrayed Christ to the public authorities for a paltry thirty pieces of silver.[97]

There can be little doubt as to which community members were obliquely being discussed in these articles. Almost certainly, George Cragin, a member of the central committee and one of Noyes's earliest and closest followers, stood in the place of Judas; his wife, Mary Cragin, who first inspired Noyes in 1846 to begin the actual practice of complex marriage, was represented as the wayward Mary, whose devotion to Christ brought her everlasting glory; and, of course, John Humphrey Noyes, God's special representative, served symbolically as Christ.[98]

Noyes's relationship with Mary Cragin had always had strong overtones of idolatry, the sort of selfish "special love" that he so strongly discouraged in his followers. It must have been galling to George Cragin to be, for all intents and purposes, supplanted by Noyes in his wife's affections, especially when both the Noyeses and Cragins were living together in Brooklyn between 1849 and 1851. After Mary Cragin died in July 1851, Noyes proved almost inconsolable. For more than a year, nearly every issue of *The Circular* contained fulsome tributes to her character, examples of her writing, and the like. In 1853 *Bible Communism*, the final important summation of Noyes's sexual and marriage theories, would be dedicated obliquely to her memory: "To Mary of Nazareth, the blessed of all generations, who so beautifully yielded to the will of heaven, though it contravened the fashion of this world, and, at the hazard of her good name and of all earthly affections and interests, became the mother of Christ, and so the mother of Christianity, this work is respectfully and loyally dedicated."[99]

The recognition that Noyes continued to be emotionally involved with Mary Cragin even after her death must certainly have disturbed George Cragin. Tensions were also clearly present between the small, relatively comfortable, elite Brooklyn group that printed the newspaper and the larger group of struggling Perfectionists at Oneida that provided their financial support. That Noyes apparently slipped his emotional moorings after Mary Cragin died did little to maintain community confidence in him or his ideas. In addition, he was extremely sensitive to external conditions and needed to validate the truth of his own ideas by seeing them accepted by his followers. Thus, his emotional instability at this time probably reflected both the internal and external tensions that he and his followers faced.

In an attempt to overcome these personal and internal communal conflicts, Noyes launched a wholehearted effort to reestablish common values among his following. His newspaper printed repeated exhortations to unity and also systematically reprinted articles from the mid-1840s that had originally been written to prepare the minds of his supporters for closer communal living and complex marriage at Putney. Individual and communal purification were stressed as part of a larger effort to achieve God's objectives on earth.

These and other measures apparently proved effective. The final Hubbard suit was terminated on July 27. On August 1, an article by George Cragin reaffirmed his total submission to God's will (as mediated through Noyes).[100] In the next issue, an article on "The Character of Peter" noted that although Peter's denial of Christ might appear culpable, Peter had nevertheless come back to become Christ's "devoted follower."[101] Throughout August, a new optimism was evident in the newspaper. The tone rose to a radiant crescendo in the August issue with articles such "The Resurrection King," "The Light Shineth in the Darkness," and "The Heart Satisfied." Most important, that issue contained Noyes's "Theocratic Platform" (reproduced in full in chapter 29), which announced to the world the reestablishment of complex marriage and close communal life at Oneida. Among the planks of the platform were "abandonment of the entire fashion of this world—especially marriage and involuntary propagation"; "cultivation of free love"; and "dwelling together in association or complex families."[102]

Supervising the Practice of Complex Marriage

Although materials relating to the difficulties of setting up complex marriage at Oneida are found throughout the G. W. Noyes volume (the issue surfaced in a variety of different contexts), the most concentrated discussion is presented in chapter 33, "The Administration of Complex Marriage," which contains much new information on Noyes's sexual control over the lives of his followers.

Among the most intriguing discussions are those dealing with "the wishes of the unmarried young men," who had difficulty becoming part of the sexual system at Oneida.[103] That is hardly surprising, given the community's extraordinary method of birth control through male continence. Under that system, men and women were supposed to come together in sexual intercourse without the men ever ejaculating, either during or after intercourse.[104]

Noyes argued that this system—which obviously required substantial male self-control, especially for young men without prior sexual experience—allowed the sexes to communicate and express deep affection without degenerating into baser physical actions, except when progeny were desired.[105] Elsewhere, he delicately described the technique by using an analogy:

> The situation may be compared to a stream in three conditions, viz., 1, a fall, 2, a course of rapids above the fall, and 3, still water above the rapids. The skillful boatman may choose whether he will remain in the still water, or venture more or less down the rapids, or run his boat over the fall. But there is a point on the verge of the fall where he has no control over his course; and just above that there is a point where he will have to struggle with the current in a way which will give his nerves a severe trial, even though he may escape the fall. If he is willing to learn, experience will teach him the wisdom of confining his excursions to the region of easy rowing, unless he has an object in view that is worth the cost of going over the falls.[106]

As John Humphrey Noyes observed, "The transition of the young men from the hot blood of virginity to the quiet freedom which is the essential element of our Society is emphatically the difficult pass in our social experience."[107]

> Experience has shown that the usual "sale and delivery" of the woman to the man through marriage is highly objectionable. We have distressing examples of the effect of initiating young men. The spiritual collapse of Julia Hyde and Sarah Dunn, perhaps also of Sarah Campbell, Mrs. Worden and Louisa Waters may be mentioned. . . . The weaker party needs protection from the untamed lion; and if the amativeness of the young men is not civilized enough to be safely trusted, the Association is bound to protect the young women. . . .
>
> On the other hand the plan proposed last fall of introducing the young men to the freedom of the Association through the more spiritual women has been attended with difficulties. Mrs. Cragin lost her equilibrium in the attempt to carry it out, and there appears to have been an unhealthy ex-

citement in Perkins and perhaps others, which has ended in grudging discontent.[108]

Tensions also resulted among some of the adult men. A detailed discussion was made, for instance, of the case of William H. Perry, who was accused of "sensual self-seeking and concealment," including hiding evidence of venereal disease, in his overly free relations with community women.[109] Eventually, those suffering from what Noyes called "the rooster spirit" and unwilling to conform to community standards, as supervised by Noyes and public mutual criticism sessions, were expelled from the association.[110]

The community in the early 1850s appears to have responded to internal criticism of tendencies toward "licentiousness" by becoming passive sexually. As Noyes put matters in a Home-Talk on "Fear of Criticism" on June 23, 1851, "I find myself in a state of simplicity and freedom, and I act it out from time to time, but there is little response. The work of breaking through the barriers to fellowship is left to me. But unless others take hold with me the barriers are not permanently removed. The Association generally seems to have betaken itself to the passive virtues. They have ceased to do evil, and have become very dutiful and obedient. But 'cease to do evil, learn to do well' is the order of God."[111]

This type of problem does not appear to have been resolved until after the resumption of complex marriage in the late summer and early fall of 1852. On December 28, 1852, in a letter to George Cragin, John R. Miller reflected, "I think I can say with Mr. Noyes, that exclusive love with me is a thing gone by. Two years ago we were obliged to act with constant reference to exclusiveness. We had to have our watch constantly on duty to prevent our social building from being burned up by the fires of jealousy. It was the great labor of the Association. Now it is not thought of, except in the case of new members. It never enters our heads that we can offend anyone by the expression of love. This is truly one of the 'greater miracles.'"[112]

The Role of John R. Miller

Although popular writings tend to highlight the significance of charismatic founders of new religious and social movements, the key to the success or failure of such movements often depends on capable behind-the-scenes managers who are able to implement the prophet's vision. In this context, the pivotal role of John R. Miller in the early survival and success of the Oneida Community is one of the most striking revelations of G. W. Noyes's document. Without the guidance of Miller, or someone else with his abilities, the Oneida Community would never have survived its first five years.

Miller, who had joined the Putney Community in 1841 and married Noyes's sister Charlotte, was a talented individual with remarkable business and political acumen. Initially, he played a vital role in the difficult forced move from Putney to Oneida in 1847–48. From 1849, when John Humphrey Noyes and his entourage moved to Brooklyn, until Miller's own early death in 1854 at age forty, he was the key administrative head and point man for everything that went on at Oneida. In particular, he personally handled the difficult Putney lawsuits that could easily have destroyed the Oneida Community (chapters 2 and 10). The high local regard for Miller and his store in Putney was critically important in allowing him to use both formal and informal means to resolve those potentially devastating suits.

At Oneida itself, Miller gave even-handed guidance and was especially important in helping to place the community on a sound financial basis within its first five years. He did so by supervising the production and skillful marketing of community-produced products, notably the Newhouse animal traps. Miller also bore the full brunt of handling the difficult Hubbard suits and harassment that brought the Oneida Community to the verge of formal disbandment in 1852. And although he appears to have had personal reservations about the community's social (i.e., sexual) system, Miller loyally supported Noyes and by the end of 1852 had played a key role in getting that system established at Oneida, where it would continue for nearly thirty more years.

Appropriately, it was Miller's untimely death on June 16, 1854, that brings to an end George Wallingford Noyes's document and its discussion of the early development of the Oneida Community. Exactly why Miller died remains unclear, because there was no visible external disease but rather a gradual wasting away. His death may have been caused by a number of factors, including the extraordinarily high stress he faced, his underlying nervous temperament, and the way he worked himself so hard—not to mention his heavy smoking, which may have led to cancer or to some similar ailment. In any event, his death was the occasion for a major retrenchment and restructuring of Noyes's communal efforts after 1854, which reduced them from a half-dozen groups scattered throughout New York and New England to two primary communities at Oneida, New York, and Wallingford, Connecticut. Those interested in the complex interaction between prophetic leaders and pragmatic administrators in the success of new religious or social movements may find the case of John R. Miller and his relationship to John Humphrey Noyes instructive.

The approximately 450 pages of George Wallingford Noyes's typescript that cover the development of the Oneida Community from 1848 through 1854 are an editor's dream. After a bit of name overload in the first two chapters, with many brief references to individuals and events in Noyes's earlier life that are likely to be familiar only to specialists, the remainder of the document reads almost like a novel. I thus have chosen to do minimal in-text editing. Lengthy editorial matter inserted by G. W. Noyes or myself is indented from the main documentary text to set it apart, followed by our bracketed initials: G.W.N. or L.F. Less lengthy editorial matter is given in footnotes, also followed by our bracketed initials. Brief bracketed references within the text itself are my insertions. Parenthetical insertions and ellipses within the original documents are G. W. Noyes's.

Obvious typographical errors, including letter transpositions, undoubted misspellings, and some other small mistakes, have been quietly corrected in both the text and appendix, without highlighting them by using the intrusive *sic.* In cases where the intended word choice is unclear, I have printed the document exactly as originally written, with a bracketed indication of the word I think was probably meant and a question mark. An occasional omitted word—for example a missing "the"—is also enclosed in brackets. I have left in the text throughout, and without comment, divergent spelling or hyphenation of some words, including "to-day" or "today" and "to-night" or "tonight"—as well as some British spellings of words whose orthography is now different in the United States.

Although the document was virtually ready for publication before George Wallingford Noyes's death in 1941, he had not selected a title. I have tried to achieve parallelism with the first two volumes he edited—*The Religious Experience of John Humphrey Noyes, Founder of the Oneida Community* (1923) and *John Humphrey Noyes: The Putney Community* (1931)—by entitling this volume *Free Love in Utopia: John Humphrey Noyes and the Origin of the Oneida Community.*

There were also some inconsistencies between the draft contents page for George Wallingford Noyes's typescript and the internal chapter headings in the draft text itself. In general, I have followed the chapter titles given on the contents page, which usually are more detailed than the titles given in the text. I also have added dates to the chapter titles when they were provided in either the contents page or text. When the dates given in the chapter titles do not represent the range of documents actually included within a chapter, I usually have substituted dates that reflect the full coverage of the internal materials, while noting the original chapter dating in a footnote.

In cases where there was a reversal of the order of chapters in the contents page and the text—namely chapters 8 and 9, 13 and 14, and 15 and 16—I have followed the chapter order of the text and altered the contents page accordingly. Throughout the document, I have regularized capitalization and italicization of the chapter and internal text headings. The pagination of the original document is indicated by numbers enclosed in slashes.

More than three-quarters of the pages in this George Wallingford Noyes document are derived from letters, diaries, and journals that were among those destroyed when the majority of the original Oneida documents were burned in 1947. The remainder consists of excerpts from some of John Humphrey Noyes's many newspapers—especially *Spiritual Magazine* (1846–50), *Free Church Circular* (1850–51), and *The Circular* (1851–64). Certain documents, such as John Humphrey Noyes's informal "Home-Talks" to his followers at their evening meetings, which were stenographically recorded, were sometimes published in the community's newspapers as well. Together, the documentary and printed sources preserved in this typescript provide a fuller account of the early development of the Oneida Community than has ever been published.

Readers will be interested in the extent to which G. W. Noyes's typescript accurately reproduces the selections it uses from the published record. Although I have not attempted a systematic comparison of the selections from the published record with the original newspaper sources, clearly they are not always identical. As in his first two published volumes, G. W. Noyes sometimes provides a summary of the substance of an article or talk without indicating that he is not giving a verbatim transcript. Thus, readers who want to be certain that they are seeing the exact words used in John Humphrey Noyes's newspapers will need to refer to the originals. They have been published on the fifteen rolls of microfilm of Oneida Community books, pamphlets, and serials from the Syracuse University Library, available through interlibrary loan or for purchase from University Microfilm International in Ann Arbor, Michigan.

A graphic example of how George Wallingford Noyes sometimes modified his sources is his one-sentence version of the Oneida Association's 1852 statement that temporarily discontinued complex marriage. When I went back to *The Circular* for March 7, 1852, I found a lengthy article with thousands of words, not G. W. Noyes's fifty-four-word compression. In this important case I have reprinted, immediately after G. W. Noyes's version, the complete text as originally published. Elsewhere, I also have inserted a few additional newspaper excerpts (identified by my bracketed initials) that bear on internal conflicts at Oneida that Noyes did not address in his original manuscript.

Although Noyes's willingness to compress original sources without indicating he was doing so may be disquieting to Oneida specialists, the selections that

I have checked have always been true to the substance of the original published sources. I therefore have chosen not to make a full comparison with the published articles, as scholars might do if they must be certain of exact original wording. This is, after all, George Wallingford Noyes's volume. In addition, one must remember that most of the original letters and diaries are no longer available for comparison.

On other editorial matters, my original intent was to have a footnote reference in the text the first time each new name appeared. I soon realized, however, that this would be less useful than having a glossary of what I have chosen to call the "Cast of Characters." I have placed this glossary just before the start of the document itself for easy reference. The Cast of Characters lists major figures in the text and highlights some interrelationships that may not be obvious, such as the individuals who were married to John Humphrey Noyes's brothers and sisters.

For fuller genealogical information on Oneida Community individuals, see John B. Teeple's detailed *The Oneida Family: Genealogy of a Nineteenth-Century Perfectionist Commune* (Oneida, N.Y.: Oneida Community Historical Committee, 1985). Still the best overall introduction to John Humphrey Noyes and his remarkable communal efforts is Robert Allerton Parker's lively, sympathetic, and carefully researched *A Yankee Saint: John Humphrey Noyes and the Oneida Community* (1935), which is available in reprint editions.

To provide an idea of what John Humphrey Noyes, his key associates, and his early community looked like, I have included a selection of photographs and drawings of the community. I am grateful to the Oneida Community Mansion House and to Carol S. White for authorizing their reproduction here.

One final but essential reader aid remains to be mentioned. The appendix of this volume consists of a complete reproduction of the text of what is possibly the Oneida Community's most revealing publication: *The First Annual Report of the Oneida Association: Exhibiting Its History, Principles, and Transactions to Jan. 1, 1849*. This document, which to the best of my knowledge has never been reprinted in full, contains John Humphrey Noyes's controversial "Bible Argument; Defining the Relations of the Sexes in the Kingdom of Heaven" (pp. 312–34), as well as an account of the origin, beliefs, and practices of the community (pp. 297–312) and testimonials from its earliest members about their experiences (pp. 334–60). The publication is mentioned repeatedly in George Wallingford Noyes's text. Reading the *First Annual Report,* perhaps even before starting Noyes's work itself, may provide much insight into the beliefs and practices of this unusual community.

I must express my appreciation to the many descendants of the Oneida Community living in the Mansion House and in the surrounding communities at

Oneida, Kenwood, and throughout the United States today. Collectively, as I have come to know them during more than thirty years of researching the community, I cannot imagine a finer group of people anywhere. It took both wisdom and courage for them to turn over the bulk of the substantial surviving collection of private records from the Oneida Community to the Syracuse University Library Special Collections in the late 1970s so they could be made available to researchers.

Special gratitude is due Imogen Noyes Stone, daughter of George Wallingford Noyes, who preserved the two copies of his 2,200-page typescript that I know have survived, placing one of them in the Syracuse University Library, and to her daughter Carol S. White, who removed all restrictions on scholarly use of the document, thereby making its publication possible here. My deep thanks also go to Mark Weimer, curator of Special Collections in the Syracuse University Library, for his indefatigable efforts to preserve and catalog the surviving Oneida documents and make them available to others. Without his continuing assistance in so many ways, this volume could never have been published. Also essential to the publication of this volume have been my fine acquisitions editor and friend, Elizabeth G. Dulany, and many other capable individuals at the University of Illinois Press. I hope that this book can in some small measure begin to do justice to the complex group of individuals who sincerely committed their lives to the beliefs and practices of the Oneida Community.

Free Love in Utopia tells a compelling and sometimes disquieting story of one extraordinary community that sought to achieve a radical restructuring of the relationships between men and women. George Wallingford Noyes's document raises complex questions for readers who continue to struggle to come to terms with issues of personal transformation and change today.

Notes

1. My book *Religion and Sexuality: Three American Communal Experiments of the Nineteenth Century* (New York: Oxford University Press, 1981), reprinted in a paperbound edition as *Religion and Sexuality: The Shakers, the Mormons, and the Oneida Community* (Urbana: University of Illinois Press, 1984), provides a historical-anthropological analysis of the process by which alternative systems of gender and sexual relationships were conceived, introduced, and institutionalized among the celibate Shakers, free-love Oneida Community, and polygamous Mormons in nineteenth-century America. Many of the concerns reflected in this introduction were first explored in that study, as well as in my later, more sociologically oriented analysis *Women, Family, and Utopia: Communal Experiments of the Shakers, the Oneida Community, and the Mormons* (Syracuse: Syracuse University Press, 1991).

2. For John Humphrey Noyes's discussion of the shifting meaning of the term *free love*, see his *History of American Socialisms* (Philadelphia: Lippincott, 1870), pp. 638–40. An example of the hostile use of the term is found in John B. Ellis, *Free Love and Its Votaries; or, American Socialism Unmasked* (New York: United States Publishing, 1870).

3. Charles Nordhoff, *The Communistic Societies of the United States: From Personal Visit and Observation* (New York: Harper and Brothers, 1875), p. 271.

4. Among the most important scholarly studies that focus on the internal dynamics of the Oneida Community are Robert Allerton Parker, *A Yankee Saint: John Humphrey Noyes and the Oneida Community* (New York: G. P. Putnam's Sons, 1935); Maren Lockwood Carden, *Oneida: Utopian Community to Modern Corporation* (1969, repr. Syracuse: Syracuse University Press, 1998); Foster, *Religion and Sexuality;* Foster, *Women, Family, and Utopia;* and Spencer Klaw, *Without Sin: The Life and Death of the Oneida Community* (New York: Penguin, 1993).

5. For the Syracuse University manuscript holdings, which include the George Wallingford Noyes manuscript, see Mark F. Weimer, comp., *The Oneida Community Collection in the Syracuse University Libraries: Inventory* (Syracuse: Syracuse University, George Arents Research Library for Special Collections, 1986). George Wallingford Noyes's two edited collections of primary documents are *The Religious Experience of John Humphrey Noyes, Founder of the Oneida Community* (New York: Macmillan, 1923), and *John Humphrey Noyes: The Putney Community* (Oneida, N.Y.: By the Author, 1931). Constance Noyes Robertson's documentary account of the end of the community is found in *The Oneida Community: The Breakup, 1876–1881* (Syracuse: Syracuse University Press, 1972).

6. I had been trying to get the document opened to unrestricted scholarly use for more than a decade. When access to the manuscript became available, I wrote a preliminary analysis of some of the new information in a paper entitled "The Turbulence of Free Love: New Perspectives on the Early Development of the Oneida Community from the George Wallingford Noyes Manuscript, 1848–1854," presented at the annual conference of the Communal Studies Association at Oneida, New York, on October 7, 1994. This introduction draws upon, and substantially expands, that paper.

7. For the most substantial previous published account of the burning of thousands of Oneida documents that had been assembled in a specially constructed storage vault, see Klaw, *Without Sin,* p. 299.

8. The four paragraphs that follow are based on these telephone interviews and on other documentary information Geoff Noyes shared with me on January 5 and 9, 2001.

9. This document was kindly made available to me by Geoff Noyes. It will be referred to hereafter as the "Aylesworth brief."

10. Ibid., pp. 20, 28.

11. Ibid., p. 18.

12. Ibid., p. 19.

13. Ibid.

14. Geoff Noyes, in his telephone interview with me on January 5, 2001, indicated that he had played in the open safe as a child and that he remembered the documents being removed in 1947 when he was six years old.

15. Mark Weimer played a critical role during the late 1970s in convincing Oneida Community descendants to deposit their surviving documents, including a typescript carbon of the George Wallingford Noyes manuscript, in the Syracuse University Library Special Collections. The inventory to that substantial body of Oneida documents fills ninety-four typewritten pages. Before Weimer's collection of the Oneida documents now held at Syracuse University Library, scholars were largely dependent upon published sources, especially the newspapers printed by John Humphrey Noyes and the Oneida Community, under a variety of different titles, between 1834 and 1879. The complete run of the community serials, which include eleven reels of microfilm along with four other reels of microfilms of community publications and related materials, are now available from UMI in Ann Arbor, Michigan, and are described in Jack T. Ericson, ed., *Oneida Community: Books, Pamphlets, and Serials, 1834–1972* (Ann Arbor: UMI, 1990).

16. Carol S. White, the granddaughter of George Wallingford Noyes, indicated to me in a telephone interview on January 5, 2001, that she has retained what she believes to be G. W. Noyes's typescript original of the manuscript.

17. All subsequent refences to the document itself will be identified hereafter as "Noyes MS" and will cite the pages that follow.

18. Background comments are based on the analysis of Oneida presented in Foster, *Religion and Sexuality*, pp. 72–122, and Foster, *Women, Family, and Utopia*, especially the chapter entitled "The Rise and Fall of Utopia: The Oneida Community Crises of 1852 and 1879" (pp. 103–23), itself a revision of a paper originally published under the same title in *Communal Societies* 8 (1988): 1–17. For primary documentation on John Humphrey Noyes's early religious turmoil, see his *Confessions of John H. Noyes, Part 1: Confessions of Religious Experience, Including a History of Modern Perfectionism* (Oneida Reserve, N.Y., 1849), and *Religious Experience of John Humphrey Noyes*, ed. G. W. Noyes. An important scholarly analysis of the roots of Noyes's charisma and mission, largely before the start of the Oneida Community, is found in Robert David Thomas, *The Man Who Would Be Perfect: John Humphrey Noyes and the Utopian Impulse* (Philadelphia: University of Pennsylvania Press, 1977).

19. Noyes's letter, published in part in Theophilous Gates's newspaper *The Battle-Axe and Weapons of War*, included a remarkable declaration: "In the holy community, there is no more reason why sexual intercourse should be restricted by law than why eating and drinking should be—and there is as little occasion for shame in the one case as in the other." Reprinted in *The Witness*, Jan. 23, 1839, 49. Documentary background on these developments is found in *John Humphrey Noyes: The Putney Community*, ed. G. W. Noyes, pp. 1–10.

20. For a skillful presentation and analysis of these developments, drawing upon some primary materials no longer available, see Parker, *Yankee Saint*, pp. 119–42. Primary documentation on the disposition of this and the other Putney lawsuits is found in the Noyes MS (pp. 13–22).

21. Noyes first published "Bible Argument Defining the Relations of the Sexes in the Kingdom of Heaven" in *The First Annual Report of the Oneida Association* (Oneida Reserve, N.Y.: Leonard, 1849), pp. 18–42, and elaborated upon it in *Bible Communism: A Compilation of the Annual Reports and Other Publications of the Oneida Association and Its Branches* (Brooklyn: Office of *The Circular*, 1853).

22. These membership figures are based on the first three annual reports of the Oneida Association, published between 1849 and 1851.

23. This frequently repeated emphasis is most vividly suggested in "The Family and Its Foil," *The Circular*, Nov. 16, 1854, p. 594, where Noyes argues that existing patterns of monogamous "marriage" derived from romantic love were antithetical to the "family," by which he meant larger social and kinship ties. As Noyes saw it, love attachments confined to individual couples were a sort of "egotism for two," part of the same disruptive and antisocial individualism that was present in the rampant, economically acquisitive antebellum scene.

24. "Bible Argument," pp. 27–28.

25. The fullest presentation of Noyes's theological perfectionism is found in his *The Berean: A Manual for the Help of Those Who Seek the Faith of the Primitive Church* (Putney, Vt.: Office of the *Spiritual Magazine*, 1847).

26. *Third Annual Report of the Oneida Association* (Oneida Reserve, N.Y.: Leonard, 1851), p. 8.

27. Throughout his life, Noyes demanded total authority and control. This key element in his approach is discussed on pages xvii–xix.

28. For a summary of how these key arrangements developed, see Foster, *Religion and Sexuality*, pp. 93–106.

29. *The Oneida Circular* 12, n.s. (May 1875): 170, recalled: "The years 1850, '51, '52 were years of external trial to the community. First came the conflict with internal 'evils,' such as insubordination, disloyalty, and pleasure-seeking, culminating in the withdrawal of several families which seemed at times to jeopardize the very existence of the community."

30. *The Circular*, Jan. 17, 1854, p. 75.

31. Parker, *Yankee Saint*, pp. 187–89. The details of the legal challenges that the Oneida Community faced at this time are among the discoveries from the George Wallingford Noyes Papers.

32. As early as 1850, the Oneida Community publicly stated that it was not actively seeking new members, and thereafter it periodically reaffirmed this position. "Plans and Prospects," *Free Church Circular*, Oct. 21, 1850, p. 281.

33. For a fuller discussion of my earlier reconstruction of these matters based on

newspaper sources, see Foster, *Religion and Sexuality,* pp. 111–16 and pages 169–86 of this volume.

34. "The Past, Present, and Future," *The Circular,* March 7, 1852, p. 66, reprinted in full on pages 157–60.

35. Foster, "The Rise and Fall of Utopia."

36. See pages 101–15 of this volume.

37. The statement is reprinted on pages 192–93.

38. For the final phase of the community experience, see especially Robertson, *The Oneida Community: The Breakup;* Pierrepont B. Noyes, *My Father's House: An Oneida Boyhood* (New York: Farrar and Reinhart, 1937); Parker, *Yankee Saint;* Carden, *Oneida;* and Klaw, *Without Sin.*

39. G. W. Noyes, ed., *John Humphrey Noyes: The Putney Community,* pp. 25–33.

40. Ibid., p. 25.

41. *Spiritual Magazine,* July 1, 1847, 57–59; *First Annual Report,* pp. 296–361 of this volume.

42. G. W. Noyes, ed., *John Humphrey Noyes: The Putney Community,* p. 33.

43. Len Oakes, *Prophetic Charisma: The Psychology of Revolutionary Religious Personalities* (Syracuse: Syracuse University Press, 1997). Oakes suggests a typology of the development of charismatic leadership that helps place the development of the Oneida Community into a larger context.

44. Noyes MS, pp. 6–7.

45. Kenelm Burridge, *New Heaven, New Earth: A Study of Millenarian Activities* (New York: Schocken, 1969), p. 162.

46. William James, *The Varieties of Religious Experience: A Study in Human Nature* (1902, repr. New York: New American Library, 1958), p. 36.

47. The term *primitive church* refers to the earliest, and thus presumable most authentic, period of Christianity when Jesus or his immediate disciples were still alive. John Humphrey Noyes, like other "restorationist" Christians, sought to recover the supposed purity of early Christianity as part of achieving a millennium of earthly peace and harmony. The best primary account of Noyes's perfectionist religious beliefs in context is his *Confessions of John H. Noyes.*

48. *First Annual Report,* pp. 296–331 of this volume.

49. *The Witness,* Sept. 25, 1839, 78.

50. "Bible Argument," pp. 21–22.

51. Noyes MS, p. 197.

52. The allegation was that "Mr. Miller does not fully believe our social theory" (ibid., p. 61) and that reluctance was also confirmed elsewhere. *The Circular,* on October 3, 1850, featured a letter highly critical of Oneida sexual practices, as well as a relatively half-hearted defense from John Miller and other community members. "It is quote possible that John Humphrey Noyes's decision to resume formal editorship of his newspapers in 1851 was in part an attempt to avoid losing control over *both* his

newspapers and his communities in the face of deep-seated opposition to his policies" (Foster, *Religion and Sexuality*, p. 110).

53. One of the factors that allowed Noyes to achieve success was his willingness to be candid and yet judicious in stating precisely what he was attempting to do. He could never convincingly be criticized for not letting people know what he stood for or was trying to achieve in his community ventures.

54. Noyes MS, p. 215.

55. Ibid., p. 213.

56. Ibid.

57. For an overview of the role of "ascending fellowship," in which older, more "spiritual" members generally guided younger, less "spiritual" individuals, and how ascending fellowship was used to direct and control the community's sexual system, see Carden, *Oneida*, pp. 52–57.

58. Copy of letter from Theodore E. Noyes to Anita Newcomb McGee, April 15, 1892, author's possession, provided courtesy of Geoffrey Noyes.

59. Noyes MS, p. 16.

60. Ibid., p. 54.

61. Ibid., pp. 57–58.

62. Ibid., p. 99. John Humphrey Noyes's "Home-Talks" were his informal discussions with the assembled members of his communities at their nightly meetings. The talks were stenographically recorded and often published in the community newspaper as well as in the book *Home Talks*, vol. 1, ed. Alfred Barron and George Noyes Miller (Oneida, N.Y.: Oneida Community, 1875).

63. Noyes MS, p. 105. For details of the earlier triangle between Abram Smith and the Cragins, see Parker, *Yankee Saint*, pp. 76–85.

64. Ibid.

65. Ibid., p. 112.

66. Ibid.

67. Ibid., p. 115.

68. Ibid., pp. 116, 117, 118.

69. Ibid., p. 123.

70. This factor receives attention in Parker, *Yankee Saint*; Carden, *Oneida*; Foster, *Religion and Sexuality*; and Klaw, *Without Sin*. Carden, for example, tells a curious story: "In 1868, practical considerations made it appropriate to rebury her remains. Looking at her skull, 'all who knew her, recognized the contour—so beautifully feminine. [Her son George] expressed a wish that the skull might be retained. The wish was unanimous. It is to be varnished and preserved'" (*Oneida*, p. 70).

71. Those chapters cover pages 3–88 of Parker, *Yankee Saint*.

72. Noyes continued to be attracted to Abigail Merwin and made efforts, via intermediaries that included Mary Cragin in 1851, shortly before her death, to persuade her to come to Oneida (Noyes MS, pp. 89–91). In remarks on April 9, 1851, he observed that God "roused up affection between her [Abigail Merwin] and me into a

mighty force, and then made it work for his kingdom. If he had given her to me, and I had turned aside to the enjoyment and idolatry of her that is usual, no good would have been gained. I am sure that nothing but such circumstances would have given me the momentum necessary to come out with the Social [i.e., Sexual] Theory" (ibid., pp. 87–88).

73. As one suggestive instance, Charlotte Miller stated, "Some at Oneida stumbled at the expression in one of the late Table Talks, that Mr. Noyes would 'drink no more of the fruit of the vine till he drank it anew with Mrs. Cragin'" (ibid., p. 162).

74. Ibid., p. 261.

75. Ibid., p. 136–45. The primary focus of the interrogation appears to have been the community's sexual arrangements, with Tryphena Seymour's case brought up almost as an afterthought.

76. Ibid., p. 143.

77. Ibid., p. 142.

78. Ibid., pp. 145–48.

79. Ibid., p. 154.

80. Ibid., p. 155.

81. Ibid., p. 175.

82. Ibid., p. 176.

83. Ibid., p. 178.

84. Ibid., p. 187.

85. Ibid.

86. Ibid., p. 189.

87. John B. Teeple, *The Oneida Family: Genealogy of a Nineteenth-Century Perfectionist Commune* (Oneida, N.Y.: Oneida Community Historical Committee, 1985), p. 26.

88. Teeple, *The Oneida Family*, p. 14.

89. Much evidence suggests that Oneida's unorthodox sexual practices, and Tryphena's father's opposition to them, may well have contributed to her breakdown, as did having to adapt to a marital relationship with her somewhat eccentric husband, Henry. She was the first local resident other than Jonathan and Lorinda Burt to join the group and accept its sexual practices after the move to Oneida. Before so doing, she and Lorinda Burt had vociferously opposed those same unorthodox practices. Just as the opposition of the father of the fifteen-year-old Lucinda Lamb to joining the Putney Community had caused problems for the group earlier, so Noahdiah Hubbard's profound opposition to his daughter's involvement was an ongoing source of tension between him and the Oneida Community.

Other revealing discussions of the tensions associated with Oneida sexual practices are found in Jane Kinsley Rich and Nelson F. Blake, eds., *A Lasting Spring: Jessie Catherine Kinsley, Daughter of the Oneida Community* (Syracuse: Syracuse University Press, 1983); in the Victor Hawley diary edited by Robert Fogarty as *Special Love/ Special Sex: An Oneida Community Diary* (Syracuse: Syracuse University Press, 1994);

and in Robert Fogarty, ed., *Desire and Duty at Oneida: Tirza Miller's Intimate Memoir* (Bloomington: Indiana University Press, 2000). Tirza Miller was the mother of George Wallingford Noyes.

90. Corporal punishment was used in a number of cases during the first few years of the community, especially in dealing with rebellious young men. Noyes also noted that physical punishment had led Elizabeth Hawley, who had refused either to leave or abide by the community's rules, to comply with its requirements (Noyes MS, p. 144).

91. Primary information on the sophisticated means of social control possible by using the practice of "mutual criticism," for example, is found in *Mutual Criticism* (Oneida, N.Y.: Office of the *American Socialist*, 1876) and in the columns of the community's newspapers. For a secondary overview of the practice of mutual criticism, see Carden, *Oneida*, pp. 71–77.

92. Alan Estlake [Abel Easton], *The Oneida Community* (London: George Redway, 1900), p. 56.

93. "The Second Course," *The Circular*, April 4, 1854, p. 82.

94. Significantly, many of these articles coupled "disease" with "death." For Noyes's basic statement on the topic, see "Abolition of Death" in Noyes, *The Berean*, pp. 476–86.

95. *The Circular*, Feb. 1, 1852, p. 51.

96. "The Rival of Christ," *The Circular*, April 4, 1852, p. 82; "A Bible Contest," *The Circular*, April 11, 1852, p. 87. Articles written by Noyes's sister Harriet are reprinted herein (pp. 163–65) as part of my enlargement of the original G. W. Noyes document.

97. *The Circular*, April 1, 1852, p. 87.

98. One of the most incisive analyses bearing on Noyes's identification with Christ is Michael Barkun, "'The Wind Sweeping over the Country': John Humphrey Noyes and the Rise of Millerism," in *The Disappointed: Millerism and Millenarianism in the Nineteenth Century*, ed. Ronald L. Numbers and Jonathan M. Butler (Bloomington: Indiana University Press, 1987), pp. 153–72. Barkun notes (p. 162) that in 1835 Noyes's sister Joanna stated that he was "deranged when he begins to talk about his suffering for that world, and that he is immortal, &c."

99. *Bible Communism*, p. [4]. The reprint of this book by Porcupine Press prints this dedication, but the AMS Press reprint inexcusably omits it, covering it over instead with their own reprint information. The Noyes MS (p. 116) includes his comment after a discussion of the various biblical Marys in relation to Mary Cragin, "Well, such coincidences do not amount to much, but after all there is some poetry in them." Nevertheless, one has the sense that Noyes in his extended reflections about Mary Cragin after her death had a more grandiose sense of his own and Mary's roles. In the same Home-Talk on September 4, 1851, he states that Mary Cragin, following her death, had become "the female member of the dual head of the church [the heavenly part, as opposed to the Oneida part on earth]." In context, this suggests something beyond a mere poetic interpretation on Noyes's part.

100. "The Message," *The Circular,* Aug. 1, 1852, p. 150.

101. *The Circular,* Aug. 4, 1852, p. 153.

102. *The Circular,* Aug. 29, 1852, p. 170. The full text of the original "Theocratic Platform" has been substituted for the shortened G. W. Noyes version in this edition of the document.

103. Noyes MS, p. 223.

104. John Humphrey Noyes's fullest discussion of this practice and its rationale is found in his *Male Continence* (Oneida, N.Y.: Office of *The Oneida Circular,* 1872). For an assessment, see Foster, *Religion and Sexuality,* pp. 93–98. A tantalizingly brief discussion by Alfred Kinsey, Wardell Pomeroy, and Clyde Martin in *Sexual Behavior in the Human Male* (Philadelphia: W. B. Saunders, 1948), pp. 158–61, argues that men practicing coitus reservatus can indeed achieve orgasm without ejaculation. The most recent accounts emphasizing the advantages of coitus reservatus for male and female sexual pleasure are William Hartman and Marilyn Fithian, *Any Man Can: The Multiple Orgasmic Technique for Every Loving Man* (New York: St. Martin's Press, 1994); and Mantak Chia and Douglas Abrams Arava, *The Multi-Orgasmic Man: Sexual Secrets Every Man Should Know* (San Francisco: HarperSanFrancisco, 1997).

105. "Bible Argument," p. 32. In this respect, male continence could be seen as a classic illustration of Victorian American concerns about wasting male semen, as described in G. J. Barker-Benfield, "The Spermatic Economy: A Nineteenth-Century View of Sexuality," *Feminist Studies* 1 (Summer 1972): 45–74.

106. Noyes, *Male Continence,* pp. 7, 9.

107. Noyes MS, p. 223.

108. Ibid., p. 223–24.

109. Ibid., p. 225.

110. Ibid., p. 228. One noteworthy expulsion involved Charles Guiteau, the unstable man who later assassinated President James Garfield. Parker, *Yankee Saint,* pp. 224–25.

111. Noyes MS, p. 234.

112. Ibid., p. 249.

Cast of Characters

The following are some of the key individuals important for understanding this document and the early development of the Oneida Community. Further information on them and other individuals may be found in John B. Teeple, *The Oneida Family: Genealogy of a Nineteenth-Century Perfectionist Commune* (Oneida, N.Y.: Oneida Community Mansion House, 1985), and Robert Allerton Parker, *A Yankee Saint: John Humphrey Noyes and the Oneida Community* (New York: G. P. Putnam's Sons, 1935). For brevity and convenience, as well as to highlight important interrelationships, I have generally listed husbands and wives together unless there was a pressing reason to consider them separately. I also have not included the names of Noyes's many previous Perfectionist rivals, who are primarily mentioned in the early chapters of this document and do not play much of a role in the later Oneida story itself.

ABBOTT, JOHN and LAURA (BISHOP). The Abbotts joined the Oneida Community in February 1848, along with their children. They were the first members who had not had some previous communal living experience.

ACKLEY, JOSEPH and JULIA (CARRIER). Joseph Ackley and his family had joined Jonathan Burt at Oneida Reserve in November 1847, and two months later they invited John Humphrey Noyes and the Putney Community refugees to join them, providing the location for the Oneida Community.

ALLEN, HENRY and EMILY (DUTTON). The Allens turned over their family property to John Humphrey Noyes as trustee in 1851, thus providing the basis for the Wallingford Community.

BAILEY, SEBA and JANE (POWERS). Seba Bailey, without Noyes's approval but with his reluctant toleration, introduced a form of complex marriage in his own small Perfectionist group in Illinois before his death in 1855. His wife Jane and the rest of the family then joined the Oneida Community.

BAKER, JAMES and CATHERINE (HOBART). James Baker joined the Putney Community shortly after marrying Catherine Hobart. His sisters, Harriet, Ellen, and Philena, also joined the Putney Community. After joining the Oneida Community in 1848, the Bakers, in conjunction with the Wordens, helped reestablish the Putney Community in 1851.

BRADLEY, LEMUEL and SARAH (SUMMERS). Lemuel and Sarah Bradley, members of the Putney Community, came to Oneida and remained in the community until the breakup.

BURNHAM, HENRY and ABIGAIL (SCOTT). The Burnhams were Millerites in Vermont before joining the Putney and Oneida communities. Henry Burnham played a key role in setting up the sales network for the Newhouse traps, upon which the community's financial prosperity eventually depended.

BURT, JONATHAN and LORINDA (LEE). Jonathan Burt was a New York Perfectionist who owned much of the land upon which the Oneida Community was established in 1848. His wife Lorinda initially was very disturbed by the sexual arrangements of the group but became reconciled to them. Sarah was one of their children. Horace was Jonathan's brother.

CAMPBELL, EMMA and HELEN. When the sisters Emma and Helen Campbell joined the Putney Community, with Helen marrying George W. Noyes and Emma marrying William H. Woolworth, their action precipitated intense and continuing opposition to the group from their step-brother, Dr. John Campbell.

CRAGIN, GEORGE and MARY (JOHNSON). George and Mary Cragin had been involved in social reform activities in New York City before becoming converted to Noyes's Perfectionism and joining the Putney Community in 1840. The fact that Noyes found Mary Cragin attractive was a precipitating factor in the start of complex marriage practice in 1846, with George and Mary Cragin and John and Harriet Noyes constituting the initial group. After the removal from Putney, the Cragins continued to be key figures, active in both the Oneida and Brooklyn branches of the community. Mary Cragin's death in a boating accident on July 16, 1851, marked a critical turning point in the development of the Oneida Community.

DUNN, LEONARD and SARAH (KINSLEY). Leonard Dunn joined the community in 1848 and married Sarah Kinsley in 1849. He was trained as a machinist by William Insley in Newark, New Jersey, and in the mid-1850s developed techniques that revolutionized the trap-making business at Oneida. Sarah was an early "mother" in the Children's House. Julia and Fidelia Dunn were Leonard's sisters.

EASTMAN, HUBBARD. Methodist minister in Putney who published a lengthy, theologically oriented exposé entitled *Noyesism Unveiled* in 1847.

GARVIN, SAMUEL. District attorney of Oneida County, whose intense hostility toward the Oneida Community came close to causing its breakup in 1852.

GREELEY, HORACE. Influential social reformer and journalist who founded the *New York Tribune* in 1841. Noyes had amicable contact with Greeley when they both were traveling to the Crystal Palace Exposition in London in 1851.

HALL, HARRIET (BAKER) and DANIEL. John Humphrey Noyes attempted two faith cures of the invalid Harriet Hall (the second was successful), and she subsequently married Daniel Hall, joined the Oneida Community in 1849, and lived there the rest of her long life.

HAMILTON, ERASTUS and SUSAN (WILLIAMS). Erastus Hamilton and his wife Susan were among the most loyal members of the Oneida Community after they joined in 1848. Erastus managed many community activities and committees and frequently substituted for Noyes at evening meetings when he was away, as well as becoming one of the four trustees of the community. Sylvia Hamilton was the mother of Erastus Hamilton.

HAMILTON, GEORGE and PHILENA (BAKER). George, the brother of Erastus Hamilton, married Philena Baker shortly after he joined the Oneida Community in 1849.

HATCH, ELEAZER and HANNAH (BURNHAM). The Hatches joined the Oneida Community with their family in 1848. Hannah was one of the first mothers supervising the Children's House at Oneida.

HAWLEY, ELIZABETH. This forceful, opinionated supporter of Noyes sent his 1837 letter on free love to Theophilous Gates, who promptly published it, causing general consternation. After joining the Oneida Community in 1851, she remained a loose cannon and received corporal punishment when she flatly refused either to submit to community regulations or to leave.

HINDS, WILLIAM. Converted while living with John Miller's family in Putney, William Hinds joined the Oneida Community in 1849 at age sixteen, would study at Yale in the 1860s, and would go on to play a key role before, during, and after the breakup of the Oneida Community in 1881.

HUBBARD, DEXTER and LUCIUS. Sons of Noahdiah Hubbard.

HUBBARD, NOAHDIAH. Referred to throughout as "old Mr. Hubbard," he was the father of Tryphena Hubbard, who married Henry Seymour. Mr. Hubbard became one of the harshest opponents of the community during the early 1850s, and his lawsuits against the community almost led to its dispersal in 1852.

HYDE, FRANCIS and JULIA (DUNN). Francis Hyde married Julia Dunn in February 1849 but seceded from Oneida in September 1850 and, after stormy negotiations with the community, took her away with him three months later.

INSLEE, WILLIAM. Owner of a machine shop in Newark, New Jersey, and chief figure in the small Perfectionist group there that helped provide a financial base for Noyes's other efforts.

JENKINS, TIMOTHY. The largest landowner and most influential citizen in the Oneida Reserve area, he served in the U.S. House of Representatives at the time the Oneida Community was founded.

JENKINS, WHIPPLE. Lawyer who gave advice to the Oneida Community during the Hubbard suits.

JOSLYN, CHARLES. He joined the Oneida Community in 1849 at age sixteen and would later become one of the twelve young men who would be sent to study at Yale University in the 1860s.

KELLOGG, CHARLES OTIS. He joined the Oneida Community at age twelve, with his family, in May 1849. He would later become one of the four trustees of the Oneida Community.

KEYES, ISRAEL. Leader of the opponents to Noyes's Perfectionists in Putney.

KINSLEY, ALBERT and MARIA (ELLSWORTH). At Oneida, Albert Kinsley played a key role as a community contact with the neighbors during the difficult early days. Sarah Kinsley was one of his daughters.

LAMB, LUCINDA. When the fifteen-year-old Lucinda Lamb was attracted to the Putney Community in 1847, intense community pressure developed that contributed to the group's expulsion from Putney.

LEONARD, STEPHEN and FANNY (WHITE). Members of the Putney Community, the Leonards would become key figures in the Oneida Community as well, where Stephen Leonard was the head printer. He moved to Brooklyn when the printing operation moved there. John Leonard was Stephen Leonard's brother.

MEAD, LARKIN. Prominent lawyer married to Noyes's eldest sister Mary and in whose law offices John Humphrey Noyes had worked after graduating from Dartmouth College in 1829. Critical of Noyes's religious and sexual heresies, he advised Noyes and his followers to leave Putney rather than contest the 1847 adultery charges.

MERWIN, ABIGAIL. John Noyes's first convert to Perfectionism in New Haven and idealized love object, her marriage led him in 1837 to write a letter advocating free love as the heavenly state. Noyes said that had Merwin married him, he probably would not have developed his idea of complex marriage. In 1851 Noyes sent Mary Cragin to try to convince the now-widowed Merwin to join the group at Oneida.

MILLER, JOHN and CHARLOTTE (NOYES). John Miller, married to Noyes's sister Charlotte, was the single most important figure after Noyes himself and made possible the initial survival of the Oneida Community. He dealt with everything from the Putney lawsuits, to continuing financial crises, to the various internal and external threats to the survival of the group at Oneida. His death in 1854 led to a major retrenchment that reduced the "Associated Communities" to two primary ones at Oneida, New York, and Wallingford, Connecticut.

MILLER, OTIS and ELLEN (BAKER). In addition to his five-month expulsion from the Oneida Community in 1849 (chapter 6), Otis Miller was a peddler who helped start the Oneida peddling business that contributed significantly to the community's income. He married Ellen Baker three days after she joined the Oneida Community in July 1848.

NASH, DANIEL and SOPHIA (CHURCH). Daniel Nash joined with Jonathan Burt and the New York Perfectionist community to invite John Humphrey Noyes to come to Oneida in 1848.

NEWHOUSE, SEWALL and EVELIZA (HYDE). Sewall Newhouse was the icon-oclastic inventer of the improved animal traps that became used by the Hudson's Bay Company and most trappers in the West. Those traps served as the finan-cial mainstay of the Oneida Community after they began to be mass-produced in the mid-1850s.

NOYES, GEORGE W. (WASHINGTON) and HELEN (CAMPBELL). George Washington Noyes was the youngest brother of John Humphrey Noyes and also his staunch supporter at Putney and Oneida. He became the editor of *The Oneida Circular* and helped found the Wallingford Community.

NOYES, GEORGE WALLINGFORD. Son of George Washington Noyes and Tirza Miller, and a nephew of John Humphrey Noyes, George Wallingford Noyes (1870–1941) became the leading twentieth-century chronicler of the Oneida Community.

NOYES, JOHN HUMPHREY. Founder and spiritual leader of the Oneida Com-munity throughout its existence, John Humphrey Noyes was the son of John Noyes, a successful Vermont merchant and member of the U.S. House of Rep-resentatives, and Polly Hayes, second cousin to Rutherford B. Hayes, later the nineteenth president of the United States. John Humphrey Noyes had eight brothers and sisters, three of whom (George W., Charlotte, and Harriet) joined him in the Putney and Oneida communities.

NOYES, HARRIET A. (HOLTON). Reared by her prosperous and well-educat-ed grandfather, who had been a lieutenant-governor of Vermont, Harriet Hol-ton married John Humphrey Noyes in 1838. She was one of his most loyal sup-porters at Putney, Oneida, and after the breakup of the community.

NOYES, THEODORE. The only son of John Humphrey Noyes and Harriet Holton Noyes, Theodore would attend Yale University and receive a medical degree in 1867. Groomed by his father to succeed him, Theodore would reluctantly and briefly assume the leadership of the Oneida Community in 1876.

PERRY, WILLIAM. An early convert to Noyes's Perfectionism, he joined the Oneida Community in 1849 but never married or had children in the community.

SEYMOUR, HENRY and TRYPHENA (HUBBARD). Henry joined the Oneida Community in 1848 and shortly thereafter married Tryphena Hubbard. Her emotional problems, connected in part with complex marriage, led Henry to try to control her by corporal punishment, resulting in a lawsuit by her father that almost broke up the Oneida Community in 1852.

SKINNER, JOHN and HARRIET (NOYES). John Skinner, a key early convert who assisted John Humphrey Noyes in writing, editing, and publishing his newspapers at Putney and Oneida, married Noyes's sister Harriet H. Noyes, who contributed more to Noyes's publications than any other woman.

SMITH, ABRAM. Leader of a small group of Perfectionists at Newark, New Jersey, loyal to Noyes's beliefs, Smith had an affair with Mary Cragin before the Cragins' move to the Putney Community in 1840. Smith later joined the Oneida Community for several years, purchasing the Willow Place house in Brooklyn that became Noyes's headquarters from 1849 through 1854.

WATERS, HIAL and LOUISA (TUTTLE). An associate of the Ackleys and then the Burts at Oneida Reserve, Hial Waters in 1849 married Louisa Tuttle, who had come from the Putney Community. Hial Waters worked at Putney, Wallingford, and Brooklyn communities, as well as at Oneida.

WOOLWORTH, WILLIAM and EMMA (CAMPBELL). William Woolworth joined the Putney Community in 1846 and married Helen Campbell in 1847. During later years he would sometimes serve as the "father of the Community" in Noyes's absence, and he was one of the four trustees of the community.

WORDEN, LEANDER and KEZIAH (DAVIS). Brother of Marquis Worden, Leander Worden married Kezia Davis in 1840, and they both seceded from the Oneida Community in 1855, perhaps as a result of Keziah's influence.

WORDEN, MARQUIS and SOPHIA CONVERSE (DUNN). Marquis Worden, an early Perfectionist, joined the Oneida Community, along with his three children, Harriet, Susan, and Cornelia, in 1848 after the death of his first wife. The day after he joined, he married Sophia Converse Dunn, who also had joined the community after the death of her first husband, Norman Dunn, by whom she, too, had three children, Leonard, Julia, and Fidelia. Marquis Worden was instrumental in briefly reviving the Putney Community in 1851.

John Humphrey Noyes's conventional appearance in 1851 belies his unconventional ideas. (Courtesy of Oneida Community Mansion House)

GEORGE CRAGIN

HARRIET A. (HOLTON) NOYES

MARY E. (JOHNSON) CRAGIN

John Humphrey Noyes's three close followers who initiated the practice of complex marriage with him in 1846. From George Wallingford Noyes, ed., *John Humphrey Noyes: The Putney Community* (1931). (Courtesy of Carol S. White)

JOHN R. MILLER

CHARLOTTE A. (NOYES) MILLER

The intense and capable John R. Miller, married to John Humphrey Noyes's sister Charlotte, played a critical role in the survival of the Oneida Community before his death in 1854. From George Wallingford Noyes, ed., *John Humphrey Noyes: The Putney Community* (1931). (Courtesy of Carol S. White)

HELEN (CAMPBELL) NOYES AND
GEORGE W. NOYES

LUCINDA LAMB

The conversion of women such as Helen Campbell and Lucinda Lamb by the Perfectionists at Putney contributed to local hostility and the group's expulsion from Putney in 1847. From George Wallingford Noyes, ed., *John Humphrey Noyes: The Putney Community* (1931). (Courtesy of Carol S. White)

Oneida Community women participating in a bag-making bee. Note the distinctive bloomer-style dresses and short hair worn by the community women. (Courtesy of Oneida Community Mansion House)

Oneida men and women engaged in a pea-shelling bee. The men's clothing is relatively "casual." John Humphrey Noyes is on the left behind the woman with glasses. (Courtesy of Oneida Community Mansion House)

The original Mansion House of the Oneida Community, completed in the early 1850s, was far more modest than the later, expanded versions. From *Bible Communism* (1853). (Courtesy of Oneida Community Mansion House)

The expanded Mansion House as it appeared in the 1860s. From *Handbook of the Oneida Community* (1867). (Courtesy of Oneida Community Mansion House)

The "new" Mansion House about 1871. (Courtesy of Oneida Community Mansion House)

Aerial photograph of the Oneida Mansion House today shows its immensity and complexity, including the last section (four stories at right) completed in 1878. The lounge connecting that section with the tontine (a dining room–kitchen) was finished during World War I. (Photograph by Bruce M Moseley; courtesy of Oneida Community Mansion House)

The Oneida Community "enlarged family" in 1863, showing 164 men, women, and children, about three-quarters of the total membership. John Humphrey Noyes is standing with arms crossed in the right foreground. (Courtesy of Oneida Community Mansion House)

THE
GEORGE WALLINGFORD NOYES
DOCUMENT

1

Noyes Again at the Helm

Between 1834, when John Humphrey Noyes became a convert to religious Perfectionist ideas, and 1848, when his key followers started the Oneida Community in central New York state, the issue of Noyes's leadership primacy became a major topic of contention among Perfectionists. As early as 1837, John Humphrey Noyes had asserted that he would never again join any movement unless he were in charge. Eleven years later, when his followers regrouped at Oneida, Noyes once more found himself face to face with a half-dozen capable men who also wanted to lead the movement. The fight for control at Oneida became especially intense because John Humphrey Noyes not only demanded acceptance of his religious leadership but also of his control over the sexual lives of his followers. Only Noyes's most devoted supporters would eventually remain to form the nucleus of the new community at Oneida. [L.F.]*

Noyes to Harriet A. Noyes
Burt's February 4, 1848

Dear Harriet:—
I came here at the right time. [William] Gould had done nothing, except in the way of undermining me. He was keeping back the truth, and in the meantime seeking his own among the women. He resisted and threatened, as he did one day at Putney, only worse, and I cashiered him. His wife is with me in heart, and he lays all the defeats he has suffered since to her desertion of him.

---

* George Wallingford Noyes's original introductory paragraph, with Lawrence Foster's bracketed insertions, reads as follows: "After three years' experience under the leadership of [Charles H.] Weld, [James] Boyle and [Theophilous] Gates, [John Humphrey] Noyes finally in the Battle-Axe letter, January 15, 1837, declared that he would never again go on board a vessel unless he could have the helm. Eight years later his leadership among eastern Perfectionists was brought to a test in the Belchertown imbroglio [when Noyes struggled to maintain his leadership], and was sustained. Now in the gathering at Oneida he found himself face to face with a half dozen capable men who aspired to leadership. The result was another fight for control."

NARRATIVE OF JONATHAN BURT

Soon after Mr. Noyes's arrival, I went to Syracuse and invited Mr. E. H. Hamilton and Mr. Wm. H. Cook to come down for a conference the following Sunday. Then I went to Lairdsville and invited J. B. Foot to come for the same purpose. Mr. Foot was the man upon whom we had relied as the leader of our community movement. The meeting proved to be an exciting one. After a warm discussion, /2/ Messrs. Foot and Cook broke with Mr. Noyes, Cook particularly denouncing him in violent terms. The split was on the social [i.e., sexual] theory, though both had been informed of Mr. Noyes' position at the time of the [Genoa] Convention [in 1847]. Mr. Hamilton took sides with Mr. Noyes.

We continued to have thrilling scenes. Perfectionists from different parts came to visit us. In some few instances warm alliances were formed, but in most cases the result was a conflict and final separation. Mr. Abbot came about the middle of February bringing $800, which he held ready to put in as community stock. There had been considerable talk already about the transfer of the Putney family to Oneida, and Mr. Noyes had selected the present location for a building site, provided it could be obtained. Negotiations were entered into with Deacon Francis, the owner, and his whole farm was purchased, 80 acres, at an average of $42.50 per acre, Mr. Abbot's money being used for the first payment. We had before purchased a small piece of meadow land, 23 acres, on which was an Indian hut, just across the road from my house. We could not have immediate possession of the Francis place, but Mr. Noyes thought that by occupying this hut we could make a beginning of calling the wanderers. . . . A short time previous to their coming, Mrs. Burt and Miss Tryphena Hubbard called on Deacon Francis. While there he showed them an article from a Brattleboro paper giving a full account of the explosion at Putney. Deacon Francis expressed himself as regretting that he had sold his farm to such people. Mrs. Burt came home much excited, and declared that she would not have such a man in the house; if she could not get rid of him in any other way, she would burn the house down over our heads. I told her that Mr. Noyes had informed me of the whole /3/ matter, and that there was an entirely different view to be taken. I also said to Miss Hubbard that, if she was in any way acting as an adviser to Mrs. Burt, she had better as a friend advise her not to act rashly, for in so doing she would certainly bring ruin upon herself. The next day Mr. Noyes proposed that we offer Deacon Francis the chance to take back his farm and return us the $800, that I take this money to settle with Mrs. Burt, if she chose to separate from me, and that the rest of us depend upon the old sawmill for a living. To this plan Mr. Abbot heartily assented. I

then said to Mrs. Burt that my purpose was fixed to bend all my future energies to the building up of a Community, and that I had two proposals to make
to her. First, if she would stay with me, I would live in a separate family with
her and see that her wants were well provided for, but that she must expect
that my heart would be with the Community. Second, if she chose to separate
from me, I would give her the $800. After some reflection, she said we had
better keep the farm. We however, went to Deacon Francis with our offer, but
he refused to accept it. Mrs. Burt and Miss Hubbard took from this time an
entirely new turn. They became genial and happy, and with a hearty good will
went about making preparations for the newcomers. The company arrived at
the time appointed, and were joyfully welcomed by Mrs. Burt, as well as the
rest. Mr. Cragin brought another $500, in gold, which was paid for the mead-
ow lot, since always called the "Cragin Meadow."

William H. Cook to J. R. Miller
Syracuse, February 7, 1848

Dear Brother:—
I do not know how long I shall call you by the above title. /4/ Yesterday I
called on J. H. Noyes and had some talk, and sharp talk it was. I have no fellowship with or for him, until he shall renounce his course as being "of the
world, the flesh and the Devil." I have not so learned Christ.
And now let me say that J. H. Noyes is unhorsed, and that he is shortly
destined to meet a Waterloo defeat. No, Bro.
This is no small task for me, as I have said much for and about him. I
loved him very much, but if my right eye offends me, I pluck it out. And if I
ever have been called to pluck out right eyes, it has been in this case.
Should any of you think that I have been actuated by worldly wisdom, I
will say that, if this be worldly wisdom by which I have been actuated, I have
no other, neither do I desire any other. My mind in these matters has not been
prematurely expressed. I know what I am doing, and with whom I am dealing;
and whoever is found advocating Gatesism* will find me an uncompromising
opponent.
Unless I see you again by return of mail, my desire for you is that you may
fare well.

W. H. Cook

---

* The views expressed in Theophilous Gates's free-love newspaper *The Battle-Axe and Weapons of War*. [L.F.]

Noyes to Deborah Haile
  Burt's, February 10, 1848

Dear Mrs. Haile:—

As your letter does not forbid a reply, I will satisfy my love of faithfulness by offering you the cautions which your present situation demands.

From all that appears in your letter, I conclude that you have judged me and the principles of the Putney Association by the report of Mr. Haile. M. G. Devoe has been here since Mr. Haile called at Owasco on his return, and he reported that /5/ Mr. Haile endorsed Cook's bitterness against me. This surprised me much, as Mr. Haile left here with professions of Fellowship.

On one point, according to Devoe's report, Mr. Haile, either by carelessness or otherwise, grossly misrepresented my principles. He represented me as adopting the French method of controlling propagation [using condoms]. There could not be a worse mistake than this. I expressly repudiated in my conversation with him the French method, condemning them all in the strongest of terms as unnatural, unhealthy, and abominable. The method which I commended [coitus reservatus] was one which confines sexual communion to social purposes, forbidding the propagative act, except when conception is intended. This method, in my view, crucifies the fleshly lust of men, and elevates sexual communion into a social and spiritual act.

Mr. Devoe also said that Mr. Haile did not show the brethren at Owasco a declaration of principles which I wrote out and put into his hands. As you are silent about it, possibly he has not shown it to you. Now, if Mr. Devoe's reports are true (which I do not affirm, and which I am very unwilling to believe) you ought to wait for better testimony before you judge and act on this weighty matter. This is a caution to you, not an accusation of Mr. Haile. I hope he will be able to clear himself.

Beware of trusting blind operations of your mind and heart, however imposing and delightful your exercises may be. New York "revelations" are at a discount. Foot went to Putney last fall "by revelation," and acknowledged me leader "by revelation." Cook in the interval between the two conventions endorsed my theory of sexual morality "by revelation." Gould has had abundant "revelations" exactly the opposite of yours. It was no longer ago than the 31st of January that Corwin found his heart irresistibly (but /6/ blindly as it now appears) loving me more and more. Only three weeks ago Foot was pressed "by revelation" to join this Community, and was wonderfully "blessed" in coming here. Remember what "blessedness ye spake of" in receiving and acknowledging me in both of the conventions and throughout the State, and consider that at that time and for more than a year previous I and the Putney

Association had been in what you now call the "depths of Satan," and remember that previous to the Genoa Convention, where the divine power was most manifest, I had "communicated privately to them that were of reputation" my gospel. One of the wickedest worldlings among our persecutors at Putney, in a crazy fit brought on by his fury against us, came out with a "revelation" just like yours, and was greatly "blessed" by it. Though he was mild and compassionate toward us for a time, he now swears he will pursue us till we cannot say that God takes care of us. Remember, too, that you were drawn into the snare of uncleanness I escaped, and during the nine years of your captivity and sorrow I have been happy in God's approval, receiving revelations which commend themselves to all rational minds. I am still happy, moving on in revelations not of the mushroom sort but stable, consistent, enduring. Which are most likely to be true, my revelations which have made me steadily happy and consistent for fourteen years, or yours which have just gushed and are yet to be tried? Bear in mind that a temporary flow of happiness is no test of the truth of your exercises. In all such changes of spiritual condition as you have just done through, the spirit comes into union with some new principality in the invisible world, and the mere novelty of fellowship produces pleasure, whether the new principality is divine or diabolical. Enduring truthfulness alone, not pleasurable imaginations and /7/ sensations, attest the divinity of our fellowships and revelations.

I advise you to wait till I have told my story in full before you judge me. I am about to publish my views, and am as sure of casting down all opposing imaginations now as I was when I came out with the new covenant and the second coming. My prayer is that you may save yourself the trouble of a vain contest with the truth.

J. H. Noyes

W. C. Gould to J. H. Thomas of Newark, N.J.
 Oneida Depot
  Madison County, N. Y.
   February 13, 1848

To Bro. Thomas and others in fellowship:—
Two brethren from Genoa, Cayuga County, have just now called on me, and reprimanded me for not writing to them a report of my visit to Putney. This reminds me of the promise I made you in Newark that I would report to you, which I have not omitted through forgetfulness or indifference to your wishes or welfare, but really because I was not prepared to give you a full report.

I was very much interested in Putney as far as concerns Association. I found a good deal of love and harmony, kindness and true politeness among the members, but I was dissatisfied and surprised to find that Bro. Noyes's leadership as practiced at Putney was totally opposite and different from his theory as explained abroad. I expressed my disappointment to Bro. Noyes, who put me off from day to day with rather evasive answers, until I finally told him plainly that unless he satisfied me on this subject I should be compelled to make a report on his practical leadership that I thought would be unsatisfactory. He then promised that he would prove to me that instead of trampling on the claims of liberty and equality, he was the champion of liberty. On the /8/ strength of this promise I expressed myself satisfied to let the matter rest; but as he left Putney in three or four days unexpectedly, and I left the day following, I have had to wait for the fulfillment of his promise until two weeks since, when he arrived here. The next day I reminded him of his promise, when to my surprise he positively refused under the pleas that I had expressed myself satisfied at Putney. I reminded him that we had had no conversation on that subject since he made me the promise, but that availed nothing. He then demanded to know if I would surrender my choice, judgment, and will to him, and obey him even in opposition to revelations from God. I told him, as I had told him in Putney, that I would see him damned first, and then I would not; that I had always meant, and still meant to obey God rather than man. He said if I did not accede to those terms he would break with me, and he did so. He went up to Burt's, and I have not seen him since. . . .

He claims to be chief because he has the longest sword, and the sword represents truth; that generally he can convince his followers of the expediency of his measures, but as commander-in-chief he must be allowed in cases of emergency to issue orders that may appear for the time being unsafe and unreasonable. This is the theory he has held out to me for eight years. But after the strictest observation for three weeks at Putney, I am compelled to say that his government is an exhibition of the most absolute specimen of despotism I ever saw. The members are under his control in the most absolute sense in matters of the least as well as most consequence. I do not think they feel the least right of control over their property, persons, time, their wives, choice, judgment, will or affections. /9/ I heard them express not a solitary opinion in his presence until they heard his first, and then all gave in the same opinion. He treats counsel with contempt, and criticism as mutiny and treason, and all such intruders are placed under the ban of the community. And although I say it with pain and regret, yet truth compels me to say that, notwithstanding the exalted opinion I have of the privileges and advantages of Association, if I can have access to them only through worse than southern slavery, then I will face isolation with all of its evils.

But, you may inquire, is not the happiness of the Community the effect of the government? I think not, but the result of Association and that its privileges make them happy in spite of a bad government.

If Bro. Noyes was inspired on all occasions, I would say, concede to his claim of dictating on all occasions. But this he does not pretend.

Yet do not understand me as despairing of Association. I believe this order of existence is destined to supersede and control all other social and political orders. Nor do I wish to be understood as condemning Bro. Noyes as a tyrant or hypocrite. I accuse him of no such thing. I regard him, as I have always done, as the best exponent of the cardinal doctrines of our faith, and chief as well as honored agent in their development. I think he has sacrificed more than any other one for the cause of truth. I have the same sympathy for Bro. Noyes and the Putney Association in their dispersion and trials that I ever had. I simply believe that he has committed an error in the matter of leadership of such a serious nature that I for one cannot submit to it. /10/

After Bro. Noyes broke with me I did not know but I should be abandoned by every Perfectionist in the land, but having strong assurance that God was on my side I resolved to stand firm if deserted by the universe. Within a few days, however, some Perfectionists in this region either have or are breaking with Bro. Noyes. I am informed that he and Burt have contracted for three or four farms, but without a material change in opinions I cannot see where they will find occupants in this region.

Having given you as full a report as my sheet will admit, I must defer a great many particulars until another time. Should this letter give rise to any questions in your mind or with those in sympathy with you, I shall be pleased to answer them. I had hoped that the day had arrived when Bro. Noyes's claims to leadership would no longer continue to be the stalking-horse of the land, when schism and treachery would give way to quietness, peace and unity of interest, fellowship and love; and [I] still hope this interruption will not be permanent.

I have looked back a thousand times with interest to our delightful visit among the saints at Newark, and the pure and heavenly fellowship that reigned in the little nucleus that was formed while there. I hope, as Bro. Inslee has come more particularly into this union, that the strength of this fellowship has increased with your increase of numbers.

We shall be glad to see or hear from any of you at any time. Suppose you come and make us a visit with your wife. I believe this is a time of year when your business is apt to be slack. We have been expecting an answer from Clarissa to my wife's letter.

Yours in the faith and love of the gospel.

W. C. Gould /11/

Noyes to John B. Foot
Oneida, February 18, 1848

Bro. Foot:—

After a good deal of thinking and talking about your situation and the prospect of your coming here, I have come to the conclusion to write you a frank letter laying open to you the difficulties which our minds are laboring in relation to you.

The undecided position in which you stand as to the views I am advancing on a subject of great importance especially to the Association movement gives an unpromising aspect to our proposed alliance. I have no right or disposition to force you to a decision, but I have a right and am bound to guard my own relations to you so long as you remain at variance with me or in doubt about my position. I feel as I did at Putney, when you were on the one hand urging me to go into partnership with you in holding meetings, and on the other hesitating about leadership. I said to you then: "We shall not act together harmoniously till our relations to each other are definitely settled. I will not press you to judgment on my claims of office, and on the other hand you should not press me to partnership." So now I am satisfied that it is not prudent for us to marry by Association till we are substantially agreed. It is impossible to organize a harmonious and efficient administration with a second officer of opposite politics to the first. I will not ask you to agree with me, but I may fairly ask you to let me stand alone till we are agreed. If you can continue to say of a doctrine which enters so deeply into my theory of Association as the doctrine of communism of love does, that you have nothing to do with it, it is evident, whether I am right or wrong, that we are not in condition to act together. /12/

The positive and continued opposition of your wife to what I regard as the Pentecostal principle still further embarrasses our relations and renders the attempt to join our interests doubtful and dangerous.

Bro. Burt also thinks (and I agree with him) that the situation of your property is not such as it ought to be in order to your satisfactory union with the body here. We shall need a large sum to pay for the Francis farm. Abbot brings $800, Hamilton $400. About $300 remains to be provided for. At least a portion of this must be supplied by the third partner in that concern. If Bro. Burt applies the $500 which I put into his hands to that purpose, $800 will still be behind, and after providing for Cragin I cannot undertake to fill this gap. We think that if you cannot help at all in this matter, prudence dictates that we should look out for another third partner. Bro. Baker is coming with $600. Ought we not to put him in with Abbot and Hamilton, instead of extending our territory?

If you have no opportunity to sell your farm, or if your wife's right in it is such that you cannot control it, you are not to be blamed for your inability to help us. Nevertheless that inability is a fact which must be taken into account in our plans, and which will necessarily affect your position among us. We ought not to involve ourselves in heavy liabilities, and if our liabilities will be made too heavy by your coming without funds, we ought to consider whether this is not a sign of the will of God that you should remain where you are till you can control and shift your property.

I desire greatly the consummation of our union, and for that very purpose I have been thus frank with you, because I know that a right union cannot be consummated without the removal of stumblingblocks.

Yours truly,
John H. Noyes /13/

Noyes to E. H. Hamilton
Oneida, February 19, 1848

Dear Bro. Hamilton:—

Abbot says that seven years ago, when my credit was low in New York, Cook wrote him a long letter censuring him for being a "Noyesite," and disparaging me in every way. The consequence was that Abbot lost his anchorage, drifted at random, and shipwrecked on Van Epps. Again Abbot says that last year, when my credit was good in New York, Cook wrote him that "there was a bond between him and Putney that neither men nor devils could break." And on Abbot's return from Putney, Cook bluffed him off till he found out where he had been, and then received him handsomely, avowing that "fellowship with Noyes was the condition of fellowship with him." But behold! Now the wind has changed again. My credit is down again, and again Cook is writing in all directions against me.

Cook has had wit enough to keep at the head of the current of the times, but he has never really accomplished anything either for himself or anybody else. He has not the generalship or courage of a true soldier, but only of a bully. Bragging is his strength, and bragging will not answer in this war. Defeat is before him.

He has written to J. R. Miller at Putney that I am "unhorsed" etc. I have written that, as he has been my horse for the last year or two and has now flung up his heels in a fright at communism of love, I may admit that I have been "unhorsed" in a certain sense. But it has been my luck, as usual, to find a better horse ready, and the battle goes well.

In the battle on Lake Erie, Commodore Perry's flagship was so battered by the enemies' shot that it became an unmanageable wreck. In the midst of the fight he left it in a boat, took command of /14/ another ship, sailed up through the enemies' line delivering an effectual broadside right and left, and so secured the victory. Cook, I suppose, would say that Perry was a coward in leaving his ship!

The little band here is purging itself of mischief-makers, and learning the value of peace. God's care over us is manifest. I think by the first of March, when my wife and Cragin with his family are to come, we shall be in condition to receive them into a quiet and happy home. We look with pleasure for the addition of yourself and family. God bless you and direct you in all things.

Yours faithfully,
John H. Noyes

Noyes to John Haile
Oneida, February 22, 1848

Bro. Haile:—

In fulfillment of my promise to write you I will give you a sketch of occurrences since you left, and (as we used to say in revival times) "close with a few remarks."

Bro. Foot, who was here when you went, said that his experience in regard to coming here was this: He was under pressure and darkness all the week previous, and at length when he turned his face this way he was "let up," and on the road hither was wonderfully "blessed." Yet he went away without any decisive union with me, sticking as heretofore in noncommitalism in regard to the agitating subject. Corwin came with eyes partly blinded by Cook's smoke, heard me, assented to almost all I said, but objected to the practical part of my position, went away to Foot's, virtually though not formally rejecting me, and has been there ever since. /15/ Hatch and his wife went with him. Soon after this a letter came from New York (sent by Cragin) which Corwin wrote me about a month ago. It is full of expressions of confidence and sympathy without a word of doubt or censure. The following are specimens of its drift:

"It is difficult to comprehend how it is that brethren who have been in the field from the beginning, who have had all your writings, and have borne the reproach of Perfectionism, do not more readily comprehend your position: How it is that such brethren are hesitating, are doubting, are unbelieving, nay more, are absolutely opposed to the genius of the gospel touching the unity of believers, the gathering of the true church in the resurrection state. . . . In answer to a letter (sent to Putney) I have just received a very interesting and satisfactory reply dated January 22nd from J. L. Skinner and Harriet A. Noyes, and notwithstanding all the reproach that is heaped upon you by a wicked world through the instigation of a still more wicked church, I find my heart irresistibly loving you more and more, a fact which sometimes my outward senses are backward to confess."

Such was Corwin's position up to the latest date previous to his coming here. It is now, I think, quite different. Time will determine.

On Sunday while Corwin, Hatch, Foot and their wives were in hot debate about the administration here, young [Henry] Seymour from Lairdsville came to examine me. He was rather "porcupiny" at first, but soon became respectful, and finally laid down his weapons and surrendered at discretion. He let us into the secrets of the conclave at Lairdsville: said that the brethren there supposed he came to spy out our nakedness, and he knew not what they would say if he came /16/ back otherwise than full of wrath at me. He disclosed the fact that Hatch was talking bitterly against me, which I put side by side with the fact that Hatch has not made a complaint against me to my face but on the contrary has plastered me with flattery for the past ten years. And especially the last three weeks. He has constantly professed to regard me as the only man that could be depended on as faithful to the truth, and the only man that could help him out of his difficulties; and he went away without intimating anything to the contrary of this profession. But you recollect he had a terrible crazy fit Sunday evening before you left. That was brought on by Burt's simply offering to become responsible for his debts. He took this as a bribe and insult. He is the last man that ought to be "touchy" on such matters, for he has been hanging on everybody and anybody for support and dunning the saints all over the land for help to pay his debts for the last ten years to my knowledge. But so it was that he was enraged, and in his fury he abused Ackley, his best friend, threatened to drown himself, declared that he cared nothing for God and had as lief be damned as not, and swore that he would put his spear into the tallest arch-angel in heaven if he dared to touch his wife. The blasphemous spirit that thus tore him has carried him away (Corwin helping), and the remaining part of the Beaver Meadow company are heartily glad to be relieved of him. Ackley has given him up.

Those that now remain are of the quiet, steady sort, and we have good times, acting unanimously, edifying one another, fearing nothing, asking no favors of men, not anxious for customers, ready to show our spiritual goods and impart to those who call. We have cheering news frequently from Putney. My wife and the Cragins are coming to settle here on the first of March. Baker and probably /17/ my brother George will come with them to stay a few days. Hamilton and family are expected in the course of the spring. Young Seymour stayed till Monday, heard me through with steadily increasing interest, went away in full fellowship thinking seriously of coming to live among us soon. He is one of the reasoning sort that can receive a rational idea and act upon it without requiring God to tickle him to confirm its truth.

Remarks: In view of all that is going on, I am impressed more and more with the conviction that unfaithfulness is one of the worst of the bad habits of New York Perfectionists. There is a spirit in these regions which makes a light thing of entering into the engagements of fellowship, and a light thing of breaking them. Rider, when he left me in 1837, was under the most sacred engagements to cooperate with me. The next thing I knew of him he had dropped off silently into non-committalism, and soon without any change on my part or any negotiations between us he became an enemy. Dutton served me in much the same way . . . Cook did nothing in the way of executing the projects of the Genoa Convention, but on the contrary fell to devising abortive schemes of his own. . . . The somersaults of Hatch and Corwin are further illustrations of the "shaky" nature of the spirit in these parts. And I fear, in view of all the signs I see, that the general acknowledgment of me which was made with so much enthusiasm at both conventions, and the solemn covenant which many made at the last convention to take Christ in the place of death and move on toward heavenly Association, will prove to have been windy talk of men who have not the spirit of execution, loud explosions like those of training day without bullets.

I shall be found for one a follower of him who rides on the /18/ horse and is called "Faithful and True." He has taught me to have [leave?] unfaithfulness, to regard the obligations of spiritual fellowship as more sacred than those of marriage. His eyes are "as a flame of fire." He witnessed the proceedings at our conventions. He noted every man who promised to take him "for better or for worse." He will assuredly prosecute for breach of promise those who are now lightly turning away from him. I am bold to forewarn all that he is about to give Perfectionists a lesson on the subject of faithfulness that they will remember.

It is due to some (and I trust to more than I know of) and especially to Bro. Burt, that I should acknowledge having found a remnant of faithfulness in this State. The man whose response to the call of Christ at Genoa was clearest and most hearty meant what he said and has proved it by deeds.

The rewards of the Kingdom of God are offered to them that "overcome," to them that are "faithful unto death." "The fearful and unbelieving" have their part with whoremongers and idolaters and liars in the lake that burneth with fire and brimstone.

The body of believers at Genoa have heretofore given signs of more steady and substantial faith than is generally to be found in this State. I look with interest to see what turn they will take at this crisis. I hope to hear good things of you and your wife, and shall remain (till you turn away from me) faithfully yours,

John H. Noyes /19/

2

Settlement of the Putney Lawsuits

THE CASE OF NOYES'S BONDS

Noyes was arrested October 26, 1847, on a charge of adultery, and was bound over for trial before the County Court in April 1848. John R. Miller furnished $2000 bail, and Noyes was released. The case came up for trial on May 5, 1849.

State's Attorney Kirkland opened the argument as follows:

"The defendant has been indicted for two of the worst crimes known to the law. The proof was as clear and positive as in any case I ever knew. The witnesses were all his friends and disciples, who believe him to be the beloved son of God. He sets himself up to be a religious teacher and leader, to have a purer doctrine than was ever taught before, the doctrine of perfect holiness. He even believes that the Kingdom of God has come, and that they belong to that Kingdom. He is a man of wealth, talents, and education, and therefore has an unusual influence. If he was a poor man, instead of being the head of a harem in the State of New York, he would be at Windsor [state prison] hewing stone where he ought to be. If there is any case in which the full amount of the bonds ought to be exacted, it seems to me that this is the one. I go for the bonds and the whole bonds."

Mr. William C. Bradley, attorney for the defense, offered to read affidavits from the Grand Jurors showing that there was no proof before them that would convict. But Judge Kellog refused to hear anything from the Grand Jury room. "As Mr. Noyes does not appear for trial," said he, "I shall consider him guilty. If you have anything to say why the bonds should be cut down under these circumstances, we will hear it."

Mr. Bradley: "The defendant became a member of the theological / 20/ schools at Andover and New Haven at the very time when the discussion was going on between Dr. [Nathaniel W.] Taylor and Dr. [Bennet] Tyler, which resulted in the division of the church into the old school and the new school. There was great excitement. The doctrine of Perfection was freely discussed. . . . The defendant turned his attention to the Bible and found there the doctrines which he then embraced. The fact that he has adhered to these principles at all times and under all circumstances, at whatever cost and sacrifice, it seems to me will convince the Court that he is honest and sincere. It is true that his principles are somewhat antinomian. . . .

"It is not true that the defendant absconded. He went away *openly* and *manfully*, by the advice of his friends, in accordance with the wishes of his enemies, and took his proselytes with him. I visited Putney soon after, and found that the trouble was principally a religious excitement, together with a little commercial jealousy. . . .

"Mr. Noyes married, I trust, into a respectable family, and received with his wife a considerable sum of money. Before he left I requested him to put something in trust for his wife and child, a fine little boy of nine years, in case they should ever come to want. He was perfectly willing to do so, and I now hold the bond.

"He took with him his personal property, and if you exact the bonds, you will either be obliged to collect them of Mr. Miller, his brother-in-law, which will entirely ruin his business, or take it out of the portion left to his wife and child. It appears to me that in either case it can do no good. We hope that the Court will take all these circumstances into consideration, and be as favorable as possible." /21/

The decision of the Court was, that the bonds should be cut down from $2000 to $1000. "Got home," writes Miller, "about 11 o'clock Saturday evening, glad to find sympathy and fellowship. I never felt more completely used up." [G.W.N.]

THE HALL AND BAKER SUITS

On December 13, 1847, Gates Perry, Deputy Sheriff, called with two writs against Noyes of $3000 each in favor of Daniel J. Hall and Luke Baker. He put an attachment on the real estate, and undertook to attach the store but gave that up. During the ensuing month Mr. Hall made a new bid for the Community's confidence; read *The Berean*, and liked it very much; even free love, he said, looked beautiful to him. In April 1848 he publicly withdrew his suit. [G.W.N.]

John R. Miller to Noyes
August 10, 1848

I have just closed my negotiations with Mr. Baker. He will settle for $300, paid to him, to be held in trust for the benefit of the girls and their heirs. I told him that I was perfectly satisfied with this proposal, and I was confident that you would be. He said he thought we ought to do something about his costs, and make Mrs. Baker a small present. I told him that I should make no such conditions, but he would find that we should deal generously and honorably with him. He has conducted himself like a gentleman, if not a Christian, through this whole negotiation. We all have the kindest feelings toward him. Just as I was leaving him he said: "I want you should do what you can to make my family think well of me, and I want you should *all* think well of me, and I shall of you."

August 13.—I think we are getting along well. We have settled $6000 of our lawsuits by giving $300 to our own society. /22/

Noyes to John R. Miller
August 16, 1848

I am satisfied with your arrangements with Mr. Baker, though it ought to be distinctly understood that it is an indulgence to his worldly views and feelings, and not the reparation of any wrong which I have done him or his family, for I have done them nothing but good, and the injury is altogether on his side. I hope he will continue to soften and yield till he sees that he is my debtor. If he does, I shall have none but friendly feelings toward him, and shall use my influence to make his family think well of him.

As to Mr. Lamb's case, I have no very clear judgment about the amount we should pay rather than quarrel at law. If it goes before honest arbitrators, I am willing to pay whatever they say. And I would not object to paying $50, or even $100, without an arbitration. Do what you think best, and I shall be satisfied. Our policy is to give the enemy a bridge of money, over which to make a decent retreat. We can afford it, as we are "operating for a rise" in Perfectionist stock, and have plenty of signs that our calculations are sound. The Old World is certainly going to destruction just at the time when we have received orders to begin the introduction of the new Heavens and the new Earth. Our constituents all over the country meet us with new devotion of heart and property just at the time when our private resources are embarrassed.

Tell Mother and Mrs. Campbell that they will find my speculations, as heretofore, safe as well as bold.

ISRAEL KEYES' GUARDIANSHIP SUIT AGAINST MRS. COBB, A MEMBER OF THE PUTNEY COMMUNITY /23/

John R. Miller to the Oneida Association

March 28, 1849.—W. C. Bradley said, notwithstanding Mrs. Cobb had received the money on her notes, if Keyes had previously left a copy of his proceedings at the town clerk's office, all transactions afterward would be good for nothing. I went to the town clerk's office and found that the paper was left there *after* the money had all been paid. We supposed everybody knew that Mrs. Cobb lived with us, but Mr. Wheat, the constable, went to three other places first. When at last he came to our house, Mrs. Cobb had gone out and Charlotte did not know where. He found her just in time to make the service before sundown, but had not time to make his return to the town clerk's office that night.

April 6, 1849.—Yesterday was a great day for Putney. Our victory over the enemy was complete. I never saw anyone so used up as Keyes. He found that if the case came to trial yesterday he should be defeated, and to get out of the scrape he pleaded for a continuance, like a man pleading for his life. But he could not give one good reason. His main argument was that some great wrong had been committed by Miller or someone else in putting the money where they could not find it. Mr. Bradley told them, if they wanted a continuance to find the money, he would tell them now where it was. It was all in Mrs. Cobb's pocket, and if they did not believe it, he would prove it. Mr. Keyes said: "It may be there today, it may be in Miller's pocket tomorrow, and next day somewhere else."

After the Judge had decided that they could not have a continuance, not a word was spoken for five minutes. At last Mr. Kimball said: "Well, Mr. Keyes, what are you going to do?" Keyes: "I suppose the judge understands what I am going to do." Judge: /24/ "No, I don't understand." Keyes: "Well, I—hm—I—shall—hm—withdraw my suit." Judge: "Well, there is nothing more to be done."

Our trust was in God, to whom all the glory.

Yours in Love,
J. R. Miller

RUSSELL LAMB'S SUIT AGAINST JOHN H. NOYES, GEORGE W. NOYES, AND JOHN R. MILLER

"for enticing away Lamb's daughter Lucinda to the serious injury and expense of her father." The suit was entered in January 1848 before Judge O. L. Shafter as Referee, and the case came to trial in January 1850. [G.W.N.]

John R. Miller to the Oneida Community
January 17, 1850

The Court was in session two days. The house was crowded. Many were present from all the surrounding towns. The Sheriff was in attendance the whole two days to keep order. Though compelled to meet all the wrath of our enemies I had the same vigorous and cheerful spirit with which I left Oneida. I think I showed the whole town that I was not ashamed of the truth.

Mr. Bradley spoke two and a half hours, and his arguments were entirely satisfactory. He freely owned our practices, and then justified them.

Though Mr. Walker in his closing plea said everything that could be said against me, calling me a devil of the blackest character, I sat by his side and took notes of his remarks coolly and quietly, and with less unpleasant feelings than I have often had in reporting our Oneida criticisms.

L. G. Mead to J. R. Miller
January 25, 1850

Judge Shafter went to sit as referee in another case at Vernon, Vermont. /25/ He carried *the Book** with him, and as often as he had any leisure was seen to

---

* *First Annual Report of the Oneida Association*. [G.W.N.]

read it, till he read it attentively through. He was then heard to say, "*Very* original and profound, but has very little to do with the case at Putney." Old Mr. Bradley thinks he will not give one cent damages. Dorr thinks he may give slight damages for the abduction from Metcalf's on the 12th.

We all agree in one thing: 'Twas well it was not compromised. The trial places you all in a much better light than public opinion would have accorded you had it been settled. The multitude would have been ready to imagine things which Lamb, his counsel and willing witnesses could not make appear. And John will probably consider the wide spread of his opinions worth at least the expense of the trial. I think no man should be indicted hereafter for circulating a book which Lamb's counsel took so much pains to bring before the public.

Love to all,
L. G. Mead

On the facts brought before the Court, Mr. O. L. Shafter, the Referee, found that the defendants were "guilty in manner and form as the plaintiff hath alleged, and found for the plaintiff to recover of the defendants the sum of five hundred dollars ($500.00) and his costs. Plaintiff's costs $41.21."

INDICTMENT OF JOHN R. MILLER
FOR CIRCULATING THE FIRST ANNUAL REPORT

In the spring of 1849 it became known that the Rev. Hubbard Eastman, the Methodist minister at Putney, was engaged on a book to be entitled *Noyesism Unveiled*. At the same time Noyes was busily preparing the *First Annual Report of the Oneida Association*, "exhibiting /26/ its history, principles and Transactions to Jan. 1, 1849." As these rival books approached completion there was some jockeying for position between Eastman and Noyes. Eastman's book was completed in May 1849, but was not put into circulation until about the 15th of June. Noyes's book was printed on April 3rd 1849, and on the 15th Mr. Cragin placed copies in the hands of Horace Greeley and a half-dozen other prominent persons in New York City. The Court that was to try the case of Noyes's bonds was in session. Noyes said to his sister Harriet, that he would like to have Mr. Miller circulate the *Report* after the court and a little ahead of Eastman. If it should come out just after Eastman had got his book too far forward to change, he would like that well. [G.W.N.]

John R. Miller to Noyes
May 7, 1849

I told Mr. Bradley your views about putting the *Report* in circulation. He said: "I think this *Report* had better not be put in circulation. At any rate Eastman's book ought to come out first. When that comes out I think that I, being a worldly man, can write something that will take better with the public than a theological work from Mr. Noyes. I will consult Mr. Mead and see what can be done. Mr. Eastman may be so careless as to say things he cannot prove. If so, we had better pounce upon him. Our policy is to keep quiet, and see what the enemy can do first.

"Since I got hold of the doctrine I do not believe there is so much concupiscence in that whole body as there is in an equal number in respectable society in the world. There is a great stimulus taken off that raises the devil with the rest of the world. I told Mead and Horatio so."

Mr. Mead said: "I cannnot see it will do any good to make /27/ the *Report* any more public at present. On the whole I think Mr. Bradley's opinion is correct."

I thought I would write you just what they said, and perhaps you would think best to let it rest a while. We shall follow your advice about it.

I never felt the pressure of the worldly spirit worse than I have for a week past. It seems almost impossible to live under it. I have had a tremendous struggle in my own heart, caused, on the one hand, by dread of further disclosures that would create another war against us, and, on the other, a firm determination to stand my ground, defend the truth, and do the will of God at the sacrifice of everything else. My prayer is that I may act wisely before God.

John R. Miller to the Oneida Community
January 8, 1850

Was I not at Oneida called a respectable man, decent at least? I thought so. But here in Putney, where I once had a name and standing with the rest of mankind, I am arrested like a common pickpocket. While I was gone this afternoon, Gates Perry, the fat Sheriff from Saxton's Village, came to Putney to arrest me on an indictment for circulating the *First Annual Report of the Oneida Association,* notwithstanding the State's Attorney had agreed to do nothing about it till we all met at Putney on the 15th of January. Perry went immediately to Mr. Barton's without stopping to hear the stories of Israel Keyes & Co. As I was passing by about five o'clock with Mr. Barton, he came out and said he had a precept for my arrest with orders to carry me to jail. "Well," said, I, "I am ready; all I ask is that you will do your duty without giving me unnecessary trouble." /28/ He said he supposed that he must carry me to Newfane jail, but if I wished to go to Brattleboro and see Mr. Mead first, he would carry me that way. I then invited him to take tea with me at Mr. Lord's. We had a pleasant chat at the table, and at half-past five started for Brattleboro in a snow storm. I talked freely with him, and before we arrived he became very much interested. He said he would be glad to read the *Report,* and assured me on the honor of a gentleman, that if I would give him one he would make no use of it to injure me. I replied that I would give him a copy if I could do so with safety. At Mr. Mead's office we found that it was not necessary to go to Newfane: all that the law required was that I go before one of the Judges of the County court and give bail for my appearance at the April Court. Perry promised to send for Judge Clark of Brattleboro, but Mr. Mead said that Judge Arnold of Londonderry was stopping at Lord's Tavern, and he would call him in. When the Judge came in, the door was locked and Mr. Mead told him what the business was; that it was got up by Lamb to have an effect on his suit; that if the book was what it was said to be, a licentious book, the best way was to make the bail so low that we would pay it without trial. He said he was willing to give any bail the Judge thought proper, but would suggest the propriety of calling it $50.00. The Judge said he had been thinking of $100.00. Mr. Mead objected that this would bring the whole subject before the Court, which did not seem to be necessary. The Judge said he wanted to do his duty, and asked the Sheriff, who is a man of a good deal of influence in the County, what he thought of it. "I think it is damned small business," said the Sheriff, "and I would take the $50.00." The Judge: "So do I think it is small business, and I shall do it. Make out your papers." The Judge got quite interested, /29/ and said: "Just between us, I would not pay the $50.00, but bring it before the Court."

The business being done, I thanked the Judge and Sheriff for their gentlemanly treatment. The Sheriff asked me to ride up with him in the morning to Putney, and said with a laugh that he would leave me where he found me.

As soon as the Judge and Sheriff had left the office, Mr. Mead jumped up, snapped his fingers and said: "I guess John will think that God has had a hand in this," and we both had a hearty laugh. Strange as it may seem, I enjoyed the whole affair highly. I saw so plainly the hand of God in arranging the minutest circumstances, that it gave me the greatest confidence in our success.

Judge Arnold was the very man of all others in Windham County to help in this business. He was one of the Judges who decided on the amount of bonds in the criminal suit, and was in favor of putting them lower than either of the others. He lives thirty or forty miles from Brattleboro, and probably does not go there once a year, but God saw that his presence was necessary and sent him there just at the right time. Again, *we* got there just at the right moment. He was there to attend a Court, and was going to Vernon to a ball in the evening. We arrived in Brattleboro just after he got through with his Court and just before he started for the ball.

After we all got together in Mr. Mead's office and locked the door, I soon saw that I had the right company, and I felt as free and light hearted as I ever did in my life. The Judge said: "Well, I suppose we can talk this matter over freely amongst ourselves." "Yes," said Mr. Mead, "let us make a kind of family /30/ meeting of it." The Judge wanted me to give a brief history of the affair. I asked the Sheriff to do it, saying, "as you are not interested, he will be more likely to believe you." "I'll believe your story," said the Judge. Mr. Mead and I then gave our account, and I can assure you we got up a real indignation meeting against Israel Keyes, Lamb, and our Putney enemies, in which the Judge and Sheriff joined most heartily.

Mr. Mead told the Judge that we were not anxious to get rid of the indictment, that we thought the *Report* was God's truth, and would take pride in having it ably argued before Windham County Court.

John R. Miller to the Oneida Community
April 5, 1850

I called on Bradley, Sheafe, and Kellogg, all of whom thought it best to settle the indictment case for circulating the *Report*. Mr. Kellogg, the State's Attorney, said he wanted to consider the case further, but that he would promise to settle with our attorney on advantageous terms. Mr. Sheafe said he told Professor Agassi that he had a book in his possession which had caused a great deal of excitement in this State, and would like to have him examine it. Agassiz caught hold of it with both hands, and after reading it for some time in silence exclaimed: "Mr. Sheafe, this book is invaluable to me. It is the very thing I want. I have been studying this subject for years. You could not have presented me with anything so acceptable." Mr. Sheafe also gave one to Mr. Gould, a distinguished physician of Boston, and sent one to the Governor of Vermont.

April 27, 1850

Mr. Mead pleaded guilty for Mr. Miller on the charge of circulating three copies of the *First Annual Report of the Oneida Association:* and the Court, after reading and considering the /31/ book and hearing the argument, assessed a fine of $15.00 and costs of $33.99. Mr. Mead paid $49.00, and the case was discharged./32/

3

Life in the Association
January 1849*

The first three and a half years at Oneida were years of strenuous endeavor "getting started." Outlying groups of Perfectionists were invited to join, and the membership, which was 87 at the end of the first year, rose to 172 at the end of the second, and 205 at the end of the third. A rough and ready organization was formed. Lands were purchased and cleared, dwellings were erected, communal housekeeping begun. The first-comers were temporarily accommodated in a rude log hut built by the Indians. A daily evening meeting was established for the religious and social communion of the family circle, and later a Sunday meeting to which the public was invited. The children and the few adults who joined in an irreligious state were converted. The fundamental principles of the new social [i.e., sexual] order were taught. Provision was made for the care of children in the "Children's House." Education was organized, mutual criticism commenced. A beginning was made of various industries needed in a new country, farming, a saw and grist mill, store, shoe shop, blacksmith shop. Branch Communities were formed at Brooklyn and Manlius in New York State, at Cambridge in Northern Vermont, and at Wallingford, Connecticut, besides maintaining the original stand at Putney, Vermont. A few members not adapted to communism were sent away or allowed to withdraw after a sufficient trial. Athletic sports and amusements were /33/ encouraged, and much attention was given to providing the best conditions for health. Short dresses and bobbed hair were adopted by the women. The old lawsuits that hung over from the Putney persecution were cleared away: the most important one was voluntarily withdrawn in consequence of the complainant being converted and joining the Community.

In the midst of multitudinous responsibilities, the public was kept informed of the teachings and progress of the Community by the publi-

---

* The original title's dates read "January 1849 to February 1850." [L.F.]

cation of a free bi-weekly paper, three annual reports, and a special exposition of the social theory entitled *"The Bible Argument."* There was a momentary flare-up of hostility on the part of one neighboring family, the Hubbards, at the time *"The Bible Argument"* was published, but in the main the surrounding population were tolerant and friendly. As the end of this preliminary period, the members were seasoned Communists, homogeneous, compactly organized, equipped with needful religious and social ordinances, respected and loved by their neighbors. [G.W.N.]

PRINCIPLES OF THE ASSOCIATION

January 1, 1849

1. Religious principle, or more specifically the principle of perfect holiness as presented in the publications of the New Haven and Putney school of Perfectionists is the basis of the Association.

2. In accordance with the sentiment of the first Resolution of the Genoa Convention, this Association as a branch of the Kingdom of God embraces and provides for all interests of its members, religious, political, social, and physical. In /34/other words, it is at once a church, a state, a family, and a business association. Of course, it excludes from union with other associations.

3. The Association has not thus far resorted to constitutions and written compacts or rules for the regulation of its members. In the place of these, it relies on inspiration, the care and admonition of those who approve themselves qualified to be overseers, and free criticism. These have been found sufficient.

4. The officers of the Association were not chosen by vote, but are ascertained and recognized as chosen by God. They come into their places by manifesting their qualifications. Under this principle some offices have already been filled, though the organization of the Association is yet far from complete. J. H. Noyes is recognized as President; G. Cragin as Vice-President and general Business Agent; J. Burt and E. H. Hamilton as principal Counsellors, etc. /35/

TERMS OF ADMISSION

January 1, 1849

As in regard to rules and officers, so in regard to the admission of members, the Association relies on the inspiration and providence of God more than on written regulations for its guidance and protection.

At a full meeting of the Association on the 28th of December 1848, the following principle was unanimously adopted:

On the admission of any member, all property belonging to him or her becomes the property of the Association. A record of the estimated amount of it may be kept, and in case of the subsequent withdrawal of the member, the Association, according to its practice heretofore, may refund the property or an equivalent amount. This practice, however, stands on the ground not of obligation, but of expediency and liberality, and the time and manner of refunding must be trusted to the discretion of the Association. While a person remains a member, his subsistence and education in the Association are held to be just equivalents for his labor, and no accounts are kept between him and the Association, and no claim of wages accrues to him in case of subsequent withdrawal. Recorded by order of the Association, December 31, 1848, by John H. Noyes, and signed by 91 members of the Association.

ORDER OF EXERCISES

On Monday evening, January 6th, 1849, the following plan for evening meetings was proposed and accepted: At 6 o'clock the Association is called together by the ringing of the bell. /36/ An alphabetical roll of the members is called over for the purpose of giving each an opportunity to offer any criticism, suggestion of improvement, business proposal, or testimony of experience. At each meeting also a question is proposed to be answered in writing, the answers to be handed to the reader and read at the succeeding meeting. These are the standing gregarious exercises of every evening of the week.

On Tuesday evening, January 7th, 1849, a Committee was appointed to digest and propose a plan for the disposal of that part of the evening which remains after the gregarious exercises. They brought in the following schedule of arrangements:

Monday evening	Reading and Report of Newspapers
Tuesday "	Lecture on the Social Theory
Wednesday "	Phonography*
Thursday "	Music, vocal and instrumental
Friday "	Dancing

---

* "Phonography" refers to any system of shorthand based on the phonetic transcription of speech. The type of shorthand used at Oneida was an American variant of Pitman that is known as Munson and is no longer used. See Robert S. Fogarty, ed., *Special Love/Special Sex: An Oneida Community Diary* (Syracuse: Syracuse University Press, 1994), xv. [L.F.]

| Saturday | " | Reading Perfectionist Publications |
| Sunday | " | Bible class |

These arrangements, with the usual meeting at 1 P.M. on Sunday, complete our order of exercises for the present.

MUTUAL CRITICISM

It has been the practice of the Association, both at Putney and at Oneida, to devote the evening meetings from time to time to criticism of individual character. The process was this: A person would offer himself for criticism. At the next meeting, the conductor of the exercises would call on each member present to express freely his or her views of the character under consideration. The number of members became so great in the latter /36/ part of 1848 that it was found necessary to change the procedure. Instead of subjecting candidates to the scrutiny of the entire assembly, the Association appointed four of the most spiritual and discerning critics, who were first criticised by J. H. Noyes, and then in the course of three weeks criticised every member. G. Cragin, S. R. Leonard, H. A. Noyes, and H. H. Skinner were the critics selected. They devoted several hours each day to the work. They consulted first with each other and with those best acquainted with the candidate. Then they called him or her before them, opened his faults, and gave such counsel as the case might demand. They closed their labors on the 12th of January.

Early in January 1849 the following note accompanying the gift of a cigar was sent to Noyes:

"Our love to the man who led us to God."

> H. M. Waters
> L. F. Dunn
> F. Hyde
> A. Burt

Noyes's answer, addressed to "The South Garret Lodge of Free and Accepted Lovers," was as follows:

"Gentlemen:—Accept my thanks for the fragrant present you sent to me last evening, and especially for the expression of affection contained in the envelope. In order that the incense of your offering may be disposed of appropriately and for our common benefit, I shall smoke the segar [cigar] in the society of Miss Julia Dunn, our common sweetheart. Permit me to say that your united note is very gratifying to me, not only as an expression of love toward myself, but as a token of harmony among yourselves. On seeing your names together and thinking of you as a brotherly band I found /37/ new love toward you all springing up in my heart.

Gentlemen, if I may be allowed to number myself among you and offer a suggestion for our common improvement, I propose that we young men maintain our freedom from the favoritism in which many of our married brethren are entangled, and study to be liberal and diffusive in our love and attention to the other sex. Let it be our ambition to hasten the grand consummation of the courtship which is going on in this Association between all the men as one man and all the women as one woman. To this end let us consider whether we may not do good, get good, and feel good by drawing nearer than we have to certain worthy young ladies whose charms have not yet been fully appreciated, such as L. B. R. and N. Let us also be heroes in love, and train our hearts to scale the heights above us as well as to enjoy the beauties of our own level.

With much respect and affection.

Yours truly,
John H. Noyes /37/

4

The Spirit of Desertion
February to March 1849*

Oneida Journal

February 6, 1849.—Francis Hyde, Leonard Dunn, and Julia Dunn called early this morning to inform Mrs. Dunn of their intention to leave. The winds have blown, and the floods have beaten upon our house, but it fell not, for it was founded upon a rock.

Mrs. Dunn stood her ground nobly. She forbade Mr. Hyde to take Julia away. He said he should not urge her, but if she wished /38/ to go she could. Julia said she did not care what her mother wanted: she would go if he went, and if he went to hell she would go with him. Mrs. Dunn exhorted Mr. Hyde

---

* The original title's dates read "January to May 1849." [L.F.]

to leave her children alone, and Leonard to leave him and look to God. We all gave our testimony on the side of truth. Leonard said with deep feeling, all he wanted was to know the truth. May we be able to clear ourselves of every obstruction, and open our hearts to the continual inspiration of Heaven!

2 P.M. The team has been standing at the door of the new house for the last two hours for the purpose of conveying them away if they chose to go. But to our great joy we now see it coming this way, and by Henry's animated look and the victorious wave of his whip I judge things have taken a favorable turn. Henry has come in and given us some account of the state of things at the other house. All have yielded after a severe struggle with self-will and the principalities of the lower world. Now in comes Mr. Hyde: Says he thinks we shall all go when he does. Next comes in Mr. Burt and informs us that Mr. Hyde and Julia, Leonard Dunn and Sarah Kinsley are to be married this evening, meet Mr. Cragin, and return home with him. *Stirring times these!* But I can honestly say that I never felt a more quiet and confiding faith in God than to-day. We have launched within a few hours some distance out of sight of land.

9 P.M. Have been up to the Mansion House. All was quiet and peaceful. Mr. Noyes looked like a young man. He said he could not see why this was not a perfect victory. I had an interesting interview with Mrs. Cragin, by which I was much refreshed. /39/ How much do I prize her! God had restored an hundred fold to us that have surrendered father, mother, and all.

February 6, 1849.—Mrs. Dunn has returned in all the vigor of youth, and has given us an amusing account of their exploits last evening (the marriage of Francis Hyde and Julia Dunn, also Leonard Dunn and Sarah Kinsley.) About nine o'clock in the evening, we had an oyster supper with wedding cake, afterward a dance. Then the company dispersed to their several rooms.

February 8, 1849.—Mr. and Mrs. Hyde sent in their written testimony retracting everything they had said or done in opposition to Mr. Noyes, asking the forgiveness of the Association for the trouble they had caused, desiring to be restored to their favor, and expressing the most unbounded confidence in Mr. Noyes and Mr. Cragin. Mr. Noyes said he thought this should be satisfactory to us all. Here was a case where we should apply Paul's rule: "If any man be overtaken in a fault, ye which are spiritual restore such an one in the spirit of meekness, considering thyself lest thou also be tempted." It was a very delicate thing to restore a wounded conscience. The difficulty lay not in our forgiving them, but in their forgiving themselves.

"I could cry very easily now," said he: "I am unspeakably desirous that they should escape the snare of the Devil." Many expressed the most tender love for them, and I doubt not all received them into their hearts as never before.

February 12, 1849.—Messrs. Noyes and Cragin left Oneida and, after visiting Boston and Cape Cod, went to New York City /40/ and took lodgings. Mr. Noyes's principal reason for leaving home was to secure a quiet place where he might give himself to the task of preparing for the press the *First Annual Report of the Oneida Association, with the Bible Argument Defining the Relations of the Sexes in the Kingdom of Heaven.* There was considerable demand for the *"Bible Argument"* in consequence of evil reports, and Mr. Hubbard, father to one of our members, together with his son were somewhat excited. Mr. Noyes's absence had the effect of quelling the excitement against the Association, and on his return in April he found the Hubbard family quiet and friendly.

Mary E. Cragin to George Cragin
   February 13, 1849

In five minutes from the time of your starting, the house was electrified by the intelligence. Some hearts quivered and voices trembled, but on the whole it was received with much presence of mind. The bell summoned us to roll-call at the usual time, and when Mr. Burt made an official announcement all hearts were prepared to appreciate the reasons and rejoice. We had a very quiet meeting. One desire pervades every breast, to behave so well that we shall be a credit to our Commander. Mr. Burnham came in just as the last name was called, bringing the latest bulletin from you. He said that Mr. Noyes was as free and happy as a school boy, described your comfortable sleeping chairs, etc. Some of us think all this fracas was got up on purpose to give him a chance for a holiday. /41/

Afternoon.—Dexter Hubbard's wife with a young man, a cousin of Tryphena's, called upon us this morning, and requested Tryphena to go home with them. She tried to work upon Tryphena's sympathies, saying she was "murdering" her mother: "poor woman, she never slept a wink night before last." Tryphena answered calmly that she would like to see her, and went out to get ready. Henry then went in and treated them very politely, so that they invited him to go too. This was what we wanted. The woman was full of wrath, but I "came it over her," as she says, by taking her into the room where the children were. She seemed delighted with them. The gentleman took up the *Religious History* in the office, and purchased it for fifty cents. Tryphena went away in good spirits, determined to be one with John and confide in God's working through her. We are all cheerful, and business goes on as usual.

Evening.—Another good quiet meeting. Mr. Seymour gave an account of his interview with the Hubbards. The old man is chuckling over the idea of our falling to pieces now that "the old he-one of the flock is scared off," and threatens the law on you if you are caught around here. But evidently enough, their spirits are weak as water. Mr. Hamilton takes the lead of the meetings, and things go on decently and in order. We took a vote to-night to return to the old system of early rising. I think it will give us a new start in business. All seem united in the purpose to seek inspiration in all things.

*February 14, 1849.—Noon.—*Henry has just come in with good news from the Hubbards. The old man has softened down: says he believes Mr. Noyes an honest man, and he would not require bail /42/ of him: confesses that he has not been free from excitement and in a fit state to listen to reason until yesterday, when he began to feel the influence of Henry's and Tryphena's spirit. Dexter is going to Albany on some land business, and we advise Henry to push still further during his absence the advantage gained. Henry suggested to Tryphena that she relate to her father her experience in reading the *Religious History,* and offer to read it to him. In reply to some innuendo about enlarging the lunatic asylum, Henry told Dexter this morning that he thought they were disrespectful and abusive, and he would not stand it any longer. Upon this they stopped talking, and the old man backed up Henry, conceding to us as an Association the right to do as we pleased, provided we infringed on no one's rights. They have fallen in love with Henry, who behaves well. So all this hulla-baloo is likely to end in a laugh, as Mr. Noyes predicted.

Otis H. Miller to John R. Miller
March 1, 1849

We have had some external commotion lately, commencing when Mrs. Skinner left for Putney. It was in consequence of the operations against bash-fulness or shame. We kept up an incessant war for some time, during which some were pushed to extremes and some vulgar expressions were made, which were not approved by Mr. Noyes. Mr. Hyde, Mr. Dunn, and Miss Dunn bolted and made a violent effort to leave. During this time Miss Dunn (now Mrs. Hyde) professed friendship and was let into the secrets of many wild things which have lately taken place, and reported to Messrs. Dunn and Hyde, who have not been much acquainted with our sexual morality. Mr. Hyde made up his mind to leave, and went to /43/ the Castle* and told all he knew to his father, who is a violent opposer, and thence it was reported to the vil-lage. The principal thing Mr. Hyde reported was that Miss Dunn had been forced. Several informal meetings in the village took place, and we were threatened with a mob. All is very quiet now. Mr. Hubbard, who was the most

---

* The Oneida Castle, or the Castle, was the post office address of the Oneida Association. [L.F.]

violent, is calm and friendly, and comes to meeting on Sunday. I do not apprehend any further difficulty from without.

The body are very well united at present. We have some schisms once in a while. Mr. Smith left last Sunday. He would not submit to Mrs. Cragin. Mrs. Cragin made some remarks in meeting on faith. Mr. Smith made some remarks on the same subject, in which he did not exactly agree with Mrs. Cragin. He made no allusion to her remarks, however. After meeting, Mrs. Cragin reprimanded him. He took offense and boarded the cars in the evening. He did not break fellowship with Brother Noyes or the body. He said it was a matter of opinion in relation to Mrs. Cragin's position.

Noyes to Harriet A. Noyes
Brooklyn, March 16, 1849

Dear Harriet:
My proposed excursion with Mrs. Cragin, the details of which you will learn from Mr. Cragin, seems to be desirable and expedient for the following reasons, among others:

1. It will give her a needed vacation and diversion.

2. It will give her and myself a quiet opportunity of perfecting our union with each other and with the Primitive Church.

3. It will expand, or rather confirm and complete the expansion of your heart and Mr. Cragin's into the free love of the family of God. /44/

4. She will be my most appropriate companion in the preparation of the *Confessions of Social Experience* [never completed].

I anticipate results from this movement which will perfect the union between you and me, and prepare us for new cooperation and more blessed festivities. And I have confidence in you, that you will be "none otherwise minded."

Hoping that I shall see you at the Depot* Thursday evening, I remain as ever.

Yours,
J. H. Noyes

P.S. Mrs. Cragin will please provide herself with a full set of our publications, a polyglot Bible, a Shakespeare, an inkstand, needles, thread, scissors, etc.

---

* The Oneida Depot, or the Depot, was the railroad station three miles away from the Oneida Association and halfway between Utica and Syracuse. [L.F.]

On March 15, 1849, Noyes with Mrs. Cragin went on a tour to Niagara Falls. They spent a week there, and returned by way of Buffalo, Rochester, and Geneva, arriving home March 28th. [G.W.N.] /45/

Noyes to the Oneida Association
March 18, 1849

There is one feature of the Association in respect to which I am anxious for a change. The spirit of desertion has been our worst plague during the past year. As the social order of the world cannot exist without effectual guaranties for the sacredness of the marriage relation, and as an army can have no efficiency without security against the caprices of mere volunteers, so our Association will be in a precarious and crippled state so long as its members hold their connection with it in that loose way that leaves the door open for the spirit of desertion. A man who has joined the Association professedly "for better or for worse" and has consummated the union by liberties which properly belong only to the married state, is not in the condition of a man stopping at a tavern, who has only to pay his bill and depart. . . . If he has any true moral sense, he will not think of breaking the connection unless he has reasons which would justify desertion of a wife in the world.

I advise our women to consider that a man who does not first prove his constancy to the Association is not likely to be constant to an individual: and that a man who can talk of deserting the Association thereby proves that he is not married to it in heart, and can therefore be only a paramour to one whom he approaches. Without this discrimination we cannot escape the degradation of licentiousness.

As the influences working in the Association during the past /46/ year have not proved strong enough to expel the evil spirit, I am disposed to try new measures. I am unwilling to go through another year of watching and laboring to keep members from becoming disaffected and running away. My time can be better occupied. The past need not be censured. It is well that we have watched and labored against desertion for one year, for we have thereby manifested that as an Association we have no fellowship with the spirit that allows transitory connections; moreover, it was fitting in this first year that extra persuasion should be used to prevent dislocations and scandals which might have impeded our work. But henceforth we may fairly throw the responsibility of divorce on the deserting party, and leave him to his chosen course without impediment. When the *Report* is printed, our principles, organization, mode of government, and conditions of membership will be open to the view of all. None will join us under mistake about these matters and so need special nursing. I propose therefore that henceforth, while we show our faithfulness and good will to every member in every modest way, we give up urging and persuading to remain those who are possessed by the spirit of desertion. "If the unbelieving depart, let him depart; we are not called to bondage in such cases." If I cannot *obtain* friends by quiet modest attraction, I will go without them; and if I cannot *retain* friends by the same means, they may go. This is the only attitude that befits us as the representatives of the Kingdom of God. It is not the individual that confers the favor /47/ by joining and staying with us; it is the Association that confers the favor by receiving and keeping him. The dread question on the day of Judgment will not be whether this or that man had confidence in me, but whether I had confidence in him. I ask no favors. If any man thinks that he can do without me, let him be assured that I can do without him. /48/

5

Founding of the Brooklyn Branch
February to May 1849*

Oneida Journal

February 26, 1849.—After visiting the Association during the winter, Mr. Abram C. Smith on February 26th went to New York and laid his case before Messrs. Noyes and Cragin. Mr. Noyes advised him to get his property in a condition where it would be subject to his own control and used for the benefit of the church. This Mr. Smith gladly consented to do, and at Mr. Noyes's suggestion purchased a house in Brooklyn, N.Y., to be used as a station for the family of believers.

April 1, 1849.—The Community men have great games of ball every Saturday afternoon. The most splendid flocks of pigeons are continually passing over.

Harriet H. Skinner to Charlotte A. Miller
Oneida, April 6, 1849

Night before last the domain presented an Arcadian scene. It was like a

---

* The original title's dates read "May 13–18, 1849." [L.F.]

summer sunset, children in the meadow, maidens in the land, young men playing ball, one group jumping. More than fifty, I should think, could be counted on the grounds. Charlotte, I long for the time when you will quit the buckram of common society, and with a short dress and short hair become a hopping, skipping sportive child again. You will, you may depend on it. /49/

Stephen R. Leonard to George W. Noyes
Oneida, May 13, 1849

Mr. Noyes reported the appointment of Mrs. Skinner to take the place of Mrs. Cragin and Mrs. Noyes in the general superintendence of the women's department. Mr. Cragin's resignation was next reported, and H. W. Burnham was appointed to fill that part of his office that related to buying and selling for the Association. Mr. Noyes then resigned his special oversight, spiritual and temporal, of the Oneida Association. Vacancy filled by J. Burt. Mr. Burt appointed J. L. Skinner to be steward in the kitchen, and in conjunction with Mr. Burnham to fill that part of Mr. Cragin's office that relates to keeping accounts and money, and attending to foreign correspondence: E. L. Hatch to fill the place Mr. Hamilton has occupied in superintending the erection of new buildings and all other work in the carpentry line; Mr. Kinsley to superintend the farming department, and Mr. Ackley the sawmills. This arrangement, Mr. Noyes remarked, would leave him and Mr. Cragin with their wives, together with some others who had not their places assigned them, at liberty to obey any call; and he believed God would send a detachment to New York City before long, which would result in the nucleus of an Association there. He concluded by giving the Association some appropriate advice, the substance of which was, that they should be careful not to get into a quarrel with God or with him; then they would never quarrel among themselves. He said he was bound to obey God in all cases, and he felt at liberty to do so without first consulting this Association. /50/ Man's judgment was a small matter with him; the one that judged him was the Lord. And he had reached a position where he walked surely; he knew he was right before he went ahead. God would defend whatever course he took, and whoever undertook to judge him would find in the end that he was their judge.

Oneida Journal

May 16, 1849.—Mr. Cragin and his wife and Mrs. Noyes left Oneida for Brooklyn, N. Y., and on the 18th were followed by Mr. Noyes, Mr. Hamilton, and Mr. Smith. /51/

6

Excommunication of Otis H. Miller
May 20, 1849

May 20, 1849

At a special meeting of the Oneida Association, Sunday, May 20, by a solemn and deliberate vote Otis H. Miller was excommunicated. This was not done in a spirit of vengeance, but as a reluctant duty to truth. That the blessing of God might be upon us, it was necessary to put away this wicked person and purge the Community entirely of his spirit.

RESOLUTION

Whereas, we have full evidence that Otis H. Miller is governed by a selfish, lying, covetous spirit, and that he is false to his profession of fellowship with our principles and subordination to the Association, it is the deliberate judgment of this body that he has sinned wilfully after having received the knowledge of the truth and is therefore a reprobate before God. As such we declare him excommunicated from our body, and separate ourselves entirely from fellowship and sympathy with him. (Signed by all the members of the Association who had lived with him during the past year.)

From his earliest connection with the Association, he has been industriously scattering seeds of evil-thinking, especially in the minds of the weak, the young, and recent members. /52/ He seemed to have an instinct for the most assailable points, and was always there. Even when he was apparently in fellowship with the body, he never let an occasion pass where he could feed an evil thought or strengthen prejudice. On this point abundant testimony was given by those who had suffered from his poisonous infusions. Pride, sensuality, laziness and covetousness appeared as prominent traits of his character.

All his pretended difficulties about our social theory were proved to be not conscientious but selfish. He was perfectly unscrupulous in his own conduct, and he never made any complaints except when our principles touched his selfish claim upon his wife. Indeed, he was wholly destitute of conscience. He was obtuse, coarse, indecent, and he did not secure a friend while he was with us. He scarcely ever mingled with the members in study or plans of improvement, or even amusements, but affected a special dignity which was truly pitiable.

The immediate cause of the present crisis was this: Seeing in Miller's spirit the elements of danger and trouble to the Association, Mr. Noyes determined before he went away to bring his case to an issue, and cast out the evil spirit even if it broke up the Association. He therefore took measures to test his subordination. The course he adopted developed in Miller the full strength of his self-will, pride, and hypocrisy. The details of the war would show him now rebellious and abusive, then submitting only to flare up the moment his submission was put to proof; now starting off with purpose to injure us abroad, then returning like a snake; too perverse and self-willed to /53/ submit heartily, yet terribly loath to leave. Finally the Devil himself seemed to drive him on to the damning act of a direct attack on Mr. Noyes, a thing from which he had restrained himself in all former strifes. On the part of Mr. Noyes and the Association, the details would show forbearance, mercy, and faithfulness, not casting him off till he had proved himself a reprobate. Throughout the contest, Miller confessed to several persons that he knew he was fighting against God, and the effect of this judgment was apparently to render him powerless and hopeless.

The epistle of Jude is a description of his character, and of the scene of judgment we have been passing through.

Stephen R. Leonard to Harriet A. Noyes
May 21, 1849

You probably will have learned from our pedestrians by the time this letter reaches you the facts in Otis Miller's case up to the time of Mr. Smith's leaving here: How we labored with him in kindness and faithfulness for the last time, and how he left in a rage with war and threatening in his heart against Mr. Noyes and the Association. He returned about bedtime of the same day. Messrs. Burt and Burnham had gone down to the Depot in the afternoon, taking his trunk with them, but had not seen or heard anything of him. They had an instinct, however, to call on Mr. Stone and give him some account of the matter. Mr. Stone was very friendly, and assured them that he could successfully withstand any efforts Miller might make. Mr. Skinner returned several hours in advance of Miller, bringing with him Mr. Noyes's decision, /54/ which was in harmony with our own feelings. Miller threw himself on the lounge in the dining-room on his return, and we soon communicated to him Mr. Noyes's reply to his note, endorsing it in full ourselves. He said nothing to it. As it was late in the evening we did not think it best nor very safe to turn

him outdoors, so he was allowed to remain on the lounge, Hial having succeeded to his tent. Messrs. Kinsley and Perkins and the two Nashes had the
oversight of him through the night. I found him in the printing-office in the
morning. He looked as if he had been crying. He asked for Mr. Smith. I told
him he had left. He asked if Mr. Noyes had gone too. I told him all had gone
that had talked of going, that Mr. Noyes had only waited so long for his sake.
He then asked me to call Mr. Burt. I did so and Mr. Burt returned word that
he did not wish to see him. Miller then wrote the following note to Mr. Burt:

"Dear Sir:—I feel as I never felt before, and I pray that you may forgive
me. I will do anything you say. You may test it by anything you please. If under
present circumstances you think I had better go, I will, but I shall say nothing
against you. I shall not give you up. I have never had a heart, when in cool and
rational moments, to do what I have said. Mr. Stone will tell you what I said
about the Association yesterday, which he marked down in his book. I felt that
my heart was with you when I left. If I go away, I will not injure you. I will get
on my knees and ask the forgiveness of you all.

Otis H. Miller"

Mr. Burt returned the following answer:

"Mr. Miller:—After all that has passed you cannot expect the Association
to have the least confidence in your word. If you /55/ ever get their confidence
again, it must be by *deeds*. If you can prove by deeds that you are a good man,
and can get the recommendation of God, the Association will be ready to receive you; but they wish to have you go away now, according to the decision of
Mr. Noyes. You can best prove your sincerity by deeds abroad.

JONATHAN BURT"

He assented to this note as reasonable. Mr. Kinsley immediately carried
him to the canal, and our bell rang for meeting to make a final disposition of
his case. He endeavored to get the sympathy of the Association through Mr.
Kinsley, but was unsuccessful. He had a sinking turn and acted as though he
would fall from the wagon. He then brightened up, and talked against Messrs.
Hamilton and Bradley. He expressed himself several times as being in terrible
distress, and Mr. Kinsley left him on the canal the picture of despair. His intention was to go to Putney. . . . We all feel much relieved by his departure,
and I guess no one more so than Ellen and Mrs. Thayer.* The latter men-

---

* "Ellen" was Miller's wife (married in the Community with Noyes's consent). "Mrs Thayer" was a lady
friend. [G.W.N.]

tioned in meeting that Mr. Miller came to her a day before Mr. Cragin and
company started for Brooklyn, and complained of Mrs. Cragin and the whole
movement in progress against Mr. Burt as unfit to manage our affairs in Mr.
Noyes's absence. Because she sided with Mrs. Cragin, he kicked her and left
her. She said she had received a great deal of treatment as mean as this from
him that she had never opened her heart to anyone about. /56/

Postscript by H. W. Burnham, May 22nd: While passing Root's I saw
Gould going into the house, and Otis Miller sitting in the wagon. On my return Miller met me in the street. He began by saying that he could not go into
the world, wished retirement, etc. I replied that we had done with him, that he
should have left on the packet Sunday morning as he agreed. "But here you
are consorting with Gould, our sworn enemy." He said that Gould was not
our enemy, that Stone could not keep him, so he went to Gould's. He followed
me a few steps, and that was the last I saw of him.

7

Community Fanaticism and Tensions
June 1849 to February 1850*

John L. Skinner to John R. Miller
Brooklyn, June 3, 1849

At half-past ten o'clock our bell rang for meeting. At the opening of the
meeting, Mr. Burt announced that marriage was intended between Mr. Marquis L. Worden and Mrs. Sophia Dunn. The roll was then called, and after testimony from all who had anything to say, Mr. Worden and Mrs. Dunn stood
up and were married. This was a sudden movement, but such things are common, you know, among us, where inspiration is allowed to have place. Mr.
Worden has stood in a doubtful position in relation to us for a good while.
His being so connected with William H. Cook (his wife being Cook's sister)
probably had much influence on him. His wife died several months ago. He
came down here yesterday from Manlius, and brought his two youngest children. After a talk with Mr. Burt, in which he expressed his decision to commit

---

* The original title's dates read "June 3–21, 1849." [L.F.]

himself and his interests to the Association, Mr. Burt proposed to him the marriage with Mrs. Dunn, the idea of which had before come to his mind with considerable force. Mr. Burt regards it as in an important sense the termination /57/ of the war with the New York Perfectionists.

Mary E. Cragin to Harriet H. Skinner
June 4, 1849

Mr. Campbell arrived this morning with letters and news from Oneida. After reading the letters we had a silence and then a talk. The result is sending you Mr. Cragin, and if he does not answer the purpose Mr. Noyes will come himself.

Harriet, I want to give you one piece of advice, and I pray you give heed to it. Do not suffer your instincts to be overruled and choked. Remember my experience in that Mary Knight affair.* If I had been simple enough to believe John's estimate of my spirituality, I should have stood my ground, alone if it had been necessary. I wish nothing altered in the case I refer to, but I should be glad to have you learn wisdom by it and believe John when he says, as he has this morning, that he would trust you before any of them.

Mary E. Cragin to George E. Cragin
Private
June 11, 1849

Dear George:—
We received a letter from you yesterday giving a pretty full account of proceedings at Oneida. Mr. Noyes suggests that you remain either until Mr. Burt fully recovers from the spirit of fanaticism, or until you can establish an organization independent of him. If you need help from here, /58/ of course you can have it by making application. At all events, I hope you will not leave them until they are all straightened up.

Mary E. Cragin to Harriet H. Skinner
June 21, 1849

We had a double treat yesterday in the arrival of John and Theodore and the receipt of a large package of notes from beloved ones at Oneida. I think of you as all quiet and settled, each one modestly getting his or her lesson. We

---

* *The Putney Community.* Chapter XXVII. [G.W.N.]

needed John here as soon as you got through with him. How pretty it will be for him to go backward and forward between the two Associations, nursing his two babies from time to time as their necessities require!

We have gone on with our criticisms, as John told us to, and have found the spirit of wisdom and judgment descending upon us. Last evening it was Mr. Inslee's turn, and he was unanimously found fault with for a spirit that sought to please everybody. After we had got through, Mr. Noyes said: "There are certain qualities of character that everybody loves, such as affability, skill in music. That these are superficial qualities is evident because it requires only superficial discernment to appreciate them. Such popular traits of character are to be considered as luxuries. For my part, I have settled the question, that I cannot afford to be popular. This is a time of war, not a time to surround ourselves with the trappings of wealth. Sometime I may be able to keep my coach and four, but at present I am not able. To those who desire true popularity I would say, you will have the best /59/ and most enduring sort eventually. Do not expect to be appreciated by the world or by weak believers. Cultivate those traits of character that are too deep for superficial notice, and be popular with God. Christ did not seek popularity. In his reproofs he did not trouble himself to be polite. He was a lion as well as a lamb."

John R. Miller to Erastus Hamilton
Oneida, August 31, 1849

At Herkimer I met O. H. Miller. He came down as far as St. Johnsville with us. I told him the substance of what was said at the meeting the other evening; that all had kind feelings toward him, and would be glad to save him if they could, but had not confidence enough in him to take him back. It seemed to give him a good deal of comfort to know that the Community had hopes of him. He thought that the trials he had been through had done him much good, and that he was prepared to submit to everything without fault-finding again. I told him that he ought to count well the cost before he ever thought of joining us again, that he could gain nothing by it unless he was in fellowship with the Association, and that it was impossible to get Ellen away or enjoy her society on any other basis. He seemed to be fully aware of this, and gave me to understand that his own salvation was what he was seeking. He wanted I should give him what advice I could. I advised him to offer to peddle for the Association, to come there only often enough to get his goods, and to make only a short stop unless he was invited to stay. He said he would be glad to do it, and did not ask for /60/ better terms. I told him that I would report his proposal to the Association, and give him an answer when I returned through Herkimer. He then took out his pocket-book and handed me $200, saying he did not need it and wished me to take it. I told him that I would take the money, and if the Association did not accept his proposal I would pay it back. He seemed very glad to get rid of it.

Harriet H. Skinner to John R. Miller
September 15, 1849

The Association has organized itself into classes of about twelve members each with a foreman for purposes of mutual criticism and anything in the way of improvement. John appointed the foremen, and they cast lots for their members, choosing round twice first. Mr. Burnham is foreman of the class I belong to. Charlotte is in Mr. Skinner's class. Today we told experience all round, and in our class chose Mr. Ackley for a subject of criticism next meeting. The members are to write out their criticisms, and give them to the foreman in season for him to read and prepare a summing up which is to be the property of the Association, liable to general inspection. Mr., Mrs. Cragin, Harriet A. Noyes and George Noyes are left out of the classes. They are to criticize the foremen before their class. The plan is very popular. All are anticipating much improvement.

AFFAIRS OF THE BROOKLYN BRANCH
November 19–21, 1849

Mr. Noyes spent the month of October 1849 in Brooklyn. Then after three week's visit to Oneida, he returned again to /61/ Brooklyn with his wife, Mr. Burnham, Mrs. Cragin, Theodore, and Victor. The campaign opened with severe criticism of Mr. Cragin for deception, George Noyes for false love, and Harriet Skinner for carelessness.

November 21, 1849.—Noyes left Mr. Hamilton and Charlotte Miller in charge at Oneida. The Brooklyn family commenced receiving classes from Oneida, including some of the children, for more private instruction.

Mary E. Cragin's Notes from Memory
December 1, 1849

We have had, or rather the truth has had, a good time this morning firing at superstition as showing itself in telling dreams, giving heed to spiritual impressions without trying the spirits, opening the Bible without a real instinct for it. We give it the general name of fanaticism, and the special one of Langstaffism because Mrs. Langstaff is notorious for doing these things, and some of us have caught the infection.

Charlotte A. Miller to Mary E. Cragin and Harriet A. Noyes
Oneida, December 15, 1849

I will relate to you the progress of Mr. Cragin's case since I wrote you last. The following criticism which Mr. Hamilton sent him Monday evening will explain itself:

"To Mr. Cragin: I find my spirit somewhat in bondage to you. I feel in you a spirit claiming deference from me and cramping my freedom of action because of the position you have heretofore sustained towards the center. And the part you had in helping me to free myself from the world and join the Association seems to hold /62/ me back from endorsing the center's judgment of you. Also there is a spirit holding me back from acting in the simplicity of their confidence in me, tempting me to fear there are things in my spirit which will bring me perhaps at some future time under such particular judgment as you have come into. In carefully thinking over the facts, I see it is my duty to stand in the confidence Mr. Noyes, Mrs. Cragin, and Mrs. Noyes have in me. In my own strength I feel perfectly weak, but in the strength of Christ and in union with their spirit I am strong to do all that God has placed before me. My heart yearns after greater refinement of spirit than I have yet attained, but still I feel constrained to hold myself open to inspiration in the relation I am placed in to you, free from the obstruction and constraint that would naturally arise from considering you according to your former position instead of your present relation with the center. Perfect sincerity and that alone will secure union and fellowship. With sincere desire to fulfill the truth, Yours in Christ,

E. H. Hamilton"

I wrote the preceding Thursday night, not concluding whether to send it to you or not, but tonight I feel constrained to free my spirit. I disliked the spirit of your remarks tonight exceedingly. I think they came from a lofty heart seeking to save its life and popularity. I can see a spirit in you trying to drag the Association down into judgment with you. You are making a merit of your sufferings, and instead of taking a position at the feet of the Association, you are assuming a position above them. I think your reference to the necessity of making mistakes in order to learn wisdom was immodest, and the influence of /63/ your spirit has been to entangle persons in suffering and mistakes. Sincerity and the position Mr. Noyes has put me in prompt me to be thus free. I pray that God may enable you to escape the snare of the Devil, and lead you to repentance that needeth not to be repented of.   E.H.H."

Mr. Cragin thanked Mr. Hamilton for his criticism the next morning, and afterward showed it to Harriet and Mr. Leonard. He asked Harriet if she thought best to have it read in meeting. She and all of us thought it was not best, but he should rather ponder these things in his heart, and if he had anything to expose or write, write it to John. We concluded not to show him your letter unless some occasion demanded it. He has been much at the office since, and has not said anything to anyone.

Noyes to John R. Miller
   Brooklyn, February 10, 1850

Inslee is here, and reports some interesting movements in Newark. 1. The Korah crew are falling into awful gaps such as adultery and drunkenness. 2. Inslee's brother has quieted off so far as to consent to have Mr. Burt come into the shop, and is actually anxious to have him come. 3. Mr. Lynch has come fully over to fellowship with us, and he and his wife will throw their house open to the church. Their children have all left them, and his business (that of tinner and stove dealer) is running down. It has been and might be a profitable business, but he is too feeble through age and other causes to manage well alone. He is worth, when all his debts are paid, about $1000. He and his wife /64/ are ready and enthusiastic for a full surrender to the church. This we hope is the beginning of a move for a Community in Newark. They have a good house in a retired situation, which may be made a gathering-place for believers that are to be engaged in taking the city. I suggested to Inslee last night, that possibly A. C. Smith was the man to go in there in the name of the church and take charge. The question to be considered is, whether Smith with the [word missing] he has had at Oneida and with the connection which he would have with Brooklyn and Oneida would be able to serve the church safely and faithfully in such a position, and redeem his character in Newark as he has in Kingston. We need not speculate much about the future, but it is well for us to watch every present opening and faithfully fill it. If the Association thinks that the Holy Ghost calls brothers Burt and Smith to new service, and can send them away with a blessing, I propose that they come on with you as soon as is practicable. Smith has other business in these quarters, and it may be worth his while to look at the prospects in Newark, even if it is not found expedient to go in there. I think it is safe and according to the will of God, that

Mr. Burt should try the experiment of joining Inslee. We are certainly not brooding over Newark so long in vain.

Yours, etc.,
John H. Noyes /65/

8

___

Industry and Finance
August 1849 to July 1851*

A New Era in Business
August 20, 1849

The Brooklyn family returned to Oneida with the addition of Mrs. Whitfield.

J.H.N.—Within the last year toleration of our principles has been triumphantly gained. Now the time has come to enter heartily into the extension of business with a view to presenting the world a perfected model of society in all its relations, financial as well as social.

It was proposed to erect a store immediately. The worldly system of apprenticeship was discussed and pretty well used up.

Erastus H. Hamilton to John R. Miller
September 2, 1849

We had a bee today, men, women, and children, to clear up the swamp west of our house. The men pulled up and drew together in piles the stumps and logs, and the women and children picked up and carried the smaller pieces. The enthusiasm of the women would get to such a pitch that they would not be content with small attainments, but uniting their forces would seize upon a large log and place it in triumph on the heap. We enjoyed it

___

* The original title's dates read "August 20, 1849, to July 16, 1851." [L.F.]

much. Mrs. Norton, Mrs. Higgins, old Mrs. Burnham, Aunt Sally were out in short dresses and as active as any. /66/

Harriet H. Skinner to John R. Miller
September 15, 1849

For two days past the men have been engaged in cleaning out the dyke. Yesterday a company of us women filled some baskets with luncheon and took it down to those poor mudbespattered, boot-soaked but never more merry-hearted workmen. They washed their hands in the brook, and came out to the stump in the pasture, where we laid out their biscuit, nutcakes and pickles. There were as many as thirty of them. Last evening a committee was appointed to attend to the setting up of stoves, lighting the house, and taking precautions against fire. Mr. Skinner was appointed watchman.

John R. Miller to Noyes
October 4, 1849

An inventory of this date showed that the Association owned property worth $53,100.00 after deducting all debts. This did not include $2000.00 owned by Mr. Joslyn, which was received into the Association last Sunday, nor Jack Kinsley's $3000.00, nor Mr. Barron's $6000.00 or $7000.00, which we can call for any time we choose. We have also an income from Mr. Mead, Horatio, and Dr. Ransom of $112.50 annually so long as Mrs. P. Noyes lives.

During the months of October and November 1849, the Association put up a building containing a convenient store, printing office, and shoe-shop, which were occupied immediately, each department commencing operations about December 1st. /67/

John R. Miller to the Brooklyn Branch
December 5, 1849

A committee was appointed last evening to arrange our men for the winter campaign. They made the following report, which was read and accepted:

Printing-office:	G. W. Noyes, G. Cragin, Charles Hamilton, S. R. Leonard (Type set by women.)
Horse Teamsters:	W. H. Woolworth, Geo. Campbell, Daniel Knowles
Ox Teamsters:	Eli Whitney, L. H. Bradley

Wood Choppers:	Albert Kinsley, H. T. Clark, H. W. Thayer, L. Worden, John Leonard, H. Thacker, Joshua Smith, J. W. Perkins
Blacksmith:	S. W. Nash, S. Newhouse
Sawyers:	H. Burt, J. L. Baker, I. Seymour, D. J. Hall
Log Sawyers:	H. M. Waters, A. L. Burt
Care of Cattle:	C. Higgins
Wagon Shop:	C. Olds, Leonard Dunn
Watch Repairer:	Harvey Norton
Carpenters:	E. L. Hatch, G. W. Hamilton, A. L. Burt, H. M. Waters, C. S. Joslyn, John Leonard
Store:	J. R. Miller, Francis Hyde, W. A. Hinds
Kitchen:	Enos Kellogg
Wood Agent:	Riley Burnham
Teacher:	H. J. Seymour
Children's House:	J. C. Ackley
Harness Repairer:	A. C. Smith
Business Agent:	E. H. Hamilton
Financial Agent:	J. R. Miller
Shoe-Shop:	L. Vanvelzer, L. Worden, A. W. Carr, Elias Hall, Daniel Nash, J. L. Skinner /68/

It was thought to be an occasion of thankfulness to God, that such an arrangement as this could be made with perfect harmony.

Later S. R. Leonard and J. L. Skinner changed places by agreement, the former going into the shoe-shop.

Erastus H. Hamilton to Noyes
December 17, 1849

The new business arrangements work well. I think we have accomplished an important change in the shoe-making business. The repugnance with which that trade was looked upon has been overcome. Leonard and Carr are well satisfied with the business. Mr. Carr, they say, is going to make a good workman. Mr. Smith has a bench in the shoe-shop, and mends harness and straps skates. He is in a quiet, growing state. They passed a vote Saturday that their shop be known as a place of prayer, not of gossip. The blacksmith shop has commenced doing custom work, and is likely to have all it can do. We have put Mr. Newhouse in with Mr. Nash, and are having him give up his guns and traps entirely. He does nothing but what Mr. Nash sets him at. This is taking the bull by the horns, but I think we shall succeed. He appears to be doing well. I hope I shall be able to carry out your principles and wishes in all things.

Brooklyn Journal
February 18, 1850

Mr. Smith closed a bargain with Capt. Bennett for the sloop "Rebecca Ford," which is to be used to transport stone from Kingston to New York City. /69/

February 28.—Mr. Noyes is much interested in our plan of running the sloop. He lay awake and thought about it, and wished it might be manned by Community men. Then our folks could take a pleasure trip up the river any time they chose. We are all much elated at the prospects which open up to us in connection with this business. It was agreed that it should be a Community school of navigation.*

O. C. Journal
June 14, 1850

A "bee" in the parlor to stitch tracts, Mr. Bradley presiding. It went off with a perfect rush, that is with the zest and harmony of inspiration. The inference is that the publishing business will be attractive. We stitched between 800 and 900 in a little more than an hour. Then with the momentum started, all fell to and mended 25 meal bags and quit in glowing spirits. There is ever so much testimony to the healthy effects of bees. They cover aches of all kinds, and send all home refreshed and strengthened.

John R. Miller in the Oneida Journal
October 1, 1850

The work at the mill goes on beautifully. We have for two days been at work in the wheel-pit, and though it is one of the dirtiest and most disagreeable jobs that can be found, I tell you the truth when I say that it has been exceedingly attractive. I have not enjoyed myself so well for a long time as when in this work with my thick boots and overalls on, well covered with the Oneida mud. To my great delight, I find I can take hold of the /70/ heaviest kind of work, and continue it ten hours in the day, and that too without feeling tired.

---

* On July 5, 1851, the Rebecca Ford sank in the Hudson River, near Hyde Park, and two of the Community women were drowned. [G.W.N.]

O. C. Journal

November 27, 1850.—Mr. Miller writes: "We now owe nearly $1200, and our funds are nearly used up. Most of our debt is due in a short time. In addition to this, funds are wanted to finish the mill, and for our daily family expenses. But I feel sure we shall have good luck—that prosperity awaits us—that our Father, who has thus far supplied so liberally all our wants, will still see that all these things are added.

December 9, 1850.—Thus far we have had all the money we needed, and that without borrowing. I regard that money from Putney as the direct gift from God. Putney was the last place to which I looked for money, and those notes the last ones I had reason to expect would be paid. I love to acknowledge the hand of God in such transactions.

In the latter part of December 1850, Mr. J. H. Thomas, a Newark Perfectionist and manufacturing jeweller, proposed to induct the Brooklyn Branch into the manufacture of gold chain. All were interested in starting a new business, and Mrs. Leonard and Sophronia Higgins were invited to come from Oneida and learn the art.

Mary E. Cragin to Harriet H. Skinner
Brooklyn, January 5, 1851

We are driving ahead in the gold chain business. A perfect enthusiasm has taken possession of the whole family down to Theodore and Sarah. We rise at daylight to prosecute the work. /71/ and happy is he or she who finds a vacant seat at the bench any time of day. Mr. Noyes says that God has given him a spirit of industry, and he rejoices in it.

John R. Miller to Noyes
January 15, 1851

I have been engaged for several days in taking our inventory, which is now nearly finished, and will vary but a trifle from the following:

	Jan. 1850	Jan. 1851
Inventory	$65,523.39	$66,600.00
Debts	3,614.39	3,300.00
Balance	61,909.00	63,300.00

This shows a gain since last year of $1391.00. It may be said that we have not paid our expenses by our own labor, but we have been getting an education, and God has provided liberally for our expenses.

In addition to the above, there are Newark, Wilber, and Northern Vermont, amounting in all to some $15,000, which is Association property, I suppose. In Northern Vermont there are eleven thousand dollars now at the disposal of the church, and nine thousand more which Mr. Barron is quite sure of.

Free Church Circular 3:376
January 30, 1851. By a recent Act of the Legislature affecting the "Oneida Purchase" of 1840–41, the liabilities of the Association to the State have been reduced more than $2600, leaving only the small sum of $377.84 still due. /72/

Business:
Home-Talk by J. H. Noyes
Brooklyn, April 15, 1851

We are nearing the end of our resources, so far as the funds brought in by new members are concerned, and at the same time external matters are shaping for the commencement of profitable business. At Oneida they are putting in machinery, and we have already commenced industrial operations here in Brooklyn. The great question is whether we are spiritually ready, whether we have fulfilled our obedience to God so that he can allow us to support ourselves. To prepare us for the boon of self-support, God has found it necessary to put us through a long series of difficult and threatening circumstances corresponding to the experiences he gave the children of Israel in the wilderness. God intended all the time to bring the children of Israel into a land flowing with milk and honey, where they should exercise themselves in all sorts of production: but before he could do that to their spiritual advantage, he had to hold them for a long time in the wilderness, where they could learn that the rock on which they rested was not money but God. I feel that our obedience is nearly fulfilled, and that God will soon call us to take up business in earnest. . . .

God has held us back these sixteen years very much as we have held back Messrs. Smith and Long. They have been champing their bits for business, but we have steadily resisted till they are in a condition to take it up right end foremost, that is with a proper ascendancy of the spiritual over the physical. . . . /73/

The pursuit of business with us shall be the pursuit of truth. We shall be industrious because we love to be truthful and do the right thing.

I feel that it is decidedly to our spiritual advantage that we be financially independent. So long as there is a devil to take a hand in it, dependence will be bribery. Our government sends its agents all over the world, but it strictly forbids them to receive presents, and any presents that are given must be delivered into the United States Treasury. That is because to receive favors from those they are sent to influence might be an inlet of corruption. Who does not know that every minister in the land who receives a salary is under a strong temptation to suit his people? I hate to be under any such temptation. I hate to have the Association dependent on its subscribers and patriotic contributors. I should like it if we were independent even of our best outside friends. The case of Mr. Thomas brought these ideas forcibly to mind. When Mr. Thomas came up for judgment, the thought thrust itself in, now take care, it will not do to offend him, if you do he will break up your business. I, of course, repelled the thought and nerved myself to break up our benches. I was determined to sit down and suck our thumbs if necessary, rather than sacrifice a hair of truth. Probably the same thought worked in him. We refused to pay any attention to that influence, and immediately the way was opened for us to go on without his patronage. I am now not altogether satisfied with our relations to the Newark concern. There is a tendency for us to feel dependent on them for our work and wages. I hate such influence, and know that just as soon as it gets hold of us, God will break it up and bring us into something better. /74/

Then I see clearly that our business here has sustained us while carrying on discipline and improvement among ourselves. Mr. Smith would have had a good deal more influence here this spring, if it had not been for our business. It would have seemed almost necessary that he should go ahead as he wanted to do, right or wrong, for the sake of our maintenance. That would have interfered with what Mr. Smith himself now knows was for his best interest. Having something else of our own to stand on we can just hold still till the Devil gives us business on the sloop. We shall soon get a platform that will make us independent even of the Association. This plan of entering into business for the sake of gaining independence and producing a free gospel is going to wash us from worldliness instead of putting us into it. . . . Men and brethren, are you ready? (Messrs. Smith, Cragin, Miller, and others responded with enthusiasm.)

This mission to England has a direct connection with our industrial movement. It takes money that is severely wanted and puts it to a public use. It is completing our obedience, showing that we do not hold property in a separate, private way, but that we make God our partner and are free to venture all on him. My personal feelings held back for a good while—my natural timidity, the expense, the danger of leaving my flock—everything looked threatening. But I made up my mind with fear and trembling to sacrifice all to the will of God. Right in the midst of our greatest demand for money, we refuse to be small, refuse to be economical against God. That is an act of faith which I know God will acknowledge. /75/

I hope there is energy enough in the family to make our gold chain business go forward. I would recommend to all that they stir up the gift that is in them. I feel that God will encourage us in that line, and also that he will encourage business on the sloop. I should recommend Smith, Hial, and Long as crew: and since Mr. Burnham has been turned out of his pastorship in Newark, let him go as pastor on the sloop. A couple of women also will be likely to go each time.

The same principles and the same kind of advice should be extended to Oneida and should be studied by those who are particularly interested. I hope that they will catch the spirit that is growing here to do business in a godly manner. Mr. Inslee will take his talents and tools there for the establishment of a machine shop. Mr. Newhouse and John Leonard will cooperate. With other arrangements that are now in progress, we should be able to do a clean business.

And here I would recommend that we do not worry about our social relations. Our social theory does hang fire: it does not realize all that we have been led to expect. Well, don't fret but press through. Remember that the social theory divides the process of redemption into four parts: first, salvation from sin; second, salvation from social evils; third, reform of the labor department; fourth, victory over death. These are all connected, and we do not expect perfect satisfaction in any until we reach the end. Until we have conquered the spiritual and moral departments. And until we have conquered disease and death, they will be a disturbing influence over all. We can only expect to approximate the right state of things at any given point until we have conquered the Devil and all of them. Supposing we regard /76/ our operations in all these lines as the day's work, with the marriage supper of the Lamb at the end. Then dividing the day's work into four parts as indicated in the *Bible Argument,* I should say that we have reached the middle of the afternoon. We have got over the main difficulties of the spiritual and social departments, and are now in the third stage of the conflict. Supper will come by and by.

We shall have to work for the present very much as our forefathers did when they settled the country. They carried their guns as well as their hoes out into the field. If they saw any Indians, they dropped their hoes and took to their guns. Don't get so busy hoeing as not to look out for Indians.

God has been building his vessel and is apparently about ready to start. Now the question is, where are the paddle-wheels? The machinery of the vessel must take effect on sweeps or paddles working outside in the water in order to get motion. Just so we must have a system of distribution, an independent means of venting the products of our industry. I have a plan to propose that will put on our paddle-wheels. We have in the Association a number of men who have been brought up as peddlers, such as Otis Miller, Mr. Hatch, and Mr. Lawton. Then here is John R. Miller, who has had a mercantile education but lacks a suitable opening for his talents. My idea is that Mr. Miller should organize a system of peddling, providing things to sell and training men as salesmen. In this way we shall come into contact with the business world and consumers through our own men, and a system of trade will commence spreading out from the Association in an increasing circle for fifty miles around. Our men will really go /77/ not only as men of business but as missionaries. To send out our own men ostensibly to sell goods would be the best method of sending out our publications and spirit. The peddlers would ultimately turn pastors.

If we can establish such a system of distribution, God will give us wit to manufacture more and better things than the world ever saw. There is obedience among us, and obedience is genius.

Our business may properly be divided among our men. Mr. Inslee is very fond of his factory work, but has always been bothered by attention to outside concerns, getting orders, making contracts. Mr. Miller, on the other hand, is exactly suited by this part of the business. So they can play into each other's hands. To show what could be done, Otis Miller when he was away under the displeasure of the Association and in a very unfavorable state made $30 a month. If he goes out now with the blessing of God, it is to be presumed that he could make $60.

I do not see but that this scheme touches all around. It is a sign of inspiration if a good plan hits a good many objects.

Oneida Journal

May 11, 1851.—Mr. Lawton and O. H. Miller returned from their first peddling excursion today. The whole Association were cordial in their welcome and united in their interest in what seems the beginning of an important operation. They went up the valley through Norwich and vicinity, about 100 miles in all, and tell some amusing stories. Mr. Lawton made $9 and Mr. Miller $18.32, though it was thought that Mr. Miller incurred the most /78/ spiritual expense, which is a more important item than money-making. G.W.N. remarked: "If the peddling cannot be made positively beneficial spiritually, we had better not go into it. I am sure that it can be, though it will probably require patience, heroism, and considerable criticism."

June 27, 1851.—The Farm Department have adopted the plan of working in groups. Once a week names are all drawn out anew. One company of men and women go out at 2 o'clock and work two hours. At 4 o'clock they come in and another company goes out till 6 o'clock. This plan works better than having all go out at once, on account of the necessary business in the house.

A large company of men, women, and children went to the mill tonight to witness the hanging of the upper millstone. The stone weighing 2400 lbs. was lifted into place by a great crane, the screw of which was made by Mr. Inslee. At a signal by Mr. Hall, the great drum below was set in motion, and the stone began to whirl with the lightness of a top, almost noiseless, but emitting a fiery glow where it grated on the lower stone. All the machinery was made in our machine-shop and works well.

July 11, 1851.—J.H.N.: I like the plan of having Miller and Cragin make mutual reports of the state of finances at Brooklyn and Oneida. They should have a care for each other and see that a proper distribution is made. When we have Associations scattered here and there, I expect there will be a regular system of financial reports, and those Associations that have a surplus will impart to those that are in need. /79/

Remarks by Noyes
Brooklyn, July 11, 1851

I would recommend that the Association turn away from expansion and preparation, and carry through to completion the work already undertaken; also that Mr. Thacker and others in the agricultural department should turn their attention from the ornamental to the profitable enterprises. Let the ornamental come in as incidental. We must look out for three things in all we do, and in their proper order: first the spiritual benefit, second, usefulness, and third present pleasure.

I think it is well, as Mr. Miller suggests, to hold up for a while the peddling. But the more I look at it, the more I am in favor of going on and increasing that business. I feel like putting the responsibility upon Mr. Miller to see that the peddling be done in a spiritual manner, and at the same time be efficient and profitable in a material sense. The two things are not incompatible. I want him to study the experience of those that go out, and learn to criticize and give advice.

I am confident that we shall be able to report next February that we are able to support ourselves and help others. /80/

9

The Children's House
August 11, 1849, to February 2, 1851

August 11, 1849

The first principle is to avoid as far as possible giving children occasion for transgression by putting them under a multitude of laws. The second is to correct their faults, usually by addressing their reason and conscience, and winning them to obedience by kindness, patience, and gentle words. Then once in a great while, when there is a signal occasion for it, give them a tremendous rebuke, such as will leave its impression forever.

The Children's Department
August 25, 1849

Mr. Noyes alluded with thankfulness to the favorable change which has taken place in the class of older boys, with whom there had been formerly serious difficulties. The Devil came nearer to proving himself almighty in that department than in any other. But now Mr. Noyes heard a good report of that class, and it was a privilege to commend them. The victory gained there, said Mr. Noyes, stands side by side with the health miracle and the other great miracles with which God is surrounding us. It contributes, doubtless, to the health of the body; there is a better atmosphere, spiritual and bodily, in consequence of stopping the leak in that direction. /81/

In the infant department we cannot claim so decisive a victory. Nevertheless, the same God is at work there as in the children's department, and we may expect the same results. To be sure, the problem is more difficult in the case of the infants. They are feebler and more impressible to evil influences, and the parents are more tenacious of worldly fashions in respect to them. It is especially difficult to introduce the new system if we complicate it with the old one. Between two stools, we fall to the ground. If we take the infant from the mother while she has her natural feelings in full play, and is at liberty to watch and keep up a particular care over it, we make the worst possible conditions. The care of the infants will inevitably become odious if it is subjected to the keen espionage and criticism of the parents. The nurses will droop, and that will make the infants droop. This will increase the anxiety of the parents, and rouse them to more watchfulness and interference. So the evil will perpetuate itself. The unpropitious results in the infant department are not due to the fact that we have introduced a new system, but to the fact that we have *not* done it. The persons in charge are faithful and talented. I feel safe in committing my children to them. Yet we do not see the same results. Now that we are making changes, let us calmly and unanimously adjust the infant department to the new basis. Our original plan was to have but one establishment for the children. I think we can now return to it with benefit to both classes. There is a general feeling in favor of placing infants under the same roof with the older children. The infants will then have the advantage of being helped by the older children, and the older children the advantage of taking some care /82/ of those more helpless. Beyond that I propose to the mothers, to the husbands of the mothers, and to all who love the Association, that they consider the importance of allowing the Association to carry out its principles unembarrassed by worldly feelings. The essence of our principles is, that children cease to be private property and be property of the Association; and the true way to manage them is, as soon as nature allows, to place them under a system of general control. This plan has been carried out with success in the case of the older children; we demand the liberty to carry it out in respect to all the children. . . .

I feel a certain respect for this tenacious philoprogenitiveness. It is mighty, and I respect anything that is mighty. It is important to provide for it, and find a way to go along peacefully with it. But intelligent philoprogenitiveness and blind philoprogenitiveness are like fire and water, and if they try to occupy the same ground, there will surely be hissing and explosion. Hence if there [be] any in the Association who cannot heartily join us in this movement, I propose that they occupy one of the old houses and take their children with them. Let the two houses which the Association has built be devoted to the principles of the Association. There is an appropriateness in their having the old and we the new.

It is not necessary to assume that there is no chance for improvement in the children's department. If we have not perfect confidence in the character and management of those in charge, let us appeal to those who are responsible for their appointment. Instead of talking in a way to disaffect the Association, or resorting to private and unruly interference, make known the fault in a quarter where it will be effectually stopped. Mr. Cragin and /83/ I are open to complaint and disposed to see justice done.

My attachment to the principles we have published is such that, if I found myself in an Association where there was no reasonable prospect of advancing to an entire community, I would quit at once.

The Children
Brooklyn Talk, August 12, 1850

The unconverted children are the front rank of the Devil's forces in the Community. We cannot expect uninterrupted development so long as this outpost of the Devil is unconquered. It is proposed that Mr. Hamilton and Charlotte Miller go to Oneida and undertake the spiritual education of the children.

September 27, 1850.—Mrs. Skinner writes in the O. C. Journal: "There is a beautiful change going on among the children, a Bible revival. Several new Bibles have lately been bought and distributed among them, and they are much interested in reading them. The spirit of meekness and quietness have been much increased since Mrs. Cragin's visit, and I feel in all my bones that pleasure-seeking had a death-blow."

The Campaign among the Children
November 24, 1850

J.H.N.—When Mr. Hamilton and Charlotte Miller were last here, the older children were much on my mind. Discipline and sincerity had worked their way through the other classes in the Association, but when we reached the older boys and girls, a wall /84/ rose up against us. This has been the difficulty from the beginning. The children have been within the family circle, yet not to any great extent under the Community spirit; and I proposed to Mr. Hamilton and Charlotte Miller that they return to Oneida with a special commission to carry the Community spirit through that class. I foresaw that the hardest conflict would come on precisely the same point as in the case of older persons, the relation of the sexes. Therefore my plan has been to devise some method by which the church could get the lead of the children, and thus let in upon them whatever good influences are coming down from heaven upon us.

There are two guiding principles which can be applied at once to the children. One is that the spirit and actions of persons must be brought out into the light where they can be criticised. The other is that there should be a leaning toward the ascending fellowship.

These principles are sure to make difficulty with a worldly spirit. We saw in the case of Hyde, that, although he was an obscene fellow, yet he was much

offended when the Association brought out a word that is commonly considered obscene and aired it. So also the principle of ascending fellowship will
offend those whose horizontal interests are at stake. I have had to stand in the
invidious position of demanding that love should gravitate toward me. But I
am subject to the same demand. I cannot have peace with God unless I keep
the ascending fellowship predominant. So I have felt bound to introduce that
principle into the church and be the victim of whatever offense its introduction might cause. /85/

There was a clique of young men and women in the Association consisting of Hyde, Julia, and others, who were in a state of exclusive fellowship with
one another. I found it necessary to demand that they seek fellowship with
those above them, and I went right in among them offering to be their play-
mate and inviting them up into fellowship with the Association. Those who
had private property there were terribly offended. If a man would only wait
and look through, he would see that no really valuable interests are attacked;
for if he is a true man he will come within the benefits of the principle. If he
calls away from him something the world regards as private property, by the
same rule it calls up to him the love of a class below when he is fit to receive
it. Let a man wait patiently and he will find that the principle will give him a
hundredfold for all that it requires of him and will eventually fill him with
the richness of God. . . .

Children can be modest, if they cannot reason. It is a trait that belongs to
their condition, and renders them beautiful and attractive to their superiors.
Modesty in conjunction with confidence in their parents constitutes the righteousness of children. Modesty and confidence, which are feelings, should
prevail over the fondness for pleasure and other feelings; and when the two
different kinds of feelings come into collision, children should use all the
power they have to make the right ones prevail. This is their faith; it is looking
upward, and is the attitude of mind which will eventually let them into fellowship with God and his family.

I do not expect that the children will understand all the movements of the
Association. It is not possible for them to do so until their minds are enlarged.
How can two persons be at /86/ peace with each other when one is a great deal
wiser than the other? It is not possible if the inferior insists on understanding
all that the superior does. What if I should say, I cannot have peace with God
without understanding all his ways. That would not be a happy state of mind
for me. God says: "As the heavens are higher than the earth, so are my ways
higher than your ways, and my thoughts than your thoughts." How, then,
shall I be at peace with him? Why, by dropping the idea of understanding all

his ways, and having a spirit of modesty and confidence toward him. Then no matter how high he is above me, love can flow.

What I want in the children is to settle it in their hearts that I am a man of God, and that I am right whether they understand me or not. When any feeling rises to contradict that, they should stand in readiness to put it down. Feeling will at last give us strength to prevail. Mere reason will never do it. God is providing for the growth of an omnipotent feeling in the Association and in the world, that I am right, and there will be an end of the insistence upon understanding all that I am about; and I invite these boys to cooperate with God in the establishment of this feeling, assuring them that I have now in my heart more love for the boys and children than ever before.

I felt as though I had found the whole of salvation, almost, when I had settled that principle of the possibility of fellowship between the superior and inferior. Without that principle, fellowship on any extensive scale would be impossible, so long as there is such a difference of intellect. There is but one way for me to have fellowship with God. He presents /87/ me the chart of this infinite counsels, of which I can understand a very little. But I understand enough to jump the rest. I will sign it and say it is right without reading, for it will require the endless ages of eternity to read it all. I will stake my all on the assertion that he is right. "Shall not the Judge of all the earth do right?" We can in the same way find men who are inspired by God to such an extent that we can endorse them without reserve and without understanding them. Such a man is one of the greatest gifts that God can give.

The Doll Spirit
Brooklyn letters, February 2, 1851

Theodore Noyes, Sarah Burt, Mary Prindle, and Mrs. Cragin formed themselves into a Committee to study and report on the doll spirit. They came to the following conclusions: 1.- That playing with dolls is acting and speaking a lie. 2.- That we do not want our philoprogenitiveness to grow any faster than God sees is best for us, and wish to learn more of the fear of the Lord, which is the beginning of education, before we try to learn to be mothers. 3.- That playing with dolls tends to make us babies ourselves in thought and talk. 4.- That the doll spirit seduces us from helping the family and from being earnest to get an education.

This report was read to Mr. Noyes, Mr. Hamilton, and others, who heartily approved. Mr. Noyes added: "The doll spirit is connected with the worship of images."

The children were well satisfied that the doll spirit had seduced them into pleasure-seeking, frivolity, and lying, and voted that they be burned up. Accordingly, the dolls were stripped without delay and laid on the coals, all hands rejoicing in their /88/ condemnation. Mr. Hamilton noted on the Report that he hoped the children at Oneida would follow the example of Brooklyn.*

10

Battle of the Putney Rear Guard

September 2, 1849, to December 15, 1852

John R. Miller to the Oneida Association
Putney, September 2, 1849

After tea, I invited Mr. Woolworth to go with me into the street. It was very disagreeable to me to meet the Putney enemy again, but I thought that the boldest course was the safest. I first called at Mr. Perry's tavern. He expressed much pleasure in seeing me, and wished I would come back with all the rest of our folks. I next went to Chandler's store, where I found a great crowd. All appeared glad to see me with the greatest politeness, except Israel Keyes, Mr. Baker, and Mr. Ryan. I left my advertisement to be put up, and then went to Upham's store, where I met with the same cordial reception. I next went to Phelps' tavern. I met Joel Willard at the door. He caught me with both hands and exclaimed, "Mr. Miller, can this be you? I am glad to see you." I then passed into the bar room. All rushed forward and offered me their hands with many expressions of pleasure. George Robertson caught hold of both my arms, gave me a real hug, and exclaimed with a good deal of enthusiasm, "God bless you, my old friend. I am glad to see you once more. We shall never allow you to leave Putney again, unless you promise /89/ to go and bring all your folks back here." I told him it would be quite a job to do that, as I had more than 150 in my family now. He said, "I don't care for that, the more the better." I handled Mr. Phelps my advertisement and asked him to mail it. Someone asked if I was going to sell myself. I said, "No. If I was, I should choose some other market. I don't think I should sell for much in Putney."

---

* The children who took part in this holocaust were about nine or ten years old. [G.W.N.]

Someone from the further side of the room said, "You are not to be bought. Putney has tried that, but there is not money enough in town to do it."

September 4, 1849.—When I wrote you of my cordial reception in this town, I felt that there would be another story to tell. The fact is, I took the enemy by surprise, and they had not time the first night to rally their forces. But yesterday morning when I went into the street, it seemed as though all hell was let loose. Israel Keyes attacked me in Chandler's store in the most insulting way possible. It was all I could do to live, but God was my strength. I told Mr. Woolworth that I did not see how he could possibly live here, that I would flee as Lot did out of Sodom, if my wife turned into a pillar of salt.

Yesterday was a curious day. I never was so well treated by the publicans and sinners, and never so abused by the scribes and Pharisees.

I thought I would not tell you that I had a very sick night, but I have concluded to tell the whole story. I have scarcely been able to sit up this forenoon, but I think I shall be able to attend my auction. The poisonous atmosphere of Putney is the only cause, I am sure.

September 5, 1849.—I have received more insults and abuse during the last two days than I have before for the last two years. /90/ Before my auction commenced, I kept away from the crowd as much as possible, but I could not hold up my head. When the people and the auctioneer came, and I saw that I must meet the situation, I sprang into a wagon I was offering for sale, and made a short speech. I felt my spirits rise at once, and after that I had no difficulty. Our property sold low, but as well as I expected.

It will be remembered that in a double wedding July 12, 1847, George W. Noyes was married to Helen Campbell, and William H. Woolworth to Emma Campbell. The girls, especially Emma, were isolated by the events of the following fall and winter, and went through great perturbations of spirit before yielding themselves to life in the Community.

Harriet H. Skinner to John R. Miller
Oneida, September 15, 1849

Today has been a victorious one for God over the power of Putney unbelief as it has been expressed in Helen's feelings for the last two years. She has come out into a state of grateful submission to God and love for the Association and its principles such as has made Mrs. Cragin exclaim joyfully: "The millennium has come! Praise God for his goodness in the great congregation." George expressed himself satisfied with the result of two years of conflict and suffering, and Noyes remarked: "If you conquer the Campbell spirit, you have conquered the world." /91/

John R. Miller to the Oneida Association
Putney, September 22, 1849

I met Dr. Campbell yesterday morning, and he looked the very picture of despair. In the afternoon, I met him again as I was coming out of Chandler's store. He said: "How do you get along working miracles and laying on of hands out in your Kingdom of God?"

M: If you want to know about our affairs, I can probably give you all the information you wish.

Dr: I find out enough by your publications to know that you are as corrupt as the Devil.

M: You may have occasion to change your mind on this subject.

Dr: I shall never change my mind, d—n it all.

M: Let God be the Judge between us.

I see that God does not intend that I shall get in love with Putney. After all the insults I have received from that man, I have hardly been willing to give him up; but now the last cord that bound me to him is broken, and I am prepared to rejoice in his case, let it be decided as it may. I think I have been too willing to overlook his faults, but I see that God is no respecter of persons.

John R. Miller to the Oneida Association
Putney, September 22, 1849

The "rear guard" are beginning to move. Emma has decided to go with us next week, and is now packing up her things. She has not been urged to go. Mr. Woolworth invited her to go with him. She refused until she found that he was in earnest. Mrs. Campbell /92/ is going too. I expect to be there Thursday afternoon.

September 24th, 1849.—There has been a great change in Emma's spirit since I came here, which fills Mr. Woolworth's heart with joy. It is nothing that I have done, for I have said but little to her. It is the work of God. I think Helen's letter produced a good effect, though she kept it to herself and has shown it to no one.

Mrs. Baker called on me yesterday; appeared friendly, though a little embarrassed. She was much pleased with the invitation to visit at Oneida. Mr. Baker was also pleased. I think the invitation must have been given by inspiration.

There is a terrible commotion in the spiritual atmosphere to-day, and I do not know how it will end, but God overrules all things and I have not the least fear.

John R. Miller to the Putney Community
September 30, 1849

After writing you at Springfield, I waited at the hotel, not knowing whether I should have the pleasure of meeting our Putney friends or not, but on the arrival of the cars to my great joy I found they were there.

After dining together at the American House, the party decided to go on by way of New York. At the Brooklyn branch, they found Mrs. Whitfield and Mr. Perry. They spent the day visiting points of interest, and in the evening went to the theater, "which Emma enjoyed very much." The next day they went by boat to Albany, and put up at the Delavan House.

We did not take tea till half-past seven. The waiter seated us at a long table where there were nearly a hundred persons, Mr. Woolworth at the end, Emma next, and myself at the side of her /93/ After I had finished my supper and was waiting for the others, Emma turned to me and asked if I expected to meet Mr. Noyes there. I said, "No. He is not here is he?" "Don't you see him at the end of the table?" I looked up, and sure enough there he was at the head of the table beside Mr. Woolworth, and had been there all the while. He saw that I did not recognize him, so he shook hands with Mr. Woolworth, and thought he would carry on the joke till I saw him. We spent the evening very pleasantly together, I assure you. He was on his way to Brooklyn to spend a few weeks. The next morning at half-past five, I walked with him down to the boat, and bade him good-by.

John R. Miller to the Association
October 20, 1849

I hear it hinted from time to time, both while at Oneida and since I came to Brooklyn, that "Mr. Miller does not fully believe in our social theory." How far I may have given occasion for such remarks by my own weakness and foolishness, I will not pretend to say, but I *do* wish to say that to be in a state that would justify such remarks or such an opinion I consider the most disgraceful state I could be in to myself, and one of the greatest unthankfulness to God. I hope that no one will ever make, or have occasion to make, such remarks again. I hope that all will believe me when I say, that I consider our principles—our social theory—as much above anything which this world knows anything about as heaven is above the earth. /94/

Noyes's Charges against Emma Woolworth
October 30, 1849

In the name of Christ and the church, I charge upon Emma Woolworth the following offenses: 1. Pride, which is the opposite of the fear of God. 2. Railing, which is the abuse of society. 3. Breach of covenant in regard to the use of her tongue. 4. Disrespect and ingratitude toward me. 5. Cruelty toward her mother and sister.

As witnesses for the truth of these charges, I name Mrs. A. Campbell, Mrs. Helen Noyes, and William Woolworth. These witnesses are interested, if at all, in Emma's favor. "Out of the mouth of two or three witnesses shall every word be established."

The alternative in this case will be a hearty confession and repentance, or a withdrawal of the fellowship of the church. Reasonable time will be given for deliberation.

John H. Noyes

October 30, 1849.—Emma confesses that she sees that the first three of the above charges are true, and on the ground of her confidence in my judgment confesses that all of them are true, though she does not clearly see the truth of the last two. She says that she repents of her railing, that she will endeavor to clear herself of all grounds of complaint, that she wishes anyone who sees any of the above faults showing themselves in her hereafter to tell her.

Of this confession William H. Woolworth is witness. /95/

Harriet A. Noyes to Harriet H. Skinner
November 10, 1849

Your mother gets along finely, and Charlotte is beautiful. Mr. Woolworth and Emma have returned. They took the Kellogg's room. John put Mrs. Hamilton over Emma to be her mother in place of Mrs. Campbell, and had a plain talk with Mrs. Campbell about being in earnest for God and for John. Emma flared up the first day, but is more quiet now. Helen does nicely. Mr. Woolworth is to take Mr. Burnham's place in the business, and stand up and be a man. Messrs. Thacker, Perkins, and Newhouse are making a flower bed. Otis Miller appears well.

With love to you all,
Your sister Harriet

Charlotte Miller to Mary E. Cragin and Harriet H. Skinner
Oneida, December 15, 1849

The case of Helen is next in order. You know how she received George's challenge to the race in pursuit of truth. She parted from him and Harriet and me in open war. To Mr. Hamilton, she appeared more respectful. She has taken no practical steps toward reconciliation with any of us since. Mr. Hamilton copied John's last note and with some remarks endorsing it sent it to her. She has made no move since, but perhaps it is working in her for Fidelia says she has learned at least to govern her tongue and mind her own business. What she is really about, I cannot say. Shall we not expect from her an acknowledgment of the truth of John's charges before we take any steps toward her? She is in her own room mostly, quite reserved, though kind in word to /96/ Fidelia. Emma is becoming quite approachable and attractive, rising some as Helen declines. I trust we have learned not to a administer undue stimulants in such cases, but to "think soberly according as God has dealt to every man the measure of faith."

Helen C. Noyes to Dr. John Campbell
Oneida, December 20, 1849

Brother John:—

I write to you because the truth, my position, and yours demand that I should do so.

In the first place, you are laboring under the mistaken idea that I am here against my will, without confidence either in Mr. Noyes as a spiritual man and leader or his principles. You have had reason to suppose so, but it is not the truth. It is not only my duty but a pleasure to tell you the *real* state of my feelings and thereby, as far as my own testimony is concerned, repair the wrong done a righteous man.

I have abundant evidence that John H. Noyes is a man after God's own heart, and that He *specially* raised him up to establish his Kingdom on earth. I recognize the church at Oneida as the beginning of that kingdom that shall finally overthrow and break in pieces every other kingdom, and Mr. Noyes as its rightful head and leader. I know that in following him I am pleasing and obeying God. I thank God that my fortunes and destiny are linked with his. I wish for no other, no better fortune.

The long threatened imprisonments, courts of law, public exposures, the summoning before the tribunals of the dignitaries /97/ of the land, *these* frighten me no longer, for the *least* in the kingdom of God is greater than all.

Besides, I should count it all honor that I was *worthy* to suffer persecution with the children of God and for Christ's sake.

I believe Mr. Noyes's doctrine as contained in the *Report* is the true order of heaven, and that the love and unity there spoken of is the miracle that shall confound the world. I believe, also, that unless Putney repents of its persecutions of a righteous man, a worse fate awaits it than that of Sodom and Gomorrah.

God only knows what I have suffered since the first outbreak at Putney and my desertion of Mr. Noyes. The *truth* has not made me suffer; that shall make us free. It was my fighting against it that caused the suffering.

I have been looking into the past, slowly and with difficulty taking up the stitches one by one back again to my first union with God, and endeavoring to remove the obstacles that are in the way. I find that *you* were my first confidant, *yours* the first spirit that I took in, and through *your* means I was seduced from my sworn allegiance to God and Mr. Noyes. I can trace the cause of my sufferings back to the time when I left *them,* and identified myself again with what I call the Campbell spirit, which has in it the very essence of unbelief, is reckless and God-defying in its nature. It is also a proud and rebellious spirit. You were a strong man in the world, I but a babe of a few weeks in Christ. I was afraid of you then, and my spirit yielded to yours. But I can now declare the truth boldly as it is in Christ Jesus. I can go no further in spiritual progress until I am forever separated from this spirit; till it has given /98/ place to the meekness and simplicity of God.

I beg of you to do the duty you owe to *yourself,* and look more into your *own heart,* and less into the hearts of the Perfectionists. You must have found ere this, that you are not their judge, and that you are not fighting with flesh and blood but with spirits. I remember when you were a believer in the doctrine of holiness, so that you preached it to your wife. Beware lest "the cares of the world, the deceitfulness of riches and the lust of other things choke the word;" "for he that *knoweth* his master's will and doeth it *not,* shall be beaten with many stripes."

You do not scruple to handle and manage your wife's conscience to suit yourself, while to *all appearances* you have no regard for your own; she is little better than a captive in her own house, without even liberty of worshiping God in her heart without *first* consulting you. Although you take this *responsibility,* still you cannot answer for her, for each must stand before the *judgment seat* to give an account for *himself; there* every man shall be rewarded *according to his works.*

"It is a fearful thing to fall into the hands of the living God." He is a God of judgment as well as mercy.

There is a way of escape for you, if you are not too proud to accept it, in repentance and turning to God. Even the thief upon the cross repented and said, "Lord, remember me when thou comest into thy kingdom." And Jesus said, "This day shalt thou be with me in Paradise." But the other blasphemed God and died. The spirit that persecuted and drove Mr. Noyes and his followers /99/ from Putney is the same that crucified Christ. I pray that you may be like Paul, not only a *persecutor* of the church, but a helper at last.

I have done my duty; I have cleared myself, warned you, and pointed out the only way of salvation for you. As for *me,* I have set the Lord always before my face.

In faithfulness,
Helen C. Noyes

A Communication from Emma C. Woolworth to the Spiritual Magazine
January 15, 1850

Having been brought through the kindness of God to a sincere love of *truth* as my best friend, I wish still farther to invite its spirit and influence by frankly confessing and rejecting my past errors.

I was converted in the first place to a confession of Christ, not by any proselyting efforts of the Perfectionists, but by a persuasion in myself which amounted to certainty, that they were right. This was also accompanied with a distinct consciousness that God was calling on me for the last time to separate from the world and unite myself with those who, I knew, manifested the spirit which he required. Soon after this I saw in the miraculous healing of Harriet Hall a manifestation of the power of God through them, which at the time was perfectly convincing.

The excessive pride, which is natural to me, and a foolish sensitiveness to worldly honor, with other strong influences to /100/ which I was exposed (but which I now feel were no excuse), caused me in a time of temptation to abandon my faith. I was led from this into a long and bitter war with the truth and with those whom I had every reason to know were my truest friends and worthy of my fullest confidence and love. The spirit of evil which I invited by my desertion wrought out in me the most unlovely and pernicious fruits. It was accompanied with darkness, suffering and despair. These were the natural results of my own course, I have no doubt.

I am now strengthened to cast off the spell of unbelief with which I have been bound, and to place myself again in the position where I first accepted Christ. I wish publicly to resume my confidence in him as a complete Savior of my soul and body; and also to confess my belief of the righteous character of this Association, and my full confidence in J. H. Noyes as a spiritual teacher.

Emma C. Woolworth

O. C. Journal
February 15, 1850

Emma Woolworth made her maiden speech, freely, boldly, warmly espousing this cause (our social theory), confessing her past wrong-doings, her present admiration of the truth, and her desire to serve it. Helen Noyes made a similar confession, saying that this theory had been the resurrection of the heart to her.

August 8, 1850.—Emma is improving in health and spirit; is studying the *Berean,* and struggling with exclusiveness. She says, if God will only save her from this, she will call it her /101/ hundredfold. She talks freely about it, not in the way of justification but of condemnation.

Helen C. Noyes to George W. Noyes
December 15, 1852

I could hardly begin to tell the improvement that has been made here since I have been gone. The Association seems much more refined internally and externally. But I see the greatest change in their evening gatherings. Stiffness and the meeting spirit seems to have given place to the social and family spirit. Conversation is general and all seem free. I thought this would please you, as you have felt interested to have a change in that respect. Harriet Hall is in excellent health and spirit, and Mrs. Miller tells me there is not one case of sickness in the Community. Miss Burgess is an inspiring woman among the children. She seems fresh and well, although she has a great deal of care, being in school all day and at the Children's House the rest of the time. I hope to be a help to her. Emma is a good girl, docile and cheerful, and is, I think, useful and acceptable to the Community.

With much love to the household, I am yours in the faith of Christ,

Helen

George, I shan't forget the paper. /102/

11

Relations with Outsiders
1849–1853

George Cragin to George W. Noyes
  April 15, 1849

I left the *First Annual Report* in the hands of Greeley, Cleveland, James, Manning, Hicks, Miss Daniels, and a new case, Dr. Hempel, a German noted as a free-thinker, Spiritualist, and socialist. James says he is a great man. I left also with him a copy of the *Confessions.** I am to call on all these persons on my return.

Mrs. Cragin to the Oneida Community
  April 15, 1849

We had a call from a Mr. Carr, a young man who has been at Oberlin and has been a warm and strong defender of their views. But he seems to be in a state where he is ready to throw away everything for inspiration. He fell in love with Mr. Noyes, and readily accepted an invitation to come and spend a week for the purpose of becoming better acquainted. He is quite a big fish, a person of good intellect and a happy, rejoicing, teachable spirit.

O. C. Journal

September 23, 1849.—This month has brought a great many visitors to Oneida. Several of our own company have come and gone. But such things interrupt the general quiet less and less. We have learned to show hospitality without the assiduities of the world; to give the freedom of home without costly attention. Nothing puts us off our track of self-improvement. In our evening meetings, there /103/ is quite a temptation to suit the exercises to the curiosity, taste, and edification of our strangers; but we find that the true way is to pursue steadily the lessons before us. Our heresies are so confessed that we cannot be afraid of disclosures; and if there is anything in the Association

---

* John H. Noyes's *Confessions of John H. Noyes* [L.F.]

that calls for criticism, we are glad to be under all the motives to good behavior which the most open exposure to a carping world can give us.

Last evening some question of industry brought forward the subject of carelessness in misplacing and misusing of tools. Several members mentioned their grievances, and the existence of this fault was pretty glaringly indicated. Dissection went on till personalities were called for. The names of men proved to be faithful in this respect were given by voluntary vouchers, and then the names of those notorious for heedlessness. It was quite an exposure, and strangers might have said it was just the result to be expected from Association; but we can venture such criticism, knowing that we are in the sure way to overcome all our faults by this very process of coming to the light.

Harriet A. Noyes at Oneida to Harriet H. Skinner at Brooklyn
November 10, 1849

Our visitor, Miss Thomas, is still with us. She is modest and pretty, gives herself up to reading and reflection, regards it a profitable visit; thinks of returning next week.

Dr. Devoe and wife spent a day and two nights with us since Mr. Cragin left. They were quite pleased. The Doctor talked pleasantly with John, and when he left presented him with a five-dollar gold-piece. While he was in New York he went over to Brooklyn three times, but could not find Willow Place. We are /104/ hid, even in Brooklyn.

Mrs. Cragin and I are much pleased at the change proposed for Mr. Burnham, and I know you will be.

We are making some progress daily in the lessons John is teaching us, and are thankful for the opportunity of being so much with him. He says he thinks he can endure living in the Association a good while at the rate of communication he is now having with them. We do not go into the meetings, but John gives matter for them whenever he chooses through Messrs. Hamilton and Burt.

Oneida Notes by Harriet A. Noyes
November 14, 1849

Mr. Franks called this evening after an absence of several weeks. He inquired into the possibility of joining the Manlius branch. Mr. Noyes frankly told him that he would not encourage any false hopes he might have in that direction; there was no sort of prospect yet of his uniting himself with any business man; the time would come when he and such men could work together, but it was not yet.

J.H.N.—I have settled it in my heart as a sober matter of fact these fifteen years, that the business of life is to seek first the Kingdom of God and his righteousness. I stand on this platform at all hazards, and get others to do the same as fast as I can. /105/

O. C. Journal

January 7, 1850.—Two strangers called to-day and asked to see Mr. Noyes. When told that he was absent, they made a demand on the Association for $40.00 for infringement of a certain patent-right. Two weeks were requested by us for investigation, but no, they must have it immediately or proceed to law. It was finally decided by our honorable body to inform them that we had consulted God about it, and should wait not a fortnight but his time, and do as he directed us. After being told of our decision, they acknowledged that they had been hasty and done wrong. We were convinced that they could collect something, and offered them $20.00. They accepted $25.00 with a *Berean,* which they promised to read.

Probably the best of this affair is that it serves as a judgment upon Mr. Burt, who had been engaged in the patent-right business since he became a Perfectionist, and had witnessed their dishonesty in silence. He took the reproof, and was thankful for it.

Brooklyn Journal

March 14, 1850.—Mr. Henry James called on us; was very polite.*

Oneida Journal

[No date indicated].—Mr. and Mrs. L. G. Mead called. Mr. Mead said: "I like things better than I expected. There is more common sense and business talent among the members than one would expect to find. I see no reason why the Community should not prove self-supporting."

Mrs. Mead said that there was more order and comfort than she expected to find, more than is to be found in common families. She was much pleased with the Children's Department. She thought the women were handsome, and that the short dress made them graceful. /106/

---

* This was Henry James senior, father of the novelist Henry James and the psychologist William James. [L.F.]

Mary Mead to Her Mother
May 26, 1850

My recent visit to the Brooklyn and Oneida Communities, I trust, will not be an unprofitable journey to me, for my faith and feelings were very much confirmed in favor of John and his interpretations of truth. I saw nothing to weaken, but many things to strengthen my confidence, and to encourage me to wait on the Lord.

O. C. Journal

May 21, 1850.—Mr. Blakeslee of the North American Phalanx called. He reports very discouragingly of his Association. They cannot make labor attractive, are badly in debt, have 700 acres of land and only about 30 members, have an aristocracy and high-livers. The rich send their children away to boarding schools, while at the Phalanx the children are all over the house and extremely annoying. He says that our Reports are producing considerable impression there.

A few days ago, Mr. Hotchkiss, brother of Mrs. Norton, called, and he now writes advising us to pitch the printing-office and store into the creek, and turn all hands into manufacturing some Yankee notion. Every man, woman, and child could then earn his dollar a week. We could soon buy up a whole township, and put the railroad under contribution for our productions.

Brooklyn Journal

July 26, 1850.—This evening we received a call from Mr. [George] Ripley of *The /107/ Tribune,* and Mr. [Charles] Sears of the North American Phalanx. Mr. Noyes, in answer to a question about the state of feeling among our neighbors, stated that a year ago on some partial discovery of our social principles there was a hostile manifestation on the part of the Castle, but that the publication of our *First Annual Report* had an immediate soothing influence. Mr. Noyes's avowal that printing was the king of the trades and love of the truth king of the passions led to a long and interesting discussion on the Bible and Christ's kingship as exponent of the truth. Mr. Noyes said that he had arrived at his most radical theories by perfect abandonment to truth. This they complimented as a high and rare attainment, one necessary to the Columbus-like enterprise of discovering a new social world. All reformers, they said, had this consolation: if they made things no better, they could not make them worse. Civilization in New York was a horrible thing. If our system was licentious, as our enemies affirmed, Mr. Ripley said he saw every day before his eyes transactions that were infinitely worse. Mr. Ripley inquired if Mr. Noyes found his social principles in the Bible. Mr. Noyes replied that he did, though not glaringly on the surface. He regarded Christ as a thorough Associationist, and thought many modern reformers in giving up the Bible threw away their best weapon. It was not essential to the value of a revelation that it be perfect in externals. It has always been God's policy to clothe his messengers with a rather repulsive outside, that people might be induced to penetrate below the surface. Mr. Ripley thought that the ultimate state of perfection was yet centuries ahead, that he himself was 500 years ahead of his age. Mr. Noyes replied: "Then I am 1000 years before /108/ my time, but nevertheless I expect great changes soon." He went on to speak of his belief in the Primitive Church [early Christianity] as a still-existent perfected organization. Replying to a question, he said he believed the principles of the *First Annual Report* were embodied in Christ's perfected church, but of course not to their full extent here.

Mr. Ripley, to our surprise, displayed a fine portly figure, bearing all the signs of a comfortable prosperous gentleman rather than the lean Cassius-like reformer we expected. He is full of vivacity, has large language, and talks rather too much to be a good listener. He has a good deal of social magnetism. Mr. Sears looks more as if he had seen hard service in the war with society. He talks much less, but perhaps more from real thought and experience than Mr. Ripley. From his thrice saying about repose from the labor of directing an Association, we concluded that he was tired to death.

October 19, 1850.—Mr. Henry James called again. He is a rich man, belongs to the "upper ten," has a splendid intellect, and prides himself upon being a gentleman. He was so conceited and dogmatical that he did not give Mr. Noyes a chance to put in a word. Finally, when Mr. Noyes spoke of the branch Association at Manlius, Mr. James inquired if it was a farming Association, and added that he supposed farming was the basis of our business. Mr. Noyes replied that printing was the basis.

Mr. James: But you must have bread and butter.

Mr. Noyes: It is more important that we should have the word of life.

Mr. James: Without the body, we could have no conscious identity.

Quite a discussion followed, in which Mr. James rushed from one subject to another in a bold assuming manner. Mr. Noyes bore it patiently until Mr. James decidedly opposed unity, arguing that each one should have his own private opinions. Then Mr. Noyes told him plainly, that he thought he was impertinent in his remarks and in his manners. At first Mr. James seemed inclined to pass it by, but after thinking a moment he rose and said: "We certainly differ very materially in our opinion of what constitutes good manners;" and with an emphatic "Good morning, ladies," left looking white with anger.

November 9, 1850.—"Greeley," says Noyes, "is the only commanding editor in the country who has avowed in his paper his willingness that we should try our experiment unhampered. Since coming to Brooklyn, we have been providentially brought into contact with the Tribune clique. Cleveland, Greeley's brother-in-law, invited me to read our *First Annual Report* to a company of gentlemen and ladies at his house. Ripley came to see me, and took our suggestion about the "Rappings." We hear by way of the Fowlers, that Greeley has read our first and second Reports, and carries our periodical home with him.

Oneida and Its Visitors
by Harriet H. Skinner
January 26, 1853

We think Oneida is distinguished from all other Associations in respect to hospitality. Its visitors are treated according to the etiquette of a family rather than of a public institution. Sympathy with the principles of the /110/ Society or a wish to become acquainted with them is the only passport that is required to hospitable treatment. No charges are made, and seldom any compensation accepted. Entire strangers stay days and even weeks, and are made to feel perfectly welcome. It is rare that the family is without visitors. Those who stay at all are invited into the work and everyday engagements. We may be asked, How does Oneida secure herself against disagreeable intrusion, if she keeps such open doors? Not by law but by *sincerity.* If visitors are treated to the family fare in other respects, they are also in respect to criticism. Her frankness is her defense.

An Indian Concert
Oneida, January 28, 1853

Dear Friends:—
Last evening we had a rich and somewhat novel entertainment. You have heard of the Indian Vocalists, members of the Oneida tribe living in our vicinity, who have attained considerable celebrity by giving concerts in New York and different parts of the country. Some of them, having attended the Community festival last summer, seem to have remembered the occasion with pleasure and lately proposed to come over and sing with us, not as in their paid concerts but as a free social entertainment. To this we readily acceded, and last evening was the time agreed upon. The singers belong to the "Or-

chard" branch of the tribe, located east of us, from which we invited several to be present, among them THOMAS CORNELIUS, their minister.

Between six and seven o'clock they arrived, eighteen I think in all. We repaired to the parlor, they occupying one end, and /111/ our people filling up the sides and the other end, with the children in the center. The Indians sung several pieces, then our people sung; and so alternating, the evening was taken up. Our children occupied one interval with their singing. All agreed in enjoying this musical reunion, particularly the part performed by our visitors.

The band consists of three men and two women. Most of their pieces were "sacred music," though spiced with some songs. Their singing was all beautiful, and some of it, exquisite. They sang all parts, keeping accurate time, and so far as I could judge, with perfect harmony. One of their songs I cannot help alluding to. The chorus was, "Long, long ago." The words spake of "The woods where they chased the wild deer," of "The hunters, swift as the eagle in his flight," of "Their maidens that to virtue were not strangers." Sung here on the very *spot,* and by the sons and daughters of those they sang of, it was exceedingly touching. They sing both in the Indian and English tongue, but principally in the Indian. They engage in it with much earnestness, and there seems to be a *soul* to their performances. They are dignified in their manners and at ease in good society. We listened to them with attention, and at times could not resist the impulse to applaud.

A few minutes past eight o'clock, we went down to our dining-room and all partook of supper served up in true Oneida style. Before commencing, we sang our Community Hymn,
"Let us go, brothers, go."

After we had supped, they sang that familiar old tune, "China," in Indian. It was beautifully sung, and we felt it was a real act of worship. At nine o'clock they left for home, assuring us that the time had been pleasantly spent. /112/

The whole affair passed off with perfect ease and order. At half-past nine, the tables had all been cleared and reset ready for the morning, and all had retired to their rooms. It was remarked, that nowhere but in Community life could such treats be enjoyed in our own home with so little trouble and so much pleasure. We sincerely thank God for the happiness we had in it, and feel like returning it to him, and making it a new stimulus to devotion to Christ and his kingdom, which will fill the world with love, beauty, and happiness.

Your brother in the cause,
H. M. Waters

John R. Miller to the Circular
     April 9, 1853

Our fishing expedition went off very pleasantly yesterday afternoon. We had a party of five, M. Victor Considerant, Mr. Skinner, Mr. Woolworth, Mr. Newhouse, and myself. Mr. Considerant* followed our advice to leave his long, nice fishing-rod and take one of ours, as we thought it would be more convenient for fishing in the bush. After providing ourselves with bait, we started for a trout brook in the vicinity. As soon as he had looked at the brook, he insisted on going back for his own fishing-rod, saying in his bad English, "She will do very well. I am accustomed to fishing in the bush," and started off at a rapid pace for the house. Mr. Woolworth and I stayed for him while the others went on with their fishing. On his return, he asked whether we /113/ fished *up* or *down* the stream. I told him that we commenced fishing up. He said he always fished down stream—"that is my system"—and started up the hill.

As we were walking up on the bank he caught me by the arm and said with enthusiasm, pointing to the western hills, "Beautiful! It is like my own country. It looks likes the mountains of Europe." He seems delighted with the scenery here.

After going up as far as he wished, we struck down the bank and prepared for fishing. As he put on his bait, he said pleasantly, "Now I will try to catch an American trout." He has a great passion for fishing, and his hook once in the stream, he gives his whole attention to it. I was surprised to see him fish in the bushes with his long pole and twelve or fifteen feet of line without getting it tangled. He caught about twenty, which was more than all the rest of us caught.

In the evening, one of the women gave him a lesson in Phonography at his request, in exchange for a lesson in French in which we all participated. He alludes occasionally to the difficulty he has from his imperfect understanding of the English language. Before starting on our fishing trip yesterday, I was conversing with him about the fishing, when he exclaimed laughingly: "Oh! You talk like a—a steam—what is it? A steam-boat—a locomotive—that's it," which gave the company a good laugh at my expense.

In the parlor one day I called his attention to a fine French picture, a view in Paris which you recollect we brought from Putney. As soon as he saw it he exclaimed, "Ah, there is my own house," and pointed it out to me. /114/

---

* M. Victor Considerant, the well-known disciple and representative of Fourier in exile from France, was at this time visiting the Oneida Association. [G.W.N.]

12

Case of Francis Hyde
September to December 1850

Oneida Journal

September 4, 1850.—Mr. And Mrs. Cragin arrived from Brooklyn, having come by request of Mr. Noyes for the special object of assisting the Association in clearing themselves from the spirit of Hyde and Newhouse. Considering all the circumstances, Mr. Hamilton proposed that tomorrow be a day of fasting and prayer; that we suspend work and humble ourselves before God for giving place to Hyde's spirit. This was warmly seconded by Messrs. Burt and Kinsley, and approved by all.

September 5, 1850.—The family took a bread and milk breakfast, and gave up the day to reflection and meetings, with a light supper at night. Mrs. Cragin held a meeting with the children in the morning, and they all voted to join in fasting and praying God to cast out disobedience. In the afternoon there was a prayer meeting of the women in the Tent Room, and a men's meeting in the parlor. Mr. Newhouse seemed hard and unconcerned, evidently thinking the Community would do nothing more than talk. Indignation was expressed against such a spirit. Judgment also fell upon Leonard Dunn, he being evidently under Hyde's influence. In the afternoon at a general meeting, Mrs. Cragin said that she had refused to shake hands with these men, and now refused to eat with them. Mrs. Skinner, Mr. Burt, Mr. Hamilton, Mr. Burnham, and others immediately said they sympathized with Mrs. Cragin. "I do not wish to eat with them," said /115/ one. "Nor I," "nor I," "nor I," echoed many voices, until Mr. Burnham proposed a vote, and a thundering "Aye" excluded them from our table. If a thunderclap had fallen upon Mr. Newhouse, he could not have shown more abject fear and astonishment. He covered his face with his hands for a long time. Leonard Dunn said in a broken voice, "I prayed to-day for the judgment, and it has come, and I am glad of it." A good many prayed audibly and feelingly, and we realized that God was here in our midst.

In the evening Mr. Hamilton brought up the case of the boys as an illustration of the influence of Hyde's spirit. It was found that George Hatch, John Norton, and John Smith had been possessed by a lying, thievish, insubordinate spirit. The boys had gone to bed, but a delegation was chosen to invite them to get up and come to meeting. John Norton broke down and confessed in a broken spirit many things he had done. As George remained stubborn, it was thought corporal punishment would be just and salutary, and Mr. Hatch offered to administer it, if the family thought best. This was approved, and it was a thrilling scene. Mrs. Cragin said: "Mr. Hatch never looked so noble as when he stood there publicly chastizing his ungodly son, a young man almost as tall as his father; and it was a striking instance of the zeal of the church to purge itself of evil-doers." The transactions of the day cleared the atmosphere, and many testified to a strong sense of God's approbation in the matter.

September 6, 1850.—The work of judgment and execution proceeded among the children. Four of the ringleaders among the smaller boys, Charles Van Velzer, Albert Ackley, Wallace Worden, and Henry Clark, after a public criticism of the children, were chastised by their fathers with the rod. /116/

Near the close of the meeting, Mr. Hamilton presented a protest by which Francis Hyde is cut off from the Community until he shall repent and gain the commendation of Mr. Noyes. This document was signed by nearly all the adult members, among whom the first on the list was Julia S. Hyde.

September 7, 1850.—Meeting at the Children's House for further discipline and judgment. Wallace Worden, having shown that his punishment last evening had not humbled him and having manifested a lying spirit, was again chastised before the children. Henry Smith, Arthur Chark, and Eliza Burt were also chastised at the same meeting. Immediately after this, Mr. Hamilton with several of the leading men met with the larger boys in their chamber, and Mr. Hamilton, after a sincere criticism of John Smith exposing his participation in the offenses of George Hatch, administered a faithful flogging.

September 8, 1850.—In the afternoon, a meeting was called of the members from Northern Vermont, and the Dunn family was criticised. Julia Hyde especially was subjected to a most searching criticism, which brought her into the same judgment with Francis Hyde. It was clearly shown that Mr. Noyes had suffered much through the Dunn family; and it was concluded that they be considered as outsiders, until they commend themselves to Mr. Noyes.

Evening.—Criticism of Mrs. Seymour and the Seymour family. Julia Hyde's case was brought up again, and her deceitful spirit was judged. It was seen that her influence among the women had been similar to that of Francis Hyde among the men; and that as Hyde's spirit had excluded Mr. Noyes, so virtually Julia had excluded /117/ Mrs. Cragin and Mrs. Noyes.

September 9, 1850.—Further criticism of the children today. In the evening, the two Wordens and their families were criticised.

September 10, 1850.—A good note from Leonard Dunn, confessing Mr. Newhouse's influence on him. Criticism of the Kellogg family and Henry Thayer.

September 11, 1850.—Several persons were criticised this evening, viz.: Mr. and Mrs. Daniel Nash, Mr. and Mrs. Joslyn, Lady Hamilton, Elias Hall, and Fidelia Dunn, the latter exposing her deceitfulness and coquetry in love matters.

Truly the past week has been one of criticism and judgment.

September 14, 1850.—Mr. Newhouse asked Mr. Burt for work. Mr. Burt told him he might work in the swamp, where Mr. Abbott has been cutting brush. We decided in Meeting to have bread and milk once a day.

September 17, 1850.—Letters were received from Brooklyn in regard to Hyde, his hardness and non-compliance with recommendations, and his departure from there after giving Mr. Cragin a receipt in full of all demands against him and the Association. A few minutes later, who should arrive but Hyde himself. He called for Julia. Mr. Hamilton told him that we left Julia free to go with him if she chose; but she declined to see him, saying that she would not leave the Association unless we turned her away.

September 19, 1850.—G. W. Noyes wrote a letter to the Campbell family, judging the family spirit.

September 25, 1850.—Hyde came this morning, and manifested much bitter feeling. Soon after he left, it was thought best that Julia with her mother, Leonard Dunn, and Mrs. Newhouse should go /118/ down to his father's and have an interview with him. When they arrived, Francis had gone to the post-office with a letter to Mr. Hamilton demanding that his wife be delivered at his father's before 5 o'clock in the evening, also a note to Julia requesting her to come. He pleaded, demanded, and cried, but she positively declined to live with him. At last he told her she might "go her own way."

M. L. Worden and J. L. Skinner went to Manlius to make preparations for removing to that place soon, in accordance with the proposal of Mr. Noyes that we commence a branch of our Association there, as Mr. Worden could not sell his place.

September 30, 1850.—Mr. Hamilton said he had lately noticed evidences of sincerity and subordination in Mr. Newhouse. Mr. Leonard, whom Mr. Newhouse had chosen as his monitor, said that he had confidence in Mr. Newhouse, and moved that he be invited back to work and to eat with the family. This was approved by all.

October 6, 1850.—Messrs. Hamilton and Miller, at Mr. Noyes's suggestion, called upon Mr. Timothy Jenkins, and gave him information concerning Hyde and Julia. He approved of the course which had been taken with Hyde. He did not think there was any difficulty to be apprehended from him, but more from the Hubbards. He stated that Lucius Hubbard had been to see him last week about entering a complaint to the Grand Jury against the Community for keeping a disorderly house. He advised him not to do it, but still he thought they might. He gave some friendly advice, and assured our men that he would not be employed as counsel against the Community. When told of the Manlius movement, he highly approved of it, and said the sooner Tryphena went there the better. /119/ It might quiet the Hubbards to know that Tryphena had left here. When they returned home, it was concluded that Mr. And Mrs. Skinner, Tryphena, and Julia Hyde should go on the first train this evening. Then if the Hubbards came to meeting tomorrow, we could tell them that Henry and Tryphena had gone onto a farm at Manlius to live.

October 11, 1850.—Messrs. Burt and Leonard consulted Mr. Jenkins. He was very friendly. He said his advice had deterred Hyde and Hubbard from persecuting the Community. He declined to take money for this service, saying it would be better for the Community if he did not take sides. He expressed much interest in the system of criticism as practiced in the Community.

Noyes to Francis Hyde
Brooklyn, October 26, 1850

Mr. Hyde:—

A simple statement of facts in reply to your late letters may help you to see and choose the reasonable course.

When you left the Association, I sent word to Julia that she would be free to go with you, and that it would be better for all parties that she should go if she was in sympathy with you. On the receipt of your first letter of demand, I wrote to Mr. Hamilton, and through him to Julia and the Association, reiterating more distinctly that neither I nor the Association would hinder Julia by word or deed from leaving us. At the same time, I said that we had no equitable or legal right to dictate to her where she should go if she went. Since then that is about the first of the /120/ present month, M. L. Worden and his wife removed to his former residence in Manlius, and by the advice of the Association Julia removed with them, and now resides there with *her* father and mother, which I presume will be thought quite as proper as it would be for her to go to *your* father's house.

I say to you now that you are at liberty, so far as we are concerned, to assume your legal rights over her by persuasion or force. We shall not in any way hinder you, and you cannot reasonably ask us to help you. Threats of revenge will not induce us to do so base a thing as to attempt to drive her away from her mother's home. I desire peace with you, but I prefer war to such meanness. . . . If the meaning of your letters is that you wish me to drive her out of our Society and compel her to follow you, I shall never do it, because I fear the God of justice more than I fear anything that you may be permitted to do . . . .

If you can induce her to choose cheerfully to go with you, which is the only honorable way, I shall not interfere nor find fault. But if you resort to law and "revenge" to obtain her, I do not think you will be pleased with your own work or happy in its consequences. I do not believe that a civilized community will sympathize with you or that God will prosper you. But of this you must be your own judge.

I shall send a copy of your letter and of this to Julia, that she may know your position and mine, and act for herself. I shall also publish this correspondence, if you make it necessary.

Hoping that you will take a peaceable and reasonable course, and that you will ultimately recover yourself from the snares into which you have fallen, I remain, *Your well-wisher,* /121/

John R. Miller in the Oneida Journal

November 2, 1850.—My visit to Manlius was at the right time, as Julia was thinking of going to Le Roy to live with Hyde. The reason she gave was to save the Association from trouble. I told her we should carry out the spirit of Mr. Noyes's letter to Hyde by making her free, and at the same time we wished her to understand that no one wanted her to leave the Association to prevent trouble. I soon saw that her private feelings had much more to do with her desire to go than she was willing to confess, and perhaps more than she was aware of. She wanted I should advise her. We declined all responsibility, and made her confess that she felt free. We left yesterday, feeling, on the one hand, that we had made her free, and, on the other, taken away all false excuses for going with which she was deceiving herself.

Oneida Journal

December 14, 1850.—Francis Hyde drove up to the mill and delivered a letter from his attorney demanding that his wife be brought to his father's house at Oneida Castle within twenty-four hours, and threatening that if this request was not complied with, he would present his complaints in a tangible form to the Grand Jury, which convened at Morrisville the following Monday. Mr. Miller went down to the Castle and talked with Hyde, but was unable to mollify him. Hyde said he was determined to have his wife or satisfaction in some other way, and threatened to follow the Association till the day of Judgment. /122/

December 15, 1850.—Messrs. Miller and Burt called on Mr. Dodge, Hyde's attorney, and explained to him the Association's course toward Hyde. Mr. Dodge acknowledged the truth of all their arguments, but insisted that they were duty bound to advise Julia to go and live with Hyde.

December 16, 1850.—Francis Hyde went to Manlius about 10 o'clock this forenoon, and demanded that Julia go away with him, saying he would give her two hours to make up her mind and get ready. She refused to go with him. He stayed between two and three hours trying to persuade her to go, but without success. He then left, telling her he was going over to the depot, and wanted her to be ready to go with him at eight o'clock in the evening; that he had come from Le Roy to get her and was determined not to go away without her. When eight o'clock came, Julia again refused to go, and felt quite jubilant. But about nine o'clock Hyde came back with a constable from Fayetteville, and told her that, if she would go with him peaceably, well and good; but if not, he would compel her. The family left her free, telling her she must take the responsibility herself. The constable asked her to try living with Hyde for a month, and Hyde promised that she might return in a month if she chose. After resisting for three hours, she was induced at length by his threats to go with him, but she protested against his proceedings, as did also her mother and Mr. Worden. He took her away at half-past twelve at night in a snowstorm, saying he would carry her to Fayetteville, where they would take the stage to Syracuse, and then the cars to Le Roy. /123/

Julia Hyde to the Oneida Association
Le Roy, December 28, 1850

You doubtless remember the promise that Mr. Hyde made when at Manlius, that I might go back in a month if I chose. *Now* he says that I shall never go back as long as he lives; but may enjoy my own opinions about religion, and may visit my friends. I asked him when I might visit Oneida, and he said, "*Perhaps* next summer."

Noyes's Judgment of Francis Hyde
December 19, 1850

I am reminded of Paul's text where, comforting himself and the church in cases of apostasy and iniquity, he says: "In a great house there are not only vessels of gold and of silver, but also of wood and of earth, and some to honor, and some to dishonor." My prevailing opinion about Hyde is that he is a vessel to dishonor. He has had a use in the church, and he has done his work,

"Nevertheless, the foundation of God standeth sure, having this seal, the Lord knoweth them that are his." The Lord knoweth, if we do not.

In looking back, I see that Hyde is entirely distinguished from every other case we have had. We might think there was a similarity between him and Otis Miller, but we should find there was a wide difference.

In the first place, Otis Miller came into the Association by invitation from John R. Miller and myself. Hyde thrust himself in. He came up and went to work. I felt sensible of this /124/ at the time.

Again, Otis Miller married Ellen by my offer and invitation. I am well satisfied that God would not give me such an agency in bringing a man to the Association and putting Ellen into his hands, unless there was something good in him. He came into possession of his wife, about whom the difficulty was afterwards made, in a regular way by consent of parties all round. But Hyde *stole* his wife from the Association, from her mother and family, and then forgot the Association to keep his plunder.

Again, though Otis Miller showed an insubordinate, deceptive spirit that could not exist in the Association, yet so far as I know he never propagated that spirit. I know of no man in the Association except Hyde, who ever seriously undertook to serve as the Devil's missionary among us. He was distinguished for a chronic hatred of our meetings, of our criticisms, and of edifying spiritual conversation, and was eager to propagate that feeling among all our young people. . . . From first to last, he never gave any satisfactory evidence of self-improvement. The only things he was ever interested in were dancing, gossip, external labor, flirtation, sexual intercourse, eating, and drinking.

To be sure, Otis Miller went out and in the craziness of passion attempted to do us mischief. But in him it was a freak of passion, and soon died out. Hyde, on the other hand, has had several months for deliberation. First came a note threatening revenge if we did not do that which was clearly unreasonable; then after a considerable interval another; and now after several months there is a third. This is no freak of passion, but settled ugliness—the desperation of malignity, disobedience, and /125/ selfishness. Here we find ourselves in the face of the text: "If we sin wilfully after that we have received the knowledge of truth, there remaineth no more sacrifice for sins, but a certain fearful looking for of judgment and fiery indignation."

This view puts me back on a closer examination of the facts in Otis Miller's case. We fired a gun of excommunication, but I think there was some little obscurity in our minds at the time. The man appears to have taken a good turn, and we find that we were all mistaken. What is the meaning of this? My instinctive understanding of it is as follows: Hyde was in the Association at this time acting himself out in reprobate fashion as the enemy of all righteousness and truth. As I was on the point of leaving, I felt that there was a terrible adversary there, and I said, "I will mob that spirit out before I leave." The three men I pitched upon as the vessels of that spirit were Hyde, Miller, and Newhouse. I summoned all three to surrender. Hyde and Newhouse made a satisfactory surrender so far as profession went, but Miller acted himself out. Well, now we know to a certainty that Hyde did not surrender at that time. His submission was a mere mockery for the sake of escaping a drubbing, and on the whole Miller's acting himself out boldly was comparatively a decent performance, altogether better for the Association than the sly, serpent course of Hyde.

The point is this: I was driving at a spirit, but I was in the dark as to the flesh and blood that held it. I fired at the one who was most honestly manifesting that spirit, but it turned out that he was not the real man. Well, I fired close enough to scare the spirit out of him, but he himself was saved. Hyde was /126/ the real representative of the spirit that was fired at, and it will pretty likely appear that he inspired the operations of Otis Miller.

Afterwards, in the affair with Mr. Perry there was the same uncertainty as to specific aim. I thundered at the spirit which revealed itself in him. As in the other case, the spirit was working in the mass, and our shot took effect on the foremost man. But as the smoke was cleared away, we have found at last the man we were after. The emissary of Satan, the Achan in the camp, from the beginning was Hyde. We have had to fire three times to hit the right man, but this time we have slung him out.

We can see what a power of infusion Hyde had in the case of Hial Waters. When I first went to Oneida, Hial was so good-natured, so far from jealousy and ugliness of every kind, and so ready for every good work, that he commended himself particularly to all. That was his natural character. But a very good-natured man who is not furnished with the protectives that come by experience and discipline is the very man to swallow a plausible scoundrel whole. Hial accordingly was prepared to swallow Hyde, and did. By such a combination, the most good-natured man becomes the ugliest man in the world, and it is true that for two years Hial was very troublesome. By his own confession and by the knowledge of others, he was full of evil-thinking, jealousy, insubordination and discontent.

We can suppose equally well that Otis Miller in his good nature also swallowed him down. As reported from Putney and as we first knew him, he was a clever, companionable man, with nothing like jealousy in him. He received our social theory in the midst of a great excitement against us at Putney, and was almost the only /127/ person who stood up as our friend. There was evidence in him of an attraction for the truth and an ambition for improvement, a spirit that was the extreme opposite of that which he manifested afterward.

It will be found that Hyde bedeviled him just as he did Hial. Hyde had the art of oozing into every opening, and thus actually filled the Association so that I could not stay there.

I am inclined to think that the same operation that has been described took place in Leonard Dunn. He is naturally a sensible, good-natured man, and that which was said of Hial is true of him.

(Some one mentioned that Daniel Knowles laid his desertion to Hyde.)

There it is again. We shall find that he was the center of the spirit of discontent and desertion, the spirit that worked the alienation of the young people from the spiritual portion of the family. According to Mr. Bradley's observation, Hyde had an agency in influencing William Courter and Joshua Smith in the course they took.

I believe that Julia was bedeviled by Hyde in the same way as the others. It is true that she did lie, and as to external transactions seduced him. But it is an easy and common thing for one person to seduce another to seduce him in return; and the first seduction is usually carried on in spirit, while the return comes out in words and deeds. I believe that Hyde blew into Julia that which induced her to persuade him to quit the Association. She is of that free, social, generous nature that would be open to the infection of his spirit. I know that I never loved a false nature as I loved her. There was something true and beautiful in her when she first came to the Association, and although falsehood and even indecency have appeared in her since, I am persuaded that it has come from his spirit. /128/

There is another circumstance in Otis Miller's case which deserves to be noted, namely, the way in which he came back. We dashed into the reprobate spirit, and slung out Otis Miller neck and heels. But John R. Miller, the man who induced him to join us and knew him best, was not there at that time. By the Providence of God, he fell in with Otis Miller, and a train of circumstances thereby commenced which led to his restoration. I was glad when we flung him overboard, that John R. Miller was not present but was cruising outside in his boat. It was clearly our business to fling him overboard, and it was Mr. Miller's business to pick him up if he could in his skiff. This he did successfully.

But in Hyde's case, the circumstances are different. There is no boat out for him. We must not jumble things together and think that Hyde is to be saved because Otis Miller was, for we have every reason to think there is no good in him.

Mr. Nash.—I will relate an incident that illustrates Hyde's vindictive spirit. Mr. Hamilton had given me a job. I went to the shop for a board, which was brought by Abram. As the board did not prove suitable, I mentioned the fact to Abram. But Hyde immediately returned with the board, and insisted in a blustering, determined manner that it should do. I remonstrated, maintaining my right to have the thing done properly, when he declared with much heat, that if he only had me in the world, he would give me such a mauling as I never had before.

J.H.N.—There is reason to believe that Hyde introduced much greedy alimentativeness into the Association. His gluttony /129/ was most recklessly displayed in the cellar, far exceeding that of any other person. Mr. Bradley tells a story on this point: The last evening that Hyde spent on the sloop, he purchased two quarts of milk, two quarts of peaches, a loaf of bread, and a pie, and ate nearly the whole for his supper. He afterwards came to the house, and I had a plain talk with him on the necessity of his being a spiritual man. Feeling compassionate toward him, and remembering the abuse he had suffered in his youth, I sent Mrs. Cragin up to express my sympathy for him.

Mrs. Cragin:—I went to him on this errand, and proffered him our sympathy and help. For a moment he seemed to relent, but with a sudden and violent effort of will he exclaimed: "It is no use." I said: "Tell God your troubles. He has a father's heart toward you. You can pray." "I can't," was his reply, "It is all dark."

J.H.N.—Hyde was then going through the experience of Esau, who, it is said, sold his birthright for a mess of pottage, and afterward found no place of repentance, though he sought it carefully with tears. No wonder it was all dark to him, when instead of fasting, as he had been recommended to do, he ate as has been related. He is one of those "whose God is their belly, whose end is destruction, who mind earthly things."

I am convinced that the true name for this man is imposter. He has imposed upon the Association from beginning to end. And this is not the result of sagacity: it is the wolfish instinct in him. He imposed upon the good nature of those around him. He shammed a particular sensitiveness, which always secured him /130/ tender treatment. By sham repentance when he was cornered, he won sympathy. But he never gave a thing to the great purposes of the Association. His sole aim, under a mask of artlessness and simplicity, was to ravage, devour and destroy. And after his mask became worn through, it was of course his time to withdraw. What we supposed true of Otis Miller has proved true of Hyde. He is the man, and we may now go back and put in the correct name.

This study of Hyde's case is interesting to me. I do not wish to treat it as a private personal affair, but as affording us an important view of truth, which will be serviceable to us hereafter in our judgment of persons. We can from time to time find out the inner truth of cases as they are brought up. And this is our way of carrying on the war. Hyde goes to the courts below, and we to the courts above. He goes to the Devil's world, and we to God's world. /131/

13

Abigail Merwin
December 28, 1850, to July 16, 1851

Brooklyn Journal

December 28, 1850.—Elizabeth Hawley has gone with G. W. Noyes as a missionary to Abigail Merwin and the many others in that region who have once confessed Christ and have fallen from their testimony. Mr. Noyes has strong hopes of Abigail Merwin's return to the truth.

Mr. Noyes said today that he had completed the circle, having reached New Haven where he began. He says of Abigail Merwin, that her spirit is eminent for good nature, and that a strong infusion of good nature is just the thing for us all, since we have had so much criticism among us. Moreover, he says that her spirit is adapted to extension. Harriet and I have cooperated with him more in the department of depth, but if we are now going into the department of extension, her spirit is the one needed. He remarked today that possibly the conversion of Abigail Merwin was the thing he was waiting for before going to Oneida; that perhaps she would go with him, and we should all rejoice together.

Remarks by Noyes Reported by Mary E. Cragin and Harriet A. Noyes
January 3, 1851

"We wrestle not with flesh and blood, but with principalities and powers." The communication with Abigail Merwin has stirred up the principality of the marriage spirit, and probably /132/ she is suffering on that point herself. The way to treat this spirit is to go back to rejoicing in bare salvation, being willing that God should take away everything else. We must seek more fellowship with God in order that we may be sure to behave well. Abigail Merwin's coming among us will make us happier than anything else that ever happened to us. We must learn to admire a beautiful person, just as we would a picture in the Art Union, without wishing to make it our own. We must be satisfied with a good love feast once in a while, and not think we must have it all the time. We should all be most free. Abigail Merwin cannot take your place, nor you hers. Our places are distinct and appointed us by God. If we yield this point and begin to retreat, there is no stopping-place short of condemnation. "The gifts and calling of God are without repentance."

Mary E. Cragin to Harriet H. Skinner
January 5, 1851

Mr. Noyes is much elated with the prospects in Abigail Merwin's case. He says it has been the greatest trial of his faith, but he has "staggered not," and now after so long a time the promise is being fulfilled. He says further that she will be the prodigal son. Having deserted him under such circumstances, she can never claim anything of him, but must receive all as a free gift. In this way, God will make an end of the claiming spirit in the Association. . . .

I suppose you naturally inquire how Harriet and I stand affected by her approach toward us. Mr. Noyes says that we are peculiarly exposed by our situations to the marriage spirit, and /133/ ever since the movement with E. Hawley began, it has seemed as though that principality was stirred up to war. As to myself, I have been tormented more or less with fears that I should act the part of the older brother, especially as I have from time to time had to be washed from a claiming spirit toward him, or tossed to and fro by a spirit which connects happiness with place instead of with a meek and lowly spirit. I do not know how much egotism remains, but I want to have all there is tempted out and destroyed.

Remarks by Noyes about Abigail Merwin
April 9, 1851

Mr. Burnham and Elizabeth Hawley to-day attempted to call on Abigail Merwin, but were refused admittance.

I want to show why my affair with Abigail Merwin is of general interest. The issue between faithfulness and unfaithfulness is being tried out. The spirit of unfaithfulness is coming to judgment in the person of Charles H. Weld; and the faithfulness of Christ toward those who believe on him, in pursuing them unto salvation, and making them faithful in spite of themselves, the world and the Devil, is being manifested in the case of Abigail Merwin.

It is curious that believers, as they get interested in the truth, get also a singular enthusiasm about that case. For instance, Elizabeth Hawley has been there at New Haven for fifteen years without any particular connection with it; but as soon as she is waked up and brought into spiritual motion, she is right away all alive on this subject. I said nothing to her about it, but I found as soon as she came here that she would /134/ talk. . . .

As I have said, this is not an affair pertaining exclusively to me. It is vitally connected with the general interest. I loved her, it is true, but not in a way ever to swerve from the truth. I can now do without her, and have no hankerings for her; but I feel that principle requires me to be like Christ, the same yesterday, today, and forever.

Just about the time that the Battle-Axe letter came out, Abigail pulled up stakes and went back to New Haven. I got back to Smith's. I then communicated with Harrison, and he was as eager to get into the business as Burnham was. He was pressed up by an impulse of the spirit that he could not resist to go and see her. He went in the face of a worse influence than Burnham met, and renewed the note—showed her my letter. She retreated as usual into a non-committal position. Afterward, in my letter to Harriet proposing marriage, there was a paragraph not published, in which I stated my unalterable relation to Abigail.

That was the end of my practical interest in Abigail till May 18, 1849, when I left Oneida for New York. On our way here, I met an old New Haven acquaintance, a passenger, who took pains to introduce conversation about her, and mentioned his occasionally meeting her. I told him that he might tell her, if he pleased, from me, that I still loved her as well as ever, that I could not help loving her, as I remembered that she stood by me in the hardest battle ever fought.

That was all that took place till I was at Niagara last, when I received a letter from Elizabeth Hawley asking for help. /135/ I said to myself, "Now for another game with A. M. I shall enter every door that opens." And I foresaw at that time substantially all the moves that have since been made. Elizabeth Hawley's letter was received about November 15, 1849. I returned to Brooklyn on the 19th, and Miss Hawley arrived there the next day. On January 3, 1850, Miss Hawley called on Abigail and left with her all our books. She has read them, and said that she did not disagree with them, that the faith she received in 1834 sustained her through all her trials. I suppose that this communication has been secret; that there is volcanic matter in her heart that is suppressed by the surrounding pressure of her friends and the world.

There is another view of this whole matter. Amativeness is a mighty passion, and whatever is to be done it will do. If God can apply that passion to the public service, the stronger it is the better. I know that was what he did in my case. He roused up affection between her and me into a mighty force, and then made it work for his kingdom. If he had given her to me, and I had turned aside to the enjoyment and idolatry of her that is usual, no good would have been gained. I am sure that nothing but such circumstances would have given me the momentum necessary to come out with the Social Theory.

What I have said of Abigail Merwin will apply to that whole Free Church.

There are fibres of connection running down through that church. They might get rid of me if I was such a man as they, but as it is they won't. I shall twist them up. I feel in full sympathy with that text of Christ's: "My sheep hear my voice, and I know them, and they follow me, and I give unto them eternal life, and they shall never perish, neither shall any man pluck them out of my hand." It is the beauty of /136/ love to have what at first is an outside feeling refine itself into eternal faithfulness. All the external excitement that works up into that is valuable, and the rest is good for nothing.

Through Abigail Merwin I was admitted into the Free Church, and for a time the truth had free course there. And in reality, through her the door was opened for a victory over the whole city. Her withdrawal was what turned me out of New Haven. It broke the connection between me and the church and the city. As she turned me out, I demand that she reopen the door, and God will insist upon it.

Remarks by Noyes
April 10, 1851

God gave plenty of evidence in 1834, that he had appointed me foreman of his church. Finney was the leading man before, but he had gone out of the country, and his dispensation had worn itself out. His men had become independent of him. Boyle, his right hand man, came out publicly and put himself under me. The truth that I brought out and the experience that followed it bore witness of me. The church had advanced to the border of holiness, and anybody watching the course of events would have said that the crisis demanded some one to lead the way into new truth and new experience. God did send a man, but the churches rejected him. When certain federal offices are to be filled, the President makes his nomination and sends it to the Senate. If the Senate refuses to confirm the nomination, the President may send in another, or he may adhere to his first choice and send back the same. If this situation persists, the office must remain unfilled and the government comes to a deadlock. That has been /137/ precisely the situation in the religious world since 1834. God nominated his man as foreman, and the church rejected him; and New Haven, as knowing most of the facts, took the lead in that rejection. The consequence was a deadlock between God and the church. Revivals, of course, have ceased.

Mary E. Cragin at Wallingford to Harriet A. Noyes at Oneida
May 4, 1851

I have seen and talked with Abigail Merwin. I found in myself an irresistible desire to make an attempt to see her, and feeling an instinct that I should succeed best alone went to the house at eleven o'clock on Saturday morning. As good luck would have it, a lady boarder entered the door just as I ascended the steps. I followed her in, and asked to see Mrs. Platt. She requested me to sit down in the hall, and went and informed her of my request. A young girl came and asked my name. I said that Mrs. Platt was not acquainted with me, and that I would tell her myself who I was, adding that I would not detain her long. Pretty soon the lady appeared, and asked my errand. I requested a few minutes private talk, and followed her into a room. I then told my name, but she had never heard of me. I said my errand was this: "Sixteen years ago you publicly confessed the doctrine of holiness in this city, and it was through your influence that Mr. Noyes gained admission to the Free Church; and it was through your withdrawal that the testimony of salvation from sin has been repressed here. Christ has many people in this city who are captives, and you are holding the door shut which would liberate them." /138/

She refused to believe what I said as to her influence either way, and then assured me that she had not altered her position; that Christ was in her a present savior; that the doctrine of holiness was still preached. I asked her if she now confessed Christ as she did sixteen years ago when she stood up and sung that hymn. She said she did, qualifying it however so as in reality to smooth it down to just such a confession as the orthodox make; that she did the best she could from day to day; she was not perfect in every word and thought, to be sure, but Christ gave her power to overcome. It seemed to me a good deal like the testimony of New York Perfectionism.

I spoke of her deserting Mr. Noyes, as she did, without giving him any chance for explanation, and said that was not proper treatment, whatever she might have thought of him. To this she made no reply, and I invited her in his name and that of Brooklyn to come and visit us and talk the matter over whenever she felt inclined.

She told me plainly that she did not believe we were living in the day of judgment, or that the Kingdom of God had come, and furthermore that she did not believe in the abolition of marriage. I asked if she had read the *First Annual Report*. She confessed that she had not; that a gentleman friend in whom she had great confidence (Mr. Benjamin, I presume) read it, and spoke disapprovingly of it as at war with the Bible. I told her that if she lived at Oneida or Brooklyn, she would soon find out that there was a beginning of the day when the secrets of all hearts were being revealed.

We talked some of Elizabeth (Hawley). She begged to know /139/ if she was a representative of Perfectionists; (She told a lie, you remember, to get in to see her;) and spoke as though she would not admit that she knew Christ, if she should be left to do such a thing. I said silently: "The time may come, Madam, when you will find your need of a Savior to be as great as Elizabeth's." However, I told her of our experience with Elizabeth, and let her know that Mr. Noyes did not recognize her as a representative of us, and that we advised her to confess the truth about herself.

Some one called her. I merely said: "You will find my words true. First, we are living in the day of judgment, and the Kingdom of God is set up in this world; and secondly, you are, so far as your influence goes, keeping Christ as a present Savior from sin out of New Haven and these regions about."

I advised her to read the *First Annual Report* for herself, and not judge of it through others, and saying I hoped I had not offended her, to which she replied that I certainly had not in the least, I bade her good morning.

I have not repeated more than half of what was said on both sides. She is a very fluent speaker, and I can tell you I had to do my best some of the time to keep up with her. The "stick" with her evidently is on the point of marriage. She said that Mr. Noyes was a married man, and that if he had any such love for her as was represented, it was a sin in his heart; that she had had a dear good husband, and did not wish to extend her acquaintance in the direction of gentlemen; that she did not want a husband. I said: "The point is, not to help you to a husband or lover, but to have you do the right thing by Christ and his gospel." /140/

I do not wonder, Harriet, that Mr. Noyes told us we must have more tongue among us to compete in any degree with her. She quite came up to my idea of her for fluency. If Boyle is her counterpart in this gift, I some doubt our being quite ready for them yet.

I walked the streets as one in a dream after seeing her, hardly believing the evidence of my senses; but so it is. Plainly God does not mean that she shall rest in her present situation, but stirs her up from time to time.

Your affectionate sister,
M. E. Cragin

Mary E. Cragin to Harriet A. Noyes
July 16, 1851

Mr. Noyes had a long *think* on Abigail Merwin's case, and came to the conclusion that Benjamin and she had never forsaken *him*, for Boyle stood between him and them and they quarreled with Boyle. They have never forsaken the fear of God and reverence for the Bible, and are in a far better position now than Boyle is. Mr. Noyes said he should pursue her forever. If she died, if she made up her bed in hell, it would make no difference with him. /141/

14

Noyes's Trip to Europe
April 16 to June 4, 1851

In 1851 Noyes, accompanied by Robert Sparrow De Latre, an English disciple who lived in Canada, visited England and Paris. It was the year of the World's Fair in London. The Fair, Noyes said, was to be a Congress of all nations, and it seemed proper that the Kingdom of God should be represented. Still he did not go primarily to see the Fair, but to "look the world in the eye," and see what Christ wanted him to see. He was gone seven weeks to an hour.

The suggestion and development of the plan were thus set forth in a letter, March 14, 1851, by Noyes's brother, George W. Noyes:

["]Some weeks ago when emerging from the long, smoky contest with Weld and Elizabeth Hawley, Mr. Noyes said that if he could get a berth in the same ship with Greeley, he thought he would go to London to the World's Fair. All were pleased with the proposal, but nothing was done until Mr. Miller came from Putney. He entered into the plan with spirit, and the next day at the Tribune Office drew out of Mr. Cleveland in an unsuspicious way the fact that Greeley had engaged a berth on the American steamer "Baltic," sailing on the 16th of April. The "Baltic" happened to be in port, and the following day several of us went over and inspected her. Mr. Noyes selected a berth, which Mr. Miller immediately paid for. We had a fine /142/ opportunity to go all over the ship, and were filled with wonder at the extent and power of her machinery and costliness of her arrangements. As there were two berths in his stateroom, a fact which would make him liable to the company of a blackleg, it occurred to Mr. Noyes to invite De Latre to go with him. This idea grew into such an assured inspiration that Mr. Miller went immediately and secured the other berth. Mr. Noyes then wrote to De Latre stating what he had done, and suggesting that Mr. Ellis furnish the funds necessary for one of them to go with him.

["]Such is the main shaping of the project at present. It affords a natural and favorable opportunity to get into communication with Greeley. They will be shut up together on shipboard for two weeks. The voyage and change of situation will be good for his health of body and mind.

De Latre is an old traveler and an agreeable companion, and will be able to introduce him to the best society. Mrs. De Latre enters into the plan with enthusiasm, and perhaps it will react favorably on her through her English relatives. . . .

["]One object in writing now is to give notice to our English friends and others at the Association, so that if they have any interests of any kind to be looked after in Europe, they may make up their orders. Mr. Mallory and Susan Hamilton, I presume, will be interested in this move as leading possibly to the establishment of a true home in their Fatherland.

["]Their berths were on the lower deck, down two flights of stairs, a little aft the middle. Greeley's is on the deck above. All the convenient berths on that deck were taken before we applied.["] /143/

The voyage was unusually stormy, and Greeley was seasick most of the time. Opening off from Noyes's berth was a small sitting-room, not nearly so pretentious as the upper saloon, but warmed by a fire. Greeley did not know there was such a place till Noyes invited him down. Afterward he came frequently, and said it was the only place on the ship where he was comfortable. It came to be a meeting-place of the intelligentsia, and the scene of many lively debates. Once Greeley upheld Noyes in a discussion with a Swedenborgian on the second coming. In another discussion when Noyes was present, Greeley opposed Communism, but defended it to Ashbel Smith when Noyes was absent. Greeley and Noyes crossed swords on the subject of Americanism, the former declaring that if he ever got through this voyage, he would "give fits" to the desire for foreign travel, and the latter that Christ's place, if He had any, was on the sea where all nations met. One day Greeley said to Noyes: "John, the 'Marriage Colloquy' in your last *Annual Report* is the best thing you ever got up, I wouldn't have Ashbel Smith see it for a hundred dollars.["] In this colloquy "Judge North" first vanquishes "Major South" in a debate on slavery, and is then himself vanquished when "Mr. Freechurch" turns against marriage the identical arguments "Judge North" had used against slavery.

While in London, Noyes attended a session of the House of Commons. Edging up to a person near him in the visitor's gallery, Noyes asked if he knew any of the speakers. His companion said he did, and very kindly and politely gave the name of several members as they arose. Shortly he excused himself, saying he had an appointment to speak on the floor of the House, and requested /144/ another to take his place in giving information. He then left. Upon that the other gentleman asked in an awestruck voice, "Do you know the man to whom you have been talking?"

"No," said Noyes. "Well, my dear sir, that was the earl of Arundel and Surrey, son of the duke of Norfolk."

Noyes visited the Crystal Palace several times, hoping against hope to see the Queen. Many who had paid fifteen shillings for entrance had been disappointed. One day he saw certain reasons for changing the program of the next day, and went early with De Latre to the Palace. They agreed upon a rendezvous, and separated. Noyes rested a few minutes, then arose, and strolled aimlessly from one aisle to another. Observing a small group of persons interested in some object, Noyes quietly joined them. A few rods away, a dozen ladies and gentlemen were inspecting one of the booths. "Could you tell me," he asked the man at his elbow, "who the stout lady might be?" "That, sir, is the Queen of England." "And the gentleman with whom she is walking?" "That is the Prince of Prussia." Off came Noyes's republican hat. In a few moments the royal party turned, walked straight toward the spot where Noyes stood, and the Queen bowing and smiling, swept by so near that Noyes could have touched her with his hand. [G.W.N.] /145/

15

The Wallingford Branch
May 1851

In May 1851 Mr. And Mrs. Cragin accepted an invitation to visit the Allen family at Wallingford. Mrs. Cragin remained a month, during which time she established evening meetings and criticism and commenced studies of several kinds in the Allen family. She became much attached to Eliza Allen (Mr. Allen's sister), and had a good influence on Henry, Harriet, and George. From this the Allen family were practically one with Brooklyn.

For several years previous to this, Mr. And Mrs. Allen had been believers in salvation from sin. They had read Noyes's writings, taken the paper, and were somewhat acquainted with Mr. Cragin and others of the Putney family. On January 31st 1851, they went to Brooklyn for a brief visit, and on February 13th they made an assignment of their property to

Christ, naming J. H. Noyes as their executor. This assignment was published in the Community paper for March 13th.

Eliza Allen's conversion was on this wise: She observed a marked change in her brother and his wife after their return from Brooklyn. One day she overheard Mrs. Allen telling her daughter Harriet that they had never given up houses, lands, children, and all to Christ, but now they felt that "Holiness to the Lord" was written on everything. She pondered these things in her heart, and perceived that Mr. and Mrs. Allen were on a higher plane than the churches. Mr. Allen then advised her to read Noyes's writings attentively. After two days' study she came down to breakfast in the morning, her countenance beaming /146/ with joy, and said: "Live or die, sink or swim, I am for the administration of J. H. Noyes." That morning they ate their meat with gladness and singleness of heart, praising God, and felt that the true Pentecostal spirit was there. They dismissed their hired servants, and had great happiness in working together. About March 20th the Bristols, who were also believers, came to live with them.

Mrs. Cragin wrote on May 4: "This family is a very pleasant one. A docile, sober spirit prevails. I don't know what I am to do here, but feel like waiting on God, knowing that he will "keep me in all my ways, and direct my paths." [G.W.N.] /147/

16

The Hubbard Quarrel
July 26, 1850, to January 12, 1851

Oneida Journal

July 26, 1850.—Last evening a report on Tryphena Seymour was read. She has been in a desponding, unthankful state. Some of our men said that they heard remarks lately made by the Hubbards showing their continued hostility to us. The other day Dexter said to Mr. Newhouse, that in consequence of having wicked neighbors they had to have their hay washed, carrying the idea that the late flood was a judgment on us. Mr. Newhouse told him we considered it a benefit to us—it enriched our land.

September 8, 1850.—Tryphena Seymour had an interview with her father today, in which she denounced and renounced him for his enmity to us and abuse of Mr. Noyes and the Association, and declared her unity with us. Mr. Hubbard was greatly enraged, and gave vent to his wrath in much abusive language.

September 15, 1850.—The Hubbard family came to meeting this afternoon, and manifested a sneering and contemptuous spirit. In the evening, a committee was chosen to go over and remonstrate with them for their insulting behavior. They had been seen to take a knife from the Community garden, and it was suspected that they had robbed the Community melon-patch.

September 16, 1850.—A committee consisting of Isaac and Henry Seymour, Mr. Burt, and Mr. Hamilton called on the Hubbards to-day, carrying a note from Tryphena. The Hubbards were much excited when the note was read, and talked abusively. They confessed /148/ they took the knife, did not deny satisfactorily the melon impeachment, and said they should pick plums or anything else they chose in our garden. When Henry Seymour positively denied some of their accusations, Mr. Hubbard put him outdoors; and when Mr. Hamilton endorsed what Henry said, he was told to leave and was abused shamefully. Old Mr. Seymour and Mr. Burt then rose and left the house.

September 17, 1850.—Burt and Hamilton called on Hon. Timothy Jenkins of the Castle, and related to him the facts about the Hubbards. He received them in a courteous, friendly manner, and entered into a long and free conversation. He told them he had no confidence in Dexter Hubbard; that he regarded him as a man of no principle, and that he had made himself liable to prosecution for his assault on Mr. Hamilton.

September 22, 1850.—Mr. Hamilton returned yesterday from his excursion with Susan and Theodore to Cayuga Bridge, where they met Mr. and Mrs. Noyes the day before at Mr. Noyes's suggestion. They reported that they talked over the state and prospects of the Association, and the plan of introducing to a greater extent the monitorial method of discipline; also that they caught eighty or ninety fishes, which Mr. Hamilton brought home. The fishes were cooked for dinner to-day.

Dexter Hubbard came to our meeting this afternoon, bringing with him a company of eight or ten rowdies, all ready for a quarrel. We hardly knew what course to pursue, for Mr. Hamilton had said to him that he wished him not to come to our meetings until he apologised for his abuse of the Association. But there was little time for deliberation. As soon as the bell rang, Hubbard /149/ and his company went in and sat down, one of the men having a large and long horsewhip. Mr. Hamilton did not go in, but stayed in the Reception Room. Before the exercises commenced, John R. Miller whispered to Hubbard that he wished to speak with him, and asked him to step out. Hubbard readily complied, and was conducted to the Reception Room, where he was kept in conversation by Miller and Hamilton during the entire meeting. He confessed that he had come prepared for a quarrel, but his spirit grew weaker before them, and they felt that they had an entire victory over him. Meantime, the meeting went on with much order and politeness. The rowdies found nothing to quarrel with. After the meeting was dismissed, they lingered under the butternut tree until Hubbard rejoined them. When they got to the road, they halted and talked awhile. They were evidently chagrined and disappointed.

Noyes to Erastus H. Hamilton
   Brooklyn, September 26, 1850

   Considering the necessity of Tryphena's thorough separation from her family, I approved of your bold proceedings. But in any other point of view, I should think it impolite to allow them in any way to draw you into a personal quarrel. Non-resistance, generous kindness, diplomacy, and spiritual enchantments are our weapons. On the low ground of dispute and violence, they have the advantage of you. If you have provoked them enough to expose them and clear Tryphena, your best course is to refuse battle and change your ground. Combativeness must not maneuvre for you or choose your positions and times, but only fight when ordered by /150/ the counseling faculties. My impression is that it was not good policy to forbid Dexter's coming into the house. The issue made was retaliatory and provoking, and one in which you could not succeed without violence, which is what he wants. "If thine enemy hunger, feed him," and if he wants to come into your house, throw your doors wide open. If this course should bring disturbance into your meetings, my way would be to quell it by truth and suavity, or suspend the Sunday meetings. You need not fight nor surrender. You can retreat and choose your ground.

                              Yours truly,
                              John H. Noyes

Oneida Journal

   December 10, 1850.—Mr. Kinsley, on returning from a week's stay at Manlius, reported that Tryphena had come under judgment for insubordination to the church and excessive egotism amounting to a kind of insanity. Yesterday the family had a meeting, and it was unanimous judgment that Tryphena be placed under the special charge of Henry Seymour, and required to submit herself to him as her head and the representative of the church; and that she should also accept the advice of Mrs. Skinner.

John L. Skinner to Noyes
    Oneida, January 12, 1851

A favorable change took place in Tryphena the day but one before I left. She had called for Henry in the afternoon, and had confessed to him her disobedience and the wrong she had done him and others. She acknowledged the justice of the treatment she had received, asking his forgiveness and that of the family. /150a/ Henry had felt impelled the day before to treat her with a good deal of severity, administrating a remedy similar to that which Mr. Cragin applied in another case. She told Henry that soon after he took that step she began to come to her senses in a way that she had not done before. /151/

17

Burning of the Printing-Office and Store
July 5–19, 1851*

Harriet H. Skinner to Noyes
    Oneida, July 5, 1851

Harriet (Noyes) advises me to write my feelings to you, as they do not seem to settle themselves very satisfactorily. The week before George came here at the time you went to England, I was wishing he would come back to the paper. I seemed to have lost my inspiration. I don't know but it was weariness in well doing. From that time, my difficulties have increased. The effect of George's being here has been to divide my mind and make me expect a good deal from him. Then I have become involved one way and another in the affairs of the Association a great deal more than I was. When Mrs. Cragin left here after her last visit, she said: "I don't see, Harriet, as you will have anything to do now but attend to the paper." But I got drawn into this and that. I

---

* The original title's dates read "June 28 to July 21, 1851." [L.F.]

think it may have been from a lust of meddling, or that I was getting narrow and needed to be broken up. At any rate, I have drifted away and don't know where I am or what to aim at. I do not wish to have my feelings govern at all unless they are an indication that God is moving for change. I thought if you knew them, you would either criticise me and strengthen me to go on, or dismiss me from being editress. In either case, I hope to remain truly and sincerely your obedient servant.

Harriet H. /152/

Harriet A. Noyes to Noyes
Oneida, July 5, 1851

Dear John:—
Ever since I have been here, Harriet has been coming up from an old, heavy, discouraged spirit. She says so herself. I have hoped she would work back toward her attraction toward the paper, but considering that you were meditating on a new move in printing, I thought her state might have some weight with you one way or another, and so advised her to write.

Yours with good courage,
Harriet A. Noyes

Burning of the Printing Office and Store
July 5, 1851

The building which was used for our printing-office and store was destroyed by fire on Saturday evening, July 5th. On that evening, the Association were, as usual, in general assembly. It was about 9 o'clock. We had been talking about individual inspiration, and had just passed a resolution that we would every one rely on interior direction for guidance the coming week. The subject was concluded, and conversation rested. A member requested that the 13th chapter of Romans be read. The Bible was just opened when Mr. Baker came to the door and said: "The store is on fire." Upon the first rush forward, someone said, *"Quiet!"* Moderation was restored, and egress from the room was free and still. On getting outside, we saw fire streaming from the roof and garret /153/ windows at the further end of the store. All energies were used in carrying water to the garret so long as there was hope of success. Then the order was given, "All hands clear the building." The type-cases, drawers and counters, barrels of pork, tubs of butter, oil and turpentine, a large hogshead of molasses, and a jug of powder were all carried out. Some attempts were made by G. W. Hamilton and others to get things from the press room, but flames drove them back. The doors, windows and blinds were saved from the lower story. The women were very efficient in clearing the store. When further work was considered dangerous, the order was given: "All hands quit the building!" Quite a crowd had gathered by this time, and attention was turned to removing the goods to a place of safety. Horse and ox team were soon at work. A strong body of our own people were stationed as police. One company was sent quietly to watch at the mill, another to guard the barn, and G.W.N. proposed that all the women return to the house. In a short time, all the things were deposited in the house, barn, and woodshed without noise or excitement. Mr. Miller seemed endowed with special inspiration and presence of mind, and was the ruling spirit of the occasion. He went out as soon as things were safe, and thanked the crowd for their assistance, going around them talking pleasantly. A gang of fellows lingered near the house, and showed some signs of making a disturbance. They asked if they might look around the garden. Mr. Miller replied that it was so dark they could see but little, but if they would come in the daytime, he would take pleasure in showing them all around. They quietly retired. Before midnight we were all, with the exception of a few acting as watch-men, assembled in the parlor listening to a Report from Brooklyn. /154/ Coffee and lunch were passed around, and all retired to rest. The event has afforded us many profitable reflections. We take it as a "conservative fire," and are sure of profiting by this criticism from God.

Home-Talk by Noyes
   July 7, 1851

The Association should take this event as a criticism from God; and it is a criticism which seems to have been arranged for, in order to have it carried home, by the article published in the last paper. (See article, "Conservative Fire.") I expect that the Association will receive it well, and rise from it with increased love, confidence and loyalty to the truth. I have felt that inspiration was lacking in the editorial department, and only this morning had blocked out a plan for change; yet I felt that what we really needed was a breathing-spell, that we might have time to fix our course and start anew. That is now done. We have a reasonable excuse for stopping the publication of the paper. I have no thought but that we shall begin again. Death is the harbinger of victory and resurrection. We can now take a new step unembarrassed by previous operations, and it is very likely this will lead to starting our publishing enterprise at Brooklyn.

It is of course quite a property loss, yet as the goods were saved and the shoe business uninjured, and the great loss fell on the printing-office, it does not really affect our income, but on the contrary stops an expense.

This event will naturally operate as an appeal to our friends and open their hearts and purses. It will give us an opportunity to say what I have contemplated saying for some time, that we are /155/ able to support ourselves and ask no favors in that respect, but the publishing of a free paper must be a national enterprise. We are ready whenever the nation is ready for that enterprise.

The Paper: Home-Talk by Noyes
July 11, 1851

The morning previous to our hearing of the fire, I had made up my mind that the editorial department at least should be established here at Brooklyn and be under my direct personal oversight; and now that the printing-office is burned the better way will be to send the type and apparatus here, and commence printing here. We have plenty of room, and with nearly the same hands that we now have in the gold chain business, we can get out a paper and give variety to our occupation. The spirit of the times is liberal and friendly. To begin with, I think we shall carry out the project George and I have talked about so much, that of publishing a Sunday paper. As things now are, all of the Sunday papers are of the meanest and most profligate kind. Religious people are too righteous to take possession of the Sunday field, and so let the Devil have that day to himself. And it is a day when people want a paper more than ever. Perhaps some do not read a newspaper at any other time. The only daily paper, I think, that is published on Sunday is the Herald. The Tribune only publishes on six days of the week. Probably two-thirds of the Tribune's subscribers read the Herald on Sunday. After persons get accustomed to it, they miss a paper as much as they would their breakfast. If the Tribune thinks we do not want a breakfast on Sunday, we know better and the Herald knows better. /156/

George W. Noyes to George Cragin
Oneida, July 19, 1851

On receipt of your letter last evening announcing the purchase of a press, several of us went down to the Burt house and took an account of printing materials saved. . . . The examination proves satisfying. I think by using the pica, and perhaps without, you can print a larger paper now than we have ever printed, without buying a type. Apparently all that you need to buy is paper and ink. It is literally true that before the ashes of our old office were cold you had bought another press and established an office three hundred miles away.

The invitation to furnish the Brooklyn office came just in season to make an agreeable diversion for the men who have confined themselves so long to the mill, and all hands have gone to work busy as bees building stands, tables for the imposing stones, and other furnishings. They will all be ready to pack off by the middle of the week or sooner. Miller and Leonard are boxing up the type to-day. I see a beautiful providence in what we saved, as well as what we lost. How so much was saved from that building is a mystery to me.

George Cragin to Mr. And Mrs. Mead
　　[No date indicated]

We are quite enthusiastic with your suggestion of building an office in our back yard. We have sent to Oneida for Mr. Hamilton to come down immediately and superintend the building of it. We propose to have it of brick, tin roof, and the side fronting our back parlor of glass windows, so that we can look in upon the operations in the office instead of gazing at a brick wall. /157/

18

Sinking of the Sloop
July 16 to August 29, 1851

Mary E. Cragin to Harriet A. Noyes
Brooklyn, July 16, 1851

Mr. Noyes attacked me last evening in a friendly way on my fear of ghosts, and asked if it extended to the Primitive Church. I said that it seemed so natural to associate with the word ghost a white sheet, clammy touch, and mischievous intent, that it became me to see whether I connected heavenly spirits with such associations. Others spoke of the same disagreeable associations, particularly Mrs. Smith. It was noticed that the disciples were affrighted when they saw Jesus, thinking they saw a spirit. Upon examination, I was not satisfied with my emotions when I brought home to my mind the idea of seeing the forms of the heavenly church. I believed that I could control the outward expression of fear, but still there remained great awe which I knew would make me act awkwardly. Surmising that my will had considerable to do with it, and that it was a great humbug to fear them in any shape, I resolved to cut that spirit in two. Mr. Noyes said that instead of their being spectres and skeletons, they were the most beautiful beings in the universe. I thought of them as real bona fide men and women, warm, glowing, youthful, and although too modest to intrude themselves upon those who were shy of them, yet happy to visit those who were hospitable. While thinking on the subject, Mrs. Smith came in to sleep with me, and I proposed that we address an invitation to the Primitive Church to call on us in /158/ *any way* and at *any time* that they felt inclined, engaging on our part to do all we could to render the visit agreeable. I felt a good deal more at home with them than before, and had beautiful fellowship with Mrs. Smith. I slept well and dreamed of Abigail Merwin, waking with this beautiful passage in my heart: "The peace of God which passeth understanding shall keep your hearts and minds in Christ Jesus," and with a glow of love toward her and toward God. I took it as an answer to my invitation, and said to myself, "What can I want or fear so long as the heavens are open to me."

A Pleasant Reminiscence

The sloop "Rebecca Ford" was ready for her trip, and Mrs. Cragin, in the cheerful, generous spirit of enjoying whatever she did to make others happy, had consented to be one of the company on board. A group of washers were engaged in the basement. Partly for their diversion and partly from a merry inspiration of her own, she invited Mr. Noyes to accompany her with the violin in a song before she left. The effect was magical. The washers will never forget it, they say. She never sang so well. The song was "The Parting of Jeannette and Jeannot." After the tragedy at Esopus, we found the sequel to the song, which we interpret as a pledge that "when the wars are over, we shall welcome back *our* rover." /159/

Jeannette to Jeannot

You are going far away from poor Jeannette.
There is no one left to love me now, and you too may forget.
But my heart will be with you, wherever you may go.
Can you look me in the face and say the same, Jeannot?
When you wear the jacket red and the beautiful cockade,
Oh, I fear you will forget all the promises you made.
With the gun upon your shoulder and the bayonet by your side,

You'll be taking some proud lady and be making her your bride.
Or when glory leads the way, you'll be madly rushing on.
Never thinking if they kill you, that my happiness is gone.
If you win the day, perhaps a general you'll be.
Though I'm proud to think of that, what will become of me?
Oh, if I were Queen of France, or still better Pope of Rome,
I would have no fighting men abroad, no weeping maids at home.
All the world should be at peace, or if kings must show their might,
Why, let them who make the quarrels be the only ones to fight.

The Soldier's Wedding

Give me your hand, my own Jeannette, the wars at length are over;
And welcome are the wedding bells that welcome back the rover.
The Song of Peace is on our hills, and all is cheerful labor,
Where late we heard the din of strife, the war-pipe and the tabor.
Good omens bless this happy day, the sun's bright rays are shedding
Their loving light of Hope and Joy upon the soldier's wedding.
Rich fields of waving corn are seen where hostile flags were streaming,
And where the sword was flashing, now the sickle bright is gleaming.
Lie still, ye brawling hounds of war. Let peace our hearts enlighten.
Rest sword, and rust within your sheath. But let the plow-share brighten.
Good omens bless this happy day! The sun's bright rays are shedding
Their loving light of Hope and Joy upon the soldier's wedding. /160/

Mary E. Cragin to George Cragin
Rebecca Ford's Cabin,
    Friday Evening, July 25, 1851

Dear Mr. Cragin:—
    We arrived here last night about half-past four o'clock, having had a very
pleasant trip. We stopped on the way and visited some ice houses, and Mont-
gomery Lake, the scene of interesting events in Revolutionary times, if I am
rightly informed. We had a pleasant ramble through the woods, and picked
several quarts of berries. I like a sea-faring life very much. It breaks up effemi-
nate notions, and takes the starch out of folks wonderfully, and is, I think, very
conducive to health; certainly it quickens my appetite and digestion. Miss
Allen stands it well. Tonight, after we have finished our day's work, we visited
the cave, and had a fine time. Tell Mr. Noyes that things go well *interiorly* and
exteriorly, and we feel satisfied that the angels are watching over us and are full
of good will to us. We shall have one or two adventures to relate to you which

will prove it. Mr. Long is improving in subordination and meekness, and gives no trouble. I had some emotions of wonder and admiration of God's power and wisdom in bringing us through safely in the days of old, which these scenes revive. Surely after what has passed we can trust him to pilot us through anything, confident that he has machinery sufficient, only give him time.

I shall visit the stone house before I leave, but how altered are its surroundings. Where I used to sit on a green bank and read to the children and nurse Georgy while you hoed corn just behind us, stands a cluster of buildings looking unromantic /161/ and business-like enough. The old house, however, looks natural, the only spot that is untouched.

I bid you good-night with love to the household.

Yours affectionately
Mary E. Cragin

Saturday morning.—Just getting ready to start. /162/

News Item Condensed from the New York Tribune
July 26, 1851

The sloop "Rebecca Ford," owned and manned by the Oneida Community, was capsized and sunk at one o'clock P.M., near Hyde Park, while on her way from Kingston to New York City, loaded with limestone. Six persons, namely, Captain A. C. Smith, Henry W. Burnham, Francis Long, Henry J. Seymour, Mrs. Mary E. Cragin, and Miss Eliza A. Allen, were on board. The women and three of the men (Messrs. Smith, Burnham, and Seymour) were at dinner in the cabin when a violent squall struck the vessel. Perceiving a commotion but not apprehending any serious danger, the men went on deck. . . . The vessel immediately careened so as to shift her load, came on her beam-ends, filled by the hatches and cabin windows, and went down in forty feet of water. The women, who remained in the cabin, were lost. The men, by swimming and by the help of articles from the wreck, kept themselves afloat till they were picked up by Captain Hotaling of the schooner Shaw Abbilena, who went to them in his yawl with noble promptitude, and afterward generously placed his vessel at their service. Two hours before the accident, Mrs. Cragin was reading aloud to a part of the crew the 8th chapter of Romans, and directing attention with much vivacity to the last verses.

The Sinking of the Sloop: Home-Talk
July 27, 1851

Noyes: Well, I suppose all will say, it is right. /163/ I will begin with that, and not only say it, but feel it. There is something very curious to me in the coincidence that this should occur just after her visiting the old battlefield at Rondout, under Mr. Smith's care. It will be something of a trial to the whole body, but in some way or other I know that the Kingdom of God will gain immensely by it. It will teach us that, notwithstanding the truth of the principle that death is overcome, still God has not surrendered his right to strike us in that way. God is evidently bringing about a new situation with a view to far greater manifestations of his power. As the center of interest was transferred from Oneida here by the fire, it seems to me that the center of interest is now to be transferred from here to the Primitive Church. I suffered a good deal last night. I finally got my balance by turning my attention to what we must do to give this event its proper effect. I look for everyone to turn to the question, "Lord, what wilt thou have me to do?"

Mr. Cragin: (Addressing Mr. Noyes) You have done all you promised. You said you would raise her as high above her former position in the world as he had been sunk below it by the affair at Rondout.

Noyes: (To Mr. Cragin) In the flesh, the tendency of Mrs. Cragin's position has been to produce chafing between you and me and Mr. Smith; but now that she has passed into the spiritual world, I can see how her position may be the occasion of a splendid condensation. The women seem to be the heroes and martyrs in this dispensation. /164/

Mr. Cragin: (Weeping) My flesh is suffering and dying out. I will behave as well as I can though the process.

Noyes: I suffer with you. The Primitive Church say to us, "Think it not strange concerning the fiery trial that is to try you." They have been through more than this. I count this and the fire tokens of God's love, He chastens those whom he loves.

Charlotte A. Miller: I was thinking she had a fifteen-hundred-[pound] monument to go down with her.

Noyes: Yes, she had the North River for a grave, the sloop for a coffin, and their short dresses for uniforms; enough for any soldier.

Mrs. Cragin's death will lead me to overcome death, just as Abigail Merwin's marriage stimulated me to break up the marriage system. She being on one side of death and I on the other, death will be cut in two, for we shall certainly come together. Her life is the faith of the Son of God, and that is as free to work in Hades as in the Primitive Church as here. She has only gone through what our women occasionally experience, a giving up of furniture. As soon as she has settled herself, she will go to work in conjunction with us here for the advance of the Kingdom of God. Her elasticity of spirit is remarkable. She always recovers quickly from any disaster or misstep. She is a model woman, and I hope many more will be run in the same mold. She is a prodigal, to whom much is forgiven. The same loveth much. The father too loved the prodigal, and when he returned there was music and dancing. I thank God for the privilege of appreciating /165/ Mrs. Cragin and of seeing God's beauty in her. Although I might say I had a hand in making her over, yet after all it was God's work. She will now have a body suited to her character, and it will be beautiful. She is hidden from the world and all its malice. Her mother and the Putney folks will not persecute her any more. How agreeable it would be if we could be invisible and yet work for God just as effectually. Mrs. Cragin's fear of ghosts will make her a fit person to commence communication from the inner to the outer world. She knows how to sympathize with the fears of many. She is ingenious, and will contrive to appear in some very attractive way.

The first thought that occurred to us was that her death would increase our communication with the spiritual world. It has come at a crisis when everything is tending to draw us upward and inward. There is so much connection between us and her that it is not possible for us to be separated from her or lose sight of her.

Harriet A. Noyes:—I have never felt to acknowledge her position as I have today. I never felt so much fellowship with spirit.

Noyes: We shall not be compelled to argue in a substantial way, free from cant and poetry, that there is no such thing as death. In order to establish our hearts satisfactorily, we must come up to the simple truth that death is not be regarded as a distressing, horrible thing. It is overcome.

All will recollect the time two years ago when I went to the Association and took her away. I had at that time an impression of her death. . . . /166/

The only way for us to get any satisfaction in view of death is to repel all natural feelings about it as fast as possible. Flattery, respect of persons, idolatry, all such thoughts will prevent us from seeing her real value and the meaning of God in this transaction. Be still, be free to receive impressions from God. We may be sure that God appreciates whatever is valuable in her more than we do. The lesson that I learned when I took her away from the Association two years ago, and that she learned, was that the truth must take the lead of all other affections. The criticism of her at that time was a criticism of the fleshly spirit in the Association which came in through Hyde. Now just as I have declared that the Association is free from false love, her death comes as the consummation, and the outpouring of her purified spirit will follow.

Oneida Journal

July 29, 1851.—Henry Burnham and Charlotte Miller arrived from Brooklyn about half-past one this morning very unexpectedly. The reason of their coming was communicated to but few till after breakfast, when notice was given that all the family were requested to meet in the parlor at seven o'clock. After all were seated, Mr. Burnham and Mrs. Miller came in with Mrs. Noyes and a few others. Mr. Burnham began by saying, "Mrs. Cragin has left us!" For an instant it seemed as every heart stood still and no one breathed. He then went on and told us all about the capsizing of the sloop "Rebecca Ford," the drowning of the women, Mrs. Cragin and Eliza Allen, and the saving of the men, Smith, Burnham, Seymour, and Long. Mrs. Miller told us of Mr. Noyes's faith, hope /167/ and love, and of Mrs. Cragin's victories and buoyant spirit. The faith, courage, thankfulness, and elevation of soul and purpose that filled Mr. Burnham and Mrs. Miller were like sunshine to our hearts, driving back the agony that would crush us. G. W. Noyes read the 8th chapter of Romans, and thought all might accept it as Mrs. Cragin's message to us. She had read it with Mr. Burnham just before she was drowned, and at the close had remarked, "What do you want better than that?" All were exhorted to go about our business in a buoyant, cheerful spirit as the one most pleasing to God and to Mrs. Cragin.

Mrs. Miller writes from Oneida to Brooklyn: As we conversed yesterday at Kingston, Mr. Noyes seemed overflowing with faith, hope, and love, and a tenderness of feeling that melted all hearts together. On reaching here the same victory over worldly sorrow, and spiritual insight into God's wonderful providences were realized by the whole Association. We all feel it is true that victory has come in the first three divisions, and that now Mrs. Cragin has pioneered the way for the final victory over death.

Mrs. Harriet A. Noyes writes from Oneida to Brooklyn: It seems to me that we have entered upon the fourth division of the battle of God. It looks as if the battle with death had commenced in earnest. My eyes are turned toward a clearing away of the clouds of death. I know Mr. Noyes will penetrate this subject, and we shall partake of his victory.

John R. Miller writes from Oneida to Brooklyn: The first feeling of my heart on hearing the intelligence was one of agony /168/ like the parting of soul and body, but this was soon followed by a quiet trust and confidence in God, who "doeth all things well." My heart involuntarily said, "What next?" We have had the burning of the store and printing-office, and now the sinking of the sloop with two sisters, and these events have not made us doubt that God protects. What next I know not, but of one thing I am sure, it will be

nothing that can shake our confidence in God. I feel that the whole Association are becoming abandoned to the will of God, and that nothing will ever be
able to separate them from Christ, from Mr. Noyes, and from each other. This
event will only draw our hearts more closely together in bonds of eternal love.

George W. Noyes to the Brooklyn Family
Oneida, July 29, 1851

Dear Friends:—
I wish to put my heart in sympathy with you in respect to this event, and
to say, so far as it has had time to work in my experience, it has been good. I
fully believe it will be a blessed gain to us as well as to her, and that "this light
affliction, which is but for a moment, shall work out a far more exceeding and
eternal weight of glory, while we look not at things that are seen, but at things
that are not seen."
I feel respect particularly for John and Mr. Cragin in this crisis, and desire
to be with them in whatever special burden that [they] may have to bear. May
we not well hope that her sainted spirit will be a bond of new union among
us, and a new channel of attraction toward the immortals? I believe it will.
/169/ I say from my heart, it is God, our God, who has done this. The time had
come with her and with us for this change, and God out of his kindness made
it suddenly, with no shadow falling before, as I believe none will remain after.

I am yours,
G. W. Noyes

Noyes to George Cragin
Rondout, Mansion House
July 30, 1851

Dear Bro. Cragin:—
I have deferred writing to you, that I might have something definite to report. I have been very busy since I left you, and will not give an account of my
proceedings.
On my way up to Kingston, I returned to my original plan of sending Mr.
Burnham to Oneida and stopping at the center of interest myself. Monday
morning Mr. Burnham found Messrs. Smith and Seymour at Rondout and
brought them to Kingston Point. Smith informed me that most of the sloop
was some feet above water at low tide, and that there would be no great
difficulty in raising her; that he had left Long in the neighborhood to keep a

light on the mast at night; and that he had been endeavoring to get the means of raising the vessel at Rondout but had not succeeded. After Burnham and Charlotte left at noon, Smith, Seymour, and I walked to Hyde Park, about twelve miles, and sent for Long. I thought it my first business to hold a sort of inquest and ascertain the causes of the judgment we have suffered. We spent the evening at this. The result was a unanimous judgment /170/ that Long's mismanagement and cowardice were the direct cause, that the perverse spirit in him which has resisted criticism and kindness so long were the previous chronic cause, and that the loose habits of fellowship which have admitted him among us and employed him in responsible business have involved the Association in his culpability, so that this chastisement is deserved and necessary for us all.

The grounds for the judgment were briefly these: Mr. Long had been for months in a gloomy, unbelieving, non-consulting spirit. One main object of Mrs. Cragin's excursion on the sloop was to make a last effort to conquer him by kindness and advice. He was in charge of the helm and the only man on deck when the squall struck the vessel. Mr. Smith, as he ascended the companion-way, saw that Long was holding the helm the wrong way, and ordered him to put it "hard down," which he did. Mr. Smith turned to look at the state of things forward, and when, a moment after, he reverted to Long, the helm was again wrong. Smith sprang to the tiller and held it down as long as there was a standing-place, but it was too late.

I told Long that I intended to set a new example of honesty and faithfulness by confessing publicly the whole truth about the disaster, and I advised him to prepare a confession of his agency in it for the paper, which he said he would do. I then discharged him from our service with the understanding that we shall have nothing more to do with him till he proves by deeds that he is a penitent and faithful man. His unfaithfulness and cowardice were signally proved in his last service after the shipwreck. He was /171/ left, as I said, to keep a light on the mast. But there was none there when we went up Sunday night. We informed the Captain of the position of the wreck, so that our boat escaped it, but no thanks are due to Long that we and a whole boatful were not sunk. Having thus providentially detected his unfaithfulness, I charged him with it, and he confessed that he saw in the night that the light had gone out, but that he *felt so bad and the river was so dreary that he was afraid to go out and relight it!* After the inquest, Smith and I went to the wreck and placed on it a good, sufficient light. At eleven o'clock in a dark night to go out in small boat a half mile to hang a beacon over the bodies of our loved ones was as solemn a thing as I ever did, and yet it was pleasant. We spoke not a word of sorrow, but cheerfully hailed the spirits of the dead and left the scene with reluctance.

The next morning (Tuesday) Smith and I hired a carriage and went to Poughkeepsie, but did not succeed in getting help. We returned, hired a boatman to attend to the light, and left Seymour to oversee the business. We reached Rondout last night about nine o'clock. Smith had another interview with Long this morning, and more effectually expelled him. Long confessed in full the justice of our judgment, and offered to discharge all pecuniary claims, acknowledging that he owed us more than he could pay. We leave him now with God.

We traveled about the docks all the forenoon today in quest of boats, and after many discouragements succeeded in obtaining all we wanted. Tomorrow or next day at farthest, we expect to be at the wreck with men and means sufficient to raise the vessel, /172/ probably in twenty-four hours. Sometime on Saturday or perhaps Sunday, it is likely we shall recover the remains of our friends, and the question of their disposal is therefore now before us. I shall not take upon me to decide it. It belongs rather to you, and perhaps her relatives should be consulted. But I will give my opinion. Exactly opposite the scene of the wreck in the village of Esopus is a beautiful church spire, seen far up and down the river. There is a burying-ground not far off. Mrs. Cragin certainly had three homes, and this spot is nearly in the center between them. Her monument (the church spire) will be seen by all who loved her as often as they pass up and down the river which she has consecrated. It would be very pleasant to my feelings to have the remains of both the departed placed here in one grave. Furthermore, the church that I speak of belongs to the Episcopal order, and it seems to me that it would be a graceful and pleasant compromise of the diversities of sentiment which exist in the circle of friends and relatives concerned, to commit the ceremony of burial to the Episcopal clergyman, and deliver dust to dust under the beautiful burial service of the Church of England. I call it beautiful because it contains so much of Bible testimony about the resurrection. By this plan we shall avoid many disagreeable things which must attend the transportation of the dead in warm weather, and shall place the remains in the most beautiful spot in the shortest time.

If after such consultation as you think necessary you approve of this plan, send me word by telegraph as soon as possible and I will make the arrangements. You can also telegraph to Wallingford and Oneida in season to have friends come /173/ so as to be here by Saturday. It is possible that we shall not raise the vessel so soon as we expect, and it is therefore not best for many to come. But I should like to have you and Mr. Burnham and Harriet A. from Oneida, and Mr. Allen from Wallingford, come on Saturday if possible, bringing a "considerable amount of money."

We are in want of clothes, as the men lost all and are using mine, but we can get along till Saturday unless you think best to send someone with shirts, coats, pantaloons, etc. My overcoat would be agreeable.

Yours affectionately,
J. H. Noyes

Note by Noyes in *The Circular,* old series, 1:6: It is but justice to Mr. Long to say (as we are glad to be able to say) that his conduct since his discharge has been honorable and very favorable to a re-establishment of confidence. When the Rondout editor broke forth upon us, Mr. Long volunteered the defense. His services in cleaning and taking care of the sloop after it was raised were laborious and cheerfully rendered. We trust that we shall yet be able to report that he has profited by this terrible event, as we have, till the sorrows of the death that has befallen us are swallowed up in the victory of the resulting benefits. /174/

Oneida Journal

August 1, 1851.—Mr. Miller writes to Mr. Cragin: I settled my cash account this morning. It stands, cash on hand $57.49. I shall have to pay in a day or two $42.00 for insurance. We have had plenty of money all summer, and I know that we shall continue to have.

August 3, 1851.—Harriet A. Noyes to George W. Noyes: When Mrs. Mead was in Brooklyn, she requested Mr. Cragin to let her know if we got into any strait in money matters, for she still felt anxious that Mr. Mead should give the three hundred dollars. Mr. Cragin promised that he would. John suggests to Mr. Cragin that he fulfill his part of the engagement now, leaving her to do as she chooses.

I spent the day yesterday taking in the scenery of this beautiful place, and sitting down and quietly breathing John's atmosphere. After tea we walked to the burying-ground, a retired spot close by a grove with only a few graves. It is just such a spot as I think Mrs. Cragin would choose. Raising the sloop seems to be a heavy job. I hope before Henry (Seymour) goes we shall have something more definite to report. I am glad he is going. I think he will be a help in the Association, although he is weak in the body now.

In making some general remarks, John said: "We must enlarge our ideas about providences. Don't lean on special providences in the way of being petted. We want God to attend to the general interest and then, if our special interest coincides, very well." /175/

Someone asked who was to fill Mrs. Cragin's place. John replied he did not know as God wanted it filled. She was so filled with the spirit of service, so helpful to the Association, that they *would* lean upon her. It was time they were weaned, and that they should go to God for themselves. God will not allow us to get sticky to persons.

August 4, 1851.—Hial Waters and Henry Seymour arrived from Esopus. Mr. Noyes sent special word by them about the family having godly prudence. He said: "When we can fill our sphere with prudence, God will fill his with good providences." A committee was chosen by his suggestion to look after and make the grindstone safe. The committee were Mr. and Mrs. Burt, Mr. Ackley, Hial Waters, and Mrs. Baker. They went immediately to the mill and had the speed of the grindstone reduced. A good deal of anxiety had been working in the family respecting it. This circumstance gave occasion for criticising the professional spirit in Mr. Morgan.

Henry W. Burnham:—We delivered Mr. Noyes's message. It seemed to have a serious effect upon the whole. Mr. Nash had laid down his pocket-book at some place where he was making purchases, and had carelessly forgotten it. There were sixty cents in it. This with other discrepancies in his dealings with outsiders led me to propose that someone else take his place, and from an instinct nominated myself. Mr. Hamilton and others liked it. The change, it was thought, would help lessen the gossip and notoriety which our present position was exciting, I being more or less a stranger here just now. /176/

Remarks by Noyes
August 8, 1851

God is taking us at our word. Soon after I returned from England, I broached the subject of criticism, and we all, as you know, invited God to criticise us more closely than ever before. Indeed, at the time when I took Mrs. Cragin away from the Association and felt that the sentence of death was upon her, I thought we had gone as far as we could in criticising each other, and that God was beginning to criticise us. You know when criticism was first proposed at Putney, we thought it would work well if there was sufficient unity to keep us from breaking away from one another. The effect proved that we were united, and I think now that we are firmly enough united to have the bond held under serious criticism from him. We may take it as a sign of an advanced stage of experience, that God has commenced criticising us sharply, for the Primitive Church had their sharpest criticisms just before the second coming. This is a woman's dispensation, and I am thinking it possible that Mrs. Cragin's death is in this dispensation what the death of Christ was in the

Jewish dispensation. Her death was more befitting a woman, and Christ's was more befitting a man.

We are marching into public notice under cover of a funeral. It is a curious stratagem of God's to bring about this death and excite sympathy for us just as we are coming before the public. As the world looks on the funeral procession, they little think that they are looking at an army, that underneath are concealed guns and pistols. /177/

August 15, 1851.—Harriet A. Noyes writes: The sloop is not within sight of us now, but lies a mile up the river. It drifted along and stopped just opposite the burying-ground. There is a road leading directly from the wreck to the grave.

George Cragin to Henry Allen at Wallingford
Brooklyn, August 20, 1851

I returned yesterday from the scene of our late labors on the North River. After those men we employed to raise the vessel had labored 19 days, they so far succeeded as to enable us to recover the bodies of our loved ones. We found them in the cabin on Tuesday the 19th about 10 o'clock in the morning. We had provided a box, well made and varnished, large enough to contain them both, and we had excellent luck in going through all the duties that devolved upon us in disposing of their remains. Mr. Johnson, the man we boarded with, gave us a place for them in his private plot in the Episcopal burying-ground. Mr. Noyes officiated as our clergyman, using for our meetinghouse a beautiful shady grove on the bank of the Hudson nearly opposite where the wreck lay when you were there. We had an exceedingly profitable time while being detained.

The expense, of course, has been very great, probably not less than $800. We should have abandoned the vessel long ago, could we have received the bodies. I state these facts for your benefit in case the heirs to her property feel disposed to contribute out of her own funds to defray part of the expense.

Noyes to George Cragin
Rondout, August 29, 1851

Smith and I came to Rondout the day you left, Wednesday. /178/ The sloop arrived at Bishop's yard Saturday morning. Discharged the vessels at noon. Hamilton took our stone on his vessel. Long took upon him the cleaning of the sloop, which was loaded with mud. Most of the things in the cabin were ruined, but we found Mrs. Cragin's note book in good condition, have dried, it, and count it worth more than all the rest. It was to me a beautiful love-letter coming up out of that dismal ruin and finding me in the midst of warring spirits and the cruelties of the world of business. The vessel was badly damaged by mismanagement in raising. It will require some $300 to repair her, besides the cost of a new mainsail. We determined, if we could not get that, to repair her. So the matter stands. She is on the stocks at the yard of Tremper & Scott in the course of repair.

Now for the expense and a view of our finances: Hathaway's bill is $220, Hamilton's is $133, Bishop's is $692, making about $1050. We have paid $50 to Hamilton, and about $100 to Bishop, leaving about $900 to be provided for. Smith is making an effort to get funds from Abijah (his brother) who is now here, but success is doubtful. Hamilton will wait on us. Hathaway wants his money, but is not urgent. Bishop presses for immediate payment, and refuses to turn in his debt of $300.

You see the whole now. Don't stare at it much, but see what you can do for us. If you can't do anything, don't fret. /179/

Remarks by Noyes in The Circular, 1:11–15

For the sake of concluding the financial part of our story here, I will say that we finally sold the sloop for about twelve hundred dollars to Mr. Hotaling, the man who witnessed the shipwreck and rescued the survivors. Our total loss was between six and seven hundred dollars, besides the value of the sloop. We settled all, and escaped from Rondout about the first of October.

In looking over this paper on the eve of its going to press, I perceive a providential combination of matter for joyful exultation and matter for sorrowful humility. Vitality, hope, success are pictured on the main breadth of the canvass; but here almost at the center is a terrible death scene. We are rising triumphant, but where is our sweetest and brightest fellow-laborer? We are rebuked in the midst of victory. A voice of warning thrills through our spirits: *"Serve the Lord with fear, rejoice with trembling; he will not give glory to another, nor his praise to graven images."*

To exult in success, as though *we* had achieved it, is to *embezzle* the property of the government we serve. Embezzlement is the most common and the worst vice in all human administrations, but it will not be tolerated in the Kingdom of God.

The King of Kings takes no counsel from fear of the party opposed to him, nor of his own party and his own officers. They will not escape criticism under the shelter of favoritism or policy. On the contrary, "judgment *begins* at the house of God." /180/ We have accepted this condition of service. We have invited the chastisements which we feel. Let us, then, in the midst of temptations to exultation, remember the integrity of God, and beware of embezzlement. We shall escape the rod only by ceasing to need it, and we shall invite prosperity only by being able to bear it without glorying. "All the haughtiness of men shall be brought low, and the Lots alone shall be exalted."

I expressed these sentiments to the company engaged with me in the work of this paper, and they wish to join with me in inviting the spirit of sobriety and humility to preside over our thanksgivings. J.H.N. /181/

19

Mrs. Cragin's Position in the Church
September 4, 1851

Home-Talk by Noyes
September 4, 1851

I shall make a confession tonight on a subject that I lately reflected much upon. It is a matter of importance to the whole church, as well as to me, that we should as fast as possible find our permanent places in the temple of God.

There has been a general concession of my position in the church. It is well understood that God has raised me up to take the lead. But the point which has hung in suspense even in my own mind has been, who is the female correspondent. That question has been seemingly answered by facts as they have arisen in regard to Mrs. Cragin. She has grown into a position where it does not require any choice on the part of the church or any designation on my part to secure for her the unanimous suffrage of the church as the female head. I can truly say that it was no plan of mine that has made her what she had been in the church. On the contrary, God has directed my attention to another woman, Abigail Merwin, in such a way that I thought of her as destined for that position. His purpose was to cut off personal ambition and glory, that the plan might be entirely by the will of God. My mind is now free to look deeply into the matter, and I frankly say that God has put Mrs. Cragin in that position by his own choice. I now see that she is better qualified for that position than any other woman in the universe. And this does not alter my /182/ substantial faith and expectation in regard to Abigail Merwin. All that I can now see distinctly is that God has put Mrs. Cragin in that place. What he will do with others, I leave to be worked out by events hereafter.

I will now present some facts which go to show that I have been in a certain sense mistaken, and that God's choice has been purposely veiled from me.

You all know that I am pretty correct in any serious spiritual impressions that I receive, that there is reliability and prophetic certainty in them. But there have been two instances, in which I have had as serious convictions as I ever had, when I have been apparently mistaken, and yet I have not been. God has been to me "as a deceiver, and yet true." When I was at Ithaca, knowing nothing of Abigail Merwin's circumstances, I had what I supposed to be revelations from God as sure as any I ever had in my life, that she was in New York City ready for me. I sent on to inquire into it, and found nothing; and what to make of it I could not tell. Well, Mrs. Cragin was in New York City at that time. Again, when I was at Kingston I had another revelation of the same kind and certainty, that Abigail Merwin was coming to Kingston, that Smith was to bring her there. So you see that the substance of the thing did take place in both instances, but my mind was on the wrong person.

Look at the history and character of Mrs. Cragin. It is central and national beyond that of any other woman we have had /183/ among us. She was a child of the cities, educated here in the metropolis, born spiritually in the focus of the church. She was Finney's first and favorite convert in his great revival in New York. Her character corresponds to that central position. No woman is so motherly as she. I can clearly see that the church now being formed is coming out of material that is stored away in Hades and this world. God's mind is on the invisible as well as the visible material. The church has already been divided into the dualities, Jewish and Gentile, angelic and human. The duality that is now being formed is mortality and Hades, and it is appropriate that Mrs. Cragin, as the female member of the dual head of the church, should have special responsibility for Hades, the female branch of the present organization. Therefore Mrs. Cragin, instead of being thrown out of her position as mother of the church, is now put into it.

Abigail is the Old Testament name; Mary is the New Testament one. The female heads of the Primitive Church were all Marys, Mary the mother of Jesus, Mary Magdalene, and Mary whom Jesus loved. Abigail was the wife of David. Well, such coincidences do not amount to much, but after all there is some poetry in them.

I think I now see clearly enough to require me to confess it, that the thoughts I have had about Abigail Merwin have been and are being fulfilled in Mrs. Cragin. This does not conflict with God's purpose to set Abigail Merwin in the church. I believe he intends to do so. Apparently there is room for her, but in a different sphere from that occupied by Mrs. Cragin. The substantial marriage of the man and woman that is first in order and that /184/ is the seed of all the others, is by the election of God, not by the will of man, and is now consummated. The cornerstone has been laid, and will never be altered. I do not see how it is possible for any other woman to do the deed of self-sacrifice that she has done, and if God rewards every one according to his works she has a greater reward, it seems to me, than any other woman in the church. I refer to her last great deed of visiting Abigail Merwin. Just think of her going to Abigail Merwin with the understanding that she was seeking to save the woman who was to displace her! She went in the face of all the usages and almost decencies of society, thrust herself into that woman's house, and laid hold of her, believing it was the will of God. The fruit of that deed remains to be seen, but I am sure that she did what was required. She is now put into her own proper place at the head of the female branch of the church. At the same time, she is knit into the affections of this part of the church. She is in a position of advantage toward each that she could not be in if she had not put off her mortality.

Although she had a lingering desire for the position she now occupies, if she was qualified for it, yet she was not selfish. I know well from plenty of experience what that feeling is, a consciousness of power to fill a certain place, and yet a feeling that I am not called to it. She verily wished herself accursed for Abigail Merwin's sake, and I have no doubt but that in this transfer, after she has had time to think of it, she will have the impression that God has taken her out of the way of Abigail Merwin, and she will be glad of it. But she will find that God is not unrighteous to forget her labor of love and patience. She will have the desire of her heart in full. . . . /185/

Charles H. Weld, who has all the sagacity of the Devil and watches everything on the Devil's side as I do on God's, knows that the relation between me and Abigail Merwin hangs in suspense. He knows too that it is in the true organization of the man and woman that the Kingdom of Heaven commences, and he has had a secret exultation all this time, supposing that as long as the division between me and Abigail Merwin exists the Kingdom of Heaven cannot come. But the substantial thing has been done. The man and woman have come together, and the Kingdom of Heaven has commenced. He has all the while been looking in the wrong direction; and so have I, but not in a wilful way that could not accept facts as they came along. I suppose my own delusion in regard to the person was necessary to perfect Mrs. Cragin in obedience and self-sacrifice, and throw the Devil off the track.

Harriet A. Noyes:—It is a beautiful idea that the mother obtained the love of all the children before they knew who she was. I have had it shown to me clearly two or three times, I thought from God, that she was anointed of him.

Noyes:—I suppose that she is more directly the connecting-link on the female side with the Primitive Church than any other woman; that there is no other woman who will ever teach her, but that all other women this side of the Primitive Church will sit at her feet. She has suffered more than any other woman can in the nature of things, and in a way that works righteousness and brings out truth. That Kingston affair, in the low view, seems very bad, but in the true view it was suffering in which she laid down her life for the brethren. Smith, the apex of the Methodist Church and as such the head of a great branch that is to be redeemed, had become connected with me but was entangled in a net of /186/ Satan's influence. The corrupt part of the Methodist Church had set that woman, his wife Mary Ann, upon him, and she was the most perfect embodiment of the serpent spirit in the world. She had sunk him, as you may say, into the depths of perdition. I was faithful to my first love for him, and sent him word several times. Finally I went to see him and spent the winter with him. After getting a clear view of his trouble, I entered into an everlasting covenant with him and then left him, Two years later the Cragins went to live with him, and Mrs. Cragin, at tremendous sacrifice of honesty and morality, broke Mary Ann's charm. She was sacrificed to save him, and she has done it. That was one of the meanings of her death; it broke up the principality that had possession of him.

This whole affair tends to cut down human imaginations and exalt the sovereignty of God in the formation of the church. You will all find by looking at the deepest working of your heart, that you have no desire for any place that you are not fitted for. You will have a true instinct and desire that corresponds to your capabilities and to the place that is foreordained for you in the church of Christ.

There was this difference between Abigail Merwin and Mrs. Cragin. Abigail Merwin drew out my heart but did not respond to it. Mrs. Cragin drew it out with equal if not greater power, and responded to it not only with love but union. With her first of all, I have had the experience of love in all its beauty and harmony. That is the fact that will stand forever.

I do not wish to have it understood from what I have said /187/ that there is any substantial alteration of God's views in regard to Abigail Merwin. I believe that he is yet going to bring about a tremendous revolution by her. But it appears to me now that her position is a secondary one. The circumstances that have taken place are calculated to throw open the door of expectation in regard to her, but my mind has not been turned in that direction at all. My whole attention has been turned toward Mrs. Cragin. I feel that God has greatly enlarged my perceptions in regard to his purposes, and led me into a new world. /188/

20

Spiritualism, True and False
August 6 to December 4, 1851

Harriet A. Noyes to Harriet H. Skinner
August 6, 1851

John says he certainly expects to see Mrs. Cragin and hear a report from her, but he is willing to wait any length of time for it. When I told him I had been just seven weeks at Oneida, he said that was just the time he was absent when he went to England, and perhaps Mrs. Cragin had taken her seven weeks' tour. At any rate he should not be out of patience if he did not see her till after that time.

Charles Lovett to George Cragin
Westmoreland, Aug. 16th, 1851
Oneida County, N. Y.

Mary Cragin wants you should write to George Cragin and tel him John H. Noyes is not right in his views in regard to womin, and I want he should testify against it. I am in the Third Sphere.

Mary Cragin

To George Cragin of the Oneida Community

Charles Lovett
Medium for Written
Communication from the
Spheres /189/

George W. Noyes to John R. Miller
Genoa, August 29, 1851

I found myself boiling inwardly from the time "Brother Lovett" came in, and I soon put a stop to his inquiries by informing him that his letter to us about Mrs. Cragin caused us some amusement. This led to a pretty satisfactory explosion on my part. I had a good and quite unexpected opportunity to put back on him the infamous counterfeit that he is circulating under Mrs. Cragin's name . . . I told him it was a lie. I think it was an inspiration of Mrs. Cragin's spirit that stirred me up. I refused to eat with him when we were called to dinner, but as he had been to dinner, I did not have to wait. The incident will at least give Mrs. Hale a wholesome specimen of our sincere way of treating such cases, a thing which the Genoa people need to learn.

Hades and the Three Worlds: Home-Talk by Noyes
September 1, 1851

The resurrection state—the state of Christ, the apostles, and the 144,000—is to us the ascending fellowship. But Hades is the descending fellowship. Hades is to this world as woman is to man. Its only advantage over us is the advantage of weakness. This view defines our position in regard to the "rappings."* Instead of our being instructed by Hades through the rappings or in any other way, we are going to instruct them. In the order of the resurrection, the first step will be the coming up of the world and of the /190/ dead into conjunction with us; then these two worlds will move along together into the resurrection sphere.

The insinuation of Marquand and Lovett that Mrs. Cragin has changed her opinion is a lie. But if it was true, I would not change my position. Much as I respect her, I respect the truth more. Do not imagine that the dead are coming here to teach us and take the lead of us. Mrs. Cragin has gone there not to be taught but to teach. In accordance with this view, my impression is that at some early date we shall have personal communication with her, as the apostles did with Christ. As soon as she had time to turn herself, she will begin to lead Hades up into communication with us. We are now where we can have precisely the same thoughts as the Primitive Church had about the second coming. I do not know as there will be the same formalities, but the substance will be the same.

---

* These were purported messages from the dead that began with the highly publicized "rappings" of the Fox sisters near Rochester in 1848. [L.F.]

I feel modest in talking about things that are too deep for me, but I must try to understand the works and purposes of God. One thing is certain—he intends to unite me and Mrs. Cragin by all possible ties of affection. I declared at Esopus that I loved her more than any other being on earth, and I know I loved her by inspiration. For the last five weeks, God has been continually turning my attention to her, surprising me with circumstances to arouse all my attractions toward her. I see plainly that his object in this is not private and personal; it is to bring on communication between this world and Hades. A touching-point of attraction will be established, and death itself will be overcome. /191/

John R. Miller to George Cragin
Oneida, September 1, 1851

I should judge that the whole world is stirred up with the "rappings." Mr. Carr called on Mrs. Giles, whose daughter is a "medium." She had a good deal to say about our Association. Among other things, she said that Paul had the special care of Mr. Noyes till within a few years, when he left him to attend to the "rappings" at Auburn, and Stephen had taken his place. She condemned our social theory, and thought Mr. Noyes less spiritual than formerly. This we thought quite enough to prove the spirit a lying one, and we wanted no further testimony.

Home-Talk about Mrs. Cragin
September 7, 1851

I have to confess, in order to be sincere, a weakness that hangs about me in respect to Mrs. Cragin. I have no difficulty in being reconciled as to my own personal interest, and can thank God and rejoice. But there is a sadness in my heart, a feeling that I want to know definitely and exactly what has become of her. I have no doubt or fear about her salvation, but I want to know what her present state is and what she has been through. I cannot help having the same care for her that I did when she was here, and I want to understand God's dealings with her.

This whole question of life in death is to a great extent blind. We cannot trust at all to the theories that are afloat about it, but must look it all over in order to get a satisfactory view. /192/

I see plainly that there is an intermediate state. The idea that she has passed directly to the resurrection, the final state of the blessed is not authorized by Scripture. That intermediate state, the one into which she passes previous to the resurrection, I am now studying with great interest.

I suppose that from the time of Christ's resurrection to his second coming, the relation between him and the church on earth was such that as fast as believers died they joined him. There was a resurrection body forming all the while. Paul says: "I am in a strait betwixt two, having a desire to depart and be with Christ, which is far better; nevertheless, to abide in the flesh is more needful for you." Stephen, I should say, did pass right into open connection with Christ. "The heavens were opened, and he saw the Son of man standing at the right hand of God." But what took place previous to Christ's resurrection and after his second coming? It is evident that there was no such process going on previous to the resurrection of Christ. The Old Testament saints did not pass into immediate connection with Christ. Paul says: "These all, having obtained a good report through faith, received not the promise, God having provided some better thing for us, that they without us should not be made perfect." This shows that the beginning of the resurrection was at Christ's resurrection, and that there was a very different state of things before Christ's resurrection and also after the resurrection was completed at the second coming. In the new dispensation which commenced at the second coming, the experience of believers was much like that of the Old Testament saints. A second resurrection is now commencing. It seems to me that those who have died since the second coming have been stored away in God's mansions waiting for the second resurrection. /193/

If I follow reason and the Scriptures, I shall expect that Mrs. Cragin will appear to us soon. That will be the first step of her resurrection. The second step will be to rise to the mansion of Christ. Unless she is in the resurrection, she should be called asleep. That is the Bible term for the dead. I think her resurrection will take place in the same order as Christ's. She will first appear to us in her spiritual body. If I cannot take this view, I must consent to the view that she is asleep, and that is what my heart is not contented with. I have no doubt but that she has had the protection of angels and of the Primitive Church, and yet there is a desire in my heart to know precisely where she is.

We may say that God cannot take away in the fullest sense all sadness from us while it is possible for us to be separated from those we love. I am confident that we are going to be surprised with something that will be far better than anything we could have planned ourselves. Her motto was: "Expect things to turn out better than you expect."

The Lord is doing new things and strange things. We must not look back and think of the things of old. On the other hand, we must not give up our minds to false imaginations. We must wait and let God work out his will.

There is a desire in my heart that can be satisfied only by hearing from her. It is not possible for me to be separated from her in spirit. I know that the text she read just before her departure is true between her and me: "Neither death, nor life, nor angels, nor principalities, nor powers, nor things /194/ present, nor things to come, nor height, nor depth, nor any other creature shall be able to separate us from the love of God which is in Christ Jesus our Lord." That love is stronger than any other power in the universe. It will reach her in the uttermost depths of hell, or in the uttermost parts of heaven. It is in that confidence that I have peace.

At the funeral, I confessed before heaven and earth that there was no other woman whom I loved as I did her. Yet I screwed on the lid to her coffin without a pang. I could not have done that if I had believed in any separation.

The prayer of Christ that his disciples might all be one has been the prayer of my heart for sixteen years, and I have had an assurance that it would come to pass.

The true Community spirit is not limited to the circle here or at Oneida. We are an Association in which the Father and Son, the holy angels, the Primitive Church, the church on earth, and all that have fallen asleep are gathered into one house with one interest, one life, one faith.

Noyes's Vision
September 21, 1851

We are in a position exactly adapted to the working of a spirit of fanatical faith, and I am glad of an opportunity to rebuke it in my own experience. I said this afternoon that I had seen Mrs. Cragin in a dream. I now say that I have not seen her. Since I made the assertion that I had seen her, I have analyzed the whole affair thoroughly, and have come to the conclusion that it was a humbug. While asleep this afternoon, I saw the external form and appearance of Mrs. Cragin as really as I ever did /195/ in my life. But I did not see her any more than I see her in her daguerreotype. I dreamed that I saw a covered bridge or archway. I was looking into it at two persons coming toward me from within. They at first appeared obscure, but as they approached, I saw them distinctly. On my left hand was Mrs. Tuttle dressed in mourning, and on my right hand was Mrs. Cragin dressed as usual, looking precisely as she used to. She seemed to be raised up a little from where I was. I looked up toward her, ready to weep for joy at seeing her, but she returned my gaze with an indifferent stony stare. I do not recollect what I said, but my heart spoke. She said: "I am glad that you are going with me." I determined to have no mysticism, so I said: "What do you mean? Do you mean that I am going to die?" She did not answer, but shook her head. I then said I was ready to die, if it was the will of God, but my impression had been and still was that I should not die. Then I awoke.

The being that I saw was a totally different being from the Mrs. Cragin we loved. There was nothing but her form. Her heart, I am sure, would meet me with an altogether different aspect. That stony stare was not an index of her heart. Then the intent of what she said was to give me the idea that I was going to die. But there was mysticism about it, and a selfish wish on her part to have my company. Mrs. Cragin herself would never say any such thing. She would say she was glad I was not going there. Also, the company in which she came plainly shows it was not a true vision. She could not possibly have come with Mrs. Tuttle.

The inference is, that it was either like any mystical dream, or it was a phantasm which the spirits of Hades and the Devil /196/ have power to present. They may have her daguerreotype, or an evil spirit may have her form. We are in a somewhat similar condition to that of believers just previous to the second coming. Christ forewarned them that many should come in his name. The demand for Christ created a false supply. I now recommend to all who are looking into the spiritual world that they feel at liberty to analyze and criticize whatever presents itself. If any of our people see Charles Lovett and Marquand again, I wish they would tell them that I have seen the same character that sent that message, and under circumstances such that I could detect the imposition. The simple truth is worth more than all visions and revelations. We must not despise such things, but we must examine everything thoroughly and rebuke whatever is counterfeit.

Those who are swallowing the "rapping" oracles are being monstrously deluded. The mediums no doubt receive a great deal of truth, but it is mixed with a great amount of falsehood. We are at the gate of that same world, and now is the time for us to walk soberly and stick to the truth through thick and thin. Spirits that do not come with the truth on the second coming are sure to be lying spirits.

The great cheat in Hades is the preference it gives to knowledge over love. When the balance is finally struck, it will be in favor of love. That is why I am satisfied with Mrs. Cragin. False spirits may tempt her with knowledge as much as they please. She will say, "Let me know less and love more." I shall wait till I see her in her true character. /197/

Discussion of Claims to Communication with Mrs. Cragin
September 25, 1851

(Speaking of Abram Smith's and Elizabeth Hawley's alleged communications with Mrs. Cragin, Noyes said): The circumstance that compels me to distrust them and feel that there is no *prime facie* evidence in their favor is this: Elizabeth Hawley in her last letter professes to report the exact words of a conversation she had with Mrs. Cragin. She was on the most cozy terms with her—was having a private tea-party with her. In the same letter she professes to have power and wisdom given her to cure the dysentery. This is the direct reverse of the truth. Instead of her having power to cure Sophronia [Tuttle] or anyone else, she was actually the cause of her death. She came here on a special mission from the Devil. She was sick with the dysentery, and our folks had trouble to send her back, but they had enough to do with her for Mr. Burnham to catch her disorder and bring it into the family. It resulted in Sophronia's death. Now she thinks Sophronia would not have died if she had been here, and says God directed her to tell me to send for her if any of our folks were seriously sick, for she could cure them. After such a detection of the spirit that is abusing her, I say there is no presumption in favor of her pretensions to intercourse with Mrs. Cragin.

Another circumstance which lessens my estimation of these alleged revelations is that when E. Hawley was here under terrible judgment for harboring and cultivating the spirit of C. H. Weld and T. R. Gates, this very spirit of foolish spiritualism, attention to dreams, signs, and phantasms, Smith was also under /198/ criticism, and in curious sympathy with Elizabeth Hawley, so that when I struck at her he felt the blow. The fact is, Smith has been in the same spiritual puddle with her. He has had a great deal to do with Weld and Gates, and so has she. Both are irrepressible, open to such spirits, and evidently both are full of dreamy, fanatical speculations. The particular thing to be noted is that these same persons that were under such judgment last winter and were in communications with each other about it are both in the same tete-a-tete relations with Mrs. Cragin. This looks suspicious to me.

I would say here that I am not cutting them off, and I am not going to say anything that need cause any serious condemnation. But I want to persuade them to deal honestly with such things. They have been humbugged long enough, and it is for their interest as much as mine, that imposition should be exposed. This has been the curse of Smith's life. He has been imposed upon by men in this world and spirits in the other world; and I expect that this criticism, instead of leading them into condemnation, will deliver them from the spirit that is opposed to justification and peace.

My impression has been that Mrs. Cragin, instead of immediately playing the angel and going visiting, has enough to do in attending to her own affairs. She has been through a tremendous experience, and I think that she received it at first as a judgment from God, and that she has been rising ever since. Her experience has probably been similar to what it was in this world, where she rose from the lowest depths of condemnation to the highest glory. It took us some little time to understand the event, and I believe she has been through what has stretched her /199/ faith. I am persuaded that the union which existed between me and her was such that death itself could not alter it. I have felt the same care for her since she left as I did before, and I can judge very well from my own feelings how she is getting along.

Taking all these circumstances into consideration, we may ask to whom would she first manifest herself? Where would her attractions lead her, and where would God be pleased to send her. I am convinced that if she were allowed to go anywhere and there was not some special almighty force preventing her, she would first come to me; and it is the furthest from probability that she would go first to Elizabeth Hawley.

I have from the beginning looked for her. I am not ashamed of the truth, and the truth compels me to look for the second resurrection as at hand; and the truth concerning the second resurrection compels me to expect that the first step of her resurrection will be her reappearance in this world. At the same time that I have been looking for her reappearance here, I have been looking for communication with the Primitive Church. If the three worlds are coming together, and we are in the middle between the Primitive Church and Hades, we may look for open communication in both directions. But I have been very quiet and modest. I have felt that I was bound by all good sense to wait patiently. "Though the vision tarry long," says the prophet, "it will come, and shall not tarry." I can wait, and am pleased to be in this position of suspense with my heart vigilant toward the spiritual world. The believers before the second coming were in an attitude of watching and patience, and God arranged circumstances on purpose to keep them in that attitude. I have felt that Mrs. Cragin's departure has turned my attention to the spiritual world in /200/ a very profitable way.

This being the situation, I do not believe that she has introduced herself first to Lovett and Marquand; neither do I believe she is much in love with Elizabeth Hawley or Mr. Smith. If she is having intercourse with them, it must be because they are seeking it and are open to intercourse that is illegitimate. The whole world of spiritualists are now rushing into intercourse with Hades; and so far as such intercourse takes place without invitation from God and without a primary marriage with him, it is like the rushing together of Perfectionists in old times; it is fornication, a snare of the Devil. I have not the smallest desire for intercourse with Mrs. Cragin or anybody else in the spirit world, except as God is pleased to sanction it.

But my judgment is that they have had no intercourse with her, and there are signs by which we may detect the counterfeit as I did in my own case. I know Mrs. Cragin's spirit, and the thing which proves Elizabeth Hawley's message not a true one is its mysticism. It is unintelligible. Then there is nothing in what she is reported to have said that is really profitable or entertaining, though I can see that there is that in Elizabeth Hawley and Mr. Smith that such stuff would please. It is very evident to me that they have been imposed upon, and I shall hold on to that conclusion until I see manifestations to the contrary.

Now I will turn to recent occurrences among us which strike me in a very different way from these revelations of Elizabeth Hawley and Mr. Smith. You will all recollect my sending a message to Mrs. Cragin by Sophronia. One night when there was every prospect of her dying, I went to her room and told her that, if /201/ she went into Hades, I wanted she should carry a message to Mrs. Cragin. I asked her to carry our love and tell her we were waiting for her. She did not start on her journey then, but remained a few days longer. Meanwhile, Mrs. Noyes reported to her our conversations and everything that was going on up to the time of her death, so that she went to Mrs. Cragin fully charged with our spirit. Several days ago in examining spirits, I discerned distinctly something peculiar in Louisa's manner of communicating with the world of the dead, and referring to the philosophy of the rappers that certain persons were peculiarly adapted to be mediums, I said to the household that I believed Louisa was the best medium we had among us. I could not give any reason for it, but I knew it was so; and I recommended to Harriet to make some change in the household so as to put Louisa more in communication with the family and with me, which was all appropriately done in anticipation of Harriet's going away. The second night after she had been, as it were, appointed, she had an impressive, realizing dream. She dreamed that she saw Sophronia, but was afraid of her and could not speak. The dream awoke her. She soon went to sleep again, and Sophronia came to her a second time; not Mrs. Cragin but the messenger we sent. When Sophronia came the second time, Louisa had recovered from her fright and was glad to see her. Then a conversation took place between them which bears no marks of mysticism. Louisa asked questions in the same manner that she would have done if she had been awake, and Sophronia answered just as we should suppose she would. Louisa asked her if she had seen Mrs. Cragin.

S: Yes

L: What have you and she been about? /202/

S: We have not been able to accomplish much yet. Mrs. Cragin has written several articles and sent them in to the authorities. But there are laws and institutions here which prevent our having much communication with the people. Mrs. Cragin and I keep together and have very good times.

L: Is that world like this?

S: It is somewhat like it.

L: Do you know what is going on here?

The answer was rather indistinct, but Louisa received the impression that they did not know much about it, and were glad to hear from us.

Those are just the answers I should expect to get. The inhabitants of that world probably know as much about us as we do about them, and no more. I have no doubt but the conversation Louisa reports actually took place. All the circumstances favor this conclusion. Here are two sisters that are in particular affinity with each other, one on one side of the vail and the other on the opposite side; and God is through them sending messages both ways. The whole transaction looks rational.

The real object of this criticism is not to shut off communication with Mrs. Cragin but to open the way for it. So long as we entertain spirits that deal in mere phantasms, so long we are precluded from getting at the reality. We must be honest enough to refuse to accept dreams as realities unless there is positive evidence in their favor.

Mr. Smith has thrown out the idea several times that Mrs. Cragin is going to help us discover Capt. Kidd's treasure. That is just the imagination I would imagine an evil angel would communicate, and it is another evidence that the spirit he has been dealing with has imposed upon him. Mrs. Cragin is the last person that would communicate any such thing. /203/

Preparing for a Personal Meeting with Christ and the Primitive Church: Home-Talk by Noyes
October 13, 1851

If I should express the greatest desire of my heart, it is that Christ may dwell with us intimately, and if possible personally. I should be very glad to see the whole family of the interior kingdom. I desire that there should be nothing in my heart or in this house that would hinder them from presenting themselves to us. I do not wish for anything before the time, nor contrary to the will of God; but if the time has come (and it seems to me that it has) when the spiritual world is breaking in upon us, I invite the Primitive Church to visit us. I don't believe, when they do visit us, they will come in the rappings or any other mystical way. The inhabitants of that Kingdom are like little children, full of simplicity and freedom, and we ought not to think of them as ghosts in winding sheets. The freshest life that we see in this world is the nearest approximation to what we ought to look for in that world.

We will not invite them presumptuously, but will prepare our hearts to receive them.

I do not ask to have Mrs. Cragin come, and have no definite expectation of it. All I ask is that we do not drive her out of the house. The same spirit that would do that would drive Christ out of the house.

I see nothing improper in our desiring the personal presence of Mrs. Cragin in submission to the will of God. One reason why I look for a meeting of the three worlds is that I see in our experience a steady progress in that direction, yet /204/ without fanaticism. We have been surrounded by rappings and all sorts of spiritualisms, and have had dreams and visions among ourselves, but we do not allow them to turn us from the simple truth.

Family Talk at Brooklyn
November 26, 1851

Noyes: —It is just four years since we were driven out of Putney, and now how changed the scene! I should like to have Mrs. Cragin here in this victory. She was among the refugees four years ago. When is she coming back? According to my dream the other night, she is coming pretty suddenly. I dreamed that I was walking along with several of our women behind me, when suddenly Mrs. Cragin jumped in ahead of us in her usual lively manner. I said to her: "You have got back, have you?" She replied: "Yes." She looked rather pale, as though she had had a hard time, but her joy was great. . . . It will not take a great while to find Mrs. Cragin at this rate, I know.

The Mothers of the Primitive Church: Home-Talk by Noyes
December 4, 1851

My experience has taken a very favorable turn of late. A great part of the time since Mrs. Cragin disappeared, I have felt the need of her. I have not had any childish trouble from a lack of personal companionship, but there has seemed to be a real need of such a woman among us, a lack of a certain motherly /205/ element, which is desirable and necessary in a family like this. But I now find myself past that difficulty. I do not now feel the want of her much, if any. I have found that want supplied by turning my attention upward. I see and feel that the Primitive Church, "which is the mother of us all," has plenty of help for us. I find myself in fellowship with the mothers of the Primitive Church, who far exceed in wisdom and power Mrs. Cragin or anyone else among us. I feel strong and well able to meet all the difficulties that may arise, both in this family and in the larger family that we are connected with. /206/

21

Education and Amusements
August 19, 1851, to November 2, 1854*

Oneida Journal
George W. Noyes to Harriet A. Noyes
August 23, 1851

Excerpts:—The mill was finished on Wednesday the 20th. It was agreed to spend the remainder of the week in relaxation. We meet after breakfast for salutation, concentration, and any spiritual exercise that is suggested, then aggregate in some attractive bee or occupy the time as we choose. In the middle of the day, we meet for reading Cromwell and for Community studies. In the latter part of the day, we have amusements and bees. Yesterday I gave some demonstrations in Algebra, just where I happened to be studying. This noon Hial is explaining the tides. Mr. Burt and I have built a bowling-alley, simply plank bedded down level in smooth ground. This was enjoyed last evening by nearly the whole Association.

Journalist:—At 4 P.M. The family went en masse down to the mill garret, which had been cleaned out in the forenoon. First there was swinging the rope for the children, many of the older ones joining in. All were children together. After this Mr. Burt read several Psalms, and we sang songs in which all could join. Music and dance followed, after which the smaller children returned to the house. Then came another dance, and a marching of all around the room under the direction of "Capt. Kinsley" and to the house, where supper awaited us. /207/

Oneida Journal

August 19, 1852.—John R. Miller: A party of twelve, six men and six women, have gone to Oneida Lake today fishing.

---

* The original title's dates read "August 8, 1850, to December 27, 1852." Items in this chapter are not organized chronologically. [L.F.]

Noyes to George Cragin
    Wallingford, August 19, 1852

I have been studying chemistry since I have been here, and I commend it to the attention of those who have an appetite for it. It will help us much in spiritual science, besides being practically useful in industry.

The Old Serpent: Home-Talk by Noyes
    September 29, 1852

There is a curious fact mentioned in the first chapters of Genesis, which tends to confirm the theory of geologists that there were long periods previous to the creation of man, that is the subtlety of the serpent. If the days spoken of were only of twenty-four hours' duration, how shall we account for the subtlety of the serpent on any known principle? . . . It is probable that God had gradually brought up the animal race until it was in a state of high approximation to the ideal of human nature, and then he started a new race to be carried still higher. /208/

Science: Home-Talk by Noyes
    March 1, 1853

This kind of science which the *Scientific American* is so full of is the greatest obstruction to genuine improvement. . . . If you should feel around in the dark and make an inventory of all the things in the room, you would expect that daylight would bring into view many things which you had not perceived, and there would be many blunders in your perceptions. For one thing, you would have missed all the coloring. . . .

There is another part of science which is miserably untrustworthy. An immense mass of what passes for science has been handed down by tradition, and you cannot find any authority for it. The time will come when a man who believes in this mass of stuff will be considered more credulous than the oldest fogy in the churches.

We shall have to make a distinction between science and discovery. There are two sets of persons in the world, one set busy inspecting and recording facts in God's universe, and the other set busy theorizing on those facts. The latter take advantage of past discoveries to manufacture a stiff crust of science that will prevent making any more discoveries. Discovery is closely connected with use. Ericsson appears to be a man who is bent on useful achievements.

This scientific spirit, however, is not bent on useful discoveries, but on parading its own thoughts. These two spirits are inextricably mixed, but we shall be able to separate them by and by. /208a/

Absolute truth is a view taken from God's standpoint. The Bible is written from God's standpoint. This idea will expound a great part of the Bible. . . .

Persons who are searching for truth in this scientific way are trying to steal it. . . . That was the fault at the beginning: Adam and Eve undertook to steal knowledge.

I shall take the ground distinctly, that whatever is true in these pretended sciences will be traced up to Jesus Christ; and whatever cannot be traced to Christ will be found to be a cheat. Paul knew what he said when he told the church that "in Christ are hid all the treasures of wisdom and knowledge."

There is something good in all the sciences, and Christ has been teaching it to the world. If there is any truth in the Copernican system, it will be found that Christ has taught it.

Home-Talk by Noyes for Wallingford
August 24, 1853

My present anxiety for this family is to have an increase of taste for improvement of the mind . . . I have more respect for what is called "modern science" than I have for the old church religion.

Paper by Noyes
October 31, 1854

In reading the account of the creation in Genesis, one is sometimes invited to speculate and find difficulties. How did Moses, or whoever wrote that book, come to know of the circumstances which he relates concerning the origin of things? How is it about the seven *days* of creation, which geology proves to have been periods of indefinite and immense length? And /209/ about the sun, moon, and stars being made to light the earth, instead of being, as modern astronomy assumes, independent globes? And about the day and night that is spoken of previous to the creation of the heavenly luminaries? . . . In our present stage of experience, we have lost all attraction and necessity for such disputations. They seem to us needless, and our hearts are quite at rest in respect to the truth of the Bible, without attempting for the present to bring to bear upon all its statements the process of a direct logical explanation. We find in ourselves a growing patience that is willing to let some things stand *unex-*

plained. . . . We are willing to submit the Bible to the criticism not indeed of hard human intellect but of the Spirit of Truth, and see any of its statements shown to be literally not the most correct.

Paper by Noyes
   November 2, 1854

If there is a temptation sometimes to find fault with Moses' cosmogony in the first chapter of Genesis, there are, on the other hand, awful simplicities of truth running though that account that it seems to us are palpably above the production of mere human invention. There is no effort, no strain or waste of words for effect, and yet who could present a picture, for instance, of original man and his relations to God and to nature more ennobling and beautiful than is here given? There is one verse in that description on which alone we should be willing almost to stake the divinity of the Bible: "And they were both naked, the man and his wife, and were not ashamed." We do not believe that Socrates or Plato or any other Bibleless philosopher in the history of this sin-and-shame-cursed world was ever equal to the sublimity of virtue involved in the perception and enunciation of such a truth. /210/

Education in the Community
   by W. A. Hinds
      December 27, 1852

There is a school, forenoon and afternoon, for children under fifteen. The young people over fifteen have a school of several hours and a Bible class every day. Adults are divided into groups and classes for study. One class numbers nearly forty; among them are three persons over sixty, and several over fifty years of age. Some are studying German, others French. A reading class occupies an hour before breakfast. Our evening meetings are becoming more and more intellectual as well as spiritual feasts. Instrumental and vocal music is also cultivated. Improvement is the motive power here, and it is found in every department. The object before all is a universal education. This comprises a knowledge of all trades, as well as mere book-knowledge. No one here thinks of making some one or two things the business of his life. By rotation of employment, persons learn to do a great many things. This system has also entirely displaced the feeling that one kind of business is more honorable than another, and tends to cultivate unity and love between the different departments. /211/

22

Collision of the Kingdom of God with Hades
September 1851

Home-Talk by Noyes
September 2, 1851

Four years ago we declared ourselves annexed to the Kingdom of God. If our declaration has been invited and substantiated by the Kingdom of God, then the whole strength of that kingdom is with us. Christ promised that the powers of Hades should not prevail against his church. This promise proved true in the Primitive Church, and if we are truly annexed to the Kingdom of God, it will prove true with us. A collision is evidently taking place between the Kingdom of God and Hades. If the deaths that have occurred and the threatenings from the world of the dead do not discourage or frighten us, but our faith and hope increase, then the collision will shatter the attacking power. Christ undertook nothing less than the destruction of the whole power of death. His purpose is not merely to prevent death from taking any more captives, but to set free those that have already been taken. And I now renew my claim on all the captives that Satan has ever taken from us.

Dysentery, the Cause and Cure:
Home-Talk by Noyes
September 3, 1851

I am inclined to think there is an unclean spirit at work, which is at the bottom of this disease and exposes the family to it. Eating and drinking are an ordinance, and if we eat and drink without discerning the Lord's body, we eat and drink damnation. Ordinarily my stomach is clean and submissive to inspiration. But on returning here I perceive that there is a spirit /212/ connected with alimentiveness that makes it difficult for me to eat my meat with gladness and singleness of heart. Children are often troubled with worms, and there are live creatures in our bowels that operate just as worms do. There are two spirits at work in the universe, a spirit of power, life, and growth, and, opposed to that, a spirit that is parasitic. Your life has become civilized enough to expel the physical vermin, but it is still unable to expel entirely the spiritual parasite. Here comes in the tremendous significance of this text: "Be sober; be vigilant; because your adversary, the Devil, as a roaring lion, walketh about seeking whom he may devour." He does not come in the shape of a lion, nor does he give any particular notice of his approach; but he is a parasite seeking to destroy God's beautiful universe. In order to live eternally in peace and happiness, you must get rid of parasites. Your bowels must be occupied by heavenly spirits. There is just the same desire on the part of the good life to take possession of us. Christ goes about to nourish and save, and he is stronger and roars louder than the Devil.

The parasitic life in our stomachs is greedy and will make us greedy. If we feel an unnatural, greedy appetite for food, we may be sure that it is the working of that parasitic life in us, and must resist it. /213/

Harriet A. Noyes to Oneida
Brooklyn, September 9, 1851

A large share of our time and attention has been taken up by Sophronia. We have written that she was better, and she did seem brighter days, but for three or four nights past, especially the latter part of the night, her circulation would stop and she would have a difficulty of breathing, which she would only recover from by rubbing and warming. Sunday night Sarah Campbell took care of her. About two o'clock she thought Sophronia was dying, and she called Mr. Burnham, John, and me. When we saw her, we all thought the same. John went to his room and felt that he got a complete victory over the spirit which was upon her. Sarah and I looked on and saw Death do his prettiest. In the midst of her worst struggle, John came in and said he had no faith in her dying, and should not believe in it till he saw her dead. But if she should die, he wanted to send a message by her to Mrs. Cragin. He would send his love to her, and say to her, we are waiting for her to come back. Sophronia smiled and nodded. Soon afterward she revived and appeared brighter all day yesterday. Last night towards morning, she was tempted again to think she was going to die. But Mr. Noyes says we will stick to the victory we got the night before. The Devil is turned out, and is now whining around the back door. Today we have criticized the spirit in her which demands attention, and advised her to talk on God's side. All her bad feelings are only a parenthesis, to be read in a lower tone of voice, if read at all. She received the criticism well.

September 10, 1851.—Grace Worden, who has been gradually declining for about two weeks, died this evening at the Children's /214/ House. She was nearly eleven months old.

September 12, 1851.—Death of Sophronia Tuttle. /215/

23

The Utica Indictments
September 27, 1851, to December 23, 1851

An Evening's Talk about Oneida
September 27, 1851

Noyes:—Under present circumstances, I revert to our position after our dispersion from Putney. The Association at that time actually moved to New York City, and the center of operations has been here ever since. The first thing we did after coming here was to right the Newark church, which in fact was to be the nest-egg while we were called off to do the necessary work of establishing an Association in Central New York. I said at the time that though our ultimate post was to be in New York City, our true policy was to make a lateral movement until our enemies at Putney were dispersed. We have established some of our forces here at Brooklyn, but the time is not quite ripe for Brooklyn to stand forth publicly as the center. The whole concern is called the Oneida Association, and will be until the enemy is dispersed at Putney. We are now promising a movement on Putney. If that succeeds, I shall consider it a signal that we are prepared to commence operations here in earnest. Meanwhile, I beg of Oneida to take comfort in the view that their tribulations are exactly what they need to reduce them to their proper magnitude as an auxiliary to Brooklyn. My heart is soft toward them. I should be glad to shield them from all their troubles, but I am persuaded that they will yet be thankful for them. The burning of the store, the sinking of the sloop, financial pressures, Tryphena's case will all work for good in humbling them and increasing their confidence in me. I was willing, so far as my personal feelings were concerned, that the center should be at Oneida, but that was not /216/ God's will. The mischief that has been at work in the Association has all come from the spirit that separated itself from me. I believe that the body of the Association have wisdom and simplicity enough to understand the meaning of our tribulations. I suggest that they fix their eye on the movement here at the center, go on earnestly with their business, and expect that God will prosper them. That is the way I do. There is enough going on around me to take up all my attention, if I should let it. But I keep my eye steadily on the press as a means of giving Christ a thorough medium of communication with the world, and will not be turned aside by sinking of sloops, waiting on coroners, or scufflings with Old Bones.

The Hubbards are reaping the rewards of their labors. I believe, and with good ground, that if I could have had the management of Tryphena's case, she would never have been crazy. The case of Horace Burt shows that I am not overcome by insanity, but can conquer it in its worst forms. By driving me away, the Hubbards have driven Tryphena into her present state, and they must take the consequences.

I appreciate Henry Seymour, and think he has done nobly. While I have no doubt he will learn wisdom by his experience, I think he has behaved well, and I shall back him against all creation. I also want to encourage Mr. Skinner. There is real value in him that has not yet been thoroughly appreciated.

I certainly feel a nearness to the Association that I have not felt for a great while. /217/

Oneida Journal

October 2, 1851.—Samuel Hutchins reported to Mr. Perry a conversation of Dexter Hubbard with Lawyer Jenkins of Vernon, in which Hubbard said that Henry Seymour had confessed to him that he had whipped Trypehna with a rawhide every day for three weeks, that her back was in consequence as black as his pantaloons, and that one of her eyes was so badly injured that he was doubtful whether she would ever see out of it again. He told Jenkins, moreover, that there were as many as three hundred men in the town who were ready to come at any time and tear down our buildings. This morning Mr. Seymour went over to see the Hubbards, and found the family full of wrath. The old man threatened to horsewhip him, and actually went and got a large stick and shook it at him, though he did not get up quite enough courage to use it. Henry kept cool, and said what he could to quiet them, and to clear Mr. Noyes and the Association from blame. As he was about to come away, the old man said he might go home and wait till he was called for. The Hubbards show that their principal spite is against Mr. Noyes, insisting that he has been here and had the direction of things. They say Hutchins told them he had seen Mr. Noyes go away within a few days. This probably grows out of Mrs. Noyes's late visit here.

Interpretation of Our Late Experience
October 3, 1851

Noyes:—The burning of the store, the sinking of the sloop, the insanity of Tryphena, and the death of Sophronia Tuttle may seem like judgments and indications of God's displeasure. But so long as we learn the lesson, and faith rises triumphant, these /218/ trials are really like the sufferings of Christ, merely a proof that we are founded on a rock. We have been subjected to trials which have broken up other Associations, yet we have stood firm and united. God is showing us and the world that evil has no power against us. With our crude ideas about victory over death, we have been encouraged to think that disease, death, and insanity could never come to us. Now that we have felt their power, we have been tempted either to quarrel with God, or rush forward into fanatical faith. Yet we have submitted on the whole quietly, and have fulfilled our righteousness in waiting on God.

Oneida Journal

October 7, 1851.—This morning old Mr. Hubbard and his son Lucius, who is constable, called and summoned nine of our folks, viz: J. Burt and wife, Albert Kinsley and wife, J. L. Skinner, Fanny M. Leonard, Eveliza Newhouse, Sylvia Hamilton, and Isaac Seymour to appear before the Court of Oyer and Terminer now sitting in Utica, to testify relative to a prosecution against Henry Seymour for assault and battery. As soon as they could get ready, they started by team, George W. Noyes with them, and arrived between 10 and 11 o'clock in the evening. The jury questioned Mr. Skinner on our social principles and arrangements. They kept Mrs. Leonard in the chair half an hour, asking her questions about her acquaintance with the Community before coming here, the number of members, marriage, sleeping arrangements, visitors, her love for her husband and child, sleeping with her husband, also about Tryphena. They questioned Mr. Burt particularly in reference to our financial condition and property arrangements. They /219/ questioned Mrs. Burt something as they did Mrs. Leonard but not so much. It is thought all answered wisely and well. The remainder of the witnesses were dismissed without an examination. Our company took supper at the hotel, and it so happened that several of the jurymen sat opposite them at the table. G. W. Noyes says: "We had a good time with them, explaining our views and inviting them to the fullest investigation of our concern. They were at least good natured, and one of them appeared to be fairly captivated. He took a favorable view of Tryphena's case, and wished to get our Reports and other publications."

October 10, 1851.—Mr. Burt had an interview with Whipple Jenkins, Esq., of Vernon. Mr. Jenkins said that the Hubbards had been to him for help in the case of Tryphena, but he had refused. They had filled his ears with exaggerations in regard to our treatment of insane persons, saying that our rule was to whip without exception, that Horace Burt was cured in that way, that a devil as big as a woodchuck was cast out of him by whipping. This gave Mr. Burt a good chance to state the facts about Tryphena and Horace. He said that whipping had never been applied except in the case of Tryphena, and that as a family we had disapproved of the measure, though we believed her husband had good intentions in his treatment of her—he knew no better way to make her quiet and keep her from injuring herself.

October 13, 1851.—Mr. Burt went to the Castle to see Timothy Jenkins, Esq. At the outset, Mr. Jenkins expressed great regret at the circumstance of the whipping, and censured it strongly. He then professed his friendship for the Community and went on to give advice. He said that Mr. Garvin, the District Attorney, /220/ had inquired of him about us, and that he gave us a good character for honesty and regularity of life, and expressed the opinion that our peculiar views ought not to subject us to indictment so long as that was the case.

October 21, 1851.—Mr. John R. Jones, High Sheriff of Oneida county, called this morning, and delivered a warrant ordering Jonathan Burt, Henry W. Burnham, Eleazer L. Hatch, Isaac and Henry J. Seymour, Otis H. Miller, John Abbott, George W. Noyes, John L. Skinner, and Sewall Newhouse to go before Judge Root of Utica on the first Monday of December next. At a glance Mr. Miller saw that his name was providentially left out, and he told the Sheriff he would go down with them and give bail for them all. The action was for misdemeanor. When they were about to start, the Sheriff told Mr. Miller he should go alone from Vernon to Utica, and invited him to ride with him. This was just as Mr. Miller liked. He found the Sheriff a free, whole-hearted, musical character, with no bitterness towards us, but on the contrary, very friendly feelings. Lucius Hubbard of the Castle was Deputy Sheriff, and had told the Judge he would like to do this business with us, but Mr. Jones said that, as Hubbard was our enemy he would be likely to have personal feelings, and he would serve the warrants himself. He became so disgusted with Lucius Hubbard that besides refusing to let him do this business, he turned him out of his office and appointed another Deputy. He said he might have called us before some other Judge, but he knew it was best for us to go before Judge Root, as he was the cleverest Judge in the County and would be reasonable with us. After dinner they went to Judge Root's /221/ office, and after some questioning the Judge accepted Mr. Miller as bail without any hesitation. He required $200 each and $200 extra for Henry Seymour on account of his separate indictment for assault and battery. The Judge was very agreeable, and the Sheriff treated us with as much kindness as a brother could. As they were leaving the Judge's office, the Sheriff said to them: "I think we can fix this business up about right for you. A good deal depends upon the selection of the Jury." They arrived home about 7 o'clock with hearts full of faith, hope, and thankfulness.

Apparently, Sheriff Jones went to Brooklyn to serve the warrants on G. W. Noyes and J. L. Skinner. But in a Home-Talk, January 24, 1853, Noyes speaks of "the Sheriff's playing in with Mr. Miller to have George and Mr. Skinner evade the majesty of the law." [G.W.N.]

October 22, 1851.—Messrs. Perry and Hatch started out peddling in this vicinity this afternoon. We thought that in this crisis of our affairs it would be well for them to circulate in this and neighboring towns. They left in fine spirits.

October 31, 1851.—The following document has been made out and is to be circulated among our neighbors:

To the District Attorney of the County of Oneida and all whom it may concern: This is to certify that we, the undersigned, citizens of the Towns of Vernon and Lenox, are well acquainted with the general character of the Oneida Community, and are willing to testify that we regard them as honorable business men, good neighbors, and quiet, peaceable citizens. We believe them to be lovers of justice and good order, men who mind their own business and in no way interfere with the rights of their neighbors. /222/ We regard them, so far as we know, as persons of good moral character, and we have no sympathy with the recent attempts to disturb their peace.

November 3, 1851.—Mr. Miller started out this afternoon with the paper for our neighbors to sign. He called first on Mr. Parsons, who was pleased with the paper and signed it most heartily, offering to go with Mr. Miller to call on his neighbors in that direction. Mr. Miller took him in his wagon and they called on eleven respectable men, all of whom signed without objection except one, who had just moved there and knew nothing about us. Mr. Miller says: "I must confess I was altogether taken by surprise to hear so many warm expressions of friendship. As a specimen, when I read the paper to John Tipple, a man of considerable influence, and asked him if he could sign it, he replied very heartily: 'Sign it, yes, I am *glad* to, and so will every decent man.'"

November 6, 1851.—Mr. Miller called this forenoon on Messrs. Rawson, Johnson, Ney, and Ira Hitchcock. He says: "I found them all ready to sign my paper heartily. I had some doubts about asking Mr. Ney, but when I read it to him he said, 'Yes sir, I'll sign that. It is what I have always said of you!'" In the afternoon he went to the Depot and reports thus: "Messrs. Allen, Goodwin, Thompson, Soper, and Bennett all cheerfully signed my paper. They were the only ones I asked. They said there was no difficulty in getting all the names we wished at the Depot."

November 7, 1851.—Mr. Miller went over to Vernon and saw Dr. Case and sons in reference to signing the paper, and had his usual good luck. He called on the editor of the paper there, and gave him the document sent by Mr. Noyes with Mr. Burt's name attached. The editor was pleased with it, and said he would put it in next week's paper.

November 8, 1851.—Mr. Miller called on Mr. Downing and three of his neighbors this morning, and they cheerfully signed the paper. After dinner he went over to the Foundry and presented the paper to Henry Wilson and son. They were both very forward in signing it. Henry Wilson said that he had been applied to for help to get up a mob, but had replied that he would have nothing to do with it. He added, "If I know this community, it would be impossible to get up a mob here. I have heard only one feeling expressed, and that was a feeling of regret that such a thing should be contemplated. Every man in this vicinity is friend to you." /223/

November 13, 1851.—In the absence of Mr. Miller, Mr. Burt went out to get more signatures to the paper that is being circulated. The first man he met with was Mr. Withee, whom we have considered doubtful and a friend of the Hubbards. He said he would sign it cheerfully, and did. Br. Burt then called on Mr. Root, and gave him a full account of our experience and troubles with the Hubbards. Mr. Root appeared full of sympathy on our behalf, and told Mr. Burt that he not only considered us good peaceable citizens, but the best class around here and a blessing to the surrounding public. At first he said he would write to the Judge, his brother, expressing his feelings towards us, but afterward he said he was going to Utica before the day of our meeting, /224/ and he would talk with him, also with Mr. Garvin, the District Attorney.

November 22, 1851.—Mr. Miller called on the Hubbards this forenoon, and asked Dexter what would satisfy him. Dexter replied that he didn't want to make anything out of it, and would be satisfied if we would give bonds to support Tryphena during life, and make her free when she became sane. Mr. Miller told him we would do that, if it would settle the whole difficulty. At this point the old man came in and made some strong objections. Dexter then said he would think more of it, and let us know next Monday or Tuesday what he would do. He would not vary much from this proposal.

November 24, 1851.—Messrs. Burt and Miller took the first train to Utica, and met Mr. Jones as agreed at the District Attorney's office. The District Attorney said that in a criminal case he had no power to settle, but the indictment for assault and battery would be dropped if we settled with the Hubbards and paid the costs. In the evening Mr. Miller went over to the Hubbards. Dexter was gone from home. Mr. Miller waited, and meanwhile the old gentleman and lady talked pleasantly and treated him to apples and cider. When Dexter came home he said that he had not altered his mind in relation to the settlement, and that if Mr. Miller would go with him tomorrow to Vernon and talk the matter over with Mr. Jenkins, he thought they might settle it to their mutual satisfaction.

November 25, 1851.—Mr. Miller and Mr. Hubbard had a consultation with Mr. Jenkins at the District Attorney's Office. After talking for some time, the District Attorney said to Mr. Jenkins, "You go home and settle this matter, and whatever you /225/ do, I will consent to." After Mr. Jenkins left the room, Mr. Miller asked the District Attorney if he intended him to understand that if we settled this thing with Mr. Jenkins it would make an end of all the indictments. He replied: "The Court must approve of what I do, of course, but you need not have any further trouble about it." Mr. Miller told the District Attorney that if the case came to trial he need not summon any witnesses, for Henry Seymour would plead guilty; that he felt badly enough for what had happened, and would confess all that could be proved. The District Attorney replied: "I don't want he should do it, for I should have no heart to punish him."

November 26, 1851.—Mr. Miller and Mr. Hubbard called on Mr. Jenkins to try to settle this difficulty that has hung like a dark cloud over us, ready to break at any moment. They had a long and tedious conversation, but at last the following arrangement was made: We are to pay Tryphena's expenses at the Asylum, which we are already under bonds to do, and when she comes out of the Asylum we are to pay her $125 per year if she is well, and $200 per year is she is unsound in body or mind. This is secured by Henry Seymour's bond and a mortgage on the Hamilton Farm. We also agree that Mr. Jenkins may procure a divorce in a quiet way at our expense. It was understood by all that Tryphena would be free to live with Mr. Seymour if she chose to, and if she did, or if she married anyone else, that would end all bonds. Mr. Miller and Mr. Burt returned by way of Oneida, and sent the following telegraphic dispatch to Mr. Noyes: "All negotiations are ended by an amicable settlement. Terms by mail tomorrow. We join with the State in a day of Thanksgiving." /226/

John R. Miller to Harriet H. Skinner:—How clear it is now that our neighbors do not regard us as a nuisance, but quite the contrary. Hubbard himself said that he was glad to have us live here, that it was an advantage to him and to the neighborhood.

God's Criticism of Us
November 4, 1851

Noyes:—It seems on looking over our history for the past season, that God has criticised us for two faults. The first is false fellowships. That seems to be the point aimed at in the difficulties with the Hubbards, Hyde, and Long. The sinking of the sloop and deaths connected with it were to me a terrible criticism on the spirit that allowed Long to hang around the church and corrupt it with his unbelief; and Tryphena's insanity /227/ has been a criticism of what we may call the neighborhood fellowship. Then I am satisfied that God has also been criticising us for over-sharpness in criticism, and for dealing with each other in a cold, hard way. I will learn from an enemy. I understood that Charles Lovett said there was not enough patience among us. It struck me that there was some truth in this, whether he had a right to say so or not. Our system of criticism has generated more or less sharpness and severity of spirit which has precluded the softness and gentleness of Christ. You will say that these two faults are opposite and neutralize each other. If you begin by being easy in your fellowships, you will admit bad material, and will be tempted to over-severity in order to get rid of it. In the French Revolution, the Reign of Terror was preceded by a reign of universal philanthropy. For the present we have fulfilled our righteousness in the line of criticism; let us now turn our mind toward the gentleness and mercy of Christ.

All the troubles we have had with Hubbards commenced with that original mistake of criticising them for taking things from our garden. . . . The tendency with Mr. Hamilton and Mr. Bradley at Wallingford is to crack up the team of criticism.

For a year past our inspiration has looked in the direction of extending the press. The Lord, who does nothing in a hurry, began the extension by sending me to England. From that commenced a series of new movements, all of which were scientifically adapted to prepare us for what we are now going about. After my return I was stirred up to demand of the Association that they submit themselves to God for criticism, and we invited him to put us through /228/ any course necessary for our perfection. Directly upon that, the printing-office was burnt. Then followed the sinking of the sloop and the deaths of Mrs. Cragin and Eliza Allen. Since then have come the insanity of Tryphena, the death of Sophronia Tuttle, the turmoils and troubles at Oneida. All these things I take as criticism invited by us and necessary to prepare us for service.

John R. Miller to George Cragin
Oneida, December 8, 1851

In relation to our lawsuits, I am quite sure there is no "cat in the meal," and I can see only one hole by which she can crawl in. The District Attorney may throw the responsibility on to the Judge, if anything should come up which would change his mind. I am quite sure that his terms were made in good faith, that he has none other than friendly feelings toward us, and would be willing and glad to have this matter settled without further trouble. Whether two months will make the case better or worse, we must trust that same Providence who has thus far overruled everything for our good.

Talk for Oneida
December 23, 1851

Noyes.—There may be a little tendency at Oneida to feel as though our late affair with the world has produced a serious internal change of policy. I would caution the Association against any such influence. There has been no constitutional change. We have learned no wisdom contrary to our previous ideas of government. We have indeed found that it was quite possible for severity to be applied without profit and in a way to give offense to the world, and we shall be cautious about doing so hereafter. . . . In regard to the use of the rod, I believe as fully as I ever did that Solomon was right. The rod is the best of all carnal weapons, and if properly used in season will remove the necessity of any other carnal weapons. The rod rightly applied to children is a mercy to them. If it is not applied by their parents, God will apply an equivalent; and if it is not applied by God or man, they will grow up mere animals. All that should be learned in the case of Tryphena is that wisdom and power of management are required in order to apply chastisement effectually, and that the application of the rod to adults would generally be inexpedient. If a person with an adult understanding is so perverse that he cannot be managed by /229/ other influences, he will not be likely to be managed by that. Yet even in the case of adults, I have learned no wisdom that precludes me from using the rod under certain circumstances. I have had good success in the case of Elizabeth Hawley. The circumstances of that case were such that, if they could be presented to the world, I should be justified. She was here under sufferance, and I distinctly and with long patience made her know that she must submit to the family or leave the house. She came to a crisis in which she flatly refused to do either. Calculating her sensitivities to bodily pain, I followed my inspiration and attacked her body. I gave her liberty to leave the house if she chose, but gave her to understand that if she behaved like a child I should treat her like a child. The case is apparently coming to a good termination, and she will yet attribute her salvation to the plainness with which I faced her.

This same reactionary tendency may produce fearfulness in applying criticism where it is needed, and tempt the Association into over-delicacy toward outsiders, as in the case of the Hutchins girls. In view of the fact that we have triumphed over the world and God has vindicated us, I demand that there shall be more boldness than ever. We shall assume that the lion is tamed, and if he is not, we will have another tussel with him.

I object to the idea that the Association is indebted to the world for mercy. Just before appealing to the world for a certificate of character, Mr. Miller asked the Hubbards what they were going to do about mobbing us. They intimated that they could raise a mob, said that every one was our enemy, and that they should do all in their power to break us up. We went forward in /230/ defiance of them, got our certificate, and secured a vote of the public against them. Then they were very glad to settle! The Hubbards apparently held us at their mercy, and would have broken us if they could. We appealed to God and the public, and are indebted to God's mercy working through our own courage and wisdom.

Then again I utterly object to any thought among us that we have made any concession to the public in this war. On the point of our social theory, we acknowledged everything, asked no favors, promised nothing. Even in regard to chastisement, we simply acknowledged our imprudence in that particular case, but made no concession of principle. . . .

The experience at Oneida has brought about no weakening of my moral character. I feel stronger and firmer than ever. We have here lately been through a campaign with the children, in which I have pursued the old policy successfully, and with beautiful results.

The Association have now conquered the country around them. They have cleared a space which they can and should fill. Unless they do, the Devil will, and the tide will flow back upon them. This is no time for relaxation of heart with me, but a time in which I am marching on the enemies' center more boldly than ever. /231/

24

Editorial Attack in the New York Observer
January 22, 1852

Perfectionism and Polygamy

Recent revelations of the interior and total depravity of some professedly religious establishments have shocked the public mind and led to inquiry as to the tendency of religious delusions. It is hard to say whether knavery or folly, whether fanaticism or lust has more power over the Mormons of Utah and the Perfectionists of Oneida, but the facts that are now before the world in reference to both those communities are worthy of being studied as new chapters in the history of modern imposture and delusion.

It is hardly known, but it is true, that there is a weekly newspaper published in this immediate neighborhood to advocate and propagate the doctrines of the Oneida Perfectionists; that in the community of those who are led to embrace the system, all the laws, both human and divine, that are designed to regulate the marriage relation are set aside and denounced, while the unrestrained indulgence of the human passions is practised not merely as the means to present enjoyment, but as *means of grace or helps to holiness.* The founder of this disgusting order of united adulterers is a graduate of a New England college, a student in two theological seminaries, and now the editor of the paper we have referred to above.

The center of this sect is in the town of Lenox, Madison County, N.Y., where about 150 men, women, and children live together /232/ in one house, with no distinction of property, family, or authority. Each one does what seems good in his own eyes. The Bible is their nominal constitution, and how curiously they must follow its teachings is evident from the fact that they disavow all separate or individual right in "property, wives or children." Literally they have "all things in common." But the sect is by no means confined to Oneida and Madison Counties. In New York and Brooklyn and in Newark, N.J., and in many other places, there are groups of practical members of this foul body, who under the name and guise of seeking after spiritual enjoyment and professing to be perfectly holy are living in a state of vile concubinate and even worse, such as is not even thought of among the Mormons. In Utah the distinction of husband and wife is rightly maintained, and non-intervention insisted upon even at the peril of life. But in the Oneida Association and in the boarding-houses established in this vicinity, these distinctions are utterly abolished and the freest licentiousness practised as the highest development of holiness. We have been furnished with a large number of certificates signed by females of this Community stating that at first they were fearful they were not doing right, but the longer they have practised on the system here pursued, the holier they are sure to grow. On the principle, we suppose, that where there is no law there is no transgression, they have abrogated all authority but inclination, and they never sin because they never do anything but what they like. The reader may be amused at the practical operation of the Association at Lenox as we find it detailed in one of their "Reports." /233/

The children are trained in a general nursery, and "it is found to be altogether a more comfortable task to take care of six in the new way than it had been to wait on one in ordinary circumstances." "The only drawback in the operation was the temporary distress of the mothers in giving up their little ones to the care of others, which made occasion for some melodramatic scenes; but the wounds were soon healed, and the mothers learned to value their own freedom and opportunity of education and the improved condition of their children more than the luxury of a sickly maternal tenderness." This is the language of the Report.

The way they sleep is curious. One large room is set apart for a dormitory, and each bed is encompassed by a sort of square tent, so that one stove warms the entire space. "As the principles and habits of the Association are more gregarious than usual, the sacrifice of privacy is a small affair."

The women found that much time was spent in dressing their hair, so they looked into Paul's theory of long hair, and, says this Report, "the discovery was made that Paul's language expressly points out the object for which women should wear long hair, and that object is not ornament but a covering. In this light it was immediately manifest that the long hair of women as it is usually worn, coiled and combed upward to the top of the head, instead of answering to Paul's object of covering, actually exposes the back part of the head more than the short hair of men." This mode of *reasoning* was carried on till the "bolder women" cut off their hair and wore it on their necks as girls do, and soon the practice became general. In the next place the women laid aside the usual dress, and substituted a short frock and pantaloons, which was found to be altogether more convenient. The /234/ Report says: "The women say they are far more free and comfortable in this dress than in long gowns. The men think that it improves their looks, and some insist that it is entirely more modest than the long dress." This is plainly the germ of Bloomerism.*

The religious exercises of this Association consist of public meetings, when each one is called on to relate his own experience or to make such exhortations or reflections as "are on the mind waiting for vent." Different evenings are set apart for different purposes; one for music, one for dancing, one for Bible reading, etc. The religious influence is said to be wonderful on those who have joined the Association. All who came in an unconverted state are declared to have been converted, and one man who was a confirmed lunatic has been entirely cured!

The Annual Report sets forth a theory of promiscuous intercourse of the sexes as compatible with the highest state of holiness on earth so loathsome in its details, so shocking to all the sensibilities even of the coarsest of decent people that we cannot defile the columns of our paper with their recital. It must be sufficient to say that the doctrine is taught and the attempt is made to

---

* Amelia Bloomer was popularly credited with originating the bloomer outfit. [L.F.]

defend it from Scripture, that unbridled licentiousness is the law of heaven, the perfection of human happiness, and the realization of the highest style of divine virtue. There is no shrinking from the boldest and frankest avowal of this faith and practice. On this point the Oneida Associationists are honorably contrasted with the Fourierites* of this city, who refuse to be held responsible for the consequences to which their doctrines inevitably lead. /235/

The Report holds such language as this: "Variety is in the nature of things as beautiful and useful in love as in eating and drinking." Again it is held that it is all very well and often-times of great advantage to bring about "special pairing," that is, marriage of convenience. But, says the Report, this should be no barrier to the enjoyment of others. "The fact that a man loves peaches best is no reason why he should not on suitable occasions eat apples and cherries."

We are able to give only the vaguest and most distant intimations of what is set forth in these pages, and we are now fearful that we are trespassing on decency in these quotations. The perversion of Scripture is oftentimes so blasphemous as to chill the blood, while a scheme of social life under the name of virtue, nay of religion, is here taught that the foulest days and darkest places of Roman Catholic iniquity never conceived. The beasts of the field are better in their habits than these people profess to be. If the orgies of the heathen are re-enacted in the City of New York in public, they cannot fill the mind with more horror than every virtuous person must feel when contemplating the "interior life" of this Oneida Association.

When we now bear in mind that the persons thus living in this beastly manner were but recently members of orthodox evangelical churches, some of them well educated and most of them respectably connected, we cannot fail to regard their history as in the highest degree instructive, tending to show the danger of error and the infinite necessity of holding fast to the truth. Loose teaching from the pulpit and the press is destructive to the principles. The only safety is in steadfast adherence to the good old-fashioned morality of our fathers and mothers, on whose principles the first half of the nineteenth century has made no improvement. /236/

* The major communitarian movement of the 1840s. [L.F.]

25

The Putney "Senate"

October 2, 1851, to February 17, 1852

John R. Miller to Noyes
Putney, October 2, 1851

Soon after it was announced in the street yesterday morning that the Wordens and Bakers were coming to town, I saw the veterans of the war of 1847 gathered at their old headquarters in front of the Post-Office with Israel Keyes at their head. But how changed! They looked more like old war-worn soldiers petitioning government for a pension than soldiers fresh for the fight. . . .

Yesterday was the happiest day of my life. The consciousness of the presence of an invisible hand guiding all our affairs filled my heart with unspeakable joy. I never rode through Putney street in such a victorious spirit as I did last night with our friends from Oneida.

Meeting of the Putney "Senate"

The inhabitants of the village of Putney met at the vestry of the Congregational Meeting-house on the evening of the 23rd day of January 1852 for the purpose of taking into consideration certain letters published in *The Circular* edited by John H. Noyes at Brooklyn, N.Y.

1.—Organized by appointing Israel Keyes, Esq., Chairman, and John Kimball, Secretary. /237/

2.—On motion of David Crawford, Esq., appointed a Committee of seven to draft and report some appropriate resolutions at a future meeting. Israel Keyes, Esq., John Kimball, Esq., David Crawford, Esq., Rev. Amos Foster, Rev. L. C. Dickinson, Dr. John Campbell, and Thomas White, Esq., were appointed said Committee.

3.—On motion adjourned to Friday evening, January 30th, 1852.

Friday, January 30.—Met agreeably to adjournment, and Dr. John Campbell reported the following preamble and resolutions, which, after being discussed, were unanimously adopted:—

Whereas, John R. Miller, one of the leading and principal associates of John H. Noyes, has recently published in *The Circular* a letter bearing date at

Oneida, N.Y., Dec. 23, 1851, wherein he writes as follows:—"As it is generally understood that we were driven out of Putney, Vt., in 1847, I think it is right that your readers should know of the changes which have taken place there during the last four years." "A great change has come over the spirit of the place." "If this is not so, I hope the people will *express* it before we go further. Unless this is done, we shall take if for granted that they have *retracted* the movements of 1847, and shall act accordingly."

And whereas, the said Miller writes to said Noyes in a letter bearing date at Putney, Jan. 4, 1852, as follows: "Our friends here were much pleased with the last *Circular,* and many appeared delighted to learn by my letter published in that No. that we thought of returning to Putney."

Therefore, 1.—Resolved, that in answer to the above request of said Miller and his associates we, the people of Putney, have /238/ not "retracted the movements of 1847," or the resolutions then adopted.

2.—Resolved, that *we* are not "delighted to learn" by the letter of said Miller that he or any of his associates have thought of returning to Putney unless they shall "retract" their principles and reform their practices regarded by us as a "Nuisance."

3.—Resolved, that now as heretofore we adhere to our penal enactments for the suppression or punishment of "offences against the peace and dignity of the State."

4.—Resolved, that the editors of the *Vermont Chronicle* and the editor of *The Circular* be respectfully requested to publish the proceedings of this meeting, and that the Secretary furnish each of them a copy of the same.

Israel Keyes, Chairman
John Kimball, Secretary

Putney, January 30, 1852

Mary J. Mead to Noyes
Brattleboro, February 14, 1852

Dear Brother:—

As I was making my pies this morning I had a long talk with you, and feeling quite a disposition to write to you I concluded it was best to obey the feeling and send you a few of my thoughts.

I was thinking of the proposed return of some of the Community to Putney, and it occurred to me that Paul prayed that he might be delivered from unreasonable men, and I don't know as it would be right to tempt God by expecting him to work a miracle to deliver those who put themselves in their way. /239/

Then there is pride of opinion, a feeling among the people that they would have to acknowledge (at least by actions) that they had done wrong, and that can only be effected by a miracle of grace in their hearts. It does not seem to me that those who troubled you before have changed their minds in the least. I think the New England Puritan character, which has been so ready in former times to contend earnestly for the truth, is as slow and obstinate in receiving new truth, and requires long patience.

When I made up my mind to write you I supposed this would be the substance of my letter, when whom should I receive a call from in the afternoon but Mrs. Nichols. She wished to have a private conversation with me; said she had received three exchange papers which had copied the piece about you in *The New York Observer,* and wished to ask me plainly the truth in the case. She said she had too much confidence in your religious character to believe that you would do wrong, and she had never believed the reports. I told her frankly all that I understood about your doctrines and practices. She did not seem alarmed or disturbed. She has arrived at the same conclusions on many subjects that you have. She has had experience to show her that the relations between man and woman need reforming. We had a familiar talk of two hours. She said she had said things to me that she had never said to any other, and I certainly said things to her that I never did to any other woman in Brattleboro. We parted with great good feeling. You are so ready to see a meaning in events that pass unnoticed by others, that perhaps you will say Mrs. Nichols' call was a rhyme.

Love to all friends. Your affectionate sister,

M. J. Mead /240/

Noyes to Mary J. Mead
Brooklyn, February 17, 1852

Dear Sister Mary:—

You will see by the enclosed copy of a letter which went to Mr. Miller yesterday, that I did not so much need your kind and judicious suggestions, received this morning, as you perhaps imagined, for which nevertheless I sincerely thank you. I perceive as usual that critical emergencies call you out into thought and action. I trust you will turn some of the good sense, which the present alarm has aroused in you, toward the favorable opening for truth which Mrs. Nichols is giving you. While I appreciate your care for our safety manifested in holding *us* back from imprudencies, I assure you that you can do more to shelter your brothers and sisters and friends from harm by *stepping forward yourself* and helping Mrs. Nichols out into the utterance of her deepest convictions in the face of Windham County and the world. We shall not be imprudent, but we shall be firm and faithful to the truth, and the ultimate chance we have of escaping the wrath that crucified Christ is the possibility that prejudice will yield to the spirit of truth and the age of reason commence. We are in the lions' den, and that not by our own wilfulness or imprudence but for reasons as good as Daniel had, and we can be saved not by getting out or by shrinking into corners but only by the lions' mouths being stopped. If you can do anything to stop their mouths, you can help us. Think of this in all wishes and efforts for our good.

Your affectionate brother,
John H. Noyes /242/

26

A Concentric Convention
February 1 to October 31, 1852

The Circular, Old Series, 1:50
February 1, 1852

As conventions for the purpose of reform are the order of the day, and as it is desirable that such conventions should be accessible to all adherents, which is not the case with any local gatherings, we propose to our scattered friends a *Concentric Convention*. What we mean is a gathering of spirits on the plan suggested in Col. 2:5.* A convention of this kind will not only admit every believer, however distant and embarrassed, but may be attended by delegates from the Primitive Church and from Hades, the two other worlds with which we are cultivating interesting relations. We will not enlarge for the present on the feasibility and hopefulness of this project, but will simply name the 20th of February next as a good time for the gathering, and so leave the

---

* "Though I be absent in the flesh, yet I am with you in the spirit." [G.W.N.]

subject to the meditations of our readers till we have matured what more we
have to say.

Business for the Convention
The Circular, Old Series, 1:54
    February 8, 1852

We propose to publish a free paper giving to all who ask the benefit of the
grace given to us. We propose also to advance, as we shall be able, in the business of publication till we can send to the church of God a *daily* message of
truth and love. For the support of our press, we have proposed the plan of
systematic, /242/ free contributions on the part of those who find themselves
stewards of God's property and are disposed to invest, according to their ability, in the stock of Communism. We expect this plan will prosper because we
believe that the heavens are interested in it, and are able to turn the hearts of
men toward it; and because our gospel, in attacking and annihilating selfishness instead of creeping about under it and asking favors of it as other causes
do, is sure to unlock the hearts that hold the treasures of the world, and so to
live by its own legitimate conquests.

Our readers have now before them an outline of our projects and hopes.
We respectfully submit them for the consideration of all hearts at the Concentric Convention proposed in our last number for the 20th of February. We
believe that there will be an actual and interesting meeting of three worlds at
that time; and we believe that whoever has a heart big enough to attend that
meeting has a heart big enough to comprehend the enterprise we are engaged
in, and to cooperate with us and heaven in its fulfillment.

About the Convention
The Circular, Old Series, 1:58
    February 15, 1852

As physical beings we are so accustomed to think of all things as subject to
the laws of space that a proposal for a Concentric Convention seems chimeri-
cal. But let us try the experiment. Improvement and discovery are going ahead
in things spiritual as well as temporal. Perhaps we shall find better means of
communication than railroads and telegraphs. "Where there is a will there is a
way." /243/

If any one asks, where shall we meet? We answer by the question, Where
do you meet Christ? If you know where to find him, you have access to all that
are in him. Paul has given this direction: "Say not in thine heart, Who shall

ascend into heaven? (That is, to bring Christ down from above;) or, Who shall descend into the deep? (That is, to bring up Christ again from the dead.) But what saith it? The word is nigh thee, even in thy mouth and in thy heart." And Christ says of his second coming: "Neither shall they say, Lo here! Or lo there! For behold the Kingdom of God is within you."

As to means and appliances, we offer the following recommendations:

1. If your circumstances permit, devote the day, and especially the evening of the 20th to spiritual attention. Make it a matter of as direct and earnest effort to meet Christ and his church in your hearts as you would make to go to an interesting convention at Brooklyn or Oneida.

2. Read again the article on "Concentric and Extrinsic Vision"* in our 11th number; also "Condensation of Life"** and "Our Relations to the Primitive Church"† in *The Berean*.

3. Seek to realize the presence not only of Christ but of the angels and the general assembly and church of the first-born. See Heb. 12th.

4. Think specifically of all believers that you know in this world or in Hades, "making mention of them," as Paul says, "in your prayers." Of course we shall not forget Mrs. Cragin in this meeting of three worlds. /244/

5. Endeavor to enter into not only the pleasure but the business of the Convention, which will certainly be to take measures for the fulfillment of the two celebrated petitions of Christ: the petition for the unity of all believers, and the petition that the will of God may be done on earth as it is in heaven.

6. Do not forget the suggestion about business in our last paper.

7. Note your exercises and observable spiritual events of the occasion, and send us reports of whatever may be generally interesting.

Coup D'Etat:
Home-Talk by Noyes
February 28, 1852

It is not five years since we adopted the principles of our *First Annual Report*. We have now come to a time when the public is taking notice of us. The Oneida Association has been indicted, and it is quite possible that the agitation which *The New York Observer* has stirred up may compel the authorities at Utica to prosecute the indictment. Now in view of the fact that we have, on the one hand, asserted our liberty of conscience toward God, and, on the oth-

---

* *The Circular*, O.S. [Old Series], 1:44. [G.W.N.]
** *The Berean*, p. 487. [G.W.N.]
† *The Berean*, p. 497. [G.W.N.]

er, are now faced by public opinion distinctly expressed toward us in the newspapers, I am led to inquire whether we cannot meet the good treatment we have thus far received in the State of New York with concessions on our part in the general desire for peace. The principle that governed the Primitive Church in regard to Jewish ordinances and marriage was a principle of accommodation. They could take two or three courses /245/ according to the necessity of the case. That principle is ours. We are not fighting for this or that form of society. We are seeking liberty to serve God, and we have insisted that we will not be the slaves of form. On these grounds I would propose to the Association for discussion the question of whether it might not be comely and in harmony with the position in which we find ourselves to adopt for the Lord's sake and for peace the fashion of this world in respect to marriage.

If an entire exposure of our manner of life were made, the fact would be shown that there has been far less freedom in sexual intercourse among us than there is in ordinary society. The taking away of restrictions has brought into the field principles and feelings that have operated as restraints, and we have all been more Shakers than Bacchanalians. Still it is true that we have abandoned the fashion of the world, and there has been among us what the world would call transgression.

Let us understand just what the *coup d'etat* is. In the first place, it does not dissolve our Association, for that is lawful. Secondly, it does not forbid spiritual circulation of love and the freedom of speech that we now have. Thirdly, it does not prescribe any permanent course. We do not promise what we will do hereafter, except that our course shall be governed by the same principle as hitherto, our allegiance to God first of all. If people wish to have us set a time, I should say it is not at all likely we shall resume our operations until public opinion allows it. As long as the world is as friendly to us as it has been, we shall recognize our solidarity with it. /246/

I am not going to allow this *coup d'etat* to come upon me as a law and snare. If it does in any case, we must find out the will of God about it. I take this as spiritual advice from Christ, and believe that whatever he wishes to have done he will enable us to do easily.

This move will be a puzzle to the Devil. He has got his officers out after Perfectionists as it is described in the newspapers, and he will have to return on his writ, *"non est inventus."*

Two Kinds of Adultery:
Home-Talk by Noyes
   March 1, 1852

   It will be well for the Association to prepare for difficulty with the world similar to what they had last fall. It will not hurt them to slacken business in some degree and study how to face the newspaper excitement throughout the country.

   By way of indicating the offensive measures to be taken, I will refer the Association to my previous advice, that they keep themselves well-aired and in rapport with the world around, that they take every opportunity to blow peace in the face of opposers, that they exercise lion-like boldness and a faith in God that expects miraculous changes.

   The source of all this wrath and misrepresentation is the nervous, irritable feeling which folks have about adultery, a feeling that is utterly at variance with Christ's estimate of this sin. Christ defined adultery, and very rigidly too. He said: "Whosoever looketh on a woman to lust after her hath committed adultery with her already in his heart." When the /247/ Jews came to him asking his advice, he said: "Whosoever shall put away his wife saving for the cause of fornication causeth her to commit adultery; and whoever shall marry her that is divorced committeth adultery." He was more rigorous than even the scribes and Pharisees so far as the extent of transgression was concerned. But what was his estimate of the magnitude of this crime? Sometimes a man commits an offense, the case goes to law, the jury brings in a verdict of guilty, and the judge with solemn countenance awards damages of one cent. That is the way Christ treated adultery. Not one word of Christ's against adultery except by implication can be found in the four gospels. When a women "taken in the very act" was brought before him, he made her accusers' consciences the jury, and then, as Judge, brought in one cent damages: "Go thy way and sin no more." His favorite women were two that had been harlots; and he held up with commendation the prodigal son, who spent his substance in riotous living among harlots.

   Here we have the gnat that public opinion makes a monstrous camel. Now let us see if we can find the camel that the world swallowed so easily. "He that believeth not shall be damned." Unbelief is worldliness. That is evidently the sin Christ hated above all others.

   We must insist upon it that there are two kinds of adultery, one referring to the human relation, and the other to the divine. The world charges us with the lower adultery. We have principles that clear our conscience, and we therefore deny that we are guilty. But waiving that advantage we are willing to stand trial if Christ's estimate of the crime is accepted. We shall then /248/ charge them with the higher adultery, and bring them to trial before the bar of Christ.

Manifesto of the Oneida Association
The Circular, Old Series, 1:66
   March 7, 1852

In view of the fact that sexual liberties of the Association are looked upon with jealousy and offense by surrounding society, it may be understood henceforth that the Oneida Association and all Associations connected with it have receded from the practical assertion of their views, and formally resumed the marriage morality of the world.

> The G. W. Noyes manuscript only presents the preceding single-sentence compression of the substance of the revealing manifesto of the association, which is reproduced below in its entirety, including original punctuation, italics, and capitalization. [L.F.]

The Past, Present, and Future

The Concentric Convention on the 20th ult., seems to have been well-attended, and to have produced everywhere, a feeling of increased intimacy with the universal body of Christ. The 20th of February is the anniversary of our movement—the commencement of the spiritual year; when we are accustomed to make up our Annual Report—get a new observation, and take a fresh departure. The present year especially, many things seemed to point to that period as forming an important crisis—and hence the idea of a 'Concentric Convention,' which should bring together in spiritual counsel all who are interested in the kingdom of heaven in the three worlds. The Community took occasion to submit their interests and affairs to the interior church for criticism and advice. The result is a somewhat interesting change of position, to which we would now call the attention of our friends, and whomsoever else it may concern.

THE PAST

Our position as a Community in regard to marriage and the relations of the sexes, has always been more or less an offense to the world, and has been much aggravated recently, by the gross misrepresentation of sectarian opponents. But it should be observed on the other side that we have been from the beginning perfectly frank in the avowal of our principles, and as we believe not illegal in our practices—at least according to the laws of this State.—At the outset of our movement at Oneida, we placed a copy of the First Annual Report, containing a full disclosure of our Social Theory, in the hands of the Governor of the State, and various high functionaries, including the distinguished Representative of our district in the national Congress. No objection was made in any quarter to our movement, and the latter gentlemen, we understood, expressed the opinion that we had a right to proceed on our new social basis, without interference. By openly publishing our platform in three successive Annual Reports, and by special advertisement of the highest general and local authorities, we satisfied in equity, if not in form, our obligations to the State. This was clearly evinced by the fact that for four years we lived undisturbed. It strikes us as rather ridiculous for the New York Observer, at this late day, to sound the alarm of discovery, and call on the legislature to put down Perfectionism as a new found heresy!

As our course has not been seditious, neither has it been unchaste; and those who are fond of imputing indecency to us, simply by inference from our free principles, only show that they have no confidence in their own virtue, except as it is secured by law. 'Mormonism,' 'Mahometanism,' 'heathenism,' are epithets easily applied by surmisers of corruption; but they are all false as applied to us. A legal scrutiny of the household habits of the Oneida Community during any period of its history, would show, not a licentious spirit, but the opposite of licentiousness. It would disclose less careless familiarity of the sexes—less approach to any thing like 'baccanalian' revelry—vastly less unregulated speech and conduct than is found in an equal circle of what is called good society in the world. That we disclaimed the cast-iron rules and modes, by which selfishness regulates the relations of the sexes, is true; but with these conditions we affirm, that there was never in that Association, one tenth part of the special commerce that exists between an equal number of married persons in ordinary life. This statement can be substantiated by the oath of the Community, as our general modest behavior may be verified by the testimony of disinterested persons who have often visited their friends there.

And if this is not enough, let the proof of our morality be found in the broad fact of the general health of the Association. No death of an adult member has ever occurred at Oneida, and not a doctor has been employed; many who joined us sick have become well; and the special woes of women in connection with children, have been nearly extinguished. The increase of population by birth, in our forty families, for the last four years, has been considerably less than the progeny of Queen Victoria alone. So much for the outcry of 'licentiousness and brutality.'

THE PRESENT

Still, with all this ground of vindication in reason and conscience, our liberty on this subject is looked upon with jealousy and offense by surrounding society. And in view of the fact, we have decided to forego it, and withdraw from the position that we have held. *It may be understood henceforth that the Oneida Association, and all Associations connected with it, have receded from the practical assertion of their views, and formally resumed the marriage morality of the world, submitting themselves to all the ordinances and restrictions of society and law on this subject.* This definite concession made in good faith, we trust will be satisfactory, and give peace. It may be observed that the late disturbance of the public mind, has not been occasioned by action of the authorities, but is merely the work of a newspaper mob. The State, and all its agents, have treated us with the most considerate generosity through the whole course of our residence at Oneida; and we think we have gained hearty toleration from those best acquainted with us—the most intelligent and respectful of our neighbors. We should regret to have this cordiality disturbed, or to have the magistrates seem compelled by a newspaper gust (which sometimes blows away common charity for the time being) to interfere unpleasantly with our affairs. We prefer to reciprocate the courtesy we have received, by withdrawing the occasion of difficulty. As our neighbors have tolerated us in our way of living, we will now adopt theirs, on the only point that could create offense, and wait for the change of public feeling, which is gradually extending the 'area of freedom' and the reign of truth.

Those friends who inquire the spiritual meaning of this movement, will find in the twofold obligation of Paul's morality; which requires, in the first place, entire emancipation from human judgment in respect to meats and drinks and holy ordinances, and, in the second place, requires considerate abstinence from offense. By our four years' experience—wrestling, not with flesh and blood, but with the powers of law and selfishness, within and without, we have gained the first point; and now we can turn to the fulfilment of the second. Our experience has been carried through successfully, both subjectively, as relates to our own education, and objectively, as developing the principles of heavenly society. The main thing is gained; and we have graduated in a sufficient state of spiritual freedom, so that we can now afford to accommodate ourselves to others and seek the salvation of all. Having learned, at all hazards to please God, we will now endeavor to preserve a good conscience toward men. With Paul, 'we are persuaded that nothing is unclean of itself;' but, on the other hand, we agree with him, that 'if meat make our brother to offend, we will eat no meat.' Both these principles are necessary to make a spiritual freeman; and having learned the first, we will freely practice the last. WE ARE NOT ATTACHED TO FORMS; and in no way could we express this victory so well as by our present movement. To substitute for the fashions of the world, cast-iron fashions of our own, would be no gain—To be able to conform to *any* circumstances, and *any* form of institutions, and still preserve spiritual freedom, is Paul's standard, and what we now claim.

THE FUTURE

We land from our long voyage of exploration, improved and refreshed, with large stores of various experience, which we shall be glad to distribute for the general benefit, as they are called for. *That* voyage, with its gales and icebergs and elemental perils is done—passed into history; and we emerge now under new circumstances, ready for new enterprises. Our present transition is like that of the insect passing from its chrysalis state revived by experience, and shedding its envelopment. The forms that we leave behind are mere cast-off *exuvia* which the New York Observer may tear to pieces at its leisure. We shall be found elsewhere.

The Community organization will remain, bound together more firmly than ever by the ties of a common faith and imperishable regard. The Community as a corporate institution is perfectly legal, and in fact popular, where it is best known. We expect now to have our hands loosened for vigorous movements in business and improvement of all kinds, *looking toward the central object of a Free Press.* And among the objects that now fill the future of our attention, is a movement towards the ABOLITION OF DEATH. This will evidently demand a separate and special campaign; 'it is the last enemy that shall be destroyed.' We conceive that what is past has been a necessary preliminary engagement; spiritual emancipation from human laws and institutions must be won before any successful attack can be made on the King of Terrors. Our past experience has gained us this spiritual freedom; and now, while we accept any form that is most convenient, for the Lord's sake, we will address ourselves to the final conquest of Satanic power.

These topics will be more fully presented in our forthcoming Annual Report, together with the general results of our four years' experience.

Oneida Journal

March 7, 1852.—Last night a letter came from Mr. Cragin criticising the Association for not carrying out the "new move" promptly. Today may be said to be the first day the new move has taken effect.

The Present Crisis
Family Talk at Brooklyn
March 24, 1852

Several mentioned the fact that since the late movement there has been in certain quarters a peculiar attraction between husbands and wives.

Noyes:—I mean to win our liberty from the world to go on in our former freedom, but for the present I am willing to show the world and myself, that I am not bound by custom. I do not /249/ imagine we shall be defrauded in the long run, but quite the contrary. I have perfect confidence that the Primitive Church are superintending our movements and understand every want; and it is my wish to give them the lead. I am waiting with curiosity and deep interest for a new movement to the Concentric Convention. The wheels have been stopped, and we are now waiting for a more splendid advance into liberty than we have ever had. My idea has been to keep things in order and not make any great changes of any kind till we get a program from the Primitive Church. If there are any cases in the Association such as Paul describes, not having power over their own will, they should receive proper attention.

I do not think the Association at Oneida or at Putney have had any true idea of the danger they have been in, what a tremendous sea was rolling when this move was made. We were here in the very heart of it and felt the whole mass of public opinion. The whole State would have been down upon us before this time if we had not made that move. It was as perilous a time as it was when we left Putney. I think the Association, after having gained a local victory, to go about their business, enjoying themselves and neglecting their solidarity with the rest of mankind.* It is a good thing to get peace and quietness, even if it is merely local, but we must have a general victory before we can be at ease.

Mr. Miller told us of his visit to the Oneida bank with Mr. Burnham. Mr. Noyes, Mr. Cragin, and others said they were heartily glad matters had come to such a crisis; perhaps there was too much of a tendency to lean on the banks.

Mrs. Miller:—Some of the husbands and wives at Oneida are in perplexity; do not feel very free with each other, and /250/ hardly know what to do.

Noyes:—I should think those who have been through our school ought to have gained their freedom by this time, so that they could accommodate themselves to any circumstances. They will have to get that freedom sometime.

---

* Part of the sentence apparently is missing. [L.F.]

Mrs. Miller:—Some wanted me to find out what the fashion was here.

Noyes:—That is the very thing we want to break up. We want to free our-selves from fashion. Each one must follow inspiration and good sense.

G. W. Noyes: It seems to me that what the Association needs is to start the ascending fellowship.

Noyes:—That has been the effect of the crisis upon me. I was satisfied that the move when made was as necessary for our internal good as for the danger from without. We put on the brakes at exactly the right time. The only possi-ble way to get out of difficulty is to walk in the spirit. It does not make so much difference what people do if they keep free from doubts. "He that doubteth is damned if he eat." Whatever you do, do it decisively, with a will, not in a half-way, doubting manner, in which passion pricks you on, and con-science holds you back.

I have never had such a sense of the Primitive Church as I have since the 20th of February. We came into their presence at that time. There was a meet-ing of the three worlds that will never be broken up. It was as great a time to me as when we proclaimed that the Kingdom of God had come. /251/

Mrs. Miller:—Some at Oneida stumbled at the expression in one of the late Table Talks, that Mr. Noyes would "drink, no more of the fruit of the vine till he drank it anew with Mrs. Cragin."

Noyes:—I never put myself under law in any such way. The most I ever said was to apply that saying to free love. In that sense I might still say the same.

I do not feel like deserting my post, though it sometimes seems a very difficult one. I fully believe that the Primitive Church will inspire me with vig-or to throw off all unnecessary burdens and demand that others bear burdens as well as I.

George Cragin:—I think the time has come for a change in the Association in relation to sustaining the center. Oneida learned that just as soon as they started an ambition to sustain our press in temporal things, they were blessed in their business. I do not see why they should not take the same view in re-gard to assisting the center spiritually, instead of calling upon the center for spiritual strength to sustain them. Mr. Noyes stands as the center point to be shot at from all quarters. The Associations should not only walk in the spirit themselves, but give actual life and strength to the center by staying up the hands of Mr. Noyes and inspiring those that write for the paper.

Mr. Noyes:—I like Mr. Cragin's remarks very much. So long as we are deep in the newspaper enterprise and are in the way of enlargement, I should be somewhat released from carrying the spiritual interests of the Associations, and the Associations should be a support and strength to me in the work. /252/

Items by Harriet A. Noyes
Brooklyn, March 25, 1852

In this family I don't know as there has been any (or if so, very little) of the marriage spirit aroused by the change of position. I did not feel like expecting any more attention from Mr. Noyes than formerly. We certainly have left the marriage spirit behind, and I hope we shall never return to it. I expect to be directed by the Primitive Church in all my fellowships.

The Abolition of Death
The Circular, Old Series, 1:82
April 4, 1852

The following notice from the New York Daily Express, will be amusing to our readers. . . .
"We trust our friends up in Oneida will meet with all manner of success, in the new scheme of Abolitions they have chalked out—the Abolition of Death! . . . As it is likely to be an arduous job, the sooner it is undertaken the better. . . ."
Strange and funny as it may seem to him,* we propose to advance from marriage reform, to the attack of another venerable institution of society— death. If this is madness, the Editor of the Express will find on inspection that there is 'method' in it. [Newspaper excerpt for April 4, 1852, added by L.F.]

The Rival of Christ
The Circular, Old Series, 1:82
April 4, 1852

We have good evidence that Judas Iscariot was not merely an unprincipled traitor, but that he was a positive *rival* of Christ. . . .
The antagonism between Christ and Judas was particularly on the point of *covetousness.*— . . . no other characteristic is mentioned of him. . . . His anger was excited because Christ did not chide the profuseness of the woman who broke the alabaster box of precious ointment, and poured it on the head of her Savior, filling the house with its odor. He went out immediately after, and gratified at once his malice and his cupidity, by selling Christ to the Pharisees for thirty pieces of silver. . . .
We see then in Christ and Judas, the rivalry of faith and covetousness—of

---

* The editor of the *New York Daily Express*. [L.F.]

the love of God and the love of the world. . . . . Christ knew his betrayer; and Judas must have chafed constantly with Christ's course, and smothered a great deal of jealousy and torment. The drama of their warfare ended in a duel, so far as life was concerned. Judas fired, and Christ received his shot; but Judas fell even before his own ball was spent. [Newspaper excerpt for April 4, 1852, added by L.F.]

The Character of Mary
The Circular, Old Series, 1:87
April 11, 1852

The contrast suggested in a late article of the Circular, between Judas, and the woman whose generous oblation provoked his resentment, is very interesting. . . . What was her sin, compared with his? His was the idolatry of covetousness. Hers (it is supposed) was the idolatry of affection. She had been a false worshiper; but how much the shrine to which she bowed was better than that of mammon. She worshiped, at least, the image of God. He worshiped 'filthy lucre.' . . .

It is apparent that Mary had little worldly prudence. Her love exceeded her discretion. She was found at Jesus' feet, absorbed in his discoursing, while her sister cumbered herself with much serving. Mary's abstraction at this time shows how abandoned she was to the attractions of her heart—a dangerous susceptibility in the case of misplaced affection, but her glory as a follower of Christ. This led her, at the loss of her dignity, into that wonderful expression of gratitude and love, which Christ promised should be recorded of her as a memorial of praise to all generations. . . .

But Judas was indignant at the scene—the sentiment was too refined for him to appreciate. He saw no value in her tribute of affection. It was, to his gross calculation, a waste. Thirty pieces of silver bought all the loyalty and nobleness he had. [Newspaper excerpt for April 11, 1852, added by L.F.]

Things Proved
The Circular, Old Series, 1:110
May 23, 1852

The Oneida Community has in a certain sense, discharged its mission, and may be looked upon as in the past. By its change of position last winter, it surrendered the distinctive and peculiar characteristic which constituted its individuality, and fell back within the lines of worldly toleration, and under the forms of selfish law. Of course, it is no longer, as to outward force and feature, the original Oneida Association. Let us treat of that as in the past; and without broaching the question of whether its principles will again be asserted in the world, let us inquire what the demonstrated results of that movement were, when it did exist. [Newspaper excerpt for May 23, 1852, added by L.F.]

A New Observation:
Home-Talk by Noyes
  May 31, 1852

Some inquiries have come from Oneida and intimations have been given that there was a good deal of circulation of social life which would naturally demand expression. That, I suppose, would be a matter of course, and it is not to be deplored at all. I shall do the very best I can to help all to walk in the spirit.

The change of course, which we took on the advice of the "Concentric Convention," February 20th, was not taken as a moral obligation but as a matter of expediency with reference to public sentiment. That pledge we may call a general debt of honor to the public, and we have faithfully discharged it on our part. But that offer of peace implied a response on the part of the public. What response did we get? Mr. Miller went to District Attorney Garvin and called his attention to that document. "That is nothing," said he. "It is worse than the original offense." He would not accept it, and there has been more stir and trouble about the Association than there was before. The *New York Observer* said: "We do not believe they will keep it; we have no confidence in /253/ them; credat Judaeus." Joshua Leavett said: "That don't help the matter any." We hear also that the minister at Wallingford takes the same ground. The compact therefore is not consummated, and we are discharged from all obligations under it. I feel myself perfectly free to take another course without asking leave. The public we have tried to pacify is not a public that will talk reasonably with us. They have no sort of respect for us. The most conciliatory and respectful thing we could possibly do they repulsed with sneers. I do not feel under any obligations to notify that public of my future intentions, or shape my course with reference to their opinions. They stand wholly as our enemies, and I do not feel bound to put weapons into their hands. On the contrary, I feel at liberty to deal wisely with them, and outwit them if I can in an honorable way. There is another part of the public that have been reconciled and feel friendly toward us, but if we examine thoroughly we shall find that they would not be displeased with us if we should go on with our former freedom.

While I say all this, I do not say it is expedient for the people at Oneida to return to their former fashions. I can do no better than to refer them to the remarks I made a few evenings past on the necessity of assuming individual responsibility. It seems to me that I and the counselors of the Association should not be called upon to dictate or give specific advice in this matter. It should be referred throughout to individual responsibility. Every individual must have faith for himself. /254/

John R. Miller to Noyes
   Oneida, July 8, 1852

I thought I would let you know how we stand on the social question. With all the freedom we have enjoyed for the past few weeks I do not know of a single transgression of the law in this Association. I think no one has felt under law, but still something has prevented any move in that direction.

   In an article entitled "The Message" in *The Circular* on August 1, George Cragin reaffirmed his complete commitment to Christ (and by implication to John Humphrey Noyes as the agent of Christ) as "the only channel through which we can reach God." In the following issue on August 4, an article by John Humphrey Noyes's wife Harriet discussed the "Character of Peter," noting that although Peter's denial of Christ might appear culpable, Peter had nevertheless come back to become Christ's devoted follower and the rock upon which he built his church. In the August 29 issue of *The Circular,* a series of articles with titles such as "'The Light Shineth in the Darkness,'" "The Resurrection King," and "The Heart Satisfied" provides the backdrop for "The Theocratic Platform" (printed in full in chapter 29), in which the resumption of complex marriage is joyfully announced to the world. [L.F.]

Advice from the Concentric Convention:
Home-Talk by Noyes
   October 22, 1852

We are in a universal crisis. There are thunders and lightnings between the Congregationalists and the Presbyterians. To-night we hear of the death of Daniel Webster. This month is the time appointed for the uprising of Europe. It would not be surprising to hear that Kossuth has set his train on fire. Louis Napoleon may make his *coup d'etat.* Our year's work advocating the sovereignty of Jesus Christ is coming to a close.
   We now feel that God is advising us to enter upon a new series of criti-

cisms on a larger scale, the criticisms of Associations. This idea came to us by inspiration very much as the call for Concentric Convention did. We offer ourselves as the representatives of the Kingdom of Heaven in this visible sphere, and invite the criticism of the church above. We shall need the criticism and advice of that church in the present crisis.

I have an impression that a criticism is needed among us as much as last spring. Our social theory is not working altogether right in some quarters. The throwing out of Mr. Lord indicates that there is a dangerous element at Putney. Then there is friction between Albert and John Kinsley in the Northern /255/ Vermont Association. And I have felt that there was need of putting on brakes at Newark. Also there are signs of looseness at Drummondville. I do not feel about Oneida as I did last spring, but among the new Associations there is grating in the machinery. I would recommend for the present crisis while we are offering ourselves for criticism, that we withdraw from horizontal fellowships, and wait for a new impulse from the Primitive Church.

We did not stop the train last spring from fear of the world. We had passed through the worst of the hurricane, and we took our course freely under a suggestion from the "Concentric Convention." But after a while the original impulse was partially obscured. We came to feel that the restriction was imposed by man. Thus our purpose was vitiated. Our instincts then were throw off the yoke and insist upon our freedom.

Dr. Newberry wanted to know why we did not put our principles "right straight through." But the truth is, we have never taken any position that obliges us to practice our social theory. Our only plan is to obey orders—learn to walk in the spirit.

We are indeed surrounded by dangers. But if we will let the Lord have his way with us, he will school us through these crooked turns in safety. This little "Modern Times" gale* shows that we must be ready to reduce sail and shift anchor at a moment's warning. Suppose, for instance, that there should be a general commotion about the Modern Times Association and its iniquities, and a tremendous accusation should be launched against us for holding radical social theories. Suppose now at the right moment we hold up and live on ordinary principles. "All correct with us!"

The wisdom that Paul had in accommodating himself to circumstances while still keeping his honesty is one of the highest [end of sentence missing]. /256/

It is a good time for us to fast and pray for a season—not long enough to let the Devil tempt us for our incontinency. I have no doubt that the "Concen-

* Modern Times was a highly individualistic community founded in 1851 on Long Island. [L.F]

tric Convention" have in view to give us a new start in edification after we finish this volume of the paper; perhaps not a daily paper quite yet, but something in that direction.

In looking upward to God we may extend the hand of fellowship to the widow and desolate in the world, and to those in the Association who are more or less out of the circle of free love. Remember them that are in bonds as bound with them, those that are bound by old age or by the fashions of the world. There are precious spirits, plenty of them, that cannot enjoy our freedom.

Mr. Worden's proposition to invite Mr. Lord back leads to some general reflections. We must never forget that our organization is voluntary and spiritual. We are bound together not by laws, constitutions, agreements, or circumstances, but by attraction. Our rule should be to make it difficult for folks to get in, and easy for them to get out. . . . I shall be glad to see the time when a man can go out without any ill will on either side. . . . As to Northern Vermont, I do not want to have our folks stand there against the wishes of Mr. John Kinsley and wife. They can go back to Oneida. I do not feel any anxiety to establish a station in Cambridge. Every Association we have can fall back now on Oneida. /257/

Close of the Volume
    October 31, 1852

We have been able, as was proposed, to issue a weekly paper, free to all, and devoted to the sovereignty of Jesus Christ. We have had our daily bread not as hirelings and by dint of anxious care, but as the children of Providence and by the gift of warm-hearted friends. With a large family we have frequently come to the end of our resources, where there was nothing in hand for our next day's dinner or to buy the paper for our next week's printing. But in these circumstances we have been kept from any unpleasant concern, and at the right time remittances have been received which met all our wants. To meet the expenses of the volume, we have received in subscriptions and donations from persons outside the Community about $1000. /258/

27

Hostilities Renewed
April 1 to July 6, 1852*

Article in the Brattleboro Semi-Weekly Eagle
 April 1, 1852
  Be Sure the Fox Is Dead

 Messrs. Editors:—

 The article published in the Eagle of the 18th ult. on the "Progress of Perfectionism" reminded me of a little incident which once occurred, in which a
shrewd old Fox acted a somewhat prominent part. The story about Reynard
runs thus: One John Skillins, a downeaster, was a noted fox-hunter, and usually
had his traps out for those mischievous animals so annoying to farm-houses.
At one time an old Fox came to his trap, ate off the bate, and went away. John
went out to his trap, looked and said (for he was always talking to himself):
"What! Does that Fox think to outwit John Skillins?" So he fixed the bed, and
set the trap the other side up, to outwit the Fox. But it was one of the cunning
old Foxes, and he managed to get off the bait, spoil the bed, and get off again
without being caught. John went to his trap and looked astonished. But he
was not to be outwitted by a Fox: he would show them that he knew more
than the whole tribe of Foxes. So he borrowed another trap, and set two, so
that while the Fox was in one he got his hind leg in the other. When John
came to his trap, he said: "Good morning, Mr. Fox. Did I not tell you that it
was no use to attempt to outwit John Skillins?" He then took up a pitch knot
and whaled him on the head till the Fox lay down and appeared quite dead.
He then turned to fix his traps, but as he happened to look around he saw the
Fox's tail just going out of sight among the bushes! /259/

 The present posture of affairs among the Oneida (formerly Putney) Perfectionists indicates the necessity of giving heed to the caution standing at the
head of this article. If the Fox is really dead, it is presumed the public will be
perfectly satisfied, and will apprehend no further danger from his carnivorous

---

* The original title's dates read "April 1 to September 14, 1852." [L.F.]

propensities, and suffer no more inroads upon their farm-houses. But that is the question to be settled. *Is he dead?*

Noyes to John R. Miller
Brooklyn, April 4, 1852

The story of John Skillins, which I suppose you have seen in the Eagle, is after all an unfortunate one for the Doctor. John had not skill enough to catch the Fox. If we beat the trappers at Putney as handsomely as Reynard beat John, we shall do well enough. And I think we shall, for Christ beat the Jews in this very way. They "whaled" him till they thought he was dead, but in three days they caught a glimpse of him through the report of their sentinels just as he was "disappearing in the bushes," and fifty days afterward he was making havoc in their farm-yards worse than ever.

Oneida Journal

April 18, 1852.—Last evening Lucius Hubbard, constable, called here with a summons for Messrs. Noyes, Cragin, Burt, and the two Seymours to appear at Oneida Castle before Esquire Dodge within twenty days. Messrs. Burt and Burnham went immediately to see Dodge, and found that the Hubbards were attempting to prove seduction in the case of Tryphena. They told Mr. Dodge the story of our settlement with the Hubbards last fall, and he said, if they told the same story, he would have nothing more to do with it. /260/ In this move the Hubbards, with no provocation, have broken their voluntary pledge to keep the peace. The news was sent to Brooklyn and Putney as soon as it could be got ready.

Henry W. Burnham to Noyes:—Mr. Burt saw Dexter alone. Asked him what new provocation there was to cause this fresh prosecution. Dexter replied that the statement in *The Circular,* "Past, Present and Future," that we had published our social principles at the beginning of our career at Oneida was not true, and that it had offended his father.

Noyes to Henry W. Burnham
April 19, 1852

In your report of the new prosecution, I see that the offense which we have given Mr. Hubbard lies in the statement made by George in the article "Past, Present and Future" that we were "perfectly frank from the beginning in the avowal of our social theory." I have thought myself that this statement in some of its particulars, though honest and substantially true, is liable to misconstruction. For instance, that article says that we placed copies of our Report in the hands of the Governor and other authorities "at the outset of our movement." This language, strictly construed, is not correct, as we did not publish our first Report till the end of the first year. But the word outset is popularly used in a liberal sense. The first year of a four years course may properly be called the outset of that course, just as we speak of the fore part of the week, meaning Sunday or Monday or even Tuesday. We published our Report as soon as we were fairly organized and in motion and had material for report. /261/

It should be observed that George had his eye on our relations to the State, and not on our relations to our immediate neighbors, in the paragraph complained of. His argument is: "The State authorities have had notice of our principles for three years, and it is late in the day [for] the *New York Observer* to call on the Legislature to put us down." We simply say that we have dealt fairly with the State authorities, which is certainly true. If Mr. Hubbard has private grounds of complaint against us for our want of frankness to him as an individual, this is a separate affair.

On this point, I will give my views as candidly as I can. Mr. Hubbard undoubtedly reasons that, because he was not aware of our views at the outset, therefore we must have concealed them. We may with equal justice reason that, because we certainly disclosed our views, therefore he must have been aware of them. But this is not fair reasoning either way. I may disclose a thing which my neighbor does not take notice of. His ignorance cannot convict me of concealment.

The facts are these: At the very outset, during the first days of my residence at Oneida, our social theory was the subject of open and violent discussion between myself, Burt, and others, on the one side, and all the leading Perfectionists who deserted us, on the other. Cook, Foot, Corwin went abroad from those discussions with all necessary information and plenty of excitement against us. We had a right to assume that they would apprise the community of our position, and we believe they did quite extensively.

In the course of a month or six weeks after my arrival at /262/ Oneida, I wrote the entire *Bible Argument* at Mr. Burt's house. While I was writing it, the sheets lay openly on the table in the parlor. Mrs. Burt and Tryphena, who were then not only outsiders but decided enemies, read this Argument of their own accord. We did not entice them to do so, nor did we hinder them. The prospect was that they would report us to the neighborhood, especially to Mr. Hubbard's family, and we took no measures to prevent it. Whether and how far they did report our position, I know not to this day. We did not feel bound to thrust our peculiar views upon our neighbors individually, but we took no pains to conceal them.

Information about our principles and practices was sent in various ways from Putney and blazed abroad at the Depot and the Castle. A legal summons charging me with our peculiar offenses was served on me by the postmaster of the Depot within a few weeks after my arrival, and he was unfriendly enough to us to be a good servant of the Putney hostility.

The Bible Argument, when it was finished, was read openly in our meeting at the shoemakers' shop. Mr. Stone of the Depot was present.

So much for our side of the story. Yet it is true that we never read that Argument or communicated its sentiments individually to Mr. Hubbard at that early period. And it is also true that he never asked us to do so, or examined us on those sentiments. After Tryphena became friendly to us, we naturally left it with her to decide for herself how far she should carry discussion with her father and friends. When Mr. Hubbard at last demanded information, we gave it without reserve.

In view of these facts, I cannot see but that our dealings with /263/ individuals as well as with the State have been honorable.

Whipple Jenkins to S. B. Garvin
Vernon, April 24, 1852

S. B. Garvin, Esq.,
Dear Sir:—
The bearers, Messrs. Miller and Burt, have called on me for a letter to you stating what was done in the matter about which I had some talk with you against the members of the Oneida Community.

The suit for a divorce of Mr. and Mrs. Seymour and the arrangement for her support then in contemplation were carried through and carried out by the Community in perfect good faith, and it was my understanding that this would settle the indictment against Seymour for assault and battery, and as to the other indictments, I do not remember that anything was said, though I've no doubt they understood that these were also to be abandoned.

Yours truly,
J. Whipple Jenkins

John R. Miller to Noyes
    Oneida Postoffice, 3 1/2 o'clock
        April 24, 1852

Dear Bro. Noyes:—

I arrived at Oneida at 1 o'clock this morning. After talking with our folks, I called on Mr. Hubbard. Mr. Burnham will give you an account of the interview. As soon as possible after dinner, Mr. Burt and I went to Vernon and called on Mr. Whipple Jenkins. He wrote a letter to Mr. Garvin giving his understanding of the settlement with the Hubbards, and Mr. Burt and I came /264/ from Vernon here for the purpose of taking the express train for Utica at 4. I will send you a copy of Mr. Jenkins' letter by the next mail. His memory was not quite so good as I wished, though on the whole it was tolerably satisfactory. I don't feel that we shall have much difficulty. My hands are so cold that I can't write decently.

Yours in haste,
J. R. Miller

John R. Miller to Noyes
    Utica, 6 o'clock P.M.
        April 24, 1852

Dear Bro. Noyes:—

We have had an interview with Mr. Garvin, and I am perfectly surprised to find how his feelings toward us have changed since I saw him last. He now says that he can only settle the case of the assault and battery, and he shall prosecute the other indictments if directed to by the Court. I told him that I supposed the Court would do as he said, and as he understood the whole settlement I had no doubt he would be willing to advise the Court to drop it. He said he should say nothing about it; as he had said, he would do nothing more about it; he should keep his word. He said he did not think we began to understand the feeling there was against us by all respectable people through the Country. He said he regarded us as a nuisance. I replied, "I don't suppose you will allow your personal feelings to come in when doing your duty as a public officer." He said he should somewhat. I asked him if he received the 17th No. of *The Circular.* He said he did, and that he considered that as bad as the original offense. He advised us to see Judge Root and make /265/ our peace with him. He promised, on leaving, to give us next week to arrange it before summoning any witnesses. We are now waiting at Judge Root's office to see what he is disposed to do, though I have no expectation that he will show any mercy, unless the powers above compel him to.

We have concluded to go home and wait no longer today for Judge Root, as the cars leave in fifteen minutes.

Yours in haste,
J. R. Miller

John R. Miller to Noyes
Oneida, April 25, 1852

Dear Bro. Noyes:—

Mr. Burnham and I called at Oneida Valley Bank yesterday and paid our note of $275 due May 3rd, which was the last note against us here. We are thankful to God that we are so well prepared for the coming storm. There has been no time since our commencement at Oneida when we were not in debt, but now we are free. If the State deals with us as justly and honorably as we have with them, we shall be able to meet all their demands without difficulty.

Enclosed you will find Mr. Jenkins' letter to Mr. Garvin. I was not satisfied with it nor with his spirit when I was there; and when I got to Utica, I found that it was no better than white paper. I have no doubt there is a perfect understanding between him and Mr. Garvin, and that he would be glad to see us broken up.

Mr. Garvin gave us to understand that others had complained besides Hubbard, but would not tell who. /266/

This may yet all blow away like smoke and end as that affair with Jones did last fall when he came to Brooklyn, but I feel that it is important to give you all the facts as they appear.

With much love to all the family,

I am your brother,
J. R. Miller

John R. Miller to Noyes
Oneida, April 26, 1852

Dear Bro. Noyes:—

On our way home I stopped at Hubbard's as I had agreed, to get his terms of settlement. Dexter said that he and his father and Lucius talked it over yesterday. His father refused to make any terms. He was determined to have it go to trial, and thought he could get a large sum. I asked him how much the old man thought he could get. He said, $5000. Dexter did not think he would get so much. He said he was anxious to have it settled, but has concluded there was no use, for his father was determined to break us up. I told him then that I had nothing more to say, and got up to leave. He called me back and wanted to know what I was willing to pay. I told him that I was not willing to pay anything, that we had done them no wrong. I concluded from the whole talk that they were quite anxious to have it settled, and only wanted to get all the money they could out of us. My opinion is that we had better let the matter rest till after the other indictments are disposed of. If they should be decided in our favor, it will greatly weaken his cause.

Yours truly,
J. R. Miller /267/

Oneida Journal

April 27, 1852.—Yesterday Messrs. Miller and Burt called again on Mr. Whipple Jenkins of Vernon. He met them at first quite coldly, but after some talk, there seemed to be a change in his spirit. He thinks he will not make out much with the ten indictments. At any rate, they can go no further than to fine us. He thought we ought to have a good lawyer, and about the same as offered his own services. Mr. Miller thinks there was a crisis Saturday in the public feeling toward us. We do not know how it will come out.

John R. Miller to Noyes
Oneida, April 27, 1852

Thinking our circumstances might demand some sudden moves, I advised our folks to have their clothes in condition to go to Court or anywhere else at an hour's notice.

Our cash is reduced to about $8, but I know we can get all the money we shall need in some way, though I don't see how. You will make your plans without any reference to the state of the treasury.

Oneida Journal

April 29, 1852.—Yesterday Messrs. Miller and Burt went to Utica to see Judge Root and District Attorney Garvin. They could get nothing from Judge Root, as he said it was against the law for him to say anything about it. They found nothing hard in his spirit, but Mr. Garvin was full of foulness and venom against us. They could see no way to avoid a trial but to forfeit /268/ the bonds. Mr. Burt returned, but Mr. Miller went to Brooklyn, expecting to return to-night. Mr. Burt's report was very interesting, and there was a calm, triumphant spirit throughout the meeting.

John L. Skinner to Oneida
Brooklyn, April 29, 1852

Well, Mr. Miller has paid us a flying visit, and is gone. I hope that by this time he has safely reached Oneida. Mr. Noyes too is gone, having left with Mr. Hamilton this morning for Wallingford.

Susan Hamilton to Putney
[Wallingford, April 29, 1852]

We were all taken by surprise this afternoon by the appearance of Mr. Noyes and Mr. Hamilton. Mr. Miller arrived at Brooklyn last night at one o'clock, informed Mr. Noyes of the state of things at Oneida, and returned at five this morning, taking Mrs. Newhouse and Milford with him. Mr. Noyes then decided to come to Wallingford with Mr. Hamilton and stay awhile with us. We shall be very happy to make a quiet, pleasant home for him. He looks remarkably well and bright, and not at all cast down or disturbed by the prospect of a scatteration at Oneida.

John R. Miller to Noyes
Oneida, April 29, 1852

Thanks be to God who giveth us the victory. I called on Mr. Garvin to-day at Utica. I told him that I should like to see him alone a few minutes, but he was in the same spirit as yesterday, and said: "If you have anything to say, you can say it here." I then stepped up to him and said in a good-natured but decided tone, at the same time slapping him on the knee: /269/ "I called, Mr. Garvin, to find out whether you would be satisfied if we quietly withdraw, and whether you will settle the indictments by our paying the cost, and whether you will give us time to arrange our affairs. We are going to take an honorable course. We are not going to run away, but you will find that we shall act above board." "What do you mean?" said he, looking up with perfect astonishment. "I mean that we have made up our minds to do all that we can honorably to satisfy you and the authorities of this County. I have been to Brooklyn since I saw you yesterday, and we have decided to break up our Association, if that is what you want, and if you will give us time to do so quietly." He replied promptly and pleasantly: "I will tell you what I will do. I will have the indictments all put by till the next Court, and see what progress you make." I told him that I was satisfied with that, but added: "I don't suppose you will expect us to leave our houses empty; we should of course leave enough to carry on our business." Then without waiting for him to reply I said: "We won't arrange that today, but I will see you again after we have commenced our arrangements." "That will do," said he pleasantly, and when I said good-by he responded in the same polite spirit and manner that he did last fall.

This was truly more than I expected or asked for. I never was more conscious of the presence and power of God giving us victory over our enemies. It was like opening the prison doors to my spirit. I can assure you it is good news to the Association.

Harriet A. Noyes to Putney
   Brooklyn, April 29, 1852

Mr. Noyes had several times spoken of the possibility of our /270/ breaking up—that it might be God's design to scatter as missionaries all over New England and New York—so he was ready to consent to an offer being made to the District Attorney, that the Community should be dispersed if all suits should be withdrawn, and that we would settle with the Hubbards if $1 or $500 would do it, they giving a bond to stop all further prosecutions against us. Mr. Miller did not go to bed at all, and most of the family were up with him. Then Mr. Noyes thought he would like to retire for a few days to a quiet place where he could look the whole field over, await the moves of the Hubbards and make arrangements for the future. After the issue of the present number of the paper, we shall wait awhile till affairs are settled.

John R. Miller to Putney
   Oneida, April 30, 1852

This is a beautiful day, externally and internally. We feel that the enemy's line is broken, and there is a quietness and calm that succeeds a tremendous battle. I think now that we can go on and make our plans with reference to the general interest and not from necessity. After seeing our willingness to submit to the "powers that be," I don't believe they will have any heart to crowd us.

The idea of having half of our Association, or more, leave here looks very attractive to us, and I should vote for it, if the world would consent to let us remain in peace. But I feel too much exhausted to enlarge to-day.

Noyes to John R. Miller
  Wallingford, April 30, 1852

  Dear Bro. Miller:— /271/
  In this quiet retreat, my thoughts are clearer than they were at Brooklyn. Some of them may be useful to you.
  I am satisfied that our true policy is to avoid a trial, as we did at Putney, by paying whatever price is necessary. The law is not our chosen field of battle. The Devil would like to force us to fight there, because with public opinion against us he can do what he pleases with us. The unreasonable result of the Lamb suit shows how we may expect to fare on that field. And then a trial, if public and reported to the newspapers, converts a local difficulty into a general scandal. We are dealing with the enemy on the field of public opinion, and our hope is that we shall finally overcome prejudice by common sense, sound reasoning and good behavior. The introduction of our private quarrels with such folks as the Hubbards would injure this operation. As good strategists, therefore, we should steadily decline battle on the lawfield, and pay the costs cheerfully, at least till we can change public opinion so as to make sure of fair play.
  My opinion therefore is that, if the enemy will make no terms, those who have been indicted should disappear, and let the bonds be paid. All together they do not amount to the sum that I was bound for. So I would pay Hubbard $500, or even $1000, if you cannot do better. And if he will make no terms, I would let the case go by default. The property at Oneida will foot the bill of our four years' education, and money-losses will not bleed us as they do the Mammonites.*
  It is further to be considered in favor of declining battle on the lawfield, that we have no time to spend about it. We have other things to attend to. I detest the idea of having our minds /272/ occupied with consultations and preparations of witnesses and lawyers, and thoughts and doubts about a dirty quarrel got up by malicious and treacherous men. They shall not get possession of me in that way. I shall pay my toll and pass on.

                                        Yours truly,
                                        John H. Noyes

* Those in love with Mammon, the power of money personified. [L.F.]

The Greater Miracle
April 30, 1852

Noyes:—There have been many miracles first and last in the history of the Association. In fact the existence of such a Community is a miracle, a demonstration of what is considered impossible, the abolishing of selfishness. But I think that the crowning miracle which we shall have the privilege of presenting to the world is that of breaking up and dividing our property without quarreling. I have full confidence in the Association that it will be done. The public spirit will superintend the whole operation. There will be no grudging, and the best thing will be done that can be done for every individual. Our external organization will disappear, and we shall be resolved into an invisible association—lose our locality and develop a spiritual organization.

John R. Miller to Noyes
Oneida, May 10, 1852

I came to Rome this morning, and went to the District Attorney's room in the Court House. He met me with all the politeness I could ask. I asked him if this case of assault and battery could be disposed of so that I could return by the mail train. He said that he would attend to it immediately after the Court was organized. I then went up into the Court Room and waited /273/ quietly till the Court was organized. As soon as this was done, Mr. Garvin arose and presented the case of H. J. Seymour and several others. He said to the Court that in the Seymour case a divorce had been obtained and security given to the satisfaction of the complainants. He then came directly to me and said it was disposed of and the costs were $10. After paying this sum, I told him that we had begun to disperse, that one or two had already left, and others would go soon. He replied pleasantly, "All right, sir." I told him that I would see him again and report as soon as we had arranged our affairs. He said, "That will do, sir." I then asked him if it was necessary for me to pay any attention to the other indictments. He replied, "No, those are disposed of." I then left, after we had bid each other good-by pleasantly. I had no idea that the costs would be less than $25, perhaps twice that.

Talk by Noyes for Oneida
May 15, 1852

Concerning Mr. Burnham's plan to go west I have nothing to say, except that some time ago I felt a desire to send a mission there, and spoke of it. I am pleased with the idea. I choose that he and Mr. Carr should act on their own inspiration. I will help all I can and expect they will have a good time.

In regard to the Newark project, the most I have to do is to keep the genial influence over it. I cannot dictate in detail, but must have confidence in the men that are concerned. If this movement toward Newark succeeds, it will be transferring an important part of the Association into an important position. We shall send our forces in there not for the benefit of the Newark brethren but for the sake of the cause. A strong phalanx there at the present /274/ time will be worth more to us than it is at Oneida. I commend the project to the free, good will of the whole Association. Take one thing at a time. The more moderation and deliberation there is, and the more heartily we do the thing now to be done, the more concentration and unity there will be in our action, and the more success. Their present circumstances will try their faith in God. I have been through that trial in a thousand times worse circumstances. I know God is faithful. I am not afraid, and I expect to have an army of men around me that are not afraid—that can stand unmoved, devoted to the public inter-est in circumstances that would tempt common people to snatch and scatter each one for himself.

Mr. Mallory has been tempted to a worldly spirit, but I believe he will get into the line, be quiet and wait on God. It is important that there should be no fright, no spirit that would down with the boats and off.

There is no absolute need of dispersion at present, and very likely there will be no severe necessity for it at all.

Let each one propose to himself the question where he would choose to go, and also the question where the Lord would like to have him go; where each one could stand most efficiently serving the public interest. The Lord has a use for every one, and will find a place for him.

John R. Miller to Noyes
Oneida, May 19, 1852

Yesterday I went to Vernon on business. As I was riding through the street, Mr. J. Whipple Jenkins came out and spoke to me very cordially. He inquired about the settlement of the indictments /275/ at Rome, and asked what we had done with the Hubbard suit. After I had given him a frank statement of the facts he said he would tell me something which might be of service to us, though I must not mention it. He then said: "I told Mr. Hubbard that he could not maintain an action against you. A few days ago he called at my office with Mr. Rose of Albany to consult me about his lawsuits to recover the ten percent on the land discounts. Something was said about your case, and

Mr. Rose wanted Mr. Hubbard to explain it to him. After he had done so, Mr. Rose told him at once that he could not maintain an action against you. I guess you will find them pretty moderate in their demands." Mr. Rose is the Albany lawyer and clerk of the [state] House of Representatives who called here with Mr. Hubbard a week ago last Sunday. I thought it quite providential that we should get access to the private counsels of the enemy just as we were expecting to make a settlement. I told Mr. Jenkins that we were making arrangements to disperse, and gave him the reasons for it. He appeared perfectly astonished, and said, "Is it so?" He dropped his head, as if in deep study, and then repeated, "Is it so?" He seemed to want to say something more, but did not, except that he thought it ought to satisfy the authorities. He promised to come down and buy some of our Rustic Seats as soon as he could.

Oneida Journal

May 22, 1852.—Last evening the last of the Newarkers left for Brooklyn at quarter before twelve.

Hial Waters writes: There is some misunderstanding between Mr. Inslee and Brooklyn in relation to the women's going on immediately, Mr. Inslee expecting the women to accompany the men. /276/ Mr. Inslee felt himself criticised some for want of clear understanding and union with Brooklyn in the matter. But it all turned out well—better for a little criticism. The remark was made that if they went out with a broken and contrite spirit, they were sure of success. On the second sober thought, they were all decidedly in favor of going without the ladies.

Hon. Timothy Jenkins to John R. Miller
Washington, May 24, 1852

Dear Sir:—

I have your favor of the 16th inst. and only have time to write you a line in answer thereto.

I have always advised our people not to molest your Community, and after you settled the assault and battery with Mr. Hubbard's people, I supposed that no further trouble would ensue.

I think in the process of a little time, this difficulty will pass over. It may be that persons opposed to you are desirous to coerce you to sacrifice your property at Oneida, perhaps with a view of benefiting themselves. However this may be, I think you had better keep your property, as I have no doubt you will, by the exercise of prudence, soon be able to get along without molestation. I think Garvin will not eventually be unreasonable, as he is a naturally well-disposed man.

With kind regards to yourself and the Community, I subscribe myself,

Yours truly,
Timothy Jenkins /277/

George W. Noyes to John R. Miller
Brooklyn, May 28, 1852

An idea has just occurred and been talked over with enthusiasm, which I will report for the consideration of Mr. Thacker and all interested. There is policy in war, and why would it not be a grand stroke of policy to devote all your strawberries this season as a peace offering to the neighborhood? Circulate a general invitation at the Castle and elsewhere for everybody to call and partake of strawberries and cream. Perhaps it would be thought best to set a particular day at the height of the season when the Community will be happy to entertain the public. Such a course, it is thought, would be an acceptable offering of our "first fruits" unto the Lord, would clear ourselves of covetousness, and show our neighbors that our prosperity, if we are allowed to go on in peace, will not be a selfish, isolated affair.

We think the plan would be worth the cost. If approved, let Mr. Miller and the rest lay their heads together and bring it to the right conclusion. It will make entertaining matter for the paper. I should love dearly to be with you.

We must tempt people back to God with the fruits of the earth, as Satan first tempted them away. After our talk Mr. Noyes opened the Bible to the account of the interview between David and Abigail. 1 Sam. 25:17–44. /278/

Oneida Journal

June 1, 1852.—This morning the Kinsleys left for Northern Vermont. No company that has left Oneida since the dispersion has affected the heart of the Community as this departure of the Kinsleys. Contributing largely in the darkest financial hour, and coming on with his whole family and effects, Mr. Kinsley has been truly a pillar in the church. He has the warmest love and the perfect confidence of the Association. At the table this morning before they left, there was a melting yet cheerful scene. Mr. Kinsley called for the song, "Let us go, brothers, go," which was sung with the sincerest feeling.

John R. Miller to Noyes
   Oneida, June 18, 1852

Mr. and Mrs. Burt called on Hon. Timothy Jenkins this afternoon. Mr. Jenkins said that Mr. Hubbard wrote to him at Washington trying to engage him to defend his suit against us, which he declined. After he came home, the old man called on him and asked him if he could sustain an action against us for seducing his daughter. He told him, No, decidedly. Mr. Jenkins then told him that he could get a writ, if he chose to, but all it would amount to was, that in the end he would have to pay his own costs. "Well," said Hubbard, "they dread the law, and I will make them believe I am going to bring them to trial, and then at last get what I can."

Mr. Jenkins said he would advise us not to go near them but wait for them to come to us, and then not refuse to settle, but offer then say $50, what it would cost us to go to trial, but no more. He said: "Don't offer them too much." /279/

He said there [was] no need of our dispersion, and that he knew we could go along without trouble, that there was no excitement against us now, but on the contrary, good feeling.

He says further that they cannot sustain an action against us for keeping a house of ill fame, and he told Mr. Hubbard so. He advised us not to leave here, wished us prosperity, advised getting Whipple Jenkins to draw up a paper to end all future trouble.

George W. Noyes to Brooklyn
   June 25, 1852

Our Strawberry Festival yesterday was the most exquisite thing of the kind that we ever witnessed. Early in the morning, some of our people constructed a bower of sweet-scented cedar in the children's playground, capacious enough to seat one hundred persons, with tables interspersed. Another party engaged in picking and preparing the strawberries, of which over seven bushels were gathered before noon from our garden beds. Groups of rustic chairs and tables were arranged in shady spots about the grounds. About eighty families of our neighbors and of citizens in Vernon, Oneida Castle, and Oneida Depot had been invited. Soon after three, our guests began to arrive. The house was thrown open, and they were invited to stroll through the gardens or amuse themselves in their own way. The company soon took their way to the arbor, where an abundance of strawberries, cream and sugar awaited their acceptance. Parties continued to arrive for about two hours, and the number of guests, it was said, was about three hundred. The attendance and singing of the Community children added to the pleasure of the occasion. /280/

John R. Miller to George Cragin
Oneida, June 25, 1852

We had some fears the night before that we might come short for strawberries. We thought we should want five bushels, but we picked seven from about 2/3 of the beds, and could easily have picked five more. We had six pails of cream, one hundred lbs. of white sugar, and plenty of nice biscuit and butter. Everything was in order about 2 o'clock, and the next hour was spent in "fixing up" for the occasion. We had enough of everything to give a rich treat. Many thought it was the most beautiful place they ever saw.

Nearly all of our neighbors were present. From Vernon came Mr. Norton, the editor of *The Journal,* Dr. Foot, the Cases, Mr. McIntosh, Mr. Jenkins's sons. The merchants and lawyers came from the Depot and Castle, Dodge among the rest. Mr. and Mrs. Dexter Hubbard were here, and seemed to enjoy themselves as much as anybody. They called again this morning to eat strawberries. How can they fight after this?

John R. Miller to Noyes
Oneida, June 27, 1852

Yesterday I went to the Depot and Castle with Messrs. Kellogg and Newhouse to sell strawberries and peas. We sold both very quickly. I was pleased to see how good-natured everybody was. People flocked around us from all quarters to buy. Several came to meet us for fear we should sell out before we got to them. All said our pic-nic was the pleasantest party they ever attended. Their good report of us now is as much /281/ exaggerated as their evil report was three months ago. We have decided not to sell any more strawberries at present, but to make a finish of our peace offering with them. I feel that God will be better pleased to have us use them in this way than to have them all sold for money. I desire to deal with others in the same liberal way that God deals with us.

William A. Hinds to John R. Miller
Brooklyn, June 27, 1852

Mr. Noyes says in relation to dispersing, it will not do to act simply on Mr. Jenkins' talk or form your judgment entirely from it. Garvin is the man with whom we have to do. If he is opposed to our remaining, the good feelings of the whole neighborhood would not warrant us in doing so. Therefore, it might be well to see Mr. Garvin and ascertain his present mind.

George W. Noyes to Brooklyn
Oneida, June 29, 1852

Yesterday we spent an agreeable afternoon in a strawberry festival given by the Community to the Oneida Indians. The Indians have been good neighbors from the commencement of the Community here, and we were glad to show our appreciation and respect. We commissioned their minister, the Rev. Thomas Cornelius, to invite the whole resident nation to meet in the Community grounds. About seventy sat down under our arbor to partake of strawberries and cream. Among them were several members of the Indian Minstrel Company, who favored us with several hymns in their own tongue. We answered them with songs, after which they adjourned to the garden and strawberry beds, and then took their way home. /282/

John R. Miller to Noyes
July 6, 1852

I went to Utica to-day and had another interview with Garvin. As soon as I entered his office, before I had time to make known my business, he asked me how we got along moving. I told him what progress we had made. "Well," said he, "you had better be off." I then told him that I had called to report to him as I had agreed, and also to invite him to visit us. He said that he should not visit us, that he considered our Association worse than any whorehouse. He went on with the most abusive language he could possibly utter, saying every little while that he was determined to break us up, and if we were not off before the September Court, he would give us "such an overhauling as we never had yet." After pouring out his wrath for some time, I said to him: "Whatever your opinion may be, Mr. Garvin, about our Community, I think we are entitled to respectful treatment when we call on you on business by your own consent." He replied: "I never shall treat you with the least respect. You are not entitled to it. I consider myself insulted every time any of you come into my presence, and I wish never to see any of you again." After a few minutes' talk, he said three or four times, "I wish you would leave," and "I wish you would leave *now.*" I supposed he meant the Community, but as he repeated it with emphasis and pointed to the door, I began to understand that he wished to turn me out of the office. I said: "What do you mean? Do you wish me to leave your office?" "Yes," said he, "now. Will you go?" "Certainly I will," said I: "Good day, sir," and left his office." /283/ He made no reply that I heard. This talk all took place in the presence of several strangers, who stared at me with perfect astonishment. At the Utica Depot, I met Judge Root. As soon as he saw me, he turned his face the other way. I soon passed again where he was standing, and spoke to him. He answered me in the shortest way possible, and turned around without offering to shake hands. I saw clearly that he had the same spirit that Garvin had.

The Community received the news in a cheerful, victorious spirit. /284/

28

Victory of the 27th, July 1852

Remarks by Noyes
July 7, 1852

There is no need of going over the old exhortation to faith. The constitutional principle in such cases is well understood.

It is plain as can be that God reigns, that the Concentric Convention is carrying on the game. I don't know what God will do, not what the Devil will do, but I can see that there is real sport to the powers above. Whenever I can sympathize with their spirits, I have a tremendous tendency to laugh. Then when I look at the case on natural law principles, there is a tendency to cry. We shall have some good laughs over it by and by. We have just got a pretty clear verdict of the people delivered by their foreman, Jenkins, and if the lawyers and Pharisees choose to go on and thrust us out, they will be kicking against the pricks. It is now simply a question of jurisdiction. We told Mr. Hubbard, to begin with, that we were living in the Kingdom of God. He answered that he was living in the State of New York. It is a long game, and Mr. Hubbard will have to wait with the rest of us till it is fairly through.

My impression still is that the Lord wants to scatter us. There will be no hurry; the retreat will be conducted in good order. It is sure to lead to an expansion as decisive and sweeping as that on the day of Pentecost. Christ always plucks victory out of defeat.

Tryphena, the exciting cause of the disturbance, was our /285/ first convert at Oneida. Thus the element of dispersion was in the Association from the beginning.

The true interpretation of all this is not that the Lord is straitened for means or power. He could strike all enemies dead, if he chose. But his policy evidently is to work into the world peaceably; if the ruling powers oppose, to blow peace in their face and give way. I am anxious to carry out that policy—keep the peace in spite of everything, so as to save all that can be saved. If we should get into an open quarrel with the authorities, we should scare away multitudes that are now imprisoned and that we shall ultimately get at. We are like a steamboat, which is bound to turn out for everything. We must do anything to avoid a collision. We have plenty of sea room.

I hope the Community will have a good flash of healthy love before they quit.

John R. Miller to Noyes
July 15, 1852

Hubbard offers to settle for $350. I offered $100. I thought I had better report to you before taking any further action. My opinion is that he would settle for $100, or $200 at most, rather than go to trial. But I would by all means pay the $350 if that would end the indictments.

Noyes to John R. Miller
July 17, 1852

Hubbard's demand is not so unreasonable as we were led to expect, and the negotiation appears to have been conducted in a good, peaceable spirit. He is willing to reduce his demand. /286/ I propose then to settle thus: We will give him $150 now on the receipt of a certificate from such as you proposed, honorably discharging all of us from further claims and expressing his wish that the indictments be dropped; and we will give him $150 more, if by that certificate and other influences which he and his family can command, those indictments shall be stopped so that we shall have no further trouble. This is $150 for half a peace, and $300 for a whole peace, which I think the Hubbards can give us if they are disposed.

It seems to me the likeliest way to quash those indictments is to set the Hubbards to work as our attorneys, and pay them well for it. But perhaps even this will fail.

By the way, what security have you that the indictments will be dropped

even if the Community disperses? Garvin has not explicitly promised anything. His language was, "I will see how you get on," or something to that effect. And even if he had promised, we know how he got off from his first engagement. In the mood of his last talk, it would be just like him to pursue us
after the dispersion, and collect the bonds or force a trial. If he will not hear
you respectfully, would it not be well to get Whipple Jenkins or McIntosh to
see him and ascertain definitely what he intends to do? For if he means to
prosecute at any rate, we need not trouble ourselves to disperse, but may turn
our attention to getting ready for trial. If he engages to let us alone on condition of dispersion, then I should be in favor of commencing the movement
immediately. God will make a way for us through the Red Sea of scoun-
drelism. I shall trust the whole matter to you and Mr. Burt. But take care not
to leave any loose ends. /287/

If you settle with the Hubbards and get their certificate and influence in
our favor, and then on top of that are able to convince Whipple Jenkins or
whomever you employ, that there have been no illegal proceedings in the
Community since last Spring, and also to show that the people around us respect us and do not wish to have us broken up, you make a strong case for
Garvin's reconsideration. I wish you would get Timothy Jenkins' leave to report his views of our case. It would almost be worth while for Mr. Burt to
make a trip to Washington, if you see that anything can be done by it.

John R. Miller to Noyes
July 22, 1852

This morning I wrote a note to Old Mr. Hubbard requesting him to call.
At 11 o'clock he came with Dexter. . . .

When I had read your letter to them, the old man said he thought his offer
to settle was low enough. They both said they would sign such a paper as we
wished. They would not give much to have the Tryphena matter settled unless
the indictments could be settled too, because . . . the door would be left open
for future difficulty. They didn't want to have anything conditional, but were
ready to do what they could to end the indictments now.

I then proposed that Dexter should go with me to Utica tomorrow and
use his influence to have the whole settlement made now. I proposed further
that we should employ Mr. Whipple Jenkins to go with us, as he might get access to Garvin when we could not. The Hubbards consented, and Mr. Burt
and I went to Vernon this afternoon.

We found Mr. Jenkins in a half-hearted state, fearful of /288/ losing his
reputation by engaging in the case. We told him frankly our position, but did

not urge him. He finally asked the privilege of thinking of it till Monday before deciding. We consented on the condition that we should be free in the meantime to pursue any other course we might think best. . . .

We have not made up our minds yet what we shall do precisely. I know that God will help us. I say to our folks, "Let us be prepared to scatter, every one of us, and then all that comes short of that will be clear gain."

Mrs. M. E. Newhouse to Lemuel H. Bradley
    July 23, 1852

The present state of the Hubbard matter is that Hubbard has offered to settle for $350 and "ground arms" as he says, permanently. The old man and Dexter will give a written pledge to that effect. They decline accepting Mr. Noyes's offer, preferring, as they say, to have the whole matter squared up before settling.

John R. Miller to Noyes
    July 23, 1852

"Samuel B. Garvin, Esq., District Attorney: We, the undersigned, having understood that a prosecution in behalf of the people against several of the prominent members of the Oneida Community had been commenced and is now pending, beg leave to say, that in our judgment, if there has ever been any cause for such a prosecution, it has been wholly removed, and does not now exist, and in our opinion it is not demanded or deemed advisable, on the part of the people at large out of that Community best acquainted with their present management and conduct, that the prosecution should be further carried on against them, and we recommend that it be discontinued. Dated, July 23, 1852." /289/

The above is a copy of a petition drawn up by Mr. Whipple Jenkins, which he thought we had better have signed by the most influential men at the Depot, Castle, and Vernon. Mr. Burt and I took it to the Hubbards this morning, and they both signed it without hesitation; and Dexter offered to take it down and ask Dodge and Root to sign. About 3 o'clock he returned, saying that Dodge utterly refused to sign it, and that Root wanted others to sign it first.

It so happened that Hon. Larkin G. Mead, Noyes's brother-in-law, of Brattleboro, Vermont, who had given invaluable counsel and aid during the troubles at Putney, came to the Community for a visit just at this time. He immediately began casting about for a chance to help. Remembering a former school-mate, Dolphus Skinner, brother of John L. Skinner of the Community and an influential man in Utica, he called on him and discussed the situation. Mr. Skinner agreed that further prosecutions were not needed and would do more harm than good; and he promised to talk the matter over in this light with District Attorney Garvin and Judge Root, both of whom he knew. [G.W.N.]

John R. Miller to Noyes
July 24, 1852

Yesterday a dark cloud seemed to hang over the Association, but today the sun shines again. On our way home from the Depot last night, Mr. Burt and I called on Mr. Root, and made a frank disclosure of our position. He said at once, "The people in this vicinity will not consent to have you disperse." He then took the paper and signed it heartily. He said he was sure that Garvin /290/ never would bring us to trial. After our return Mr. Burt took the paper to Mr. Downing, who signed it without hesitation. This morning Mr. Burt and I went to the Depot and presented our paper to the leading men, who signed it cheerfully and heartily. The following are the names of those who signed: O. P. Root, R. Downing, J. C. Sloan, J. M. Messinger, J. C. Thompson, H. J. Wetmore, S. Riverburgh, B. B. Stoddard, John C. Sherwood, Noahdiah Hubbard, Dexter Hubbard, J. Newton Messinger, Erasmus Stone, Sidney J. Breese, S. H. Goodwin, S. Kenyon, Niles Higginbotham, Edmond Hills, Daniel Lamb, Robert J. Stewart, John W. Allen, James Tomlinson.

While in the Post Office at the Castle on our return, we learned that Hon. Timothy Jenkins had just returned from Washington. This truly looked like the interference of the invisibles in our favor. We went at once to his office. He received us very cordially indeed. We told him just our position and showed him the paper without asking him to do anything for us. He said that Mr. Garvin never would bring those indictments to trial—that we had got the names of the very first men in this neighborhood. He advised us to get Whipple Jenkins to go with us to Utica. We told him how he felt about it, and that he was to give us an answer Monday. He said he should see him this afternoon, and would advise him to go. He added: "People are ready to get hold of anything to injure a public man, but if it is necessary I will interfere and stop it." He advised us to make no preparation to disperse; said there was not the least necessity for it. He then went into a free talk about our affairs. He said it was a public benefit to have us here, and gave as one reason the attention we are giving to horticulture—more than any single man /291/ could afford to give. He said that he should turn his attention more to that business when he got through at Washington, and thought it would be a great help to him to have us here. He came home to attend the Commencement, as his sons both graduate, and is to return next Friday.

John R. Miller to Noyes
July 28, 1852

Mr. Burt and I went to Vernon last evening, found Mr. Whipple Jenkins at home and that everything had been arranged at Utica to our satisfaction. Mr. Garvin gave his pledge that the indictments would be ended at the next Court. At first Mr. Garvin was quite hard and determined to prosecute. Then he wanted time to think the matter over. But Mr. Jenkins told him that the question must be settled now; that he lived nearer us than Mr. Garvin did, knew us better, and knew better how the public felt toward us, and that he should demand that Mr. Garvin take his statement. He left Mr. Garvin with good feelings. Mr. Garvin told him about his treatment of me. He thought that Mr. Garvin had acted honestly in the matter. From all that Mr. Jenkins said, I couldn't help thinking that Mr. Garvin requested him to see that we had good feelings toward him. We were satisfied with this explanation.

You will see that we got a great deal better terms now than we should have asked when Mr. Garvin turned me out of his office. I was about to make a bad bargain, and was sent home for further instructions. We are now at full liberty to remain here and have as many more as we choose. When I reported the other day that we had already reduced our number nearly one-half, nobody was pleased /292/ with it. The people, so far as we are known, do want us here, and are determined that we shall stay. . . .

Old Mr. Hubbard called here this morning on other business, and was much pleased to learn that this matter was settled. He said he was glad on Tryphena's account, she would feel so much better to know that we had settled and were good friends.

Victory of the 27th
July 28th, 1852

Noyes:—What has saved us? To the view of faith we have been saved by a manifest and sublime movement of the armies of Heaven in our favor. God has saved us with no thanks to Hubbard, Garvin, or any of the men who have abused us. They have let go of us not because they feel a better disposition toward us, but because their hold has been broken by God almighty. He has vindicated us, and brought us out white as snow before the surrounding public.

John R. Miller to George Cragin
    Rome, N.Y., September 14, 1852

After dinner I went to the Court House. Mr. Garvin treated me with all the kindness I could ask. At the first moment he could he invited me up into the Court Room. After he had talked about five minutes with the Judge and Clerk in a low voice, he came where I was sitting and took hold of my arm. We walked out of the room together. As soon as we were seated at his desk he said, pleasantly: "The Court says you must pay $20 costs," I made no reply, but threw down a $20 bill. He handed me his receipt and said: "You can get a certified copy of the *Nolle Prosequi* from the Clerk of the Court." I have been thus particular to /293/ show you that we have not only got out of the clutches of the law, but that there has been a great change in the public mind toward us. We sold one Rustic Seat and three bushels of potatoes in Utica for enough to pay the bill. We won't find any fault with the authorities for indicting us, so long as they only charge $2 each and take their pay in potatoes at a shilling a peck. Providence has favored us with a good crop of potatoes this year, so I think we can live well and grow fat while the potatoes last. /294/

29

The Resumption of Complex Marriage
August 29, 1852*

Theocratic Platform
The Circular, Old Series, 1:170
    August 29, 1852

The Editor of *The Circular,* in a recent letter sketches the Platform of our new state of Society as follows:

---

* The full text of the August 29, 1852, manifesto here replaces the less complete version in the G.W.N. manuscript. [L.F.]

SOVEREIGNTY OF JESUS CHRIST, dating from his Resurrection, and manifested at his Second Coming.

CO-SOVEREIGNTY OF THE PRIMITIVE CHURCH, raised from the dead at the Second Coming.

UNION WITH CHRIST AND THE PRIMITIVE CHURCH, by faith and love.

UNITY OF ALL BELIEVERS, in this world and in Hades, with the one kingdom in the Heavens.

RESURRECTION OF THE SPIRIT, resulting in salvation from sin and selfish habits.

RESURRECTION OF THE BODY, preventing or overturning disease, renewing youth, and resulting in the abolition of death, and the loosing of the captives in Hades.

COMMUNITY OF PROPERTY of all kinds, with inspiration for distribution.

ABANDONMENT OF THE ENTIRE FASHION OF THE WORLD—especially marriage and involuntary propagation.

CULTIVATION OF FREE LOVE.

DWELLING TOGETHER IN ASSOCIATION or complex families.

HOME CHURCHES AND HOME SCHOOLS.

MEETINGS EVERY EVENING.

LORD'S SUPPER AT EVERY MEAL.

CULTIVATION OF FREE CRITICISM.

HORTICULTURE the leading business for subsistence.

A DAILY PAPER as the gathering point for all separate Associations.

This may properly be called the Theocratic Platform. The ideas suggested, will be found to comprehend the main features of the Revolution which we believe in as the kingdom of God. Our readers we are sure, will study it with interest, and agree with the remark of Mr. Noyes, accompanying the above, that "a Discourse, or Series of Lectures, which shall develop these ideas in their true proportions and connections, so as to make an available science of them, will deserve a premium."—The different points and subjects of this sketch, will engage the warmest attention of *The Circular,* and offer an inviting field of discussion to our correspondents.* /295/

---

* For selections from the seven Lectures on Social Freedom, see chapter 32. [L.F.]

30

Constitutional Christianity

Article by George W. Noyes, [The Circular], O.S., 2:62, 65, 70
    January 8–15, 1853

We have insisted that the marriage question is to be settled not by experiments of expansion or contraction, as polygamy, divorce, Shakerism, but only by death. The only alternative or modification of the marriage system which the Bible anywhere recognizes is a resurrection state in which "they neither marry nor are given in marriage." The only question that remains is, whether the commonly recognized form of death is the only one. And here we have expressed the opinion that it is not—that there is a better and more effectual way of dying than to be sick and call in the undertaker. It seems to us that the very sum and substance of the gospel of Christ is its ability to put us on the other side of death and in possession of the privileges of a posthumous state, i.e., freedom from sin, from law and evil relations of every kind. Paul everywhere assumes this, and his only labor was to develop to the minds of the church the consequences of that change. Christ stands in the place of death to those who receive him. This is the meaning of Paul's great doctrine of "Christ crucified," which to the Jews was a stumbling-block and to the Greeks foolishness, "but to them which are called, both Jews and Greeks, Christ the power of God and the wisdom of God."

We get the simplest and surest idea of the gospel as a radical organizing force by fixing our attention on the central /296/ fact in its history, the death and resurrection of Christ. A man who had lived in this world for a time and gathered about him a company of disciples, died; and in a short time afterwards arose from the dead and reappeared to his disciples; and this resurrection-man by the distribution of a spiritual influence became the head of a church. The church, having as it were dropped their own lives and taken his, claimed his death and resurrection as their own. The assumption of a posthumous state and position in this world involved ultimate consequences of the profoundest character, and it is a matter of history that the Primitive Church did not develop *all* the consequences of their constitutional principle. The apostles did not wish to spend their force or that of their hearers on secondary elements. Hence they chose not to place themselves in a direct quarrel with slavery or with civil governments. Of all the recognized institutions of the *present* world, probably the only one that was directly attacked by the Primitive Church was *sin*. They struck at the root, and neglected the branches. But the constitutional principle of Christianity was a growing, expansive thing, which must finally break up everything foreign to the resurrection. A resurrection vortex was then formed, around which all men and institutions from that time began to circle, and into which they must all sooner or later plunge. Those that belong to the heavenly state will survive; those that do not will go down. /297/

The Primitive Church did attack one institution growing out of sin, and that was property. The account, therefore, to speak accurately, stands thus: The Primitive Church, standing on the constitutional principle of unity with the death and resurrection of Christ, subverted first of all and chiefly *sin;* secondly subverted the ecclesiastical system of Judaism. So far they made thorough work. Then thirdly, they practically manifested temporarily the resurrection-principle against private property. Fourthly, they advised against marriage, and were averse to entangling themselves with it except so far as was absolutely necessary. Fifthly, they left slavery and civil institutions in general undisturbed.

Noyes:—I have gone through a regular course on this subject. I began with salvation from sin and the second coming, came from that to the abolition of ordinances and legality in general, then to communism and emancipation from marriage, and finally to emancipation from death. All of these doctrines grow out of this central one of the cross of Christ. I have labored round and round this doctrine spiral-fashion for many years, and that little article for the first time preaches it plainly and satisfactorily. It is the best thing that has come out since 1834. It is just what I have wanted to bring out, but George has brought it out better than I should have done.

I have known perfectly well the central nature of this truth since I began, but I have had hard work to make anyone else appreciate it until now. All these other doctrines are /298/ but spokes to the wheel. At the end of 1852 we finished our discussion of salvation from death. Then came the time for us to put the hub into the wheel.

Spiritual Ventilation: Home-Talk
September 25, 1851*

I think the attempt to bring up a family in seclusion is impossible, however beautiful in theory. And it is right that it should be so. God's object is the educa-

---

* This talk was inspired by a letter from Mr. Delatre to his son Herbert. [G.W.N.]

tion of mankind, and whatever individuals gain is an advantage only so far as it goes to benefit the mass. Persons brought up in that way could not have a wholesome, robust life, either spiritually, morally, or physically. The effect would be the same as to live in a closed room without ventilation. The only way to be healthy is to harden our nervous system and not be afraid of the surrounding elements. As children grow toward maturity, their social nature demands exercise, and there is an absolute necessity for their taking a place in the world. So the individual results at last go into the general mass. And the more perfect the seclusion has been, the more disastrous the consequences are apt to be.

The circumstances of our Association have in some ways made us liable to this same mistake, but the tendency of God's dealings with me has been to counteract that liability. In the first stages of my education, I lived in close seclusion from the world, but as I advance God more and more calls me /299/ to face the world and not be afraid of it. We must calculate that ultimately we and our children will be turned back into the world, that we may spread abroad the truths we have attained. So long as we are in a state of seclusion, we are liable to certain diseases. One point, in respect to which I wish to have the good sense of the Association directed, is that of our peculiar social doctrines. It may be necessary in the early stage of our experience, that there should be a kind of secretiveness. But I want to have all feel that this is only a military measure, not a permanent principle of the Kingdom of God. There will ultimately be nothing of the kind, but the direct contrary. It is very desirable that the Association should feel free to make known their principles on all points, and have no secrets. I wish that they would treat Tryphena in such a manner that they would be willing to have the whole world know, and that they would allow the opinion of the world to come in as one consideration to modify their treatment. We need all of God's teachings and the pressure of social influences to keep us right. There is a great deal of good sense in the world, and I want all the help I can get from it. I think the time has come for us to become slowly a little more confidential with the world.

The peddling scheme is one of the best measures we have ever introduced in the Association, on account of its ventilating qualities. It is giving the men that have engaged in it more ruggedness toward the world. The trouble now in the Association is lack of ventilation. The world will not hurt us after we get a little indurated. My experience has been very satisfactory in this respect the last year. The true /300/ policy now is to feel friendly towards the community around us, and do business with them as though they were one with us in everything.

We shall not signalize ourselves by destruction but by quiet construction. Whatever destruction is necessary will take place gradually. I do not want to have these old institutions vanish in a moment. I like Paul's prayer: "I exhort, therefore that first of all supplications, prayers, intercessions, and giving of thanks be made for all men; for kings, and for all that are in authority; that we may lead a quiet and peaceable life, in all godliness and honesty." (2 Tim. 2:1, 2) That is a prayer that foolish fanatical folks have no taste for. They would pray for the destruction of the powers that be. We shall find that these powers will crumble fast enough.

I do not wish to have the least spiritual members of the Association catch at what I have said, and run into gossip with the world. But if the strong, spiritual members give scope to God, I believe that he will lead them to ventilate more. All the real good sense and civilization there is in the world is on our side. /301/

31

Industry and Finance
August 1851 to January 1853*

Oneida Journal

August 16, 1851.—Notice was given at the dinner table that the new flour-ing-mill be started at about four o'clock. Accordingly nearly all went down to see it. They were satisfied beyond their expectations with the performance of the machinery. G. W. Noyes writes: "We all felt that the subjective profits of building this mill were the most valuable thing about it. A great deal has been done in the way of spiritualizing the labor department. Organization and uni-ty have been introduced among the men, and the professional spirit has been broken up."

August 18, 1851.—Young Mr. McGregor called to-day, and says the work we did for his father's grist-mill gives entire satisfaction. This was a job amount-ing to $80.00 for fixing the shafting, the first job of any importance done in our machine-shop.

August 25, 1851.—Mr. Nathaniel Potter of Erie County came to instruct our men in making his patent bee hives.

September 20, 1851.—Notice was given last evening that there would be a general bee on the swamp northwest of the house. Accordingly at 2 P.M. All

---

* The original title's dates read "August 1851 to August 1854." [L.F.]

assembled under the Butternut Tree, men, women, and children, even our visitors having arrayed themselves in short dresses and old clothes; and with fife and drum all marched to the scene of attack, followed by horse and ox teams. The stumps and logs were drawn into piles, filled up with brush, and set on fire. It was a jolly time, and long to be /302/ remembered as our first bee in clearing up the swamp.

October 9, 1851.—The prospects for business are opening more and more. Mallory and Hall are champing their bits for action at the mill. It has been suggested that we shall soon need a shop of our own at the Depot to sell our flour, vegetables, shoes, and other productions.

October 18, 1851.—Our blacksmith-shop has taken a new start in business lately. The grist-mill too is doing a good business. Martin Kinsley has gone in to assist. Our mill has already gained the reputation of being the best one in this region. We have received an order from the Depot for from ten to fifteen bbls. per week. Our customer tells us that our flour sells the best, and at 25¢ per bbl. Extra.

October 20, 1851.—A new order from Oneida for seven bbls. of flour. It was decided to have Daniel Knowles go into the mill, and for the present to run day and night. Our flour is put up in bags and gives employment to some of our women.

October 20, 1851.—Mr. Miller says in a letter: I sold the Seymour mortgage without difficulty for $900. This gives us all the money we want both here and at Brooklyn for the present. It will enable us to carry on all our business successfully, besides paying our debts. How manifest it is that God is prospering us! I won't ask him to show me one day ahead how I am going to have money or food.

November 17, 1851.—Noyes writes: I think the peddlers should confine themselves pretty strictly to their business and not take it as a proselyting operation. It is not fair to do so. I want to be able to say to the world, we are honest in this thing as well as in all other things. We do not go out as peddlers /303/ and take advantage of that profession to steal in as preachers.

Wallingford Journal

December 31, 1851.—Among the products of 1851, mention is made of 1650 brooms, worth $184.25. This industry was carried on at the old log house by Mr. Thacker as foreman, assisted by W. H. Perry, Samuel Lord, and Daniel Abbott, with occasional help assorting the broom corn. John Leonard assisted in making the machines.

John R. Miller to Noyes
Oneida, January 24, 1852

The traps are going ahead finely. They have commenced one thousand. Five hundred of them will be ready for market in a few days. I think we shall have some very nice traps. We have made great improvements, so that we can make them much cheaper than Mr. Newhouse used to. For one thing, we have made a machine for bending the jaws. They are bent in an instant and are all exactly alike. Mr. Newhouse used to bend them all with a hammer. I think we shall make this a very profitable business. Has anything been done about selling them in New York? We keep an exact account of the cost, and when the first five hundred are finished, I can tell you what it is. /304/

John R. Miller to Noyes
Oneida, January 29, 1852

I have just finished our annual inventory. You will see that, notwithstanding the burning of the store and printing-office, the sinking of the sloop and all the expenses attending it, using money with perfect freedom, and publishing a free paper, we have during the year increased our property $778.62. It is true that the Wallingford property has been added to the inventory, but this is as it should be.

In the place of the store, the peddling business has been introduced with splendid success. We can make more with a capital of $300 in this business than we could in the store with a capital of $3000.

We have kept an exact account of our expenses for board the past week, and find that it cost 50¢ for each individual. We buy less than half of what we use, which is a great improvement on former years.

In February, 1852, Mr. Miller sold 250 traps in New York. The Oneida Journalist said: "This is quite a business and opens up." [G.W.N.]

John R. Miller to the Brooklyn Family
Oneida, February 8, 1852

I went down to the mill this morning immediately after breakfast to mark a load of flour for Putney. The scene I witnessed I am sure would have pleased you much. The mill /304/ and machine-shop hands were all busy: Mr. Perry and I marking flour; Mr. Kellogg and his team at the door ready to take it away. At the Burt house half a dozen farmers were putting up oats to be sent away this morning. Just across the street in the log cabin, another company were employed making brooms to finish out the load, and in front of the door were Mr. Carr and others loading the brooms.

Oneida Journal

February 10, 1852.—Mr. Ellis, with Mr. Hatch and John Leonard for apprentices, is engaged in making rustic seats.

March 23, 1852.—Near the close of meeting Sunday evening, Mr. Reynolds spoke expressing his confidence in the Association. As he concluded, he rose up saying he might as well join the Association now, and emptied his purse on the table. There were $143.20 in gold and silver. He was invited to help wash, and was toasted this morning by the ladies. Henry G. Allen was awakened this morning by the merry song of the washers. They arose at four and finished about eleven.

Items by Harriet A. Noyes
Brooklyn, March 25, 1852

Mr. Noyes was speaking to-day of the trap business. He said he was pleased with it on the principle of exterminating wild beasts. Rats are the wild beasts we have here, and these traps are good to catch them. We have been much troubled with rats. In the night they play their pranks all about the house. Saturday night a rat got into Mr. Noyes's room and kept him awake all night by jumping on and off his table and then hiding in the fire place. The next night a trap was set and the fellow caught. /305/

Henry W. Burnham to George Cragin
Oneida, May 6, 1852

Dear Brother:—

I am still thinking about going west, and as my thoughts are taking more of a serious turn, I have concluded to lay them before you and, if you think best, before Mr. Noyes.

To begin with, it seems to me that if Mr. Miller remains here through the summer there will be no necessity for my presence. The responsibility of disposing of things at Oneida naturally rests on him, and would if I were to remain. The idea, however, of cooperating with him would be attractive if this is my place.

If it was thought best, I could visit the Howards at Perrington, Ellis and Delatre at Drummondville.

I see by *The New York Times* that a railroad has recently been completed between Toledo and Chicago, a distance of four hundred miles. This, I should judge by the map, would carry me within twenty miles of Geneva, where Maria Clark lives, and directly on my route to Seba Bailey's, who lives perhaps twenty-five miles further. He has, from his first introduction to us through the paper and that without the advantage of personal acquaintance, adhered closely to our cause. He has for a long time expressed a wish for some of us to visit him, and particularly in his late letter to you that we should do so this summer. From what I can gather, he has been instrumental in turning the attention of quite a number toward us. I have an impression that a missionary among them at this time might do good service. . . . /306/

You have before you one side of my proposal. The next suggestion is to take along three or four hundred traps and a good quantity of silk for sale. As to traps, Mr. Newhouse says that Chicago is a good place to sell them. A dealer residing there, who is acquainted with his traps, has offered to buy on a large scale. This intelligence I get from Mr. Burt. The silk would probably sell for a higher price in that region than here, and Mr. Miller suggests that it be sold principally to merchants.

Charlotte says that I shall want a companion, and I have thought of Mr. Carr as a suitable person. He was reared at the west, I believe, is familiar with its geography and habits, is a lucky peddler, and would be, I have no doubt, a lively companion.

You have now my cogitations in full, entirely submitted to your consideration. They are approved by Mr. Burt, Mr. Miller, and Charlotte, and Mr. Carr is ready.

With love, Henry W. Burnham

George Cragin to Henry W. Burnham
Brooklyn, May 10, 1852

Dear Brother:—

Your proposal to go west accompanied by Mr. Carr was laid before Mr. Noyes after his return from Wallingford. He favored the plan, and proposed the following notice to be published in the next *Circular:*
"Notice to Western Friends.

Henry W. Burnham and Mr. Carr of the Oneida Community, having occasion to go west on business, will be at Chicago, Ill., /307/ and vicinity about the first of June. Wishing to make themselves useful to believers in that region but not intrude upon them, they take this method of giving notice of their visit in order that any who desire a call from them may have an opportunity to inform them. Letters addressed to Henry W. Burnham, Care of Seba Bailey, Grand Detour, Ogle County, Ill., and mailed any time in the present month will find Burnham and Carr at the end of their business tour, and will determine their subsequent movements."

I am much pleased with Mr. Noyes's suggestions about circulating among believers. He said he never had any fellowship with the old policy of Perfectionists in thrusting themselves even upon their friends without an invitation. He is decidedly favorable to having business of our own, too, as you propose. You will do well to take Bereans and Circulars.

Affectionately,
George Cragin /308/

Oneida Journal

May 20, 1852.—Brothers Burnham and Carr left to-day for Chicago via Drummondville. They took with them $253 worth of silk and 343 traps, their baggage in all weighing four hundred lbs. We all feel much interested in their mission. It is particularly a Community move. May God speed them, is our prayer.

John R. Miller to George Cragin
Oneida, May 24, 1852

Dear Bro. Cragin:—
I proposed to make a note for $250 payable at the Bank of Vernon in ninety days, signed by Mr. Burt and myself, and, if they had any doubts about it, endorsed by Mr. Leete. When I presented the note to the cashier, Mr. Case, he said he would rather wait and lay it before the directors. "There is some prejudice against your Community," said he, "And I presume some of the directors partake of it. The last two notes I discounted on my own responsibility. I consider the note perfectly good." After putting the note in my pocket I had a pleasant talk with the Cashier about the Community, but said nothing more about the note. Just as I was ready to leave he said: "I will take that note." I told him that I had no wish to have him take it if the directors didn't consider it perfectly good; I would get an endorser. He said: "I consider the note per-

fectly /311/ good, and if the directors are not satisfied, I will endorse it myself."
I left with the feeling that God had unlocked the Bank for us against the will
of the directors.

John R. Miller to George Cragin
Oneida, June 2, 1852

Enclosed you will find two letters from Messrs. Burnham and Carr. I have
been much interested in that mission and in their letters, but my impression is
that they have got into a discouraged spirit about business, and are hurrying
too fast to the end of their journey. I cannot help feeling that Br. Burnham has
allowed Mr. Carr's business experience to take the lead of his inspiration; that
they think too much of going by the quickest and cheapest route, and not
enough of the business part of the mission. They seem to think the country is
supplied with silk, and there is but little use in trying to sell. I think there is no
reason for this, and that so far as they have tried to sell they have had good
success. I wrote my impressions to Mr. Burnham yesterday, and thought I
would keep open with you.

Letters from John R. Miller
Oneida, June 5, 1852

To Putney:—Mr. Burnham writes that they sold the traps in Chicago at
$4.50 per dozen, and the prospect is that we can sell there at that price all we
can make. I am satisfied that Chicago is our market for traps, and that we can
do a good business in that line. /309/

To Albert Kinsley:—Their customers were much pleased with the traps—
call them the nicest in that market. They have sold over $60 worth of silk, so
you will see they are having pretty good luck, their total sales amounting to
about $200.

To Noyes:—I shall be in favor of having all the traps we can, say four or
five thousand, ready for the next spring's sales. The stock for a thousand traps
would cost less than $50, and they sell for $375, so you can see most of the in-
vestment is our own work. I think it will be well for us to keep stock on hand,
and let our blacksmiths work at this business when not otherwise engaged.

I shall expect money from the peddlers the first of the week, and shall then
forward some to you. At present we have about $2 in the Treasury.

I received a letter from Mr. Mead night before last saying that they would
probably have money in a short time now, and could let us have the $1000 we
have talked of. My first thought was that we could do without it, but then I

thought we had better take it. That will supply Brooklyn and Newark, buy wheat for our mill, and give some more capital in the peddling business.

Oneida Journal

June 11, 1852.—Since the last record the care of God has been especially over us in respect to our finances. A week ago last Monday we had $180 to pay, and no visible means of raising such a sum. But God helped us by his providence. Old debts were paid, sales of superfluous property were made, and to our astonishment we had at night the sum required and $1.53 over. /310/

A True Reason for Loving Labor: Home-Talk by Noyes
June 27, 1852

If I can give a good reason for devoting myself to intellectual pursuits instead of ordinary labor, I can feel justified in going on as at present. But I will not have any laziness in my heart. If I cannot get rid of that in any other way, I will go to making shoes with John Smith. I believe that secretly [secret?] laziness is the motive of many who take advantage of their opportunities to shirk work and become "gentlemen," and I know what a curse it is.

I have set up Harriet A. for my model in regard to service. I envy her readiness for anything and everything. She had opportunities that would have allowed her to be quite a lady. But she had chosen a course which is not only useful to the Community, but also to herself.

The four and twenty elders in Revelation "cast their crowns before the throne." That is what all those in high places must do. My face is steadily set in that direction. As fast as I get crowns I shall fling them at Christ's feet. Life is a growth, and I cannot make sudden changes. But I am growing toward the simplicity of service, away from everything that distinguishes a gentleman from a commoner.

To work under law is bad, and not to work at all is bad. /312/ But to work under inspiration is good. With inspiration every kind of work is good, and there is no important distinction between them. In Fourier's system, unattractive labor was to receive a higher rate of pay. But if we get a firm hold on inspiration, I cannot see where there is any unattractive labor.

John R. Miller to George Cragin
Oneida, August 19, 1852

Enclosed you will please find $25. I felt an instinct this afternoon to send you this amount, and proposed it to Mr. Burt and Charlotte, saying that we could trust God to take care of us. While we were talking on the subject and all were hearty in sending it, a letter was handed me from Albert Kinsley with $50 enclosed. /313/

Charlotte Miller to Harriet Skinner
September 29, 1852

(After describing a call from a Mr. Webster, Mrs. Miller adds:) He leaves tonight, taking every dollar in the treasury to send him home. I write this (Mr. Miller says he hates to have me) just to show that we do from time to time come down to the bottom. That is always the sign of a special influx. The more the demands, the more we have. This was never more true than it has been this summer. All pretensions to being our own keepers of anything but receivers of daily bread are taken away.

State of the School
December 22, 1852

The Brooklyn family numbers twenty-seven members including children, and is mainly employed in publishing *The Circular.*

The Newark family numbers thirteen members, and is principally engaged in machinery. Its shop employs about eight men.

The Oneida Community comprises about 130 residents, who are occupied with gardening and farming and, to some extent, with manufactures, merchandise, and milling.

The other three Associations are mainly agricultural, tending toward fruit-culture and gardening. Wallingford has a family of seventeen, Putney fifteen, and Cambridge six.

Total number of members in the six associated families, 208.

John R. Miller to George Cragin
Oneida, December 27, 1852

I have this morning paid our last debt, except about $800 state debt, which we can pay at our convenience. We have been through all sorts of financial experience, but I think this is the first time we have been free from debt since the commencement of this community.

Business Organization
January 15, 1853

The following is a statement of the different kinds of business at Oneida, with the distribution of men to each: /314/

Grist-mill	3 men	Steel Traps	4 men
Saw-mill	2 "	Silk Peddling	4 "
Rustic Seats	5 "	Shoe-shop	2 "
Broom-shop	5 "	Miscellaneous	9 "
Teaming	4 "	Kitchen	2 "
School	1 man	Children's Dept.	1 man

These several trades have grown up quite naturally in the Community, and afford a pleasant variety adapted to the different tastes and faculties of the members. Changes are frequently made, so that persons can go through the whole circle of employments if they choose. As Spring opens several branches will be dropped, and many of the men will go into gardening and building operations. Several of the trades were brought in along with the other private attainments of members and, being adopted by the Community, have thus far proved pleasant and successful. The Community received a silver medal at the New York State Fair for specimens of their rustic seats. It is proposed to make $1000 worth the present winter. The steel traps are ordered in large quantities by hardware dealers to supply the trappers of the Far West, the pioneers of civilization. In the silk business several men are constantly employed in traveling, not on foot as formerly, but on different lines of railroad, supplying merchants and others in the villages. This brings us into contact with business men, and affords a good recreation for those who wish to go out. The trips are generally not over a week, and by that time the men are glad to hie homewards. The women of the Community are principally occupied in household affairs and in the needle work necessary to supply the other Communities with clothes. In summer they mingle freely in the outdoor labors of the garden and farm. The children all attend school. /315/

32

Seven Lectures on Social Freedom
November 26, 1852, to January 15, 1853

First Lecture
November 26, 1852

A true confession of Christ gives control of the passions, and is a necessary preparation for study of this subject. Perfect contentment with the minimum, bare salvation, is the qualification for the maximum, a state where every passion will have its perfect development. All our advances toward the maximum will be by God's gift, not by our own right.

Second Lecture
November 29, 1852

Oneida has come up out of great tribulation, and I would gladly have them manage so as not to get into it again. For this purpose we should study our experience. We have just discovered that Harriet Skinner came under a dreadful influence in her dealings with Tryphena. When I see such an effect from a long-past cause, I realize the necessity of inspiration to understand the scenes we go through.

We must connect our sexual experience with that which is sacred. In the world there is a great gulf between sexual love and divine love, and so long as this exists, sexual love must be profane. Our social theory is an important means of grace, to be put into the same category with the Lord's Supper. We propose to the world two institutions, the daily press and local associations, which constitute the service of the word of God. But the *Bible Argument* shows that Association is impracticable without our social theory. Fatal stumbling-blocks will inevitably /316/ arise from exclusiveness and marriage spirit. Thus our social theory takes on all the sacredness and importance of the institution of which it forms a vital part. If Association is a means of grace, then our social theory is a means of grace.

But let us go farther. We have found by plenty of experience that our social theory is exactly adapted to producing conviction and conversion. Whoever comes among us with the intention of becoming a member at once finds himself brought to the point of giving up all those things that the ministers told him he ought to give up, wife, children, property. Then our social theory is a means of grace, not only in the negative sense of giving up the world, but in the positive sense of producing in us a Community spirit. If the Primitive Church could discern the Lord's body in the meat and drink of the Lord's Supper, how much more naturally can we discern the Lord's body in each other, and in all our interviews receive each other as members of Christ! By giving us means and occasions of communion, one with another and with Christ, our social theory fulfills the law of love which binds us exclusively to God.

The great danger in the administration of our social theory is that the least spiritual are apt to be the most active and get the most influence. "Fools rush in where angels fear to tread." When I was at Oneida I felt the responsibility of taking the lead myself; and I know that things cannot go right until the most spiritual do take the lead.

Kindred to the above is the danger that women will take the lead. It is a false situation where the women get the lead in such things. /317/

Another danger arises from the fact that the young are the most attractive. It is so and cannot be helped. But if persons follow simply their attractions, they mingle too much with those that have life and magnetism but lack discretion. Yet our law is that the young should mingle with the old. So there is a necessity for inspiration that adapts itself to present conditions and discerns when evil effects are developing.

Let them at Oneida not be in a hurry. If they will hold still a little while and keep their hearts open to me, I think I shall be able to help them. I do not see any better way than to give them a course of lectures. Standing at this distance perhaps I could have more freedom than if I were there. It will be good for Oneida to study the Table Talks with a special reference to our social theory.

Oneida should not think that I distrust them. I feel great confidence in them. Inspiration is flowing there. We have had Association criticisms. Now let us rise into Association courtships.

Third Lecture
December 4, 1852

I am seeking the secret of happiness, the play of the passions that makes people perfectly happy in heaven and can make them so on earth. . . .

The great difficulty as things are in the world is that happiness generates a desire for more happiness of the same kind. A man can go to work to make money. When he has made as much as he would once have thought enough, he finds that he has generated a desire for more; and when he had got more he wants more still. /318/ Desire constantly outruns enjoyment. There is no happiness in this. We must learn the secret of enjoying more and desiring less. This nothing more or less than the attainment of contentment. God wants us to appreciate the good we have to such an extent as will reduce to a moderate amount our desires for good that is absent and future.

To be securely happy we must have the power to withdraw instantly from any specific form of enjoyment and turn directly to some other form of enjoyment. This power is something like the reciprocating feature of a steam engine. The steam acts first on one piston, then there is a shifting of valves and it acts on another piston. And the alternation is entirely automatic. The same force that drives the pistons shifts the valves. Similarly a man acting under the full force of passion may be connected and regulated by an inner law so that his operations will be safe and effectual. . . .

God made us to enjoy everything in succession. If we try to get all our enjoyment from one thing, we shall find ourselves out of gear with the universe.

We have found in the Association that when a man's amativeness is excited he can withdraw but it is a hard job! The steam is not cut off short. His passions do not go "click, click" like a watch. Herein lies the whole trouble about jealousy. If a man could control himself so as to withdraw the whole force of his life from that particular channel, and turn it instantly into some other channel, he would never be jealous.

We must not think that it is right to pursue some particular pleasure till we have exhausted our susceptibility in that direction. /319/ We must learn to withdraw in the midst of pleasure, when our susceptibility is at its height, not only without pain but with positive enjoyment. This is carrying contentment to the mountain tops.

My rules for happiness are these: Make desire subordinate to enjoyment, and break up habit.

Fourth Lecture
December 19, 1852

There is much dispute in the world about "Solomon's Song."* Some think of it as a bawdy song, and wonder that it is in the Bible. Others say it is an inspired poem descriptive not of sexual love but of love between Christ and the Church. Paul in his epistle to the Ephesians speaks of marriage between man and woman in the same terms as between Christ and the Church. He says: "Husbands, love your wives even as Christ also loved the Church." Love

---

* The Song of Solomon, a book in the Old Testament. [L.F.]

makes man and woman members of each other, and in the same way makes us members of Christ. In Paul's mind there was evidently no impropriety in transferring the view from one to the other. So I should say that Solomon's Song was a beautiful description of love between man and woman; and also a most poetic symbol of love between Christ and the Church.

The question that now arises is this: If the images and suggestions of love between man and woman are really unclean, are they fit symbols of the love between Christ and the Church? I believe that we have in Solomon's Song the true, literal treatment of the human form, and that it is not unclean. The best taste will lead us to glorify the works of God in that way. In fact the poetical treatment of the human form in connection with human /320/ passion is strictly holy and according to the design of God. We must expel from our minds the base associations connected with the human form before we shall be fit to receive Solomon's Song as a symbol of the love of Christ.

Artists contrive to hand a veil over the central parts. A free spirit will throw aside that veil, and introduce poetic conceptions to the very last act. That is where we must seek the source of all poetry.

If you examine yourself you will find that one of the most difficult things in the world is to represent the sexual act in a way to satisfy your sense of beauty. Suggestions from below prose, down in the regions of the Devil's poetry will thrust themselves in. It would be worth years of labor to get the imagination righted in this respect. If we gain that, we shall gain fellowship with heaven.

It would be a valuable exercise if each one of us should write down the most savory, clean, wholesome objects to which the sexual organs can be compared.

If we wished to show our position on our social theory, I would take as my text the story of Shadrach, Meshach, and Abednego.* The fact is, our social theory is a furnace that has always burnt folks. It is calculated to burn them. But in the case of these men, a fourth person was there. They trusted in God, and had a good time undoubtedly—a first rate time—because they had Christ there with them. The smell of fire was not on their garments. /321/ That is almost literally true of us, both externally and internally. We enter the furnace, and are not consumed.

I suppose there is a veiled allusion to sex in the description of the river and tree of life. John says he "saw the holy city coming down from God out of heaven, prepared as a bride adorned for her husband." There is a curious mixing up of ideas: a city, and yet it is a bride. The tree of life has twelve manner

---

* Heroes of the Old Testament Book of Daniel who survived their ordeal in the fiery furnace. [L.F.]

of fruit, and yieldeth its fruit every month. That seems to me to relate to the laboratory of love, the sanctuary where life begins. And there are allusions to the same things in the interior of the temple, in the ark of the covenant, and the cherubims of glory, which Paul saw but could not utter, when he was caught up to the heavens. There is a preparation for all these things in sanctifying our imaginations.

I, for one, was brought up in the "nurture and admonition" of the Devil on this subject. But you cannot say anything about these things in the presence of children. And since that branch is not taught in schools and families, the children form schools among themselves, and the Devil volunteers to teach them.

As a postscript to this discourse, I will offer an illustration of my own. As a man is said to know a woman in sexual intercourse, why may we not speak of the telescope with which he penetrates her heavens, and seeks the star of her heart?

Fifth Lecture
December 24, 1852

Christ's answer to the Sadducees about marriage in the resurrection*
brings to view the most important factor in the working of our social theory. He says: "Ye do err in your hearts not knowing /322/ the Scriptures and the power of God." The power of God! That is what we must know to understand Bible Communism. That alters the whole problem. People who understand the power of God may reasonably expect to find things easy which to others are difficult or impossible.

Sixth Lecture
December 26, 1852

If we confess Christ, we must insist upon having the first result of the confession of Christ. It will make every one free, unembarrassed and bold. The very fact that Christ is in us all makes us the most intimate friends. I do not wish to force social freedom, but on the other hand I do not wish to have it obstructed by unnatural contraction of the heart. I want "faith that worketh by love" to have free play. This is a quality of character that I very much covet, and I should like to have examples of it held up to view. I can think of one person, Mr. Mead, who has a freedom and boldness combined with decorum

---

* Matthew 22:15–22, Mark 12:18–27, and Luke 20:27–40. [L.F.]

in mixing with men and women that is highly valuable in society. It is a pleasure to him to get into the cars and become acquainted with everybody; treat
men and women in the most familiar way, and yet not be impertinent. He
simply acts out his social freedom. I don't know as we shall become as skillful
as Mr. Mead right away, but we can all acquire a great deal more of that facul-
ty than we now have.

There are certain persons who have a natural talent for that kind of music,
and there are others who do not have so much. If you let things take their natural course, this first class will branch out and occupy the whole field, while
the others become merely passive. I don't believe in that state of things. I belong myself to the bashful class, and I will head an insurrection /323/ against
the aristocracy. Let us claim our right to a part in this talent for making fun.

We must bestir ourselves. If we are going to take the lead of a daily press,
and become the center of public opinion, we must feel at home anywhere and
everywhere, ready to go into society and teach everybody.

Seventh Lecture
January 15, 1853

Since reading Greeley's article in *The Tribune* this morning, I have felt a
strong desire to do justice to our women. One great point in dispute between
Greeley and others is the comparative responsibility of men and women in
regard to chastity. Greeley takes the ground that women have the special
charge of chastity, and they ought to have it, and that they ought to bear the
heaviest portion of blame if they go astray. I go clear over to the opposite side
and insist that man is more responsible than woman. Man is bound to take
care of himself and of woman too. If men are chaste, you need not trouble
yourself about the women. That is the doctrine embodied in our social theory,
especially in the distinction between the amative and propagative departments. It is impossible for a woman to exercise sufficient influence to protect
her there.

In the stand that we have taken before the world, the women are the sufferers more than the men. The world condemns sexual offenses in women
more than in men. The fact that the women have so loyally and faithfully
stood by us in this fight calls for thanks.

I feel bound as a Christian lover to see that I do not injure any woman
morally nor physically. A man must secure a /324/ woman from fear. He must
win her confidence, because he has the power to do her mischief.

I vow to the Lord before you women in the name of all the men, that we will do the fair thing by you. We will try to understand and appreciate you, and remove the torments and encumbrances between you and the men. We will make room for you, and you shall have all the chance you want. Before God here tonight, we give you free papers.

If men know their interests, they cannot take any other course than this. You can never have any satisfaction in love as long as women are under bondage to fear. Every disadvantage you put upon women is a damper upon their love. If you make women your slaves, you will have to put up with pretty poor fodder in the love line. /325/

33

Administration of Complex Marriage
June 1849 to December 1852

Mary E. Cragin to George Cragin
  Brooklyn, June 11, 1849

Another suggestion of Mr. Noyes's: That if Mr. Bradley is in a good state (as I should judge he is by what is said of him in Sarah Burnham's note), he have liberty with Ellen and Philena if he wishes it. Sarah (Bradley) will no doubt be pleased to help her husband to fellowship with others. You must be the judge of Mr. Bradley's state, and have an eye to things. Also hint to those girls that they exercise some conservatism, and not allow themselves to be made too free with by all sorts. . . .

Since the receipt of yours, Mr. Noyes says I may say to you *privately,* that although he does not invite Ellen, yet if she chooses to come, and circumstances make it expedient *on her own responsibility* remember, she may come if she wishes to.

With regard to the state of things between you and me, I am well satisfied. God has our hearts in his power, and I have no complaint to make of his administration. When he thinks best, he will give me that attraction which you desire; and until he does think best, as there is some excellent reason for withholding it, let us say, "Thy will be done."

John R. Miller to His Wife
CONFIDENTIAL
Brooklyn, July 25, 1849

Dear Charlotte:—
Your letter of last Saturday was received this morning, and I need not tell you that it gave me unspeakable pleasure. /326/ Furthermore, it did me a great deal of *good,* as I will explain when I see you. You must not for a moment think that I intended to find fault with you for not writing me sooner. Instead of complaining, I feel very thankful that you have written me as often as you have.

When I said I had "a thousand things to say to you," I was in great distress of mind, and my heart was full of things I wished to write you, but did not feel free to. I have thought lately that I would write you regularly once a week and no more, but I cannot endure it. I want to write you *twice a day,* and should if I followed my own feelings, for I always have enough to say. I should not fail to write you once a day, if I could make up my mind that it was not foolish. What do you think about it?

I feel an interest in all you *do, say, or think,* but I have not the least curiosity to pry into your affairs. And here let me say that I have utmost confidence that you will do exactly the right thing.

You did not exactly like my warm love letter, did you? Perhaps I was a little too free in expressing my feelings toward you, but I wrote just what was in my heart, and I cannot say that I am sorry for it. When I write I am obliged to keep my heart closed, for if it once opened there is no knowing how much would rush out.

You ask how I get along. Since I wrote last, I have been quite sick. One day I thought that I must go to Oneida, that I could not possibly stand it any longer. I proposed it to John. He left me at perfect liberty to do as I pleased. I /327/ thought I would wait a little longer, and finally gave it up. For a week past I have really felt that it was doubtful whether I lived or died. But today I am quite well.

There has so far been nothing particularly interesting in my *private history.* The first week I was here I went to bed between eleven and twelve o'clock, and got up at half past four in the morning. The last week I have retired about the same time, but get up precisely at five. I do not think I have slept over two hours in twenty-four since I left Oneida. I have tried to sleep in the daytime, but have found it next to impossible. I hope to improve in this respect. I suppose one reason why I could not sleep was because I was so lonesome. I have had no company except one night and part of another when I was sickest and it was hardly thought safe for me to stay alone.

And now I am about to make a confession. There is a lady in the block opposite with whom I have been perfectly charmed. I have looked at her for half an hour at a time, and could hardly keep my eyes off from her. She is decidedly *beautiful.* She has been at her window while I have been writing this letter. Don't you think I am getting in love? Now for the secret of the story. The peculiar charm is that she looks like you. She wears a dress which at this distance looks like your gingham. Her hair is combed like yours, and when she sits with her face partly turned from me I should almost be ready to swear that it was you. I could not muster courage enough to look at your likeness till I had been here more than a week. Now I take great pleasure in looking at it.

I hope when you write you will always tell how the children are. Give my love to them and kiss them for me. /328/

I do not think I shall write you another letter like this. I will endeavor to have them "Community letters."

No more, so good night, dearest C.

Yours as ever, J.R.M.

The Marriage Spirit
August 30, 1849

The good luck, good health, good feeling, which we find among us, attends the Community spirit, the spirit that cleaves to and acts out the principles of the *Report* we have published. If there is a good spirit here, as those who come here testify, it is the spirit that acknowledges God as our owner, and resolves us all into one family. But this good spirit has worked its way in the face of tremendous opposing forces. We cannot judge what would have been the result if our principles had been unobstructed. There has been thus far only a half-way surrender to the truth we have proclaimed. If a man comes into this Association with a wife that he has to watch and reserve from others, he has brought a cask of powder into a blacksmith's shop. It is the business of the shop to make sparks, and no wonder he is miserable. But it is not fair to charge his unhappiness upon our principles. I say to such persons: "If you cannot be persuaded to be rational in this matter, I will be patient, and insist only on keeping the theory clearly before us." Sometimes a ship coming into harbor against wind and tide sends a small boat forward with the anchor; then when the anchor is fastened wraps up to it by pulling on the cable. We will take our theory as an anchor and wrap up to it as fast as we can. /329/

Our theory is that there is no marriage in heaven. Not merely this Association but Christ himself has made this declaration. Even if the Association goes to destruction, God will find a way to break up marriage. Death at any rate will end marriage. This Association preaches Christ as having the prerogatives of death, and invites you to volunteer in that course to which you will be dragged at death. A people who have learned that they need not wait for death to be delivered from sin should expect to learn that they need not wait for death to be delivered from those things which are built on sin, that is selfishness and exclusiveness. The family relation of brothers and sisters is to take the place of the artificial relation of marriage. I am anxious to see these principles fairly tried, but we cannot do this so long as the Association, or part of them, are holding back.

I am convinced by experience and observation that God does not favor marriage. Love is an infusion from God, and I believe that there is very little warm, genial love between the married pairs in Association. The parties are not to blame; God does not send his love in that channel. Almost every married person in the Association is in love with somebody besides their married companion, and they are sensible of an electricity about it not to be accounted for by the working of their own spirits alone. It is the free love of heaven, and it is directed by the living God.

Marriage has a proper place in the Association. It establishes our rights against the world, the same as the law of property does. You avail yourself of that law to say to the world: /330/ "This is mine." Then you turn to the Association and say: "This is yours." We make the same use of marriage. By marriage you place yourself and your partner in a position where you are protected from the interference of outside society. Moreover marriage for the present may be the best method of introducing the sexes to each other. The time may come when we shall have wit enough to invent fashions that are more natural and beautiful. Meanwhile the world offers us a convenient method, and we will avail ourselves of it. I have never assented to any marriage that gave one an exclusive right to another. All our marriages have been matters of convenience and policy. Marriage may be wise in some cases for purposes of care and oversight. Besides these reasons, I see no further use for marriage.

The principal ground of exclusive companionship does not exist in this Association. In the world a woman secures her support and protection by marriage. A man becomes responsible for her, and on that ground claims a right to her exclusive affection. But there is no woman here who is dependent on one man for support. Another ground of exclusiveness in the world is the idea that a woman who has once married has lost her attractiveness, and her husband must love her and take care of her, for she has no other chance. But this is not true here.

While a man stands in the ranks of society as a candidate for the favors of the other sex, he is under the strongest stimulus to cultivate amiable manners and honorable ambition. He looks well to the quality of his goods. But when he is sold in marriage, there is an end to all care about quality. He has got a woman, whom he has a right to make his companion whether she will or no, the right of a master over a slave. /331/

I should be glad, at any cost, to see this whole Association come on to courting ground; to see every man put himself into the market for what he is worth. There would be a good deal more attention to quality. A man who has a wife has the privilege of being lazy; he has all that is necessary to satisfy his sensual appetite and social craving, and he is contented, though he may be as poor as poverty. He is in no condition to do justice to other women. It costs something to court another woman, and he cannot pay the price. But the real happiness and beauty of love lies in the courting attitude of mind. This shrinking back from the energy necessary to become attractive is the natural outworking of the marriage system. Let us all come into the market with no rights or claims. Obtain love by love and by presenting attractiveness. "Owe no man anything but love." Never think of paying that debt once and for all. God rewards every man according to his works. Marriage is a refuge of lies that people cover themselves with to get a reward that they do not earn.

All that we need to be a healthy, happy community is to let God's love have free course among us. God's love is not contracted and egotistical, but expansive and universal. God loves the whole Association without respect of persons. All secondary affections based on marriage and kindred must submit to the primary and take their place at last by the favor of the primary. False love, whether manifested in the form of licentiousness or the marriage spirit of philoprogenitiveness, is characterized by a feverish, groveling anxiety for one's own pleasure and an evil eye on the pleasure of others. /332/

Love between the sexes is not a mere privilege or luxury but a debt. Every man as such owes a debt to every woman, and every woman as such owes a debt to every man. You may say it is impossible for a man to stand in love relations with every woman. How do you know? Eternity is before us. If you cannot pay down, perhaps God will hold a note against you toward every woman to be paid on demand. Dare you put yourself in a condition which precludes you from paying your social debts, and dare you put anybody else in that condition? A man who has the marriage spirit is precisely in the condition of a fraudulent debtor; he has given all his property to one preferred creditor, and is cheating the rest.

There are men in the Association who have talents for social music and

ought to be glorious distributors of God's love, but who are crippled by daintiness and cramped and made miserable by marriage adhesions. Then there
are women who can and should love the whole Association, but whose husbands stand watching and jealous and grumbling if their wives pay a cent to
anyone but themselves. Many persons are not only precluded from paying
their just social debts, but are starved; and society is not only deprived of their
love but of their efficiency. A man is not a man unless he is in the free exercise
of his affections. True love is essential to health. It is the fire of life.

You will not be excused on account of daintiness from paying your social
debts. You may say you have no taste for anybody but your wife. But your taste
may be diseased. God will not have those in his kingdom who cannot love all
that he loves. Christ loves us not with distant benevolence but with intimate
union. /333/

I have not only no right to refuse paying my own debts, and no right to
hinder others from paying theirs, but no right to allow anybody to make me a
fraudulent debtor. Every man must give an account of himself to God, and
those who are held in a fraudulent position by selfish partners must still pay
their debts.

While the world is predicting that our principles will result in confusion
and licentiousness, the difficulty has actually been on the other side. It has not
been enough to set the doors open; we have had great labor to get folks to
come out of their cages.

Noyes to the Association
November 8, 1849

I find in my heart commendation and gratitude toward the Association for
its faithful observance of that part of our social theory which relates to propagation. Our principle of Male Continence makes a large demand, especially in
our present incipient stage of education, on self-control and self-denial, and is
doubtless the occasion of some trials and temptations. It would not have been
strange if instances of violation had occurred among us. But I am thankful that
we are able to say that no involuntary, unwholesome impregnation has taken
place in this Association during nearly two years of its existence. The Association will also allow me, on behalf of myself and others, to tender thanks for the
respect and kindness with which those strangers who have come among us
contrary to law (though not by chance) have been received.

John H. Noyes /334/

Charlotte A. Miller to the Brooklyn Family
   Oneida, November 26, 1849

Did ever the telegraph convey such electrifying news? The rebuke and re-proach are taken away indeed, when they had produced the desired effect, that of expelling frivolity and cant. This has been a sober week, and the spirit of judgment has been active and searching in many directions.

Our meeting this evening was extremely interesting. The news was re-served until after the reading of a confession from Mrs. Ackley and remarks by Mr. Hamilton; and when the audience could fairly catch their breath, it was responded to by clapping of hands, laughter, and exclamations of joy, with episodes of embracing and kissing between Mother and Mrs. Campbell and Mrs. Seymour. After a second reading Mr. Hamilton called attention to the coincidence between the date of this crisis with that of the flight from Putney two years ago.

Mr. Hamilton then related some of his experience the past week, which proved that God had not only carried the Association through a dangerous crisis, but had placed a man at its head whom he could make behave well, not suffering him to be puffed up or swayed from his upright course. Mr. Burt expressed his satisfaction with Mr. Hamilton's position, as one which bore decidedly on W. H. Cook's ambition to attain the same place.

There was a general looking back to the events of past years. Mr. Hamilton related the manner in which his confidence in John first began, was destroyed by the Wilders, and again restored and confirmed by John's writings. The ef-fect on the whole was exhilarating but quiet and serious. /335/

My heart appreciates brotherly love more and more, and my union with John is becoming more satisfactory.

I am yours forever,
Charlotte

Mary E. Cragin to the Oneida Association
   Brooklyn, November 26, 1849

I have thought it might not be uninteresting to you to know some of the exercises of mind through which I passed before my deliverance. When Mr. Noyes came home, and wished me to dismiss the Association from my mind, and quietly sit down and wait on the Lord, although it was just what I had been wishing and praying for, yet I found that while I could seclude my body I could not separate my spirit, which had a strong centrifugal tendency. I prayed God to separate me from the spirit of flattery and false love at any cost, for I was anxiously seeking fellowship with the Primitive Church, but found myself fettered and bound in a descending direction.

About this time Mr. Noyes wrote his first note to the Association. When he read it to me, I felt as though I ought to tell him that I had reason to suspect myself, but I was so unwilling to believe such a thing, so sure that I had been careful and that all others concerned had been equally so, that I laughed at my own fears. But I could not get rid of them by the efforts of my will, and at length gave it up and asked God to hold me in suspense just as long as he pleased, or to make me believe it, or to make it true if I could not learn the lesson which he wished me to in any other way. From that time the conviction fastened itself on my mind, and I mentioned it to Mr. Noyes. Then I went through the most terrible ordeal of criticism which I ever did. I disclosed /336/ to him all the secrets of my heart and abode the judgment of God. For two days I was in great doubt whether Mr. Noyes had strong enough hold of the center of my life to break the snare which held me, and I felt myself hanging over hell at God's mercy. Before I got through I was much more anxious to learn the lesson which God had set me than to be released from the consequences, and said in my heart, I will not accept deliverance until this lesson is learned. I prayed God for repentance which needed not to be repented of, and he gave me that which wrought in me clearing of myself, indignation, fear, vehement desire, zeal and revenge. He has made me *sincere,* and in your thanksgiving to God on my behalf I pray you to thank him for this more than anything else. For this sincerity has brought me to Him. I find the same love in my heart, the same sober, earnest tone which I had when I was first married to God at nineteen years of age. God has brought me back to my first love, and in doing so he has displayed the nice skill and fearlessness of a surgeon and all the attractions of a lover. While he cut me loose from idols mercilessly, he charmed me with love. He has willed me into sincerity by making me feel that every time I open my heart and let in the light upon the secret places, it lets in his love upon me. And now I ask for nothing else, need nothing else to make me happy and lovely. This beautiful sincerity is making me true to my inner instincts, true to my real self which is the voice of God in me. Sincerity will save me from flattery and false love, and will make me single-eyed. I shall be such a lover of true pleasure that I shall put up with no shams. /337/ Ascending fellowship will charm beyond all possibility of being seduced by those below me.

In looking back at the dealings of God with me from my youth up, I see that he is in earnest in his love. He never forgets the covenant he made with me then, and all he has put me through has been necessary to bring me where I could rejoice in his love and appreciate his faithfulness.

The agony of heart through which I passed at Oneida in view of the probable consequences of false love, and the terrible judgment through which I was delivered cause the question to spring involuntarily, What shall I render to the Lord for all his goodness to me? My heart answers, I will render sincerity. I have no secrets from those above me. I will be true to my inner instincts at the risk of being singular and unpopular. He who has proved himself my best and most faithful lover shall have my whole heart; to him will I abandon myself without looking over my shoulder. I love Mr. Noyes because he knows more about God than I do, and can teach me how to please him, and I reverence him as God's agent in bringing me to him.

I must say a word about the second note which Mr. Noyes sent you. I felt when he read it to me, that my death-warrant was signed. I gave up the life of the body for the sake of my spirit, and gave up all the love I had from you, and was willing to be an outcast from the church as I have long been from the world. To my utter surprise I found myself in an ocean of tenderness and love. Oh, by this love let me implore you to be sincere, be true to your instincts, be sober, be in earnest, love truth better than your life, if you would be happy and have /338/ fellowship with God.

There is a hymn in the Lyre which expresses God's dealings with me, which perhaps you will like to sing. It begins: "Hark, my soul, it is the Lord."

I wish you a joyful thanksgiving.

Truly yours,
M. E. Cragin

George W. Hamilton to Noyes
Oneida, November 28, 1849

The day you left Oneida, I was in a tumult of feelings. The advice you gave me served to quiet me and cause me to look at my character to see if I could find the spirit you said I was possessed of. I saw very plainly that you had hit the mark. That evening I stayed in my room, and had more heart-felt fellowship with Christ than ever before. I gave myself up anew to God, willing to take any position he would put me in. I can say this without any cant. I found a frivolous, pleasure-seeking spirit in me, and was surprised that I had not seen it before. The next day I prayed God, if he could not free me from those spirits in any other way, to take the love of the Association from me entirely. That evening I read your *Religious Experience*,* and it seemed to me that I

---

* *Confessions of John H. Noyes, Part 1: Confessions of Religious Experience,* 1849. [L.F.]

could swallow every word of it. I have never felt such a strong desire to read your writings as I do now. Friday evening I was thrown into trials and suffering. I felt as though I was nearly enveloped by the Devil's spirit and could not be saved. All I could do was to confess Christ in me, and say, I am God's property. I find that every part of my character is being judged. /339/

The other evening I was cut by your sending for Philena Baker. But I can thank God for it, for I feel it is cutting into the egotism I am possessed of. I have been trying to pass myself off for more than I am worth, but God has detected the spirit. I can now say I do not wish to be appreciated for more than I am worth, and I do not want any love but that which God directs. My desire is that God will carry out the work he has commenced in me, and I am confident that he will do so.

In looking at the proceedings of yourself and Mrs. Cragin in this late affair, I could not help being forcibly struck with the way that both of you took it. My confidence has been greatly increased in you. I have never loved you before with such pure and sincere love. I would like to thank you for the criticism that came from you. I rejoice heartily in Mrs. Cragin's deliverance from danger, but pray God it may not be the means of my forgetting the lesson that he set before me. I would take up with Mrs. Cragin's advice, to sit at the feet of Jesus and learn.

Charlotte A. Miller to Mary E. Cragin
    December 15, 1849

Your letter concerning George Hamilton will receive our earnest consideration. I am persuaded that what you have suffered in this affair will prove a bulwark of salvation between him and Helen Noyes. In her case I know that I was dazzled by a superficial glare of beauty, and was drawn into a flattering spirit toward her. /340/

Oneida Journal

March 2, 1850.—Just as our men were through their breakfast, the cry of *fire* was heard and the blaze and smoke of a burning house was seen in the direction of Mr. Hubbard's. All sallied forth, and arrived on the spot just in time to save Mr. Dexter Hubbard the loss of his barns, worth several hundred dollars. George Hamilton took a position on top of the barn, where they had to throw water on him to keep him from burning.

As George Hamilton was the hero of the morning, "dauntless in the fire," so he was the bridegroom of the evening, "gallant in love." Just before meeting Mr. E. H. Hamilton received Brooklyn's approval of George Hamilton's marriage to Philena Baker, and communicated it to the parties, both in a state of innocent simplicity till then. A beautiful spirit of unity and sympathetic happiness pervaded the ceremony.

Note by Noyes:—This was in the transition period of our social system, before we had entirely abandoned marriage; but the knot was not tied very tight.

Noyes to E. H. Hamilton
Brooklyn, March 4, 1850

I have not overlooked or forgotten the suggestions that have been made from time to time in regard to the wishes of the unmarried young men. I have reflected much on their position. In fact the problem which I undertook to solve last fall in relation to their admission to the freedom of the Association has been continually before me. I have had plenty of good-will for removing all difficulties, but having no special /341/ inspiration on the subject I have refrained from writing. I find that in a difficult spot the best thing I can do is to stand still; and evidently the transition of the young men from the hot blood of virginity to the quiet freedom which is the essential element of our Society is emphatically the difficult pass in our social experience. I have not much new light on the matter now, but after receiving your application for advice in regard to mating George Hamilton and others, I have thought it best to state distinctly the difficulties which have constrained me to stand still, that you and others may act fairly in view of them and may understand the spirit of my administration in this respect hitherto.

In the first place, experience has shown that the usual "sale and delivery" of the woman to the man through marriage is highly objectionable. We have distressing examples of the effect of initiating young men. The spiritual collapse of Julia Hyde and Sarah Dunn, perhaps also of Sarah Campbell, Mrs. Worden, and Louisa Waters, may be mentioned. I surmise that the possessive feeling, when it gets a foothold in the midst of the counter influences of such a society as ours, by no means abates its usual energy. The husband's ownership of the wife seems stronger in these cases than in the cases of those who brought wives into the Association. The past warns us against sale and delivery, and though I approve of your motion for mating George and Philena I protest in advance in the name of the Association and on behalf of the weaker party against such appropriation as in the former cases has disabled and almost sunk the women. Here I stood last fall. Here lies the secret of /342/ my dealings with Fidelia and Abram. Here I stand still. The weaker party needs protection from the untamed lion; and if the amativeness of the young men is not civilized enough to be safely trusted, the Association is bound to protect the young women. I am willing, as I have been, to suffer odium in this quarrel.

On the other hand, the plan proposed last fall of introducing the young men to the freedom of the Association through the more spiritual women has been attended with difficulties. Mrs. Cragin lost her equilibrium in the attempt to carry it out, and there appears to have been an unhealthy excitement in Perkins and perhaps others, which has ended in grudging and discontent.

So then whichever way we turn we meet a difficulty. What precisely is the difficulty? It is nothing more nor less than the fiery, ungovernable condition of amativeness in men whose ardor has been stimulated by the unnatural training of the world but not drawn off by marriage.

This difficulty is by no means so formidable in the case of the young women. Amativeness in them is naturally less ferocious than in young men. The danger of pushing love into ownership as well as into undesirable propagation is by the position of he parties chiefly on the side of the men. How is this difficulty to be overcome? It cannot be conjured out of the way by any civil request, nor by any ingenious modes of mating. It must be resisted, like all other forms of uncivilized passion, wisely but firmly and heroically, /343/ and success must be sought and patiently waited for in the growth of spiritual strength in the Association. As we become mighty in the power of the resurrection we shall be able to hold the passions even of young men quiet, and introduce them to the freedom of love without danger. Till then we must try experiments and wriggle through our difficulties the best we can; and in this transition period the young men must consider the difficulties, be patient, and help as much as they can by self-discipline. I sympathize with them, and would be glad to see them all enjoying the full freedom of love, but while trying to do justice to them I must look out for the interests of the Association. They cannot possibly enjoy the freedom of love until they have conquered themselves; on the contrary, they are liable to be themselves the greatest sufferers from the perils of the crisis which they are so eager for. I demand therefore for their own sakes that they give us time for study, and themselves time for self-improvement.

Possibly the true solution of the problem, so far as it can be solved by social contrivances, will be found in a combination of the two plans, namely, introduction to free love by the ascending fellowship, and mating horizontally. This combination was tried in the case of Abram and Fidelia, and the results are the best we have had yet. If all the young men will court as well as Abram did, they will have no difficulty so far as my feelings are concerned in obtaining a free relation to the church and the special companions they desire.

With these observations I leave the whole matter to your discretion. /344/

CASE OF WILLIAM H. PERRY

Noyes to William H. Perry
Brooklyn, April 24, 1850

Bro. Perry:—
Mr. Leonard has reported to me facts which show that your amativeness is in a bad state, and I am bound for the church's sake as well as for your own to deal plainly with you.

Your sexual history previous to your connection with us reveals unusual corruption. Though you had been a church member and a Perfectionist, you had been a secret whoremonger and had several times contracted the venereal disease. Without any disclosure of these facts, and of course without any hearty repentance of them, you availed yourself of our free principles and exposed two of our women here at Brooklyn to the poison still lurking in your system. Self-seeking and concealment thus far marked you as an unclean man. Your secret was drawn from you, and you passed through a judgment which I hoped would give you a new sense of the sacredness of love and make you an honorable man toward the other sex. But it now appears that, in the face of my counsel, and in the face of your own conscience (since you found it necessary to walk in darkness), you have dealt with Mrs. Smith as you dealt with Mrs. Whitfield and Mrs. Langstaff, exposing her to distress and distrust, if not to disease. Sensual self-seeking and concealment are as manifest here as heretofore, and you have now added to them gross insubordination. You are not a safe man, and you will not be till you have had a far deeper work of repentance, and have thoroughly laid to heart God's /345/ judgment of whoremongers. In view of this discovery of your character, I see why I have not been able to forward your negotiations with Mary Mabie. As an honorable man, I cannot advise you to offer yourself to her in your present condition. You are diseased in spirit if not in body.

Now is the time to overhaul your accounts and make a thorough settlement. The act in question is not the thing to be judged. It is the spirit betrayed in that act. That spirit has blunted your sense of honor in love, and you must get rid of it or your place will be without among dogs and sorcerers. God does not tolerate it, and you shall not bring it in among us if I can prevent it. If you ask what you are to do, I answer: Turn away from all women to God, judge yourself, and open your heart to the church. If you are faithful, you will find business enough of this kind to occupy you for some time. Moreover, I counsel you now and forthwith to apprize the whole Association of your past history. Such a disclosure is due. We must demand such disclosures from every man who proposes to enter our circle, otherwise we are open to all the plagues of licentiousness, spiritual and physical. Every woman ought to know your condition as evinced by the facts which I have referred to. Every man ought to know women have had intercourse with you. If there is one thing above all others that ought to be prized in such a community as ours, it is perfect frankness, especially in sexual matters. Our only hope of safety lies in throwing all open to the light and allowing spiritual criticism to do its work. God will insist that sincerity shall go before liberty. Expose yourself to /346/ the "Flaming sword that keeps the way of the tree of life," and you may yet win our confidence.

Yours faithfully
John H. Noyes

Oneida Journal

April 27, 1850.—The Holmeses of East Hamilton, after a week's trial, have decided that they are not ready to join, and must leave. They were scared away by the requirement that husbands and wives should sleep apart.

Harriet H. Skinner to Mary E. Cragin
Oneida, April 28, 1850

If ever there was an illustration of Paul's philosophy, a little leaven leaveneth the whole lump, we are seeing it now. A spark of hell-fire has come in through Mr. Perry that would sweep the Association if it was not quenched. The engines are at work to-day in good earnest. Mr. Perry received John's letter Friday evening. He communicated it to Mr. Burt, and Mr. Burt to George and others. Last evening George called a meeting of the leading members, read the letter, and brought out facts showing that a licentious spirit had been disclosed in other quarters. Mrs. Smith confessed yesterday that she had been with Hyde without Mr. Skinner's knowledge while she was professing to confide everything to him. This brought Hyde into judgment. Julia and Jane confessed that he had been trying to seduce them, and he confessed to Julia that night before last he was with Mary Pomeroy during the evening meeting. It appears that he has been completely drunk with sensuality for some time, and all the while in special fellowship with Mr. Perry. /346A/ Hyde, Mrs. Smith, and Mary Pomeroy have of all others in the Association been close to Mr. Perry, and have had a thorough run of his spiritual disease. You can see what a mean transaction that was between Hyde and Mary Pomeroy, because it is notorious that he has a great repugnance to her.

It was thought best, as Mr. Perry had consented, to read John's letter before the whole meeting and invite the spirit of judgment. George said that this spirit of licentiousness was imported by Mr. Perry from New York City, and was foreign to the Community. Hyde came out with an apparently broken-hearted confession of being under its influence and forsaking it. Several confessed what struggles with that spirit they had lately been through, and George said he believed the whole Association had felt it. The evidence that it had been withstood in a good measure was encouraging.

This forenoon the Association met by appointment. There were some circumstances that connected Mr. Perry directly with the present disorderly state of the children. He was observed this morning to be fondling Ellen Lord in an unbecoming way, and Ellen Lord and Ann Eliza have been identified as the leak among the children that lets in the pleasure-seeking spirit. They have lately had all the appearance of girls brought up in the city, roving about, calling at the store and shops, and spending their time in the streets. Mr. Perry has been in the way of giving them sweetmeats at the store. Mr. Carr said that he had been obliged to criticize Mr. Perry sharply several times for coming to him with the complaint that the center of the Association monopolized the amative privileges. Testimony /347/ is pouring in about Mr. Perry. He has been in love with Sarah Johnson, or rather has been trying to seduce her. She came out in the meeting with a desire to separate herself from his spirit. He was not present at this meeting, but we were scarcely out when he was seen to give Ellen Lord a bunch of wild flowers; then Philena told that last night, as she was washing her hands at the sink, he came along and said he wished somebody would wash his hands. She did not know that he was under special criticism, and playfully told him she would. When she had washed one, she felt an involuntary disgust and told him he could wash the other himself. But he wanted to pay her, and forced her to receive a kiss. This after John's letter, you see. Mrs. Smith has come out openly to him, and seems disposed to take sides with the judgment of God, though it is hard. She has been tempted from the first to excuse herself and throw the blame upon the Association in one way or another. Finally she said that George, Mr. Skinner and the rest of us made a serious matter of her affair with Mr. Perry, but she could not see what harm there was in it. This spirit of blindness and confounding false love with true has been like a nightmare on us all; we could feel that city spirit which attaches no sacredness to the expression of love. Charlotte said that this practical lesson was to be learned by the whole Community, that all amative expressions not proper according to common rules should be reserved for true inspired love, but that lascivious freedom characterized the common interchange of those under rebuke. /348/

About a fortnight ago Charlotte went through a judgment and self-clearing about her connection with Mr. Hyde, so that she was in a condition to criticize him in a way that she never has been before.

Altogether this affair has let in the judgment most seriously. It has thrown Mr. Hatch and Fidelia into the fire for things that have come out about their freedom months ago. And Charlotte says it will throw Mary Pomeroy into perfect obscurity for a while; she is taken out of the kitchen. Mrs. Smith, who has been in the kitchen, has expressed her inclination to retire from observation, but Charlotte advised her to keep herself as much in the light as possible; if she retreated to her room in a spirit of pride and hypo [hypochondria], it would be bad for her. Mrs. Smith takes the advice and is very meek.

Oneida Journal

April 28, 1850.—Two meetings were held today to dispose of Mr. Perry's case. Further investigation showed a lack of subordination to Mr. Noyes and the Association, also an absence of sincere repentance; and it was determined by a general vote of the Association that he be expelled from our body until he make a full proof by deeds that he is cleansed from that false spirit.

July 2, 1850.—Mr. William H. Perry, on the advice of Mr. Noyes, returned to Oneida. Mr. Noyes stated that Mr. Perry had given proof of his subordination and faithfulness, and that he with the other members of the Brooklyn family could unanimously recommend him to the Association. (Conclusion of the Perry Case.) /349/

Harriet H. Skinner to Mary E. Cragin
Oneida, May 18, 1850

I thought I would communicate to you some thoughts which have been passing through my mind today, as they might perhaps be suggestive in some way to John. It seems to me that what he says is true, that amativeness in the Association is in a negative state, and that a heaven-inspired activity of the affections is needed. This negative state is not natural or healthy, and I have thought there was something like a mutinous feeling in several members, the feeling which possessed Mrs. Smith and Mr. Perry, that the center monopolized the amative privileges, and they had a right to help themselves. These persons, I imagine, feel some like the hungry *canaille* of Paris in the time of the Revolution. There seems to be a great stricture. Amativeness has been under so much judgment that the sexes are more divided, if anything, than in the world. As Charlotte says, all criticism and no love does not work well. It seems as if there must be some way by which the extremities can be warmed and vitalized. At present the men keep bachelors' hall, and the women are kind of forlorn. I think of you as the mainspring of love, and have anticipated your return as a season of quickening and improved circulation.

> *May 20, 1850.* Brooklyn's response to Harriet Skinner's appeal was to send Mr. And Mrs. Cragin and Harriet A. Noyes to Oneida for a visit of ten days. They returned to Brooklyn with several others of the Oneida family on May 31st. [G.W.N.] /350/

Conversation at Oneida after Reading Noyes's Letter about Mr. Burnham's Case
June 6, 1850

G.W.N:—This is an encouraging letter, but it has a degree of criticism in it. I am sensible that the criticism is just, and I am prepared to act heartily on the suggestion made. I should like to have perfect freedom of expression on this subject.

E. H. Hamilton:—I consider this criticism just, not only with regard to others but with regard to myself. I have found that what Mr. Noyes calls the rooster spirit has occasionally worked into my experience and has hindered the perfecting of my relation to the Association. It has stood between myself and him, and I am thankful for this frank offer of himself to us as a free gift from God. He is in deed and in truth our brother, and this feeling of fear that we have been under is false. He is not a man to be feared but to be loved. I have had a good deal of conflict with a temptation to think I was overshadowed when I was in his society. But I thought last night, that before I left Oneida I should like to give my testimony on this subject. Instead of being overshadowed by him I have been prospered. All my prosperity in love has been owing to the inspiration and guidance I have received from him. I for one feel like opening my heart to him, and I hope the Association will appreciate him as a gift from God to lead us through the difficulties that lie in the way of true free love.

Isaac Seymour:—Formerly I regarded him as a distant oracle, but I have lately regarded him as a brother. /351/

Henry Seymour:—We need to wake up to a sense of our obligation to Mr. Noyes. If we remember that he has been the means of delivering us from the evils we were subject to in the world, and also of showing us the glories of free love, we cannot feel too thankful to God for the gift of Mr. Noyes.

Jonathan Burt:—Those suggestions of Mr. Noyes came home to me as the

out-gushing of a large heart, and though not given in a spirit of complaint
they are a severe rebuke from God. His feelings toward us now, as they ever
have been, are those of a tender brother, and I invite him with all my heart to
be free on this subject.

Henry W. Burnham:—This discussion is very timely. It is quite evident that
there has been a stoppage in this department. In this letter we have the key to
the mystery. I feel anxious that the whole Association open their hearts to the
leaven of his spirit. Without the life and strength of true love, we cannot prosper. I feel barren, and I want to apply heartily the truth that Mr. Noyes is our
brother. He is a bright spot that we can look to in our temptations and trials.

Albert Kinsley:—I feel that the criticism is just, and I wish to clear my
heart of everything that stands in the way of the life and inspiration of God
that I know flows through Mr. Noyes to us.

John L. Skinner:—I desire that there may be a better appreciation of Mr.
Noyes as God's gift to us, and I hope there will be an expulsion from the Association of the spirit of jealousy and fear of him in relation to love. /352/

George W. Noyes:—I do not know as there need be any reflections cast
upon the past. I am perfectly satisfied that the Association stands higher on
the scale of spirituality than ever before, and that we have a sincerity and earnestness that will enable us to do justice in this matter. I know there is deliverance for every one of us, and I thank God that the crisis has come.

Otis H. Miller:—I have unbounded confidence in Mr. Noyes on this subject and every other.

William H. Woolworth:—It is all-important that we appreciate Mr. Noyes's
character as a brother and as a pioneer. I am conscious that my love for him is
increasing. It is cheering to me that we have such a leader.

Amasa W. Carr:—I esteem it a great privilege to avail myself of Mr.
Noyes's experience in love matters.

Several other men expressed themselves as appreciating Mr. Noyes more
and more as a brother and leader.

Noyes's Remarks on Mr. Burnham's Case
July 2, 1850

I surmise that the root of Mr. Burnham's difficulty is the same as Mr.
Bradley's at Putney. Mr. Bradley had made a surrender of private claims to his
wife so far as fellowship was concerned, but when he learned that Mrs. Cragin
was to have a child by me he began to act like a madman. On the point of pro-
gagation, he was quarreling with God. The community spirit had not pervaded that recess, and consequently there was a chance for poison to work out

into all his social relations. Mr. Bradley finally came over to a right view of the /353/ matter, and was happier for it. I imagine there was a great deal of secret quarreling with God on account of that child, and I would inquire whether that same supposition did not enter Mr. Burnham's mind, that I might possibly intrude on his private interests. I stand as the champion of the right of every man to have children by those he loves. That right is not yet won by a good deal.

Oneida Journal

July 10, 1850.—Mr. Newhouse, who has been suffering from jealousy and the marriage spirit in its intensest form for some time past, gave way to his feelings and committed an assault upon D. P. Nash and Mrs. Newhouse as they were walking in the garden after meeting. He followed them, and violently demanded an explanation of their course, telling them that murder was in his heart. Mr. Burnham, hearing the noise, came to their rescue. He drew Mr. Newhouse away, and slept with him all night.

July 11, 1850.—Mr. Burt and G. W. Noyes have labored with Mr. Newhouse today. By some exertion he confessed his faults in the meeting, and wrote a communication to Brooklyn exposing his past life.

George W. Noyes in the Oneida Journal

July 16, 1850.—The body has been under considerable pressure for a few days past. I called out Leonard Dunn, who has been suffering from the marriage spirit. He frankly expressed himself, referring the cause to that Burnham *Report.* He has never been tempted with murder in his heart toward Mr. /354/ Noyes. He has written a note to Francis Hyde judging the spirit. Mr. Isaac Seymour confessed his difficulty with that *Report.* He did not see any right or propriety in Mr. Noyes's assuming peculiar privileges or a peculiar interest in propagation. This brought down a regular tempest upon him from Mr. Burt and others, and he backed out in a rather [be]draggled condition.

There are of course occasions of trouble enough of other kinds, and well there may be so long as confidence is not externally declared in Mr. Noyes. How can we expect God to be very much at home with us while Mr. Noyes cannot?

July 17, 1850.—Mr. Burnham made a confession acknowledging the truth of the *Report* on his case, and making a full surrender of his wife to the church of God and Mr. Noyes.

July 18, 1850.—At a meeting of the men, the report of Mr. Noyes's discourse called out by Mr. Newhouse's confessions was read. G. W. Noyes spoke with earnestness and power, urging the necessity of carrying sincerity clear through to the bottom of our hearts. If the surrender of our rights to God was not carried through to that ultimate point of an entire surrender of our wives, the Association might fail. Evil-thinking and distrust of Mr. Noyes such as was brought out by old Mr. Seymour must be thoroughly expelled. We should not get free from troubles and distresses till we got sincerity and confidence in Mr. Noyes that would invite him heartily here and make a genial home for him among us. Others agreed with this. Mr. Newhouse said he was thankful for Mr. Noyes's criticism. /355/

July 21, 1850.—A free meeting in the evening, in which the spirit of truth seemed to be present. Mr. Isaac Seymour confessed himself wrong in his doubts of Mr. Noyes. He said that, having such abundant evidence that Mr. Noyes was called of God as a leader, he ought not to doubt him in specific things.

October 17, 1850.—A daughter, Grace, was born to Mrs. Kesiah Worden this evening. Mr. A. C. Smith is the father. This is the first accidental birth, or false-ness to our principles. Both parties have had a sincere criticism for their un-faithfulness to Christ and the truth.

Charlotte A. Miller to Mary E. Cragin
Oneida, March 6, 1851

I have been wishing to write you, not out of a desire to burden you with complaints (for I truly feel that I have all and abound), but rather to express to you, and through you to John, the increase of my first-love devotion to him—the gratitude that melts my heart for his loving kindness and patience, the loyalty that gathers strength constantly from a remembrance of the past, and will, I am sure, reign over all other affections. You guessed rightly that his expressions of love and commendation toward Harriet and me would be joy-fully received. . . .

I think that under Mr. Cragin's spirit a far more genial feeling prevails, yet there is a great deal of what may be called loyalty to Mr. Hamilton as a man, that sets him up as the standard of character, and is cold, cramping, and dis-trustful toward others who are his superiors in many things. This spirit /356/ crept over me. I was in a spiritual contest much of the time to keep in fellow-ship with him as a co-worker, and yet keep my independence. I remembered your advice to be sincere with him and not submit to his claim of right to fa-vors. The first time I had a collision with him I told him that I did not think he ought to expect Harriet and me to follow his lead without consultation, and that it would be the worst thing in the world for him to be in circumstances where he could break down all opposition. He said he had an impression that Harriet and I walked in the letter of John's instructions, but did not get at the spirit as he did. The last difficulty I had was in reference to Consuelo. He had her up in his chamber about a week. Susan took care of her under his directions with Mrs. Hatch in consultation. I broke through a spirit which made me feel small and tempted to evil-thinking about his movements, and went up and told him how I felt. I said that I believed it was more healthy for him and me to work together than for him and Susan and Mrs. Hatch; that I was not tempted to flatter him, nor he me; and that my spirit was a necessary mixture with his. He acknowledged that I was right, and changed his policy.

I welcomed Mr. Cragin here with much joy, for I was in a rather haggard condition. Since then I have had an increase of hope and fellowship with John, Mr. Cragin, Mr. Burt, and others. When Mr. Hamilton left, there was a clearing out of all old grudges, and we parted with peace and fellowship so far as our personal relations were concerned. I saw clearly from the confessions of Philena and others and from my own feelings, that there was a spirit here that would belittle Mr. Cragin and indeed /357/ almost any other man as compared with Mr. Hamilton. The other day I had a free conversation with Susan. She acknowledged that loyalty to Mr. Hamilton was what John had more difficulty with than anything else, and that she thought Mr. Hamilton knew that he could always find a home in her heart if he was cut off everywhere else. She had hated to have him criticised, particularly by a woman. She knew that Mrs. Hatch almost worshiped him.

Fear of Criticism: Home-Talk by Noyes
June 23, 1851

We proposed last evening to pursue the subject of the fear of criticism in its bearings on love. There is no point on which the Devil seems nearer almighty. But I expect to beat the Devil there at least, no mistake about that. I must go back to foundations, and show the tremendous importance of love. Love is more interesting to me than all the sciences and arts. God will give us but little instruction in smaller matters until we have attended to the more important ones. We may say that love more than anything else has come under criticism, and the best thing we can do is to do nothing about it. I have suffered as much as anybody, but I shall never forget that love is life. To be turned away from it by fear of criticism is to be turned away from the tree of life. Let us meet criticism, the "flaming sword" which God has placed "to keep the way of the tree of life."

I find myself in a state of simplicity and freedom, and I act it out from time to time, but there is little response. /358/ The work of breaking through barriers to fellowship is left to me. But unless others take hold with me, the barriers are not permanently removed. The Association generally seems to have betaken itself to the passive virtues. They have ceased to do evil, and have become very dutiful and obedient. But "cease to do evil, learn to do well" is the order of God.

We have difficulties both in individuals and in the Association. But instead of hiding from one another and from God, we should say, "This experience has given us safer and better grounds than before. We will take a new start and perfect ourselves in this science."

This discouragement that has spread itself over the Association proceeds partly from fear of criticism, and partly from laziness, a shrinking from difficulty. Personal enthusiasm has dwindled down to nothing. There are but few cases of attraction among us. Perhaps this necessary in the present transition stage. The head members of the Association are hardly out of this trouble themselves. Let us have an end of this matter without further jaw. A more manly stand must be taken, doing all things in the name of Jesus. The spirit of heaven is wrestling with the spirit of darkness that is brooding over the Association, and will be cramped up neither by the men nor by the women. Greeley's spirit about going to sea is the spirit of the Association on this subject. They have been seasick, and have come to the conclusion that it is best to "reduce this intercourse of the nations." You may say, if you please, we have had one hard voyage, but I am going to sea again, let who will puke. /359/

Women need not think they are going to sail into heaven as pinks of propriety. What is considered propriety here is impropriety there. I would advise all to adopt the motto "Evil to him who evil thinks," and make each other free to commit improprieties. Cultivate sincerity. Whenever in a sincere spirit you cut through the spirit of the world on this subject, you will hear all heaven shout.

Criticism of Mr. Hamilton
June 24, 1851

Mr. Hamilton:—I am greatly implicated in this spirit of fear of criticism. It has lately worked in me a feeling of barrenness, a feeling that I had created great expectations toward me, and had not fulfilled them. I felt as though Mr. Noyes stood ready to criticise me all the while.

Noyes:—I never had any such evil thoughts as you describe. I think you are a hard critic of yourself, and would fare a great deal better in my hands.

Difficulty in Carrying Out the Social Theory:
Home-Talk by Noyes
    June 25, 1851

A change has come upon the Association, a sort of stoppage, fearfulness, discouragement; a feeling that the social theory is a good thing but not feasible. If that spirit has carried away everybody else, it has not carried me away. I have the same confidence and interest in that theory that I ever had. I shall not be turned aside from a straightforward course of serving Christ with my amativeness. I have a perfect consciousness of safety and feel well able by the grace of Christ to avoid both licentiousness and legality. But the Association /359A/ has got into a fog. Mr. Hamilton mentioned my advice to him to "beware of novices." Mrs. Smith* and Mr. Perry were novices, persons who had not learned to walk in the spirit, yet they took the lead in love matters. They brought in the spirit of daintiness, exclusiveness, secretiveness, and shame. There is need again of classification, making a distinction between those who walk in the spirit and novices. There should be faith enough in the spiritual class to take the lead, not by suppressing and withdrawing, but by filling the market with the true article. If our leading men like George, Hamilton, and Cragin are discouraged and afraid to stir, and the novices are active in the outward parts of the Association, you are in a state of fever, sick and weak within and hot on the outside. Somebody must get faith enough to make amativeness public property. I must have men enough of this character to monopolize the market, or all will go wrong. Let us take no counsel from fear. Mr. Hamilton is in a wrong state, legal, discouraged, fearful. It shows itself in his countenance and the tones of his voice. There must be good sense enough not to jump out of the frying-pan into the fire. Jump onto the hearth. If you get out of the way, try again. Up and at it, trusting to the grace of God, who giveth liberally. This talk is adapted to such cases as I have mentioned, and probably to Harriet Skinner and many more in the Association.

I am bold to say in the name of Jesus Christ, that so far as any outward thing is concerned, the use of amativeness is what is going to drive the Devil out of the world. I mean to learn the trade, and beat the Devil on that point. Without /359B/ purity in that department, you cannot approach the Holy City. As at the beginning, they are naked there and not ashamed.

The Devil has "done his darndest" to swamp us in both ways, by licentiousness and legality, and we have beaten him. We shall certainly have an Association that is free and pure, able to stand against all the wiles of the Devil.

---

* Wife of "Smith" who was on the sloop. [G.W.N.]

We have endured persecution and obtained toleration; and we shall have purity, freedom, and money.

Harriet A. Noyes to Noyes
Oneida, June 28, 1851

Dear John:—

I felt like writing to you this morning, and now come to write the day of
the month I see it is the anniversary of the day on which we were married. It is
very much such a day as that was outwardly. I should like to celebrate the day
with thanksgiving to God for permitting me to fill the station that he called
me to at that time, and for the measure of faith he has given me in overcoming the marriage spirit. I thank you for your love and patience. Your spirit of
freedom from care and looking on the bright side of things rises up in me
from time to time above all dark appearances, and I enjoy myself very well
here. . . . I feel like going against the fear of criticism, and opening myself to
you in all my thoughts. Yours for the service of God,

Harriet

Commendation of Mr. Mallory: Home-Talk by Noyes
July 22, 1851

We are about sending Mrs. Mallory home to Oneida. One reason is that
her eyes do not stand the chain work very well. /360/ But the principal thing
that led me to the proposal was this: She and Mr. Mallory have been separated for a great while, and I thought, if the trial had gone far enough for their
good, that I should be very glad to have Mr. Mallory see some of the beauties
and benefits of our system. I do not feel disposed to interfere with or break up
permanently any affection that has a soul in it. Mr. Mallory stands out in my
mind as an instance of faithful submission to the truth which is highly com-
mendable. He has been put to a hard trial in being separated from his wife. Yet
we have heard no complaints from him; on the contrary, he has gone through
with it with a hearty good will. It seems to me that he has proved himself a
man in whom loyalty to God is stronger than any other affection. I should be
glad to have Mrs. Mallory meet him with new confidence. Let the Association,
if possible, get them into a new honeymoon, cautioning them not to get
sticky. /361/

The Social State of the Association: Home-Talk by Noyes
July 22, 1851

Mr. Mallory's case led me to look at the state of the Association with re-gard to jealousy. We used to have a great deal of difficulty with it, in such cases as Mr. Bradley, Otis Miller, and Mrs. Hatch. Where is it now? "Echo answers, Where?" It is not to be found. There may be smouldering embers, but I am not aware of them.

To look a little further, I feel free from a certain special jealousy that exist-ed toward me. There was a pretty general feeling that I had special privileges, and was getting the women's affections away from the other men. That feeling has all vanished. . . .

Mr. Miller was long in a touchy state where it would not do to order Char-lotte to any particular post without reference to his feelings, and so it was gen-erally. But now, if you should order any husband or wife in the Association to a post separate from the other, I do not believe there would be any objection. There is a good spirit among us which is showing itself in various symptoms of health. It has not yet brought on much active freedom between the sexes in a still and safe way, but it will last.

Harriet A. Noyes to Brooklyn
Oneida, July 30, 1851

After hearing particulars of the late important event (sloop was sunk) we went right on with the matter in hand, the routing of the old maid spirit and prayer for a revival of love. Old imaginations had stepped in between Mr. & Mrs. Newhouse, and Mr. Mallory in a wilful way was suffering his wife's past treatment /362/ to hide her present love of him. In our morning meeting, Mr. Mallory was thoroughly criticised, and toward night he wrote a letter to Mrs. Skinner and me, saying that he knew that obedience was the way to the tree of life, and that he thankfully submitted his will to Mr. Noyes and the Associa-tion. Finding that Mr. & Mrs. Newhouse were ready to join with Mr. & Mrs. Mallory, we concluded to celebrate the marriages and have some bread and butter and honey. I was delighted with the turn things had taken, and thought there would be a simultaneous burst of joy in the Association. Well, when George introduced the subject of the evening meeting by reading Mr. Mal-lory's letter, and a few of us had expressed our sympathy with it, there was a dead calm and such a heavy spirit that it seemed like lifting a great weight to speak. Then we turned about and endeavored to show up that spirit that would not sympathize with love or receive love itself. The situation showed the Association more clearly than ever before the dry, barren spirit they were in, and one after another came out against it. Mr. and Mrs. Kellogg's case was mentioned, and it was thought a good opportunity for them to carry out what had been proposed to them some weeks ago. After a manifestation of will on Mr. Kellogg's side, and shyness on Mrs. Kellogg's, George said to Mr. Kellogg: "Will you accept of love?" He answered: "I will try." "But *will* you?" said George. "Yes, I *will*," Mr. Kellogg replied. So they joined the marriage. George said, "Fetch on your cake," and all were treated with bread and butter and honey, the three couples sitting together. After this the three couples went into Mrs. Newhouse's room and conversed in appreciation of love and /363/ against the opposite spirit. They then retired to their rooms. The next morning they were quite free in their reports. Mrs. Kellogg said she had entirely new experience; Mr. Kellogg said that he was quite refreshed; Mrs. Mallory that their experience was very satisfactory, etc. I have heard a number confess that they had an increasing attraction for their husbands or wives lately, but were afraid to speak of it for fear it was of the old exclusive sort.

Charlotte A. Miller to Brooklyn
Oneida, September 18, 1851

There is a gradual warmth of life diffusing itself through the Association that seems healthy and true. Criticism is at work in some cases, and the fear of criticism and of the ascending fellowship are under judgment.

Practical Suggestions on the Subject of Amativeness:
Home-Talk by Noyes
September 20, 1851

It appears from the report received this morning from Oneida, that we are to have more difficulty with amativeness. As the free spirit begins to circulate again after the chill we have been under, the Devil rallies his forces for another skirmish. I think that a healthy spirit is on the whole prevailing in the Association, though there are symptoms of disease in particular members.

I want to assert in a distinct and somewhat extended form the principle which lies at the foundation of our social system. It is that in all safe, healthy fellowships the ascending fellowship must prevail. Though we may be baffled, slandered and /364/ abused, we shall at last establish the principle that the way to induct the young into a true state of amativeness is to have them mate with older persons. There is a natural attraction between superiors and inferiors, the old and the young, the spiritual and novices, and it is an attraction that is necessary and desirable for both. The time will come when a young person, with no forcing, will naturally be led by the hand of some older person in matters of love; when the idea of persons that are not spiritual embarking on the tempestuous ocean of amativeness without a pilot will be regarded absurd.

Another principle which I wish to suggest is that of intellectualizing love. I well remember that as the Lord led me along in my love for Mrs. Cragin, one of the first symptoms was a strong instinct in me to intellectualize her. I wanted her to educate herself and become a good writer, and I insisted that she could learn any of the sciences. That element ran through our whole career together, and the results were most splendid. Little facts that are occurring just at this time remind me of this principle. We have an attraction going on between William Hinds and Harriet Worden,* and it manifests itself in their sitting down together to study. They are not ashamed to show that they are attracted to each other. It is a beautiful example. There should be first a marriage of hearts, next a marriage of intellects, and last a marriage of bodies. When persons fall in love, I would suggest that they manifest it not by sneaking around flirting in their chambers, but by quietly seating themselves in the parlor at study. /365/

Criticism of Mrs. Worden
September 30, 1851

Christ must control the attraction of the young. The whole war at Oneida was upon this point. Hyde withdrew from the Community spirit, and sought to introduce secret love between the young. I at last outgeneraled him and drove him out of the Association. Now I am driving his spirit out as fast as I can. It is the working of that poison that has caused all the troubles of the Association. It is that spirit that is now tormenting Mrs. Worden. It is that spirit that has made Tryphena crazy.

Commendation of Harriet A. Noyes:
Family-Talk
December 13, 1851

Noyes:—I feel myself in better relations with Harriet than ever. She has gained a power over her feelings that makes her cheerful and happy, and she is a great help to me in the household. She is quiet, peaceable, and faithful. I like her very much—not as a wife; I don't care anything about her as a wife—but

---

* Aunt Harriet M. Worden. [G.W.N.]

as a co-worker in the Kingdom of Christ. Marriage between us has certainly worn out in the right way. New and better relations have come in. I have not had much to do with her for a good while. She has gone on independently, as I have desired she should. But I watch her, and see that she walks in the spirit and helps me.

Harriet:—I feel very thankful for this expression of confidence. It shows that looking from the outside you cannot take a correct view. When looking from that direction it seemed as though I was going farther away from you.

Noyes:—You need not be any concerned about that. /366/

Harriet:—I have felt my heart drawn out toward Mrs. Cragin a good deal of late, with a desire to be a help to her and to you.

Noyes:—Well, I can say that you do help me, all of you. I feel that a spirit of faithfulness and obedience to the truth prevails in the family. There is growing sympathy toward me, which is right.

Noyes to John Norton

Oneida, January 22, 1852

Brother John:—

Seeing in a letter from Mrs. Sarah Campbell some account of your trials and criticisms, I thought I would say a few things to you by letter. You say you cannot forget Helen. I do not wish you to forget her, nor to love her less. But cannot you love her without *claiming* her, and quarreling with us and with God about her, and almost shooting yourself on her account? This is not the right kind of love. It is not strong enough. When you love her thoroughly with the love of God, you will be thankful that God made her, not for you but for himself, not to be used up as Hyde is using up Julia but to grow forever more and more beautiful in His garden; you will be thankful for the acquaintance with her which God has already given you, and for the hope of future more intimate fellowship; you will be thankful for her privileges here, and for her love toward others and others' love toward her. I cannot forget Mrs. Cragin. Yet I will not quarrel with God because I am separated from her, nor shoot myself, nor do anything of this kind. On the contrary, I will be thankful for the past, and patient and hopeful for the future. /367/ You and George Hatch both love Helen.* With that old, greedy, worldly love, how would you ever reconcile your respective claims? Do you not see, that it is best she should be here away from both of you till you both learn to love her in the Community spirit? You have a good opportunity to learn the great lesson which I learned long

---

* The Helen mentioned in this letter was Helen C. Noyes. [G.W.N.]

ago by the same kind of experience you are now going through, that God owns all things, even our sweethearts and ourselves. I trust this lesson will make you young men now, while your hearts are fresh and pliable, devoted to the principles of free love, that so you may be saved from the distresses and insanities which you see among those who have come into the service in later life. Your wing of our regiment has been troublesome to us in past years, but I expect to see it pressing into the front rank of loyalty and self-conquest. Write me, if you please.

Yours truly,
John H. Noyes

Four Years of Complex Marriage: Home-Talk by Noyes
March 9, 1852

The impression made upon me by the budget of testimonies read last evening is that there has been a great amount of abstinence in the Association. There has been serious self-denial in such cases as Mr. Perry that is highly meritorious. Many have undoubtedly been robbed of the freedom that we have enjoyed in the world. I feel too that there has been no constraint; all has been done in a joyful, patriotic spirit. I pledge myself to see that all who have been faithful to our principles shall have an hundred fold. I feel like expressing myself in the /368/ language of Isaiah: "Let not the eunuch say, 'Behold, I am a dry tree.' Even unto them will I give in mine house and within my walls a place and a name better than of sons and of daughters. I will give them an everlasting name that shall not be cut off." (Is. 56:3–5) There is time enough to have all these accounts settled. I feel very thankful to the Association as well as to God for the results these papers disclose. I am satisfied too that there has been a great deal more happiness on the whole than if there had been more sexual intercourse. There has been in reality no loss. But I can conceive of a state of things in which there would have been more positive gain. Like Mr. Mallory, I do not regard the state of things during the last four years as in any measure an example of the heavenly state, but only of a transition state toward it.

We will now square up all accounts, close the books, and wait on God for a new start. Our next voyage may be much better than this.

A statement of the amount of sexual intercourse among us as compared with that in the world is the best showing we could make. We have developed principles that look radical and licentious. These testimonies establish the conservative nature of these principles. Now we will go on in the fashion of the world for such a time as God pleases, devoting ourselves to establishing a character in the eyes of the world for continence and good behavior, and so fairly work out our freedom.

This disclosure shows that a great amount of good has been done by our principles. Many have been saved from bondage, /369/ health has been secured, and the troubles of the flesh prevented. I am delighted to see so many distinctly express the fact that our principles have led them to regard their social nature as sacred. I already see a great harvest of good, but we will turn it all under, calling it seed grain, and wait for a much larger harvest in the future. I am encouraged to go on with our principles and practices as soon as it is judicious and we get advice to that effect from the heavenly church.

Henry W. Burnham to George Cragin
Oneida, March 24, 1852

Young Shedd came here last night. Whether his presence had anything to do in developing the following fact I do not know. Kesiah Worden this morning reports a secret Mrs. Morgan disclosed to her about a year ago, viz: that previous to her coming here, she had connection with this Shedd. This, I thought, threw light on the whole matter. I told Morgan about it, and Fanny talked with Mrs. Morgan. He was as hard as a millstone, and justified himself by insinuating that, when the whole truth was brought to light, *you* would be found to be a bad man. I asked him what he meant, and he refused to tell, only that he and his wife were ready to face you. I came back to the house feeling almost used up. Just before dinner, he came to my room and said he was ready to tell his story. Accordingly, after dinner he and his wife came in, and before a number of us said that some little time previous to Mr. Morgan's coming to the Association, Mrs. Morgan had taken the venereal disease, and that it was traceable directly to you. They corresponded about the matter while he was here, and during that time she consulted a doctor in Leverett. I asked /370/ if that was all, and they both said, yes. She reports that she is now clear from that disease, but was not until after her connection with the Association.

March 25:—Dear brother, don't think that your reputation suffers any from recent disclosures. I verily believe you were never appreciated in the Association as now.

Charlotte A. Miller to Fanny Leonard
Brooklyn, March 26, 1852

John and Mr. Cragin are talking about the Morgans and venereal disease. John says: "I have had my eye on this disease from the beginning. I knew that Satan would do his prettiest to get that thing going. The world predicted it. But I am inclined to think that the spirit of the Association has cured that disease. I am persuaded that it breeds in darkness and shame. Let the Association go into an inspection, as we did in the itch. I can report myself sound. I have got back from the voyage safe." "So have I," say Smith and Cragin. It was remarked that Mr. Cragin's faithfulness had saved the Association from the disease.

John says: "If Mrs. Morgan had not confessed her connection with Shedd, her story would be more plausible. But that fact, taken together with the fact that she is cured by coming to the Association, and that Cragin never had it, makes the case very clear. The Lord had a meaning in Shedd's coming to the Association. I should advise not to quarrel with Mrs. Morgan. Read to her that part of Mr. Cragin's letter that refutes her charge, do it gently, and then take no responsibility for either Mr. or Mrs. Morgan." /371/

John L. Skinner to His Brother Alanson
Oneida, March 30, 1852

The actual amount of sexual intercourse in the Association for the last two or three years has been scarcely one seventh (and many of the members judge it has been hardly one tenth) of the amount that occurs in ordinary married life in the world. This statement is verified by the testimony of all the married men and women of the Association. They all state, moreover, that they have had intervals of several months at different times of total abstinence from sexual connection. The ordinary practice in the Association is for men to sleep with men and women with women.*

The amount of smutty talk or indecent behavior of any kind is far less in our Community than in ordinary society that is called respectable in the world; so much so indeed that these things are scarcely seen or heard of among us.

The effect of the principles and practice of our Association on the passion of amativeness, instead of making it irritable and ungovernable, has been to produce the opposite result, that is to quiet, civilize, and purify it.

---

* This refers to the same-sex sharing of sleeping rooms, not sexual relations. [L.F.]

One member writes thus: "Previous to joining the Association, my amativeness was in a very excitable state. I was to some extent addicted to the
practice of masturbation. I can say with a thankful heart, that the influences
of free love have cured me of that evil and made me entirely free from inordinate excitement." Several other members, who were formerly addicted more
or less to masturbation, testify that they have experienced an effectual cure of
that evil since joining the Association. /372/

Introduction to the Bailey Affair

Mr. Seba Bailey of Illinois had long been a subscriber to the paper,
and was regarded as belonging to the inner circle of outside friends. There
had been some talk of forming a Community in the West, and it was
thought that the Bailey family might be the natural nucleus. When
Messrs. Burnham and Carr projected their trip to the West, they planned
to make the Bailey home their headquarters for a time, and notice to that
efffect was sent to western subscribers. On their arrival Messrs. Burnham
and Carr learned that steps toward a western Community had already
advanced farther than they supposed. Mr. Bailey had, with Mrs. Bailey's
consent, had a child by a young woman named Olive, and Olive was about
to be married to Mr. Conant, a member of the Bailey group. The child, a
daughter, was named Virtue Conant. She was brought to the Community with the rest of the Bailey-Conant group when they joined in March
1856 after Mr. Bailey's death. At a later period, Virtue was a much-beloved
sweetheart of Dr. Theodore R. Noyes. [G.W.N.]

Noyes's Judgment in Mr. Bailey's Case
July 1, 1852

I have purposely abstained from forming any hasty judgment in Mr.
Bailey's case, for I knew that sympathy with the world's exaggerated estimate
of such things would be likely to affect my judgment at first. I know that I do
not now approach the subject with any disposition to condemn. I feel perfectly goodnatured and established in the charitable attitude that Christ has set us
an example of; and the higher and lower adultery occupy their true places in
my mind. /373/

With these preliminary remarks I will now frankly state how the case
strikes me. In the first place, I like the faithfulness and frankness manifested in
this letter, the evident disposition he shows to submit himself to the criticism
of the church and abide its decision. Then there are some things in his account of the transaction that look as though God was taking measures to cov-

er his retreat. The fact that the woman found a man who was disposed to marry her under such circumstances is a striking one.

So far the case strikes me favorably. On the other hand, there are several things that I do not like. For one item, I do not like the fact that he was not in frank, confidential communication with the church before he took this course and at this time. It produces an inevitable temptation to distrust when we find that he has been making important moves under the cover of our principles without acquainting us with what he is about. Mr. Bailey ought to be a pillar in the church, a man that we can have perfect confidence in, but after this affair several repairs will have to be made to give us that confidence.

Another thing that I do not like is that, according to his own account, he acted under the instigation of women. His wife and the girl moved him. He puts this fact as though it was in his favor. It would have been against the proceeding, to be sure, if his wife had been opposed to it. But the fact that his wife was in favor of it and urged it reminds me of several cases we have known where men were pushed into foolish moves by their own wives. In general I have settled it as a principle that men should not justify themselves by the urgencies of women. It is /374/ going wrong and foremost when such things are proposed by women. I should have more confidence that Mr. Bailey acted by inspiration if he had taken the initiative himself. As the case stands, it looks as though his principal inspiration came from women, and that is rarely safe.

Again, the thing proposed was not judicious. It was a woman's plan, one that could proceed only from a reckless affection, not from true judgment. Olive was going to be separated from him by request to have a child by him. It was venturing out into a stream where they had reason to expect a shipwreck.

I have not been talking about the morality of the act. I am looking at its wisdom. When our measures come from Christ they turn out to be wise. Good generalship will be manifested in them. I do not think there was a proper regard for the results of their action when they placed themselves in a situation to stir up the wrath of her relatives and of the world.

If Mr. Bailey's position is truthful and God protects him in it, I shall certainly be glad to see him get out of his difficulty without injury. But my impression is that they will suffer. If so, they will get good out of it by being humiliated.

In the honest spirit which Mr. Bailey seems to have, I do not wish to judge him. I wish to have him judge himself. Let him reread the last paragraphs of the *Bible Argument,* and if he thinks he is right up to standard, I will not quarrel with him. Of one thing I am certain, however, that Christ will not be responsible for anything he had not authorized. Everything that is done under mere natural impulses will be criticised.

I must confess that Christ has not instructed me to expect /375/ that persons outside of our circle will have independent inspiration on this subject. So far as I have received instructions, they teach me that for the sake of unity Christ has committed the charge of this whole subject to me. Persons who undertake to go before me or aside from me without consultation will find themselves beyond their depth.

The question is not one of morality but of expediency. I imagine that Mr. Bailey acted more from social than from a military point of view. If he finds that he cannot fairly claim inspiration in the whole matter, I hope he will have the good sense and patriotism to acquit Christ of responsibility, and acquit us publicly.

This proceeding will tempt him to concealment and self-deception. Love is a great hand to cheat in the world, and it is a high attainment among believers to get deeply in love and yet be truly honest. I would say to Mr. Bailey: "Be sure to get your vindication honestly, do not let your wishes swerve your judgment, swear in your heart tht you will have the truth, the whole truth, and nothing but the truth on this subject."

Persons in such circumstances are liable to misjudge their own attainments, and imagine that they can sail smoothly where we know by a good deal of experience that skilful navigation is needed. If they can sail along smoothly in this sea, [they] are entirely in advance of us. /376/

Practical Suggestions for Regulating Intercourse of the Sexes: Home-Talk by Noyes
September 22, 1852

The first thing to be done in exchanging the fashion of the world for that of the Community is to put off entirely the marriage spirit, which claims private property in love. Civilized amativeness is as unselfish in respect to love-property as in respect to any other. The Community must learn to put hearty sympathy into the very place where jealousy usually manifests itself. In suggesting the following general rules, I assume that this preliminary conversation is past.

1.—The sexes should sleep apart. Their coming together should not be to sleep but to edify and enjoy. Sleeping is essentially an individual function that precludes sociability. Probably the truest fashion would be not only for the sexes but for those of the same sex to sleep apart. We need not insist upon reform to this extent until convenient, but for the sake of love it is best that sexes should ordinarily sleep apart. Overfamiliarity dulls the edge of sexual passion.

2.—Proposals for love interviews are best made not directly but through a third party. This method is favorable to modesty and also to freedom. It allows of refusals without embarrassment. If the third party is a superior, one in whom the lovers have confidence, calm wisdom will enter, as it should, to give needed advice and prevent inexpediencies. The third party will also be helpful in arrangements. This method excludes selfish privacy and makes love a Community affair.

3.—Short interviews will be found the best. Lovers should /377/ come together for an hour or two, and should separate to sleep. If they part before over-excitement, they will think of each other with pleasure afterwards. It is an excellent rule to leave the table while the appetite is still good.

4.—It is not according to truthful taste to spend much time in talk. The tongue has its field to itself all day. Why should not the other members have their turn? I imagine that the impotence, which some of the men complain of, may be connected with over-activity of the tongue.

5.—Cultivate the habit of sagacious, reflective observation. In the midst of passion, watch for improvement. So shall the spirit of truth go with you and perfect you in the heavenly art.

Our Victories:
Home-Talk by Noyes
　　November 21, 1852

If we were to examine ourselves, we should be astonished to find what victories we have gained almost without knowing it. Take, for example, our social system. I do not know how it is with others, but the feeling of exclusive love with me is a thing gone by. It is as far off as the shores of the Old World. And I do not hear anything of it in the Association. I have a quick eye to detect anything of that kind in myself or anybody else, and I do not see anything in our Association but what makes persons just as free and polite to one another in sexual privileges as in any others. We have the same freedom on that subject as on eating and drinking, talking walks, or any other kind of enjoyment. Thus we have got where we possess our amativeness instead of being possessed by it. There is not only no quarreling among us, but there is no temptation to quarrel. All troubles too about involuntary propgagation are at an end. . . .

A lighter work is given to us than was given to the Primitive Church. It is for us to get the victory over enjoyment; they had to get the victory over suffering. Christ kept his heart steadfast through enormous suffering, and his righteousness was fulfilled in that department. The Primitive Church followed after, and filled up the measure of his sufferings. There is as much temptation to nervousness in enjoyment as in suffering, and as much need of faith. We must lay hold on the faith of Christ and the Primitive Church, and let their glory go forth into the world as the fame of their suffering has. They are through with shipwrecks, judgments, stonings, and whippings. They want to see some fun in this world, as well as shouldering crosses and traveling through the world dripping with blood.

There is a growing spirit of faith in me that turns every way. The enemy is on the retreat, and I feel like putting on the cavalry. It seems very silly, after all that has been done for us, to be cast down by any bad experience we may have. When in trouble, if you drop all care and fall back on Christ, you will find in your heart a deep consciousness of power that makes no demonstrations nor requires any. It looks into the chaos of the Devil's creation with a kind of exultation, as an old salt /380/ does when he sees the wind come in a gale. He says little, but proves by deeds that he is competent to take care of the situation.

John R. Miller to Noyes
Oneida, November 25, 1852

When the Report came, "Advice from the Concentric Convention," it seemed to be accompanied by a spirit that drew all hearts upward to seek fellowship with Christ and the Primitive Church. There was no longing for the things that were behind. I felt distinctly that the Community offered up their amativeness to God, and that he accepted and was well pleased with the offering. There was a spirit of quietness and rest on this subject that was truly delightful. There was no turning towards husbands and wives, as in the "Coup d'Etat," but we felt called by God as to a fast. This was the experience of the Community for about three weeks, when our amativeness seemed to be returned to us purified and refined. I should judge that there was as much life in that direction as ever, though peaceful and quiet. The fast was a sincere one, but it has ended in heart though not in form.

John R. Miller to Noyes
Oneida, November 29, 1852

Before coming here, Mr. Howard was very much in love with Emma, and told his wife several times that he would like to have an interview with her. It put Mrs. Howard into some suffering, but she thought it was right, and proposed it to Emma, who consented, and it accordingly took place. They told me of it with some trembling for fear they had done wrong, but I thought they had a good spirit about it, and told them that I would endorse it, which seemed to set their hearts at rest. Mrs. Howard told me she had no idea that it would cost her such suffering to give Mr. Howard up. She thought it would be a relief to her to have him free, but she found that she didn't know what it was *to die.* She didn't sleep any for nearly a week, and cried a good deal of the time. It brought fresh to my mind our first experience at Putney, and I heartily thanked God for freedom. I was glad that the deed was done, and that *Mr.* Howard had taken the lead in it.

John R. Miller to George Cragin
   Oneida, December 28, 1852

Mr. Noyes's remarks about exclusive love are full of encouragement. I did not realize till I read that *Report,* the victories we had gained in that respect. I think I can say sincerely with Mr. Noyes, that exclusive love with me is a thing gone by. Two years ago, we were obliged to act with constant reference to exclusiveness. We had to have our watch constantly on duty to prevent our social building from being burned up by the fire of jealousy. It was the great labor of the Association. Now it is not much thought of, except in the case of new members. It never enters our heads that we can offend anyone by the expression of love. This is truly one of the "greater miracles." /381/

34

Tilt with Tobacco
1853

Newspaper sketches of the Oneida Community in its day seldom omitted to mention that the Community abstained wholly from tobacco. But during the first five years of its existence, the Community had its full quota of smokers and chewers. More than half the men, including some of the most prominent, upwards of forty by actual count, were, as they put it, "wearing the chain." Spittoons were in every public room. Tobacco was bought in Brooklyn by the half barrel along with other subsistence stores. The selection was entrusted to a brother of the Founder, who was thought a man of good taste. "But in the year 1853," wrote Harriet H. Skinner, "The chains fell off." The Community awoke one morning and found themselves rid not merely of the habit but of the appetite. The psychology of this change is revealed by contemporary documents, and forms one of the most interesting episodes in the history of the Community. [G.W.N.]

Tobacco Experience of John Humphrey Noyes, Founder of the Oneida Community

My father always chewed in the daytime and smoked evenings. My mother took snuff during my early years, but set a good example afterwards by breaking away from this habit. A cousin older than myself, with whom I worked and slept all through my boyhood, was a steady chewer. My associates and roommates at an academy which I attended when I was eleven years old thought it smart to take snuff and smoke, and I learned of them to enjoy a little excitement in these ways. But my grandmother, with whom /382/ I boarded (good soul!), reprimanded me faithfully for drinking too much tea and for carrying a snuff-box, and I was temporarily frightened back into steady habits.

But my term of slavery came at last, probably in my thirteenth year. In vacations, pleasant as home was, I had hard work to kill time; and once when I was complaining of this to my mother, she suggested, not exactly as advice but rather as a sagacious reflection, that tobacco was what I needed. I took the hint and found something to do. I remember well the very place out in a lane between the house and the barn where I tried my first chew. It made me very sick. Dizzy and trembling I ejected it, and almost renounced the attempt to find comfort in this terrible way. But I did not vomit. This rather elated me. I soon felt all right again, and was ready for another chew. After a few trials my stomach and nerves submitted to their new master, and I entered into a life of slavery which lasted, with some brief intermissions, till my forty-second year when Communism set me free.

The general course of my life with tobacco was that of the man who has a quarrelsome wife, and can neither live with her nor without her. The habit was always encroaching, and I was always resisting. There was a regular succession of quarrels, regularly followed by reconciliations. The number of chews or pipes per day would steadily increase till intolerable disorders of the stomach and nerves would set in. Then would come a sharp struggle between reason and appetite, and I would get back to moderation to begin the same course over again.

Sometimes these quarrels would proceed to the extremity of an attempt at divorce. I remember on one occasion, when I was /383/ lodging in the third story of the Seminary building at Andover, my conscience got so stirred up that I determined to break off all relations with tobacco. I had a hand of Cavendish in my pocket. Raising the window, I hurled it out as far as I could. A storm of rain was drenching everything. It was Sunday and the stores were shut. I had no more tobacco, and apparently no possibility of getting any for that day at least. Can the reader guess the sequel? Just at dusk, when the old love began to whisper most seductively and conscience began to relent, I went out in the rain and searched the ground patiently for that hand of Cavendish, and found it! The "lover's quarrel" was made up, and I passed a pleasant evening with the poor half-drowned plug.

The pitch to which tobacco-slavery carried its exactions is truly astonishing. I often watched and speculated on its encroachments, and always found that it was satisfied with nothing short of a devotion that would have no pleasure in anything without it. The old tobacco-user must think of his idol and provide for its accommodation when he sits down to study, when he visits his friends, when he takes an excursion, even when he goes to a religious meeting. The wise say, "We must eat to live, not live to eat," but tobacco, when it fairly gets the upper hand of a man, says that he must live to chew and spit! I have often seen the time when the principal charm of a good meal lay in the quid of "fine cut" that was to come after it.

But religion did at last conquer. When I was in the Seminary at New Haven, prayer and Bible influence strengthened me till I broke away from tobacco and escaped. The struggle was long, and sometimes it seemed doubtful whether I should not sell my soul for the morsel that was so sweet to roll under the tongue; /384/ but the good spirit prevailed, and for a year I was free. During this period, I did my best to raise public insurrection against tobacco-slavery. We instituted an anti-tobacco society in the Seminary, and among other efforts sent letters of inquiry and appeal to the heads of all the colleges. I was appointed to correspond with the President of Williams College. My letter after some days came back, scrawled over with filth and profanity (doubtless by some student into whose hands it had fallen), and on a space that had been left blank I was informed that "a meeting of the students was to be held on the next Thursday to pray for my eternal damnation!"

After I became a Perfectionist, my theories about the ways and means of reform were entirely changed; I became distrustful of laws and human resolutions, and jealous for the grace of God. In short I got into a quarrel with legality, and came to hate it as a more subtle and dangerous seducer than tobacco. In the struggle with this new enemy, I went back to the use of tobacco, and had a second course of domestic infelicities similar to those I have already described. Perceiving that my previous reform had not been a true divorce but only a voluntary separation, I consented to live with tobacco a while longer and wait for an effectual release by the powers above.

Home-Talk by Noyes
November 4, 1851

I am trying in some way to help Mr. Burt, George, and others in regard to the tobacco habit. We have adopted the confession of Christ as the best way out of trouble, and confessed Christ in our eating, drinking, and sleep. I propose to /385/ Mr. Burt and George that they confess Christ in chewing tobacco.

I feel a sickly spirit in respect to that habit. Whatever there is bad in it we may as well put into Christ's hands to correct. He is prepared to take charge, and is not afraid. We can dispense altogether with the services of the Devil.

Christ does not forbid the use of tobacco. On the contrary, he claims it as his property. His policy is to take possession of tobacco the same as of food and music. But we will not set up any barriers to prevent him from changing our course and breaking up habit. The first step toward abolishing the tobacco habit (if it is to be abolished) is to give Christ charge of it. We must have faith enough now to do that. We will chew tobacco heartily as unto the Lord, and insist that Christ shall have his way in everything. Then if there is anything evil in the habit, Christ will cure it. Let it be a Community matter. In this way those who do not use tobacco can sympathize with those who do. I would exhort those that do not use it to have compassion on those that do, and not think evil of them. Let us see if there is not a way for those that have this habit to be as clean and free from condemnation as those that do not have it. I offer myself as Community property in dealing with this principality.

I feel that all things are lawful for me, but not all things are expedient. Is the use of tobacco expedient? I think we shall have to be redeemed from it. Is this to be done by such means as Greeley and other legalists would recommend? I think not. I can understand Mr. Burt and George a great deal better for using tobacco myself. I have been an old soldier in /386/ this war, and can brag some.

I shall never cease to watch tobacco as a tremendous principality. It is altogether more difficult to deal with than rum. It is far too subtle to be conquered by law, but it is not too subtle for Christ.

Home-Talk by Noyes
March 5, 1853

The gospel method of reform is to take persons just as they are, in bondage to whatever evil, and set before them ultimate complete deliverance as the hope of their calling; then in such gentle, moderate ways as can be used without legality begin to assume control. This is a combination of two methods

that are used separately in the world. On the one hand, legal reformers set before people a rule of present action and summon them up to immediate attainment. On the other hand, liberals deal moderately with the passion to be
overcome but have no hope of their calling toward which they are moving. . . .

There is a principle which makes it necessary that deliverance from evil
should be gradual. If you cut any evil short off, you will cut away more or less
good with it. Where the life of individuals is combined with evil principalities,
the process of separation requires nice dissection. If we cut ourselves off from
the use of tobacco at once by pure force of law, we shall find that the mischief
is in us in a latent form still. It is the truth that makes us free.

We may fix our ideal by the calculations of absolute truth, without any
interference from present infirmities. Then we will make up our minds to attain that ideal without law if it takes /387/ forever. The ideal will work itself
into our life in many free ways and leaven the whole lump.

This method of reform precludes self-condemnation. The very fact that we
are bound for a perfect ideal and keep our eyes on it brings us justification. /388/

Home-Talk by Noyes
March 27, 1853

"It is good that the heart be established with grace and not with meats."
The whole world are establishing the heart with meats, that is, seeking comfort from outward things that stimulate and soothe. Eating and drinking are
the primary, universal method, but as the world has grown older it has found
ways of stimulating the flesh more powerfully, the two greatest methods being
by opium and tobacco. . . .

It has been impressed upon my mind that the time has come for us to discuss freely and thoroughly the subject of tobacco. For my part, I am ready to
deliver tobacco-slavery up to judgment. We are coming to a crisis that I have
been looking for, when the truth, not law, shall make us free. I do not want to
put any one upon a violent effort to get free from the use of tobacco, but I
want every one to consult the Spirit of Truth and charity faithfully before God
about it.

I think there is considerable credit due to those who do not use tobacco for
keeping quiet and not judging those who do. The women have shown wonderful patience and willingness to accommodate themselves to things as they are.

Legal opposition to stimulants, and bondage to them, are much the same
in essence. Law is effectual for a while, but has to be repeated and re-inforced,
and is just as sure to fail at last as other stimulus.

I am charged with Christ's treatment of such vices. There is no harsh criticism in him. He is heroic and helpful, and asks nothing from us any faster than he strengthens our hearts. Tobacco stimulates the flesh and drowns the spirit. /389/ Christ stimulates the spirit till it overcomes and drowns the flesh.

You will find that your want of tobacco is not merely natural want; it is a positive supernatural injection from a spirit with which you are in rapport. Your life is being sucked by some evil spirit that has the benefit of your tobacco-chewing.

I would propose that the Association contemplate as the hope of their calling the entire breaking up of this bondage. I am in no hurry about measures. If we have a faith that leads to the end, we shall be warping up to it in one way or another.

To come to something practical, I would recommend first, that those who are free from tobacco should keep their freedom; second, that all who can drop the habit without any serious quarrel with themselves should do so; and third, that those who are thoroughly enslaved should fast next Sunday. As a means of grace let's quit it for one day, and give attention to the Lord's mind about such matters.

In accordance with Noyes's suggestion, April 3rd, 1853, was named as a day of fasting from tobacco. The effects of the fast may be seen in the following letters and talks. [G.W.N.]

Harriet A. Noyes to John R. Miller
Brooklyn, April 4, 1853

We had a very pleasant fast yesterday. Most of us went without our dinner to sympathize with the tobacco men. /390/

John R. Miller to Noyes
Oneida, April 4, 1853

This is the second day of the tobacco fast. We were conscious yesterday that we had to contend with a great principality and, though we felt happy and strong, still we had to *fight*. Last evening we had an interesting time telling our experience. Some are chewing today and some are fasting. All are free.

Harriet A. Noyes to John R. Miller
Brooklyn, April 5, 1853

On hearing what you said about the tobacco war in your note yesterday, Mr. Noyes said he wanted now to see the Community rid of tobacco in the right way. He suggests that abstinence be not carried so far as to produce a reaction; that no one leave off with the nervous system in such a state of want that hereafter the remembrance of tobacco would be pleasant and a temptation to return to it sometime: that we make up our mind that God can take away the appetite. He himself has not kept up the fast, but used some yesterday and today. He says: "Watch for things that you can do to cross the spirit in a frisky way." When the suggestion comes up to take tobacco, he says to it: "Now do I want it? Am I not happy enough without it? Would it not spoil the enjoyment I now have to take it?" We gain on the spirit every time we argue with it in this way.

Remarks by Noyes
April 5, 1853

I am distinctly sensible of a change in the general /391/ atmosphere and my own feelings about tobacco. I think the agitation of the subject and the fast have already resulted in weakening the tobacco charm. . . .

We shall be delivered from bondage to tobacco and all such external excitements by having such an abundance of the fresh life of God that we shall not feel any need of them.

Poverty of life is the soul of vice.

If our hearts are open and fearless toward God and man, free from legality, this bondage to tobacco will drop off from us like a dry snake-skin. If you flay a snake while his skin is firm, he dies in the operation; but if you let him alone, a simple, genial, vital action will go on until the skin dies and he runs out of it.

I thank God that he has not allowed us to quit the use of tobacco in a premature way. He has reserved this habit on purpose, that we may work out the true philosophy of reform with a chance to experiment. It is worth everything in such studies to have a concrete case on hand for illustration. We shall find that all habits are under the same system of spiritual laws that governs this.

John R. Miller to Harriet A. Noyes
Oneida, April 7, 1853

There is but little tobacco used here now. Several have left off entirely and others use it moderately. We keep the thing in the light by telling our experience in the meeting every evening. I have just taken a quid since I commenced this paragraph, which is the third I have indulged in since the day before the fast. I stand midway between the ultras and the conservatives, so you may judge the state of the Community on this subject. /392/

John R. Miller to Harriet A. Noyes
Oneida, April 8, 1853

Mr. Noyes's tobacco talks are very interesting. I am satisfied that he has got the true principle. I left off entirely for three days, when I commenced again because I felt that I was coming under a spirit of legality. Mr. Woolworth's and Mr. Thacker's experience was the same.

Brooklyn to Oneida

Many, and those the most inveterate, have broken off. Messrs. Kinsley, G. W. Noyes, Leonard, Hamilton, and others have quit, and find pleasure and sport in it. They feel free to use tobacco when they want to. Mr. Leonard says he has taken a chew twice since he gave up the habit, but for the most part the appetite is gone. Mr. Noyes has not quit entirely.

By the first day of May 1853, a large majority of the "tobacco slaves" had already been liberated. A half dozen or so remained still in prison rather than give undue advantage to legality. The battle now died down for a few months, while fresh psychologic reinforcements were being brought up. On the first of the following December, Noyes again raised the flag of rebellion, and this time it was not furled until every "captive" was free. [G.W.N.]

Home-Talk by Noyes
December 1, 1853

If you want to be saved, you must "put off the old man with his deeds." You must put *him* off; not merely put off his deeds leaving him there to bring forth another set of /393/ deeds as bad as the first; but put off the old man with his deeds, and chiefly put off the old man that you may put on the new man. Here there is no legality and no quackery, but sound truth which we must learn to handle aright.

Communism is going to be a powerful auxiliary of Christ in enabling us to put off the old man with his deeds. I was interested in that experience old Mrs. H. related in a recent letter. She had been thirty years attached to her pipe, but when she went to Putney she found herself in such close relations with persons who did not like smoking, that in order to make harmony she gave it up. This is an illustration of the natural effect of close association. Whoever enters Communism understandingly must go through a washing and scrubbing that will end in his being purified of everything that is disagreeable to those around.

Another principle that will cooperate with Christ is this: The line between what we shall eat and what we shall not will not be between clean and unclean, nor between meats and vegetables, nor between bolted and unbolted flour, but between those things that are adapted to Communism and those that are not. I should like to see that principle clearly defined, and as fast as possible put into practice among us.

Still another foundation principle is, that the things best adapted to Communism are the cheapest. We should put ourselves on a scale of living that is accessible to the greater part of mankind. Luxuries will either be cut off by Communism, or they will be taken into the Church and given to all. /394/

The fact that Tobacco is not a Community element is weaning me from the appetite more than any motive I have ever had. This Community motive will root out the love of tobacco, liquor, and everything that isolates and separates. Paul worked upon this plan. He said, on the one hand, "Let no man judge you in respect to meats and drinks," and on the other, "If meat make my brother to offend, I will eat no meat while the world standeth."

I shall content myself with these two motives of reform, Communism with Christ and Communism with one another. I believe they will work out every problem of morality.

With this inspiring tocsin, the men of war in all the Communes rallied for a last desperate assault on the tobacco bastille. Soon a breach was made. And the remaining captives came forth into the light of day. [George] Noyes and Daniel Nash at Brooklyn, we are told, left the crumbling walls without injury on the very day of the above Home-Talk; Miller at Oneida "signed himself free" on December 7th; all but one at Oneida were away on the 14th; George Hamilton and Seymour Nash at Newark made their escape on the 18th; Daniel

Hall at Putney took his last chew on the 19th; and when on the 23rd of December 1853 a message was flashed to Brooklyn, "Oneida uses no tobacco," a shout of victory and thanksgiving went up from all the Associated Communes. /395/

35

Tea, Coffee, and Other Stimulants
1854

Brooklyn Journal

March 20, 1852.—The family unanimously resolved that we would for the present pleasurably abstain from tea and coffee. Mr. Noyes said he would allow no legal restraint in the matter, neither would he submit to tyranny of habit.

April 2, 1852.—Putney and Wallingford have unanimously abolished tea and coffee for the present at least.

John R. Miller to George Cragin
　　Oneida, January 18, 1854

Dear Brother:—
We contrive to enjoy our fast from tea and coffee, though we find that we were more in bondage to it than we were aware of. It has really been a more serious matter than leaving off tobacco. We are confident that it will be profitable, and our experience has already convinced us that a fast of this kind was necessary. I have no quarrel with tea and coffee, and believe that they are among the good things that God gives us, but I will not be brought under the power of any. I think there were not more than a half dozen cups of tea drunk last night, and the same number of cups of coffee this morning, though it was passed to all and all were made free to drink it. I noticed this morning that a cup of coffee was carried the whole length of the long table without finding market. It is interesting to see a whole Community cheerfully consent to any such self-denial for the truth's sake. The spirit I have seen manifested /396/ on this subject has given me a new love for the family.

A Girdling Axe for the Coffee Tree:
Home-Talk by Noyes
  January 20, 1854

The gospel of reform may be compared to the girdling of trees. . . . A tree is dead when it is girdled, though it may stand for some time and look like a live tree. . . . This is the way we handled the tobacco principality. We girdled it last summer, and this winter the wind blew it over. Now what do you think of the expedience of girdling the love of tea and coffee? They seem to have trouble with that tree at Oneida. They are daily finding out that the tobacco spirit has run into the coffee-bag.

I confess I had an apprehension, when the tobacco question came up, that it would not end there. My theory has been that narcotics and stimulants are naturally connected, and I have thought that when the Lord called us to quit tobacco he would probably be looking toward a general breaking up of the use of such things.

People resort to narcotics and stimulants mostly because they have nothing else to do that pleases them. Now as God is more and more putting into our hearts the great purpose of establishing a daily press, it will be easy for us to quiet our sensual appetites. I have coveted a state in which I have no attachment to anything, but could live comfortably on parched corn; at the same time, I would be free to use the luxuries of the world, if they came to hand.

I believe that the Lord will show us and help us to do one thing after another that will directly contribute to the success of our enterprise. I have such an ambition for the /397/ work before me that I shall go into any kind of temperance that seems necessary, from *attraction* and not from legality.

John R. Miller to Noyes
  Oneida, March 9, 1854

Dear Bro. Noyes:—

The report of your remarks on the subject of prayer met a warm response in my heart and in the heart of the Community. On reading it, I felt a desire to tell you some of my experience about leaving off tea and coffee.

During a fast from these drinks of a week that we kept here some time since I suffered a good deal in my body, and had a hankering for coffee till the last day of the fast, when I gained a victory over it, and commenced drinking again from choice and not from necessity. Since that time I have held the habit loosely, bearing in mind constantly that the tea and coffee trees were both girdled and must die soon. I seldom drank but one cup and sometimes less, but notwithstanding all my crowding the other way I was conscious of a growing appetite for both drinks, and never enjoyed them better than I did after the fast. I had it constantly in mind that I should follow the example of the Brooklyn Commune joyfully, let it be what it might and come sooner or later, but I had no instinct to lead in the matter. When we learned nearly a week ago that the Brooklyn family had abandoned the use of tea and coffee, I made up my mind at once to do the same. I confess it was something of a trial and seemed anything but attractive. The next morning I awoke early, and was up some time before the bell rang, with an unusual appetite for some coffee with my /398/ breakfast. I knew I could go down to the table and willfully refuse to drink it and put myself under law, but this I could not bear to do. I went to God in earnest prayer for deliverance with a determination not to go to break-fast till I could go a free man. It was nearly eight o'clock when I went down, but my appetite for coffee was entirely removed, and I have not enjoyed my breakfast so well for a month as I did that morning. I have enjoyed my meals better ever since, and have not had the least appetite for tea or coffee.

In my meditations that morning, I felt clearly that there was no need of suffering in my body as I did before, and I asked God for such a victory over habit that I could make any change that was called for and not suffer by it. I have been conscious that my prayer was answered, for I am not aware of the least suffering in consequence of the change.

During our fast of a week, I wanted something for a substitute and some-times took hot water with milk and sugar, and sometimes milk, but this time I have taken pure, cold water, and have had no appetite for anything else. . . .

Your loving brother,
J. R. Miller /399/

36

Wrestling with Disease and Death
September 16, 1851, to July 3, 1854

On September 16, 1851, Tryphena Seymour, daughter of old Mr. Hub-bard and wife to Henry J. Seymour, a member of the Oneida Association, began to show symptoms of insanity, or what some termed hysterics, crying nights, wandering about, frightening the children, and talking incoherently. Her husband looked after her. He gave her a "short lesson in geometry," and told her not to leave her room before dinner. She was afterward in the garden and kitchen. He criticised her for her disobedience, and punished her a little, rapping her on the cheeks. But she grew rapidly worse, and for three days he could keep her from raving only by a continual use of the word of command and a slight use of the rawhide. It was difficult keeping her so, and soon she broke out again. He tried to make her yield by whipping and talking. In a letter to Harriet A. Noyes, he writes: "The responsibility of all the chastisement she has received belongs entirely to me. I give myself to God for direction and criticism. I should be thankful for help in reading the lesson God is giving us."

At this crisis, Noyes sent his wife to Oneida with the following word to Mr. Seymour: "If Tryphena continues insane, your true course is to go in a manly way to her relatives and report the case. They know her tendency to that disease, and will not be likely to blame you or us, if you deal with them wisely. After consulting them, if there is no favorable change, take her to the Asylum in Utica. The case is beyond our power. /400/ I advise abstaining from all harsh treatment. Perhaps the proposal of sending her to the Asylum will quiet her. Perhaps Mr. Burt will be able to break the spell. At all events, God is over all. Trust in Him and fear not. All the threatenings that are coming upon us constantly end in smoke. Our forebodings are daily reversed. It is darkest just before day. God bless you.

John H. Noyes" [G.W.N.]

Harriet A. Noyes to Brooklyn
Oneida, September 25, 1851

Mrs. Tobey started in the morning for home direct. She and Mrs. Howes had been expecting to go next Monday by way of Brooklyn, but she got so afraid and in such close corners about Tryphena that she went off without ceremony. She was afraid to go to Brooklyn and afraid to stay here, because if she was crazy she would be whipped. She has been crazy, and the folks here felt that it was good for Tryphena that Mrs. Tobey went away. It seemed to clear the atmosphere, and Tryphena was more composed. Mrs. Tobey was tried too on financial matters. Mrs. Howes thinks that was the main thing.

I went to see Tryphena soon after I arrived, and although she did not recognize me, and went on with her idiotic talk, I addressed myself to her inner man and paid no attention to her outer man. I set before her the truth and what you proposed doing for her. Then I told her to lie down composedly and think of it. Mr. Burt had just arrived, and he said that after we had seen what effect my talk had he would try her. /401/

Mr. Burt did not succeed in getting money, and yesterday morning, after Mrs. Tobey left, the Association had not a cent in the Treasury. I do not find any special fear about Tryphena's case here. I think Henry Seymour is learning a good lesson. All seem quite engaged in business. They have passed a resolution to contribute on the first of every month $25 to Brooklyn. It is 50c to a man. Horace Burt earned his yesterday at the buzz-saw and handed it in to the treasurer. He is quite bright, so this case stays cured. Also Harriet Hall.

This morning Mr. Burt talked to Tryphena very kindly but without apparent effect. Mr. Seymour then said he felt prepared in spirit to go to her father's and tell him about her, confessing the truth of his treatment of her. Some queried whether it would not be better to put it off a few days on account of the black and blue spots on her body. But I felt that he should go *now,* and tell them frankly that he had tried soft measures, and then he had tried controlling her, and had even held her mouth and whipped her, if he found it necessary. Accordingly he and Mr. Burt went over to Mr. Hubbard's. They found there an aunt of Tryphena's, who was coming here tomorrow expecting to find her well. Here we saw the wisdom of Henry's going over there today. At first Tryphena's father spit out his wrath, but her mother checked him, saying it was no time to talk so now; she would forget all the past, and see what is best to do. When Henry informed them of all the means he had taken, her mother inadvertently exclaimed: "You ought to have been whipped yourself." He made no reply, but afterward said he had used his best judgment and done as well by her as he knew /402/ how. She then told him she did not wish to cast any reflections on him, but wanted to do the best she could *now.* Soon after Henry's return, Dexter Hubbard, his mother, and aunt came over and saw Tryphena, and proposed to have a doctor sent for to give his opinion whether her situation was owing to sickness, or whether she was a fit subject for the insane asylum. The doctor came, and the result of their consultations was that Mr. Burt, Mr. Seymour, and Dexter Hubbard took Tryphena in a carriage to Utica.

Henry J. Seymour to Noyes
Oneida, October 2, 1851

Dear Brother Noyes:—
What you say to me and about me is most consoling. It is true that I can learn much from my experience, and see much to criticise in what I have done. My prayer and endeavor is to shield you and the church from the impu-

tations which the world is heaping upon you. I pray for wisdom. Without Christ I can do nothing. With him I can do all things.

With much love,
H. J. Seymour

Remarks by Noyes
Brooklyn, November 10, 1851

I should like to say of Mr. Jonathan Burt (and have it sent to the Association) that I have not seen the smallest symptoms of insanity in him since he has been here, and never saw him when his mind and spirit seemed more sound. The only oppressive influence I have felt from him has been connected with tobacco, and that has passed away since our tobacco talk /403/ a few evenings ago.

I should recommend to the Association not to be frightened by this squall of insanity. Fear oftentimes begets the very thing it fears. They will soon begin to see that the spirit of insanity is not almighty; it is on the retreat.

The position of things at Oneida was so critical, and Mr. Burt's position was so central, I wanted he should have a means of escape if there was any danger of his getting off the track. I should say now that the circumstances in which he is placed would naturally worry him, and I wish, when there is any such tendency, he would [be] free to slip away from the Association and come down here.

Oneida Journal

December 28, 1851.—For the last two weeks Mr. Joslyn has been growing worse. He seems possessed by an insane spirit, is continually telling what the spirits say to him, talks about the angel Gabriel, etc. There is some talk about taking him to the Asylum. Referred his case to Brooklyn.

Insanity
The Circular, Old Series 1:34
January 4, 1852

Perfectionism has been hitherto remarkably free from the reproach of causing insanity. Within a few months past, however, it must be confessed that the spirit of insanity has made several apparently successful inroads upon us. One case at Oneida passed beyond the control of the Association, and was committed to the care of the Utica Asylum. Another case there /404/ has more recently been threatening a similar termination. The family at Putney is also at this time troubled with a case of monomania. These afflictions are calling our attention to the stronghold of the spirit of confusion.

John R. Miller to Noyes
Oneida, January 22, 1852

Mr. Joslyn ran away between ten and eleven o'clock last night. Mr. Morgan and George Hamilton went after him with a sleigh, found him near Dr. Gould's in Oneida, and brought him home. While they were attempting, partly by persuasion and partly by force, to take him back with them in the sleigh, the Presbyterian minister, hearing the commotion, came up and inquired into the trouble. The next day he wrote a brief account of the affair for publication in the *Oneida Telegraph,* but at the request of Mr. Burt and Mrs. Joslyn, who called on him and explained the circumstances, he requested the editor to withdraw the article, which was done.

Table Talk by Noyes
March 2, 1852

We are now evidently in a transition state. The subject that has engrossed our attention for five years past is the sexual relation. We have now in the late movements committed the decisive act which launches us on a new course. But the transition has been going on for some time; it dates, in fact, from the death of Mrs. Cragin. Since then the central subject of interest with us has been victory over death. Marriage and death are the two great principalities to be overcome. Mrs. /405/ Cragin went hand in hand with me in the attack on marriage, and now she is put on the other side of the veil that she may go hand in hand with me to the final victory. In consequence of her death, we have come into a realizing view of Hades, on the one hand, and the world of the resurrection church, on the other. At about the same time I came back from Esopus Dr. Graham died, and I commenced a new treatment of alimentiveness. Our labor since that time has been to sanctify the table. We are coming into reconciliation with matter, so that we can eat and drink in the name of the Lord Jesus. Our new views of the spiritual world have resulted in the Concentric Convention. We are in our proper vocation here at the table in removing the causes of death. It is here that the decisive victory is to be won.

Brooklyn Journal

April 5, 1852.—Mrs. Miller mentioned to Mr. Noyes that the report Fanny was making would prove that our women, instead of contracting any of those peculiar diseases common to the sex, had been cured of all former complaints.

Noyes:—"That is splendid! That is worth a thousand dollars to me right now on the spot. To think that with our new social life, and the hazards, and the predictions, we should come out cured even of old complaints, is a miracle. It is worth telling of!"

Harriet H. Skinner to Her Mother
Brooklyn, July 1, 1852

John is particularly engaged in the conquest of death. He says, if Christ is going to be elected, we must have death /406/ out of the way. It is John's idea that believers everywhere should ratify the nomination by Kossuth.* He says he is going out to stump it. He is going to try his voice in the field of public speaking. He means to get his liberty or die.

John said last night, that he saw no kind of use in your going to Hades, you would have to come back so soon. It was so near morning, you had better not lie down at all.

Remarks by Noyes
July 4, 1852

The Lord seems to be suffering my old thorn in the flesh [hoarseness] to operate upon me to some extent, no doubt for good purposes, and I have to request that I may be freed from any necessity of talking on stated occasions at the table or in the evening. I prefer that the family undertake to edify themselves for the present and give me an opportunity to rest. I think it would be for the benefit of the family as well as myself that this change should take place. If visitors come, do not expect me to take the brunt of conversation. Let others step forward and entertain them. What is needed now is a breaking up of habit not only in myself but in the family in respect to looking to me for discourse on all occasions. It is a bad habit and might produce disease. My health in every other respect is good. This trouble is a signal to me, as it has

---

* Lejos Kossuth was a Hungarian patriot who briefly ruled Hungary after the revolution of 1848 and then fled to the United States, where he was received as a hero. [L.F.]

been before, to turn away from too much communication by word of mouth. I count it a good sign for the paper. /407/

Lemuel H. Bradley to Mrs. Newhouse
    Wallingford, July 17, 1852

Mr. Noyes is with us yet. He said at the tea-table this afternoon: "If I stay here I shall grow fat. With no letters, no newspapers, together with fine sport in swimming and fishing, God is giving me rest and refreshment. My throat troubles me but very little now." He said to me the day he came here: "Extremes meet in my case. While I am fleshy, my throat is worse than it has ever been. I am going to have a fair fight now, and if I beat this time the Devil will have to give it up." So you see he has beaten the old scamp again.

Oneida Journal

July 25, 1852.—J. Philander Abbot, a member of the Oneida Association, died of consumption on the 20th inst., aged twenty. This is the first death of an adult that has occurred at the Community since its commencement in November 1847. As the day dawns we smile over those that fall asleep, reckoning that their slumbers will be short and their dreams pleasant.

Noyes to George W. Noyes
    Wallingford, August 10, 1852

Dear Brother:—
In this green, quiet retreat I have leisure and favorable circumstances for inquiring into the causes of our maladies at Brooklyn. My motto is: "For every evil under the sun there is a remedy or there is none. If there is one, seek it, and find it. If there is none, then never mind it." In my seeking I have taken a hint from the following symptom-fact in my own experience: Yesterday for the first time since I have been here, I took up a *Tribune* and skimmed it through. My throat and lungs had been in a comfortable /408/ improving state, but before I got through the paper they were smarting with the old irritation. To-day I repeated the experiment with the same result. Reflection on these facts has satisfied me that newspaperism is the inlet of many of the plagues we suffer. Why not? The acrid selfish spirit of the Devil's world is the element of all disease, and certainly the newspapers represent and circulate it. True, we have the promise that we shall "drink any deadly thing and it shall

not hurt us," and accordingly we find ourselves alive and able to doctor ourselves after having breakfasted, dined, and supped for years on newspaper poison. But it is good to stop and consider the experiment, that we may not tempt the Lord. It has undoubtedly been our duty to acquaint ourselves with the newspapers for various objects. Our profession and projects have demanded the sacrifice. But let us not forget that it is a sacrifice to plunge thus into the depths of Satan. Have we not gained the general information and the literary helps that we needed, at least enough to last us for some time? I would suggest, by way of experiment, a fast from newspaper fare. Do for once clear the nasty sheets all out of the sitting-room, and, if possible, out of the house. Try it for a week and see if you don't all feel better. Why should we not make up our minds to quit the literature of the world, and turn our whole attention to our manifest business of creating a new literature that shall be a medium of life and joy?

Harriet H. Skinner to Charlotte A. Miller
Brooklyn, August 11, 1852

Dear Charlotte:—

We have just arisen from the dinner-table, where we had a refreshing laugh in reviewing a scene which occurred in the parlor /409/ this morning after reading John's letter. We gathered up the papers in the sitting-room, and had a game of ball with them. George expressed his disgust by kicking one of them, whereupon others joined, and flung and kicked the papers about the room right merrily. Although it lasted but a minute or two, it was an expression of feeling that cleared the atmosphere. We thought Greeley and Bennett would have stared to see their papers treated so.

Sarah K. Dunn to Brooklyn
August 11, 1852.—We are having quite a battle with consumption [tuberculosis]. Mrs. Olds is quite feeble, and others have had consumptive symptoms. But we are bright and happy in the midst of it all. Mr. Noyes thinks we are facing consumption this season in the same way we did insanity last year. If we can overcome consumption, we can death, and he advises all to confess Christ in their lungs.

August 31, 1852.—Mr. Miller in a letter to Mr. Cragin mentioned the death of Mrs. Olds.

Charlotte A. Miller to Harriet H. Skinner
Oneida, August 16, 1852

Dear Harriet:—

The funeral of Edgar Ackley took place this afternoon. Sarah Dunn and I marched right into the bedroom (the same that Philander died in and that Mr. Joslyn had occupied) after we returned, following up a suggestion from Miss Burgess that the room and the wing to which it was attached was probably haunted by Mr. Joslyn's old Hadean spirits, and determined to exorcise and fumigate it. We commenced taking down the bedstead and removing things from the room, Mr. Ackley helping, resolved that we would scent out the mischief /410/ and get up a general mob that would turn these evil spirits out, and the dolefuls too, before Mr. Miller came home. We took down the curtain that hung before the shelves, and lo! an Old Hat, which everybody recognizes as Mr. Joslyn's, the one which he wore constantly in the house and out, while in deep consultation with those foul spirits. We threw it onto the floor, and while we were talking of burning it, Mr. Ackley gave it a kick. The rest of us joined in and finally kicked it downstairs into the kitchen. Mr. Ackley then kicked it into the furnace and it was burned up. The laughter and excitement gave a completely new turn to the feelings of Mr. Ackley and the house generally. As a still further purification of the wing, we resolved to have our evening meeting there. An hour was passed in testimony. The experience of those who had roomed there and had been troubled with bad dreams and bad sleep was related. There was some criticism of the spirit that Mrs. Olds was suffering under. Then we read the 91st Psalm and some others. Mr. Burt was full of unction, and the old revival spirit seemed to circulate from heart to heart. It was half-past ten, and we were closing the meeting with singing "Sherburne" when Mr. Miller came in. A supper for all with coffee, etc., after the old Putney fashion followed and ended the day with peace and thankfulness.

Noyes to George Cragin
Wallingford, August 19, 1852

I was weighed yesterday, and found that I had gained three lbs. since I have been here—present weight 165 lbs.! That does not look much like consumption. /411/

Charlotte A. Miller to Brooklyn
    Oneida, September 2, 1852

Dear Friends:—
    We are happy to record that there are no invalids among us. Harriet Hall is better in spirit and body than I ever knew her. This has been the case for several weeks. She is very edifying, and we love her very much. She is in the kitchen, and works heartily and usefully. Her case is a Gibraltar the Devil will never be able to take.

Erastus H. Hamilton to Oneida
    Brooklyn, September 15, 1852

At the supper table, Mr. Noyes said: "Mr. Hamilton, I recommend that you write to Miller and Burt to take hold now and get the indictments against them for disease and death removed. According to accounts the Devil has been crowding them hard with these indictments."

George W. Noyes to Charlotte A. Miller
    Brooklyn, October 9, 1852

In conversation last night John remarked that there were four lines in the army of death: 1: acute diseases; 2: chronic diseases; 3: insensible diseases manifesting themselves in old age; 4: death itself. We met the first line in dysentery and cholera in the first years of the Association, and broke it. The past summer we have got a victory over the second line. John said it had been one of the hardest seasons he had ever experienced. When he went to Wallingford his throat and lungs were very bad, but he got a new baptism of faith and will against it, and feels that he can put it down. I have been in a steady skirmish with chronic troubles for the last year, and had a crisis soon after /412/ John came from Wallingford, which I think amounts to a decided victory. All the crazy ones have got well, and those at Oneida who have suffered attacks seem to be better.

Sarah Campbell to Oneida
    Brooklyn, December 18, 1852

It is quite a time just now. Some have colds, one a boil, and Mr. Noyes's throat has troubled him of late. He remarked last night that we thought we were having a hard time, but we were not. The Devil was having a hard time, and we were having a good one. There was no need of a sick spirit.

Saturday evening, 8:15. As I was looking out of the parlor window into the printing office, I thought how I should like to paint the lively scene to you. I will try: Elizabeth is at her old post, laying on papers; Ellen by her side taking lessons; John Smith in Abby's place; Mr. Leonard by his side; Anna Maria standing opposite looking on, bright and happy; Mr. Hull turning wheel; now Mr. Carr steps into his place and gives it new force; there comes Mr. Noyes out of the office with new paper in hand, and sits down in the corner to peruse it; Sarah Dunn and Sophronia have just gone in; Henry and Sarah Johnson now turning wheel they salute me through the windows; so does Ellen. Suffice it to say they all look very cheerful. There has been quite a lightening up in the atmosphere since last night. Mr. Noyes seems lively, and all around tells that it is easy to do God's will. It is nearly time to fold papers, so good evening. /413/

Home-Talk by Noyes
December 22, 1852

I will not criticize Wallingford now, because I criticized them enough while I was there. I remember my visit with a great deal of pleasure. There was a drawing out of my mind into a new love of science which characterizes the place; and withal I had some of the severest and at the same time most precious experiences I ever had in relation to sickness, both in my own case and in the case of Victor and Theodore. I date a new era in my own health from my visit there, so that the thoughts of Wallingford are very pleasant to me. I feel healthy and growing in spite of adverse influences. I had a pressing time a while ago with my throat, but I feel stronger now.

Dialogue
May 11, 1853

Q:—You have just returned from Oneida, I understand. How is the health of the Association?
A:—Very good.
Q:—Haven't they any sick ones there?
A:—No, none that are confined at all.
Q:—Did you see Harriet Hall?
A:—Yes, she was about, as busy as any one.
Q:—Don't they employ a doctor?

A:—Not at all.

Q:—One of their members was formerly a doctor, I believe, What does he do?

A:—He was tending the circular saw when I was there; but he goes from one business to another, making himself "generally useful," as the phrase is at Oneida. He is called upon to pull a tooth occasionally, and is always ready to sew up a cut or do any little office of that kind when asked. /414/

Q:—His *materia medica* is all thrown overboard, I suppose.

A:—Not a pill or potion left.

Q:—Where there are so many children I should think some of them would be ailing. Don't they have colds?

A:—I heard no coughing and very little complaint of any kind. I was told that the children had been almost entirely free from colds the whole winter.

Q:—What do the Association live on?

A:—Common vegetables and fruit; good bread of all kinds; tea and coffee; fish, salt and fresh; some salt pork; and once in a great while a dinner of fresh meat.

Q:—I see they are not Grahamites. Are they Hydropathists?

A:—No, they are too busy for that. In short the question of health is very much neglected there. You seldom hear it mentioned in any way. They seem to be so much taken up with other things that they forget to be sick.

Brooklyn Journal

February 19, 1854.—Mr. Noyes got up and ate his breakfast as usual. But he soon asked Theodore to make a fire in his room, and wrote on a paper that he had resolved not to talk at all and see if his throat did not gain by it. He quit talking on the principle of non-resistance; he could go on as he had done, but it would be a continual strife with the Devil, and he did not care enough for the privilege of talking to quarrel about it.

February 21, 1854.—A hard day in the family. Almost every one had a headache. Nevertheless we finished the paper between ten and eleven in the evening, and all felt better. Perhaps some principality opposed us that wished to hinder the publication of *Morality of War* and *Cheerful Views*. Mr. Noyes thinks those articles are grand and just what are needed at this time.

February 22, 1854.—Mr. Noyes continues his fast from talking, though I judge from his actions that he feels better. His advice /415/ on paper [letters] to the editors is to avoid combativeness. "Do not drink in Greeley's spirit. Charles should keep out of the Nebraska pow-wow. Mr. Pitt should keep his temper about antichrist. All should go back and examine the grounds on which I acted in renouncing allegiance to the United States."*

February 25, 1854.—Mr. Noyes's throat is better. He says it does not trouble him any, but still he feels like keeping his fast until he has a clear instinct to mingle with the family again. The paper went off very easily today. G. W. Noyes and others came from Newark. George had gained four pounds in flesh. He is doing a good work in Newark. He electioneers for the paper wherever he goes.

March 1, 1854.—Mr. Noyes wrote that he had received much benefit in respect to regulating that which goeth out of the mouth, and he was now inclined to avail himself of this opportunity to take a step forward in respect to regulating that which goeth into the mouth. He requested therefore that no more tea or coffee or beer or meat be brought to him. He said this should not be considered as making a rule for the rest of the family. He thought it best to have these articles on the table, certainly as long as Larkin remained with us. (There is prospect of his finding another boarding-place soon.) As Mr. Noyes was boarding by himself now, he felt free on this first day of spring, with a view to clarifying his brain for a good time of working on the paper, to make a change of diet, which he had long contemplated as to come in connection with the breaking of the reign of tobacco and other unnatural stimulants. Quite a number of the family were ready to join him in giving up the use of tea and coffee. /416/ Mr. Noyes says that this is evidence of the need for a change in our diet.

March 5, 1854.—After fasting from speaking for two weeks, Mr. Noyes last evening sat in his old "Home-Talk Corner" and spoke as follows:

"Before I returned upstairs I had been thinking of the difficulty in my throat, and one day while walking the street it suddenly flashed upon me that what I wanted was to stop talking so much to man, and talk more to God. That is undoubtedly the difficulty in all other cases. You may seek help by changing your situation and circumstances as much as you please, but you will find at last that the only way to get help is to retire from the earth and earthly things and get more intercourse with God. Mere criticism and trying to edify one another is not enough. Our conversation then is horizontal.** There will have to be a great deal more prayer. I don't know but in our social

* Early in 1837, John Humphrey Noyes had written William Lloyd Garrison concerning his hatred of slavery: "I have subscribed my name to an instrument similar to the Declaration of '76, renouncing allegiance to the government of the United States, and asserting the title of Jesus Christ to the throne of the world." Noyes went on to say that he was prepared, in effect, to accept the existence of a corrupt world, but not to partake in that corruption himself. [Quoted in R. A. Parker, *A Yankee Saint,* p. 49. L.F.]
** Between two who are equal. [L.F.]

meetings there will have to be exercises of that kind. I think there is too much reading and not enough prayer in the family. The tone of the family is not healthy on that account."

Mr. Noyes proposes to go to Wallingford tomorrow morning, to rest awhile and get out of the city atmosphere. Mr. Seymour will accompany him.

March 5, 1854.—Mr. Noyes wrote: "My impression is that the family here in the city won't gain much by leaving off meat and taking up milk two or three times a day. The milk in these markets is as suspicious at least as the meat. Let that reform come along naturally, as I think it will, when we are more cleared of the old hankering for stimulants. But you may as well make /417/ thorough work now in the drinkables. At any rate I shall recommend to Theodore to learn to love cold water as ordinary drink, instead of tea or coffee or milk, or even warm water. Let those who are disposed try it a while. We will prove all things and hold fast that which is good.

John R. Miller to George Cragin
Oneida, March 15, 1854

I was very thankful for the interest you manifest in my health, and also for G. W. Noyes's very kind note. They quite touched my heart. I can assure you that I shall give heed to the advice. I have already found great advantage in living very temperately, and quite often going without a meal. My living for the last ten days has been generally a small piece of toast three times a day, usually of brown bread, with a glass of cold water. For a few days I have given this up, and ate something which I found on the table. At the same time I have abstained from talking as much as possible. My health is greatly improved, so that I shall be able to do all that belongs to me, I am sure. I shall endeavor to be economical of my life.

On May 5, 1854, Mr. Miller arrived at Brooklyn for a short visit. Up to this time his letters have been full of business. He has been pushing the peddling enterprise, which has shown unusual profit this spring. At the same time he has been opening a market for rustic seats in New York, and for carpet bags in Utica, Syracuse, and other near-by towns. There are frequent references to "providential" receipts of money needed to pay the running expenses of the six Associations and support the tri-weekly paper in Brooklyn. [G.W.N.] /418/

John R. Miller to His Wife
Brooklyn, May 8, 1854

Dear Charlotte:

I have spent three days here very pleasantly and, I think, profitably. Mr. Noyes is full of enthusiasm in *The Circular,* the Bible games, the carpet bag business, and whatever he undertakes. The morning after my arrival, I arose at half past five and was quite surprised to find Mr. Noyes up and busily engaged in putting things in order for the day. The parlor had been swept and made ready for use, and George had gone to New York on business.

This morning I joined the washing-bee. We washed two hours before breakfast, and I enjoyed it much. I have entered right into the business of the family and endeavored to make myself generally useful. I joined our bee in making carpet bags. Saturday night I worked awhile at the Press, and then by Harriet Skinner's invitation helped Harriet A. Noyes address the Circulars, and shall continue it while here. I find plenty of employment. It is a poor place here in which to be idle. I am thankful for the privilege of making this visit.

Brooklyn Journal

May 14, 1854.—Mr. Miller has been here over a week. He is considerably under the spirit of disease, looks thin, and seems rather low-spirited. Mr. Cragin just proposed that we criticise the spirit that is upon him. He, with George and Mr. Skinner, advised him to do just as he would advise another to do in the circumstances, turn his mind away from himself, and get hold of something new.

Evening.—Mr. Miller has gone to bed feeling quite indisposed. /419/

May 15, 1854.—Mr. Miller [is] much better, thinks the crisis is past, looks better than he has since he has been here. Goes to Wallingford to spend a day or two and then return here, and in the course of this week will return to Oneida taking Mrs. Skinner with him, thus giving her a little variety and respite from the paper.

Mr. Silas Blaisdell died at Oneida on May 13th, and Mrs. Nash on the 23rd.

Mr. Noyes has just started for Wallingford. Quite a sudden start. He says he does not go from necessity as he did before.

Note by J. H. Noyes
May 16, 1854

Charles asked me if my throat was any better. I said, NO. I wish to add that, though the local disease has been quite painful for a few days past, (apparently in consequence of the easterly storm), my system on the whole had improved decidedly. My mind has gained its freedom again, and I am more free from nervousness and childish temptations than I have been since February. God has strengthened my faith, and given me a new elasticity of will, so that I am having a good time fighting with my old enemy. I thank God that now, when he is bringing my talking to an end, He has begun a revival of Bible study in the church. You can do well without me if you study Christ. The Bible game, if it continues to interest as it has done, will do more good than Home-Talks. I advise Mr. Miller to do his best to promote universal industry and the study of the Bible at Oneida, and then fear not but the Association will prosper without him and without me. If we are disabled or should even die, the good fight will go on till victory shall swallow death. Either in heaven or under /420/ heaven, we shall see and share in that victory. If God pleases, our children shall take our places and finish what we have begun.

It is now just twenty years since the present war with sin and death began in New Haven. That is only half the period which I had in mind and alluded to in the Battle-Axe Letter, where I spoke of the "long race and the hard warfare" that was before the saints. Twenty years have brought us round to where I started from, to the earnest study of the life of Christ. I thank God and take courage.

John R. Miller to Brooklyn
Wallingford, May 16, 1854

I arrived here about 4 o'clock yesterday, and found Mr. Noyes, Mr. Bradley, and the women engaged in making carpet bags. The other men were employed in different kinds of outdoor work. I enjoyed my ride here better than I expected, and found no difficulty in walking up from the depot carrying my carpet bag and heavy overcoat. I felt thankful every step I took for the strength I had gained.

After being here a short time I took a walk over the premises with Mr. Bradley, which I enjoyed and was not fatigued. I had a very good night and felt quite refreshed this morning. Mr. Bradley, Seymour, and myself are going to Paug Pond fishing today. Mr. Noyes said his throat was too bad to go. He does not talk much. He is out grafting this morning, and seems quite happy. I expect to start for Brooklyn tomorrow. /421/

Oneida Journal

May 19, 1854:—Mr. Miller, Harriet Skinner, and Mr. and Mrs. Long came. Mr. Miller retired to his room to rest. When Mr. Noyes's letter to Brooklyn was first read, a feeling of sadness came over us, but an evening or two later a second reading of it was called for, which diffused a bright, hopeful spirit among us. We had an edifying talk occasioned by Mrs. Deborah Knowles. She was in trial on account of the sickness of the leading members, and said it seemed to her as if something must be wrong. Mr. Burt said he thought the salvation of the body was as much a matter of election as the salvation of the soul; it was for God to say, who should live and who should die. God would be glorified in the dead and in the living. Mrs. Skinner said we needed such experience here at Oneida to make us more interior. Mr. Miller wrote, that he did not think he was going to die, or that Mr. Noyes was. "But," he continued, "I do say in relation to it, and I believe we must all say the same, 'Thy will, O God, be done.' If we live after the fashions of the world, we shall surely die; but if we join the resurrection army, there is at least a chance for us to live till this last enemy is conquered. If I fall, it will be with full faith in victory over death."

John R. Miller to the Community
Oneida, May 25, 1854

I have had a good many thoughts lately, especially within a few days, about our finances. I see that there is a good deal to be done to pay our present debts and keep all the machinery in motion so that the public interests will not suffer. I cannot do it. The question is, whom has God qualified to fill the /422/ place? It seems to me that Mr. Barron is the man. I think he has talent and taste for it, and would consider it no burden. The only objection I see is his lack of spiritual experience. He would be liable for quite a while to come under a worldly spirit, which would have to be criticised; but he takes criticism well. I would propose farther, that Mr. Burt, Mr. Skinner, and perhaps one more should be a board of directors, and that no debts, except for small sums, should be contracted without their consent. A small debt which Mr. Barron did not know of might seriously embarrass us for a short time.

We frequently say, when we have calls for money to supply private wants, that there is no money to spare. But this would never be thought of when there are calls for the public interest. Mr. Barron at first will not be likely to make the proper distinction. But he will learn that Brooklyn's wants should always be attended to, and so of a great many other things. He will have to be wide awake to see that no inspired proposal is stopped for the want of money.

Is Mr. Barron ready to engage in this new field?

Yours for devotion to Christ,
John R. Miller

Circuit Talk No. 1
Wallingford, May 31, 1854*

Our revival at Putney commenced with just such a state of things in my throat. There is to be a new growth after this. I don't know how. /422/

Last year I started a scheme, that once in a while the leading members ought to resign and offer themselves for criticism from all quarters. That scheme has never been fully carried out, but the Lord is not going to let me off without seeing it through. There is need in all the Associations for criticism of the leading members, to give the family a chance.

I have got command of myself now, so that I need not be afraid to go to Oneida or anywhere.** I can go and not say a word; whisper, as I do here, and not irritate my throat. Then my throat is a good deal stronger than it was. I feel stronger in every way. I shall do the Devil a good deal of mischief. I do not feel at liberty to go yet, and am not quite able to. But with a little more repairs, I could go and do good and get good.

I can see that "when I am weak, then I am strong." My most fruitful time is when I am low. Just now, while I have been threatened, I have been starting this Bible game.

Family Conversation about Mr. Miller

(Mr. Noyes proposed that we have a general talk for Mr. Miller's benefit. The letter received today from Harriet Skinner was first read.)

Noyes:—For my part I feel cheerful and good-natured about his condition and the uncertainty that hangs over him. I cannot say but he will die. I do not ask for any pledge. My principle in regard to my own health and that of others has always been that of Shadrach, Meshach, and Abednego: "The God that we serve is able to deliver us, and he will deliver us; but if not, be it known unto thee, O king, we will not bow down and worship the /424/ image thou hast set up." That is my faith about death. I know death is being overcome, and will ultimately be absolutely so. But it is evident, and has been all along, that we cannot claim to have finished that work. And my faith in regard to victory over death is not staked on any individual case. If I got my will into such an attitude as to put God under law, I should expect he would cross that will. While I say these things, I do not find in my heart any especial expectation

---

* Noyes has been suffering from throat trouble, and this "talk" is marked "Whispered." [G.W.N.]
** Noyes spoke of going on a circuit of the Communes, not for a jaunt but on business. [G.W.N.]

that Mr. Miller will die. I rather expect he will hold out beyond all expectations, and begin to rise again. I advise him and all to take a cheerful view. Yet I would not force any faith; that would do no good. Instead of that I would turn around and face death and learn to be courageous in view of it. I have found in such instances that as soon as I became perfectly willing to die, and began to make my arrangements accordingly, the Lord began to make arrangements not to have me. So I advise Mr. Miller to set about cheerfully making arrangements as though he were certainly to die, pack up his trunks as though he were going on a long journey; then if orders come that he need not go, it will be a short and easy job to unpack his trunks again.

Mr. Seymour:—That course would undoubtedly disappoint the Devil. His object is to frighten us. The fear of death is the worst thing he has to frighten us with.

Noyes:—"He that loveth his life shall lose it, and he that loseth his life shall find it." As individuals and as an Association, we must have experience of that king—must pass death as it were—must overcome death through death. I believe that the resurrection is at work in me whether I live or die, and whether Mr. Miller does. I love Mr. Miller very much, and /425/ believe God loves him. I love him too well to wish to take him out of God's hands. I am willing that God should do what is necessary for his salvation. I shall never cease to love him and remember his labors of love and faith among us. No man has done so much as he to strengthen the business department. A great gap would be left, if he were taken away, but I have confidence that God will fill it.

Mr. Seymour:—We need to get in the way of regarding death as a small matter, as you would a bridge that you had to pass on a journey. We are bound for heaven, and we shall go through at all events, toll or no toll. God has made us rich enough to pay toll if necessary.

Noyes:—Besides, he has promised us a free bridge sometime! There never was since our commencement such a freshet of diabolical influences, physical and spiritual, as there has been this spring. There have been blood and destruction in Europe, Asia, and South America, which have been constantly poured in upon us. Then there has been a continent of ice on our coast, several times as much as common. Winter has extended itself far into the Spring. All that ever had any consumptive tendency have been severely tried. Mr. Blaisdell and Mrs. Nash have been carried away by the flood.

Mr. Bristol:—The Association needs this experience. There appears to be too much leaning on Mr. Miller both for their good and his.

William Hinds:—I have always loved him a great deal, and do now. I can never appreciate too highly what he has done for me. /426/ It was a great while before I would consent to think of his dying; but I can now say, Let God's will be done. The love of life is particularly strong in him. His strong, affectionate nature has thrown out its fibres everywhere; and it would seem absolutely necessary that God should reduce him as he has done, in order to crucify thoroughly his natural life, that Christ's life may take its place.

Mr. Seymour:—Such a character would do more good by generating his spirit in others than by acting as a single person. He ought to have a great body for his soul to live and act in.

Noyes:—God has almost to kill the little body in order to give him a great one.

In 1846 I ran down lower than I am now. I was cured then by love. Now I shall have to confess that I have been cured by labor. It has been life to me. Nothing else would exactly touch the spot.

Such a man as Mr. Miller should not go out and work an hour or two in a gentlemanly way; he should make up his mind to become a workingman—change his class.

Mr. Seymour:—The Lord wants to clean up the parlor, so he invites all to go down into the kitchen. (Laughter.)

William Hinds:—That cloud of hypo seems to be rolling away now.

Noyes:—Yes, the heavens are lighting up. I have not been troubled with any hypo for some time past. There is connected with it a cross, quarreling, claiming spirit. I have had to nip my lips and hold my tongue by force to keep from scolding. /427/ If I undertook to criticise, I would be thrown into hell-fire, and would have to go to bed. But now I am free, and can criticise and feel better for it. I am sensible of having grown in peace and good nature rapidly this spring in the midst of my troubles. There has been a singular mixing up of spiritual and physical phenomena. When that easterly storm came on, my mind became as dark as the heavens, trouble with my throat commenced, and I had a violent toothache at the same time. If I took up *The Tribune* and read about the eastern war, accidents, etc., the same symptoms came on. Sometimes I could read only a few minutes.

William Hinds:—If it is true that it is the darkest time just before day, there must be a very bright day just ahead of us.

Mr. Bradley:—Whatever happens, God is drawing the bands of love and union tighter and tighter. We are becoming more and more independent of individuals. "It is not by might, nor by power, but by my spirit, saith the Lord." Not by man, nor by anything external, but by the power and purpose of God, the Association stands.

Harriet H. Skinner to Wallingford
Brooklyn, June 8, 1854

The family talk on Mr. Miller's case was received the day before I left Oneida, and Mr. Miller set right about making such arrangements as he would if he knew he was going to die. His first thought was to deed his property, the Putney mill to Mr. Baker, the store to George, the Abbott and Baker property at Oneida to Mr. Skinner, Mr. Thacker and Mr. Barron. But on consultation with Mr. Burt and Mr. Skinner, with advice of Mr. Joslyn, /427A/ he concluded to make his will, as that could be done privately, and in case he should get well would leave everything as it was. I understood he was to will his property to the same persons to whom he thought of deeding it, for the benefit of the Community.

I thought the effect on Mr. Miller was good, and the Community, which had flattened quite sensibly, straightened up and took a new tone. The Talk hit the mark all round. Mr. Miller had worn out his bad symptoms a good deal when I came away; was weak and lacked appetite, but was much more free from any distress than previously. His worst time has been nights from 9 till 2 o'clock, but the night before I left he slept quite well.

Charlotte A. Miller to Harriet H. Skinner
Oneida, June 10, 1854

I cannot speak of any apparent gain in Mr. Miller. Last night he was less feverish than the night before, but he is quite weak in mind and body. I suppose that is to be expected if a fever takes its course. I trust God and look on the bright side. As John says, "he may hold out beyond all expectation and then begin to rise." I desire to be of God's mind about his case any way. His appetite is gone, as when you left. He ate three strawberries this morning, nothing more.

Charlotte A. Miller to Henry J. Seymour
Oneida, June 10, 1854

Your information about Mr. Noyes and his recovering his voice was very cheering. I can rejoice in it as a great public blessing, and a token for good to us all. Mr. Miller is rather languishing in uncertainty yet, though hope on the whole prevails. He wishes to say that he felt very grateful for the /428/ Report from Wallingford. His case does not appear to be consumptive, but a fever of some kind hangs onto him yet. He is up and dressed every day, and sits up considerably. We expect to get great good out of his case in some way, and we find it is not hard to trust God to dispose of him.

George W. Noyes to Charlotte A. Miller
Brooklyn, June 11, 1854

I think about you a great deal nowadays, and realize more fully than before our unity in one body making appropriate the apostle's exhortation to "remember them that are in bonds as bound with them." Mr. Miller's battle I know is ours. His sufferings and victories, whatever they may be, will transfer themselves to the benefit of the whole church. While feeling the extent of Mr. Miller's trial, I have had prevailingly good and happy impressions about it, that it is a necessary chastening administered in the kindest love, and intended for his enlargement and deliverance, and not for destruction. John remarks that the present winter and spring have been a time of peculiar spiritual severity, and my consciousness has fully confirmed that fact. But I am sure that it is working a great and beneficent revolution for the church, making for us a new, and so far as it goes, a resurrection world. The official spirit and the narcotic spirit have been judged and cast down. We have got the love of useful work in the place of the love of office and stimulants. We can hardly realize yet the sweep of this blessed change, but in my case it is producing daily returns of health and happiness amply compensating the stormy experience of the transition. A few months ago I was like a shipwrecked vessel, as I thought, right onto a lee shore. I was nervous and cast down, but not /429/ destroyed; quite distressed and miserable, but it seems not wholly forsaken. From my plunge into the machine-shop I began to date a new experience. Since then I have been steadily improving in general health and spirits. My vessel is "clawing off" from the breakers that seemed inevitable. I give thanks to the grace of God and the resurrection life of Christ which are able to start a new enthusiasm in the midst of death. I was much interested in a remark of John's, that in order to get a new growth, the old seed has to die. I expect the time will come when the process will not be so severe.

On June 12, 1854, G. W. Noyes went to Oneida "to see Mr. Miller through the narrows." On June 16, 1854, Mr. Miller passed away. The funeral took place on Sunday, June 18th. It was attended by nearly a hundred from the neighboring towns.

Writes Mr. Skinner: "We had a good, edifying meeting last evening. The presence of the Primitive Church was invited. Remarks were made on the coming together of the three worlds, (Primitive Church, Hadean

World, and World) and the opinion was expressed that the partition between them was now very thin. George read the article 'Constitutional Christianity,' (See Home Talks) which was heartily endorsed. After supper we picked 145 quarts of strawberries." [G.W.N.]

George W. Noyes to the Community
Oneida, June 16, 1854

We have had a good meeting this evening. Mr. Burt commenced by a prayer recognizing the hand of God in our situation, and thanking him for chastisement. There is a good spirit of peace, acquiescence and faith in the family. I think Charlotte has /430/ done beautifully. Though she feels the affliction, she keeps about business as usual and diffuses a cheerful spirit.

June 17, 1854:—I shall stay here till next week, when we shall have had time for a response from the other Associations, and if it is thought best for Charlotte to have a change for a time, I can assist.

Harriet H. Skinner to Charlotte A. Miller
Brooklyn, June 18, 1854

The news this morning touched me, though I was not unprepared for it. With a tearful sensation on the outside my heart inside has been full of comfort today about Mr. Miller, and of rejoicing in God's dealings with us. The effect will be, I believe, to hasten the resurrection. . . . How precious the Bible is now! The parable of Lazarus has a new interest to me, and Christ's words to the thief on the cross. Christ gave his disciples that glorious promise, "Whosoever liveth and believeth on me shall never die." Yet he suffered Stephen and James and Peter to fall asleep. So we see he is not under law not to use death for his purposes.

I have thought that Mr. Miller laid down his life for the brethren, when he met the wrath of the world in the war at Oneida. His spirit was like oil on the foaming waters. You remember John said he covered himself with glory then. Does it not seem as if he fulfilled his work.

What joy, Charlotte, is before us in meeting friends that have gone the journey to Hades! Our seventh Community is there, John says. I love Mr. Miller more than ever before, and the /431/ effect is to make me feel more and more abandonment to the work before us. We too will work day and night on our appointed portion in this enterprise of bringing together the three worlds, and expect that everything we do tells.

June 19, 1854.—John, we hear, is improving very fast.

Charlotte A. Miller to Her Mother
Oneida, June 23, 1854

In the fly-leaf of his memorandum book bought in January, Mr. Miller wrote his name, and the first entry is: "I wish to commence this year with confessing the sovereignty of Christ and union with him," and on the last leaf he wrote: "To him who has the Christian's hope there is no light except what shines through the grave."

I think he has had rather a presentiment for a year or more that the trouble in his throat and stomach would be fatal, and after he was taken so unwell at Brooklyn a strong persuasion that his hour was come settled upon him. His vital energies seemed spent, and nothing seemed to get the lever of faith under him. It was fore-ordained: his work was done, and the call to depart was imperative.

I think Mr. Miller was ripened much during the last two years. His faith and devotion were more single-eyed. He was weaned from earthly things. His natural buoyancy never seemed fairly gone though much beclouded after he came from Brooklyn. . . . He was much beloved in the family. All seemed to feel that he was a father and a brother indeed. That God loved him, and still keeps him, I have no doubt. It is needless to say that I have a /432/ lively sense of all his noble, lovable qualities, and of his constant, generous affection for me. Yet I feel a rejoicing in my innermost heart, that God's will is done in taking him away. Christ is all in all, and better than any creature. We shall find all good in him.

George W. Noyes to Noyes
Brooklyn, June 24, 1854

Dear Brother:—

I came down the river last night on my return from Oneida, and shall hold my self ready for service in all kinds of business here. I had not much opening for writing at Oneida, but found the most edification in working at the shoe-making with Mr. Van Velzer.

There is a rather singular state of things at Oneida. It looks outwardly chaotic, and is accompanied by more or less tribulations of individuals, but it is the harbinger undoubtedly of new peace and resurrection. I think it the necessary casting down of the official spirit—the outward resting in persons, which has been very strong at Oneida as well as here. All will be compelled to go singly, to God. To bring this about is painful for the time being, but it will work out right. I can see in this the best promise of your being able to go there and do them good. The state of things there reminds me of the distresses that pressed upon us here during the winter, and I judge that it is an extension of the same criticism and clearing. If it is so, the result will be worth all the trouble. I am uncommonly happy and buoyant nowadays, and love God for all his dealings with us. /433/

Editorial by Noyes in the Circular
Wallingford, July 23, 1854

Dear Brethren:—
Having no occasion or disposition to mourn for the death of our brother John R. Miller, I have not been tempted to wish that we might get up a flourish of panegyric over him. But the suggestion, which has been current among us, that his death was a judgment on the Association or on his own folly in some way, has led me to give calm and serious attention to the question, what is the proper view of this event. His labors of love toward me have been so abundant, that I am in no danger of indifference or forgetfulness in reference to his memory. My only anxiety has been that I might think and speak of him truthfully and according to the best judgment of God. As I was waiting in this attitude of mind, we came in the course of our Bible studies to Paul's epistle to the Phillippians, and there I found a case which seemed to me a sound precedent for judgment in respect to brother Miller.

That epistle was a love-letter sent back to the Phillippians by the hands of Epaphroditus, whom they had delegated to carry their contributions to Paul in his imprisonment at Rome. Epaphroditus, in his zeal for the service of love on which he was sent, in some way over-worked and fell sick. He did not die, but he came very near dying, and his case might have been the subject of the same queryings that have occurred in regard to brother Miller. Now see how Paul judged the matter. He writes:

> I supposed it necessary to send you Epathroditus, my brother and companion in labor, and fellow-soldier, but your messenger, and he that ministered to my wants. For he longed after you all, and was full of heaviness, because that ye had heard that he had been sick. For /434/ indeed he was sick nigh unto death; but God had mercy on him; and not on him only, but on me also, lest I should have sorrow upon sorrow. I send him therefore the more carefully, that, when ye see him again, ye may rejoice, and that I may be the less sorrowful. Receive him therefore in the Lord with all gladness, and hold such in reputation; *because for the work of Christ he was nigh unto death, not regarding his life, to supply your lack of service toward me.* Phil. 2:25–30.

This word of Paul tells me "in demonstration of the Spirit and with power," that our brother Miller, who was truly an Epaphroditus to us at Brooklyn, and whose zeal for the work of God at Oneida really wore out his throat, died not under judgment for sins either of the church or his own, but as a good soldier and martyr of Jesus Christ.

In any case of death in the church—even in that of Stephen or of Christ himself—an accusing spirit might find reason for treating it as a judgment on the church or a punishment of imprudence. But after all there is a line of distinction which the common sense of faith can easily find. If ever there was a case of noble sacrifice of life to the service of Christ, that case was brother Miller's. /435/

37

Review of the Brooklyn Epoch
1849 to 1854*

In its earlier years the Community had eked out a precarious but rather comfortable subsistence partly from its own productive labor and partly from property brought in by new members. This was, of course, an unsound position financially. No institution could permanently "live by conquest," least of all an institution absolutely devoted to salvation from sin, and set as flint against all compromise with "the world, the flesh, and the Devil." As a matter of fact, the raw material provided by the old Perfectionist revivals had been nearly all drawn in by the summer of 1850 and, as new converts came slowly, financial pinches began to be felt. Often money was not on hand at night for the next day's necessary expenses. On one occasion, the last dollar in the treasury was given to a visitor, to pay his way home. From this time until the end of the Brooklyn epoch, economy, industry, and dexterity in converting property into cash were all that averted financial disaster.

In October 1850 the subject of needless watches in the family was discussed in the evening meeting, and it was proposed that all who could spare watches should place them in the hands of a committee to be sold. After meeting 25 watches were given up, and the next evening 15 more.

---

* All of chapter 37 is the work of G. W. Noyes. [L.F.]

In September 1851 a letter was read in meeting, proposing that the Oneida family should furnish Brooklyn with butter. "This," said the Oneida journalist, "created quite a laugh, since we have had no butter on our own table for several days."

There were many instances in those early days of what the /436/ Community considered "providential care" in money matters. For example, one day the business men could see no means of raising $100 due at the bank. After collecting all the change at the mill, the shoe-shop, the black-smith shop and store, and borrowing $20 of a visitor, a few dollars were still lacking. Says the journalist: "'Tis almost night, what is to be done?" Well, here comes the mail. And first is a letter from Mr. Miller: "Enclosed you will please find a draft on New York for $100." Here is another letter from Mrs. T. "I have got the money which I intended for you, and enclose $100, a note on the Barnstable bank." Thus after doing all we could do to raise the money without success, God has given us double the sum required.

The Community at first assumed that horticulture was to be its chief industry. That somehow seemed the most Biblical and appropriate. But when money became scarce, they began to find their way into manufactures. Among other articles of their own manufacture, they made at different times palm leaf hats, gold chain, brooms, collars, flour, bee-hives, mop-wringers, and rustic seats. While these early experiments were all eventually abandoned, the instinct back of them proved sound and led on to fortune.

The first permanently profitable business in which the Community engaged was the manufacture of steel game-traps. Sewall Newhouse, a member from Oneida Castle, a hunter and trapper and withal a mechanical genius, by improving on older English and German models had evolved a superior game-trap, and both before and after joining the Community in 1848 had employed himself during the off seasons in making these for his own use and for sale to the neighboring Indians. One day in December /437/ 1851 an order was received from a New York house for five hundred Newhouse muskrat traps. This was an unheard of quantity, and Newhouse was summoned from Wallingford to fill it. The next spring the same house took 250 more. At about this time two of the Community men made the first selling trip to Chicago, and took with them, among other things, 353 traps. The Newhouse trap proved to be exactly what the western trappers wanted, and the Community men had no trouble in disposing of their stock. In the fall Chicago ordered 530 more, including a few of the larger sizes. They were all hand-forged by Newhouse with one or two assistants, who during the intervals between orders turned their attention to other things.

The next substantial spoke in the industrial wheel was the machine-shop.

William R. Inslee, an expert machinist and proprietor of a small machine-shop in Newark, New Jersey, joined the Community in February 1851. During the dispersion at the time of the persecutions at Oneida, quite a number of the young men were sent to Newark and received a thorough education as machinists in Inslee's shop. The bearing of this on the industrial development of the Community will be seen in the sequel.

The third business which made its mark on the future, though humble in its beginnings, was extremely important in its final working out. It was peddling. In attempting to utilize the accomplishments of all the members, Noyes bethought himself of two men who before joining had been peddlers; and feeling that it was highly desirable to establish an independent system of distributing Community products, he suggested that a peddling department be started. The journalist notes that this suggestion "cut /438/ across the pride of some, especially the women;" but on further discussion the whole Community took up the idea with enthusiasm. Men and women begged the privilege of going out, and one man said he would "shoulder a razor-grinder, and joyfully too." The peddlers went two and two, on foot, like the disciples of Christ, and were usually gone not over a week. On their return they were washed from the world by the kindly offices of criticism. They bought and carried for sale silk, needles, buttons, pins, thread, combs, lace, edging, ink, and as they went preached the gospel of salvation from sin and took orders for the Community publications. After a year two, they traveled no longer on foot, but by rail; and as they became more and more exclusively salesmen of Community-made goods, their trips were extended till they covered the country. Thus was developed the Community system of distribution.

In the last year of the Brooklyn epoch, but under the influence of the new afflatus, three new industries were started, job-printing, the manufacture of traveling bags, and the preserving of fruits and vegetables. Job-printing fitted in well with the printing of *The Circular,* and maintained itself as a small department until the end. The bag business was a considerable financial aid until 1868, when it gave way to other more profitable enterprises. The "Fruit Department," as it was called, soon became more identified with the Community in the public mind than any other department. The story of its beginning is thus told by George N. Miller:

"There is a tradition that the first fruits put into bottles by the Community were packed at the solicitation of Henry Thacker, /439/ and that the experiment was mainly an amiable concession, for the sake of harmony, to what was considered a rather visionary idea. The number of bottles which Thacker was cautiously allowed to fill was one thousand, and after these were put up every one feared that a rash thing had been done. However, the goods being packed, an attempt had to be made to sell them, and one of the Community business men, who was accustomed to meeting the world, took a few samples to a distant city, and timidly showed them to a large grocer, expecting to be rebuffed or laughed at. Great was his surprise, therefore, when the grocer, having tasted the contents of one of the bottles, said bluntly, 'I'll take all you've got.'"

But the chief center of interest and romance during this period was the rise of the trap business. When Noyes returned to Oneida from Brooklyn in December 1854, he began looking about for some means of extending the industrial basis of the Community, and it was not long before he pitched upon trap-making as the most promising possibility. This business was still being carried on by Newhouse, with two or three occasional assistants, in a corner of the blacksmith-shop, the annual output varying from 2000 to 5000 traps, according to the season. Newhouse was extremely particular about the kind of help he used, but during the winter and spring of 1854–5 he admitted Noyes to the shop and permitted him to do some of the simpler parts of the work. Not content with this, Noyes pushed on into the forging, and finally into all the mysteries of the trade. Meanwhile, in October 1855 orders began to exceed supply, and Noyes, perceiving that the business to amount to anything must be liberalized, /440/ succeeded in gaining Newhouse's consent to the admission first of Inslee with his trained machinists, and then of untrained Community help. In March 1856 orders aggregating six hundred traps put the department "on the qui vive," and the following month a single order from Milwaukee for one thousand traps sent a long-remembered thrill through the whole Community. There was only one drawback: the farmers were afraid that the trap-shop would have to retain all its hands throughout the summer. However, the profits of the business were so enormous as compared with tilling the soil, that the farmers soon adjusted their minds to the deprivation. Before very long the whole Community, men, women, and children, were making traps and, with the introduction of labor-saving machinery, the output mounted to 11,150 in 1856, 25,000 in 1857, and 275,000 in 1864. To be sure, there were considerable fluctuations in the business. Following the panic of 1857 there was a year and a half of small sales. Then again in 1861–2 during the Civil War the orders dwindled until the shop had to be closed through the summer, and the profits fell below those even of the peddling department. But in December 1862 such a volume of orders came rolling in, that the school was closed, and the scholars all marched into the trap-shop on a promise of an extra week of study after production had caught up. The next year a water-power [word missing] was purchased and a factory built at Turkey Street, now Sherrill, one mile north of the home dwellings, and the trap business entered upon an expansion so huge as to leave no doubt in the minds of the Community that manufacturing rather than farming was to be its destiny. /441/

In all this enthusiasum for industry, the spiritual interests of the Community were kept steadily in view. A religious and general meeting was held in the hall of "The Mansion" every evening from eight to nine o'clock, and was attended by all the members above the age of fourteen years. The children received religious instruction at an earlier hour. "They searched one another marvelously," writes H. G. Wells, "for spiritual chastening; they defied custom and opinion; they followed their reasoning and their theology to the inmost amazing negations." Always and everywhere they insisted upon the practical subjection of business to religion. More than once an entire department of business was abandoned because it interfered with spiritual interests; and many times a successful business man was taken out of a prominent position lest his character suffer.

Nor were intellectual interests forgotten. For a time in the early days at Putney, the whole Community took the morning hours from nine to twelve o'clock, as being the freshest and best, for study. Afterward, besides a regular school for children, classes were formed which met at various hours through the day and were attended by old and young. The wife of the founder commenced the study of Hebrew after she was seventy years old. Other favorite subjects were geography, rhetoric, algebra, Latin, and short-hand. Several of the more aged members were busy with their spelling-books. Their early education had been neglected, and they seemed to take a new lease on life by going back to the beginning. Men of business could be seen drawing from their pocket a slip on which the conjugation of the French verb *savoir* was printed for home use; and a stout striker on the anvil, while waiting for his team-mate to catch up, turned his attention to his lesson in French verbs which he had pinned /442/ to the window casing at his right hand. One class was held at quarter of seven in the morning, that it might interfere as little as possible with labor; but in a business meeting, the fact was noted that teams stood idle in the barn while the teamsters attended classes at the Mansion.

Added to these intellectual pursuits there were reading circles, debating societies, dramatic clubs, occasional lectures, and especially the cultivation of music. At the very height of the industrial epoch [a band] of twenty-eight pieces met daily immediately after the noonday meal. Their half hour of practice ended, the members scattered to their work in the fields or shops. Several of the most talented were sent to New York to study under the best teachers. Cantatas and operas were learned. In the winter of 1862–3 a free weekly concert was given, to which the general public was invited.

Another powerful means of education in the Community was the paper, which not only provided instruction for all, but encouraged a considerable number to become thinkers and writers themselves.

It cannot be said that during the Brooklyn epoch Noyes became more devoted to the purpose of establishing the Kingdom of Heaven on earth, for he was wholly devoted before; but his conception of the Kingdom of God as a practical, mundane institution became constantly clearer. He had seen from the first that the Kingdom of God on earth meant religion and business united under the lead of religion. But with society as then constituted he saw everywhere religion and business united under the lead of business. How could it be otherwise, so long as /443/ business was able to make its continuous impression six days in the week, night and day, while religion could ordinarily engage men's attention only one day in seven? As Noyes expressed it, religion could only talk in whispers, while business was heard in thunders throughout the land. To shift the balance of power from business to religion, Noyes had groped his way into Communism. During the Brooklyn epoch what had before been largely instinctive became a definite, rational, plan of procedure. He proposed specifically to substitute the family relation for the wage-system. "Those who work together," he said, "ought to live together. Let every important business be the gathering point of an enlarged *family*. That family embracing persons qualified to instruct and having constant opportunity to meeting and mutual help, would become a *school*. That school, rising into the knowledge of God and having the best possible facilities for mutual criticism and religious culture, would become a *church*. By this plan we do not call people away from their homes and employments to attend to religion, nor snatch them out of the current of the world for a few days, only to drop them in again, but we carry religion home to the people, and turn their very arrangements for getting a living into the essential conditions of a school and a church." In Noyes's scheme all interests, from the lowest to the highest, were organically united in local Communities of the kind described. To complete the structure, there was need of one more influence. At the center of the system stood "the mighty engine of a free, daily, omnipresent Press, combining and harmonizing the local Communities, and distributing the bread of life to all." /446/ By means of these two institutions, local Communities based in spirit if not in form on the pentecostal model, and a central Press "divorced from Mammon and devoted to the sovereignty of Jesus Christ," Noyes expected that the Kingdom of God would at last gain permanent access to the world.

By the spring of 1854, substantial progress had been made toward realizing this conception of the Kingdom of God. There were six associated Communities, and the various instrumentalities of business, family, school, and church were in organic operation. There was also a free, central paper, called *The Circular*, which, having been issued on an average once in two weeks since 1837 [under a range of titles], had in 1852 become a weekly, in 1853 a semi-weekly, and in 1854 a tri-weekly. The conquest of the world for Christ seemed almost at hand. But as the year advanced, signs accumulated of an approaching change. In June, John R. Miller, the man whose energy, diplomacy, and financial skill had averted bankruptcy and turned aside the shafts of persecution, fell sick and died; and Noyes himself was brought to death's door by an inflammation of the throat. The over-extended condition of the Community and the lack of profitable businesses now became increasingly evident. None of the outlying families were self-supporting, and the Brooklyn family drew on the common purse to the extent of a thousand dollars a year for the maintenance of *The Circular*. Constantly recurring money pinches warned of exhausted resources, and an inventory of property showed that forty thousand dollars, out of the original hundred, had already been sunk. /446A/

Under these circumstances, a policy of concentration was resolved upon. The branches at Brooklyn, Newark, Putney, and Cambridge were given up, and all efforts were thenceforth bestowed on the two main Communities at Oneida and Wallingford; the paper was reduced to a weekly edition, and became little more than a family journal; and Noyes sounded a clarion call to manual labor. "In a true state of society," he declared, "the so-called upper classes will be sent down into manual work as fast as the lower classes are called up to education." He pointed to the example of St. Paul, who, besides preaching, labored with his hands and supported not only himself but others. "Let us go back to our first bishop," he said, "and see if his ways will not improve our health of body and mind, purge us of effeminacy and pride, and make the church strong and victorious as it was in the beginning." To this appeal teachers, editors, and religious leaders enthusiastically responded, and a new era of industrial development commenced.

Although this change of policy might seem to some a backward step, a step toward materialism, Noyes refused to regard it in that light. Speaking at a banquet in 1860, he said: "In reviewing my course, I discover that toward the close of our Brooklyn epoch my faith took on a new character. At that time, I engaged in the study of geology. Now the moral of geology is long-continued faith, patient continuance in well-doing with reference to far-distant results. In studying that science, I acquired an element of patience. Since then I have not been in so much of a *hurry* for a daily paper, for the /446B/ millennium, and for victory over death. But if I am more ready to wait, I have a surer faith in these things than ever. Since we left Brooklyn we have been, as a Community, less enthusiastic but more practical. While there we threatened the powers of evil, and boasted against them. Since then our business has been more thoroughly to carry our faith and principles into practical life." /447/

38

Concentration at Oneida
1854

Paper by Noyes
August 31, 1854

The Northern Vermont Community has occupied my attention considerably since I was there, and the day before I left Oneida I expressed to Messrs. Burt and Barron some ideas which I will put into writing to save talk.

The entire family at the North is not very strong, being composed in large proportion of children and new members. It is divided, Messrs. Ackley and Lord being stationed at J. Kinsley's. There seems to be quite a tendency toward a further weakening of the colony this fall. Mr. Burnham and Jane Kinsley are expecting to go to Oneida, and would have been there before if I had not detained them. Mr. Hamilton is going to Putney to help them in building, and he is needed at Oneida to superintend repairs and other matters. The Aikens are bound for Oneida. It is evident, as things are going, that there will be but a feeble family there soon. One of two things ought to be done. We ought either to send on substantial men and women enough to make a strong Community, and give them new buildings, or we ought to abandon that post altogether.

Several considerations may be suggested in favor of the latter course: 1. The other Communities, instead of being in condition to send men abroad, want help. 2. Our general financial state will hardly allow us to build a new Commune at Cambridge. 3. The cooperation of J. Kinsley is precluded and placed beyond hope by the position of his wife, so that Albert Kinsley's original /448/ attempt has decisively come to an end. 4. Heman Kinsley and his wife are the only other material of cooperation to be counted upon in that region, and they certainly need to be transplanted. 5. In short, there is not enough dry stuff enough (as we used to say in the swamp) to make a good pile in that region, and the logs, if we mean to make them burn, must be carried to other piles. 6. The location of the Barron farm or of the Kinsley, though good for dairy purposes and for a single farming family, is not good for a Community, which requires more variety of business and consequently free access to markets. The Northern family is the only one of our Communes that is off the beat of the railroads, and inconveniently distant from post office and markets. Manifestly it is our best policy, at least as long as our numbers are small, to keep within reach of the improved machinery of the times.

I suggested to Messrs. Burt and Barron that the question should be fairly entertained, whether it is not best to sell out at Cambridge and distribute our forces there to the other Communities. They accepted the suggestion readily and seemed on the whole to favor the view I have presented. They will correspond with the brethren at Cambridge, and they wish to know the views of Mr. Cragin and others here who have anything to say.

I wish it to be understood that I make no proposal that need affect anybody's free judgment. My intention is simply to call attention to the weakness of the Northern colony, and to urge the importance of either making a strong post of it, or of strengthening the other Communes by abandoning it. /449/

Brooklyn Journal

September 1, 1854.—Since Mr. Noyes's return to Brooklyn, he speaks often of concentrating our forces at Oneida; has broached the idea of publishing a daily paper there; says he shall obey orders from God, but thinks we may feel at liberty to pray to be returned to Oneida. Instead of enlarging our numbers, he desires to see improvement in those already members of the Association. He would like to have all the branch Communities shut up shop and go to Oneida, and spend the winter in studying the Bible and attending to some unitary business. If it were not for the cattle, such a thing might be done and would doubtless tend greatly to unity and strength; but perhaps it is not feasible. It will do no hurt, however, to think and talk about such a move. The very idea may loosen us from undue attachment to place.

George Cragin to Albert Kinsley
Brooklyn, September 23, 1854

Yours of the 20th announcing the sale of the Barron farm came to hand this morning. We give thanks to our heavenly Father for the good success attending your labors. How true it is that when Mr. Noyes makes a proposition and it is heartily responded to by the Community, good luck always follows.

Nothing more has been said about our removing to Oneida, but we feel much assurance that the Lord will open the way for us all to reassemble there when the time comes to publish a daily paper. /450/

The Circular, Old Series 3:622
December 1, 1854

Last year we occupied the short interval of suspension that followed the close of the volume in printing *Bible Communism.* This year we shall employ a similar short vacation in removing our press and printing materials to Oneida, where after a few weeks we expect to resume our regular issues. What may be our future course, whether we shall go forward to a daily or back temporarily to a less frequent issue remains to be determined. We are perfectly convinced that the movement sooner or later must be forward, that Bible Communism will both demand and sustain a daily paper.

We are well assured that our present move is the right one. . . . While the world and its institutions are being torn by treachery, defalcations, and war, we shall endeavor to kindle a back fire of confidence, faithfulness, and peace. In face of the separation and discord around us, we concentrate. Oneida at least will set an example of two hundred persons seeking not to destroy each other, but to help each other in the direction of heavenly things.

THE END

Appendix

This Appendix reproduces the complete text of the *First Annual Report of the Oneida Association* (1849), a remarkable document that is important for understanding the George Wallingford Noyes manuscript. The title page of the *Report* has been photographically reproduced, and the rest of the document is presented in a more readable style that nonetheless preserves the original spelling and idiosyncratic punctuation (except for obvious typographical errors) and indicates original page breaks (page numbers enclosed in slashes) and variations in type size.

The *Report* is divided into three approximately equal sections. Pages 1–17 of the original sixty-six-page text briefly survey the origin and history of the Oneida Association and the way it was organized and governed during its first year of existence. Pages 18–42 present John Humphrey Noyes's "Bible Argument; Defining the Relations of the Sexes in the Kingdom of Heaven," a manifesto explaining and justifying Noyes's extraordinary sexual theories. Pages 43–66 provide testimonies of some of the early members, stressing the positive impact the community and its practices have had upon them.

Mark Weimer, curator of Special Collections at the Syracuse University Library, kindly provided a photocopy of the original report, as well as the disk version, which has been compared against the original document.

FIRST ANNUAL REPORT

OF THE

ONEIDA ASSOCIATION:

EXHIBITING ITS HISTORY, PRINCIPLES,

AND

TRANSACTIONS TO JAN. 1, 1849.

~~~~~~~~~~~~~~~~~~~~~~~~~~

PUBLISHED BY ORDER OF THE ASSOCIATION.

~~~~~~~~~~~~~~~~~~~~~~~~~~

LEONARD & COMPANY, PRINTERS,
ONEIDA RESERVE.

1849.

REPORT.

LOCATION.

The Oneida Association is located in a secluded valley on the Oneida Creek, in the towns of Lenox and Vernon, and counties of Madison and Oneida, in the State of New York, three miles south of the Oneida Depot, which is the half-way railroad station between Utica and Syracuse. The post office address of the Association is Oneida Castle, in the county of Oneida. The lands of the Association are part of the territory reserved till recently, to the Oneida Indians. The State purchased the territory in 1840 and '42, and disposed of it to white settlers, receiving part payment and giving articles securing deeds to the purchasers on full payment. The Association holds most of its lands under these articles. The domain, consisting of 160 acres, lying on both sides of the Creek, is mostly alluvial soil of good quality. It includes an excellent water privilege which is now occupied by a saw-mill and other lumber machinery, and affords abundance of power for a grist-mill, machine-shop, and other works, already projected by the Association. This water privilege and the land immediately adjoining, has been paid for in full, and is held by deed from the State.

NUMBER AND CLASSIFICATION OF THE MEMBERS.

On the 1st of January 1849, (which is the date of the preparation of the material of this Report,) the whole number of persons connected with the Association was *eighty-seven*.

The following is a classification of the age, sex, nativity, religious connection, and occupation of the members.

Number of persons between the ages of 40 and 50, ten; between 30 and 40, twenty-one; between 20 and 30, eighteen; between 10 and 20, fifteen; between 1 and 10, twenty-three. Adults, (over 15,) fifty-eight; children, (under 15,) twenty-nine. Adult males, twenty-nine. Adult females, twenty-nine.

The adults were born in the following places, viz:—in Vermont, twenty-one; in New York, seventeen; in Massachusetts, eleven; in Connecticut, four; in New Jersey, two; in Maine, one; in New Hampshire, one; in England, one.

The churches out of which the adult members came are as follows, viz:—from the Congregational church came twenty; from the Methodist, seven; from the Presbyterian, three; from the Dutch-Reformed, two; from the Baptist, two; from the Quaker, one. /2/

The professions of the male members are as follows, viz:—four are farmers; two are carpenters and machinists; two are cabinet-makers; two are shoe-makers; two are blacksmiths; two are millers; two have been school-teachers; two were bred to the ministry; one [is] a printer; one is a wagon-maker; one is a gun-smith; one is a lead-pipe-maker; one has been a merchant and publishing agent. Some of the members are conversant with several other professions, such as those of editors, architects, harness-makers, masons, &c. &c.

HISTORY OF THE ORIGIN OF THE ASSOCIATION.

The Association in its present form and location, has existed but one year, and this is its first Annual Report. But the history of its actual birth, and growth to its present form, extends back fifteen years. In February 1834, John H. Noyes, a member at that time of the Senior class in the Yale Theological Seminary, and a licentiate of the Congregational Church, began to preach in the city of New Haven the doctrine of perfect holiness, and other kindred "heresies," and laid the foundation of what has been called the school of modern Perfectionism. The religious theory then developed, involved the social theory which has embodied itself in the Oneida Association.

J. H. Noyes, after laboring several years as an editorial and itinerant advocate of Perfectionism, in various parts of New England and New York, in 1838 settled in Putney, Vermont, where his father and family resided. This was the beginning of what has been called the Putney Community.—Perfectionism assumed the form of Association first in a small circle of the immediate connections of J. H. Noyes. His wife and several members of his father's family being associated with him in religious faith, and in the business of editing and printing, adopted, or rather naturally fell into the principle of community of interests. In 1840, George Cragin (who till then had been the publishing agent of the Moral Reform Society in the city of New York) joined the Putney circle with his wife, and has since had a large agency both at Putney and Oneida, in forwarding the growth of the Association. From 1840 to 1847, there was a gradual accession of members, till the family numbered nearly forty. During the same period all the leading principles of the present social theory of the Oneida Association were worked out theoretically and practically, and, step by step, the school advanced from community of faith, to community of property, community of households, community of affections.

In the mean time, the publications and other labors of the Putney Association gained favor and confidence among spiritualists throughout the country, and especially in the State of New York. In September 1847, Conventions were called at Lairdsville and Genoa, by the leading Perfectionists in this State, for the purpose of effecting a union between believers in these regions and the Putney Association. J. H. Noyes attended and took a prominent part in those Conventions. The result was the unanimous passage of the following resolutions at the Genoa Convention:

1. *Resolved,* That we will devote ourselves exclusively to the establishment of the kingdom of God; and as that kingdom includes and provides for all interests, religious, political, social and physical, that we will not join or cooperate with any other Association. /3/

2. *Resolved,* That as the kingdom of God is to have an external manifestation, and as that manifestation must be in some form of Association, we will acquaint ourselves with the principles of heavenly Association, and train ourselves to conformity to them as fast as possible.

3. *Resolved,* That one of the leading principles of heavenly Association, is the renunciation of exclusive claim to private property.

4. *Resolved,* That it is expedient to take measures immediately for forming a heavenly Association in central New York. (For a full account of the Convention, see "SPIRITUAL MAGAZINE," Vol. II. p. 126.)

In pursuance of the intent of these Resolutions, Jonathan Burt commenced a partial Association with D. P. Nash, J. Ackley and others, in November 1847, on his premises at Oneida, which are now part of the domain of the Association. Ackley arrived and commenced operations with Burt on the 26th of November.

While these movements were going forward, the Putney Association, located in the midst of a New England village, and of course surrounded by religious jealousy, was exposing itself more and more by the development of its new social principles, to the indignation and intrigues of its enemies.—Public excitement against the prominent members of the Association rose to a tumultuous pitch. At length it became evident that the only peaceable course open to them was to retire from the village, and seek a new location for the community school. J. H. Noyes left Putney on the 26th of November, and was soon followed by George Cragin and most of those members of the Association who had come in from abroad. They had no thought at that time of re-gathering at Oneida; but they afterwards perceived that the very day of the dissolution at Putney, (Nov. 26,) was the day of the first union at Oneida between Burt and Ackley. The subsequent course of events proved that the apparent overthrow of the Association in Vermont was only a kindly transplantation of it to a more sheltered spot in New York, fully provided for by the Conventions, and the train of operations growing out of them.

On leaving Putney, J. H. Noyes, with Cragin and his wife, took lodgings in New York city, and waited for the opening of a new course. The other members of the Association were scattered to their various homes. In the latter part of January following, Burt and his associates invited J. H. Noyes by letter to visit Oneida. The invitation was accepted, and the result of the negotiations which ensued was, that on the 1st of February the present Association was commenced by a full union between J. H. Noyes and J. Burt, and a transfer of $500.00 of U. S. Stock by J. H. Noyes to the stock of the new union.

Purchases of lands were immediately commenced, and the whole of the present domain was soon secured, having on it two comfortable houses, besides Burt's. On the 1st of March, Cragin and his wife from New York, and the wife of J. H. Noyes with the children of both families from Putney, met at Oneida and found a quiet home. In the course of the spring and summer, all the refugees from Putney, and a part of those who remained in that village, in all seventeen of the members of the original Association, with their children, were re-united at Oneida. /4/

Thus the Putney Association died and rose again. Many and great benefits resulted from the operation; but the most valuable of these benefits was this: the tumult and odium that attended the death, on the one hand tried and strengthened the faith and love of the victims and of all their true-hearted friends throughout the country, and on the other hand drove away from them a herd of treacherous, fair-weather followers, whose friendship had been a dead weight on the cause of holiness and union; so that in the resurrection at Oneida, the Association entered upon a period of growth, with the advantage of being exceedingly repulsive to the false, and more attractive than ever to the true spirits among Perfectionists. Thus the material that has gathered around the Putney nucleus during the past year, has been sifted.

The Association has been enlarged to its present number by accessions of new members and families from time to time through the year. Its first and strongest reinforcements came from the central counties of the State of New York. Subsequently it received a valuable colony from Northern Vermont; and later still, was joined by a delegation from Massachusetts.

The original accommodations of the Association, consisting of two ordinary dwelling houses and two small cabins, were put to full occupation in the course of the year; but their capacity, with the help of ingenuity and good will, proved to be almost indefinitely elastic, and sufficed, (with the addition of a rough board shanty early erected for the dormitories of the young men,) until more liberal quarters could be prepared.

ERECTION OF THE MANSION HOUSE.

Erastus H. Hamilton, a young man from Syracuse, N. Y., joined the Association with his family early in the spring, and having soon proved himself an able workman and manager, became the acknowledged chief of the industrial department. He had been an architect by profession, and under his superintendence, the Association undertook to build a Mansion house. With a saw-mill at command, and all the timber necessary on the domain, and with a goodly number of carpenters and joiners in the Association, this undertaking was carried through pleasantly and successfully. The whole of the work except the plastering, was done within the Association. All hands, whenever free from other necessary occupation, were merrily busy on the house. Even the women joined the sport, and the lathing was mostly the work of their hands. Many valuable lessons in regard to gregarious and attractive industry were learned in this operation. The house was ready for occupation before the advent of winter, and gave the Association seasonable and ample relief from short quarters.

A brief description of the house will not be out of place in this Report. It stands on an elevated part of the domain, commanding a very extensive view of the surrounding country. It is sixty feet long, thirty-five feet wide, three stories high, and is surmounted by a cupola. The lower story or basement is divided by partitions across the whole width, into three apartments of equal size, viz., 35 feet by 20. The first of these apartments runs back into a rise of ground on which the house abuts, and is a cellar. The second or middle apartment is the kitchen. The third or front apartment is the dining /5/ room. The second story comprises a parlor over the dining room, and of the same size, (i.e. 35 by 20,) a reception-room, a school-room and a printing-office. The third story is devoted to sleeping apartments for married pairs and for females. The garret, extending over the whole house, and without partitions, is the dormitory of the unmarried men and boys. This edifice now gives comfortable quarters to about sixty persons, and might easily accommodate one hundred.

LABOR AND FINANCES.

In connection with this main enterprise, the Association worked its farm successfully, and kept the saw-mill and other lumber machinery in operation. It did not undertake or expect, however, by these or any other labors, to meet the expenses of the year, but looked mainly to the capital coming in with its members, and to the subsidies of its friends, for subsistence and the means of building, regarding this first year as properly and necessarily one of preparation and outlay.

Mr. Cragin had approved himself at Putney as a man of ability and sound principle in financial affairs, and the Oneida Association unanimously gave him the charge of its money-matters. He adhered substantially, though not with unreasonable rigor, to the cash system, and by fair dealing, and prompt payments, secured confidence and popularity for himself and for the Association in the surrounding community. Under his management, the domain was paid for so far as the claims of the previous occupants were concerned, a liberal subsistence for the Association was provided, without incurring debt, the expenses of building were met, and debts to the amount of about two thousand dollars, with which Mr. Burt's property was previously encumbered, were cancelled. The only present liability of the Association of any importance, is the debt to the State for the lands of the domain, amounting to about two thousand dollars, the payment of which, however, it is understood, will not be demanded, so long as the interest is paid. The funds required for the operations of the year, have been supplied mostly by the members of the Association, but partly by the voluntary advances of friends in Vermont, Massachusetts, Connecticut and New Jersey.

The opportunities and prospects of the Association for profitable business, in lumbering and several kinds of manufactures already commenced or contemplated, are very good, and it is not unreasonable to expect that after the present season of necessary preparation, it will become a self-supporting institution.

PRINTING DEPARTMENT.

The printing press of the Putney Association was transferred to Oneida in July, and one number of the Spiritual Magazine was published soon after, in which the forthcoming of the "Confessions of J. H. Noyes" was announced. The First Part of these confessions was printed in the course of the fall, and is now in circulation. Two other parts are to be published hereafter. It is the intention of the Association ultimately to turn a considerable portion of its force to the business of printing and publishing. /6/

HEALTH OF THE ASSOCIATION.

The general health of the Association has been remarkably good. In the latter part of summer, most of the adults were seriously attacked by dysentery; but faith and cheerfulness, without medicine, soon prevailed over disease. One death only occurred—that of an infant, previously very feeble;* and this loss was compensated by the birth of a pair of twins. In no case has the Association had occasion to employ the services of a physician. A more extended *expose* of the condition of the Association, as to health, will be found in the latter part of this report.

ARRANGEMENT OF THE HOUSEHOLDS.

Previous to the completion of the Mansion house, no special classification was attempted in the arrangement of the households, but the several families, composed as usual of parents and children together, were distributed to the four houses of the Association, as convenience and natural affinities from time to time seemed to dictate. In the course of the months of November and December, however, when the Mansion house came to be occupied, the following classification

---

* In contrast with this fact we may mention the statement contained in the last Annual Report of the Managers of the New York State Lunatic Asylum, where they say, in reference to the prevalence of dysentery at the Asylum the last summer, that "thirty-nine, out of two hundred and forty cases which occurred, [i.e. about one sixth part,] terminated fatally." And the Report adds, "We think the mortality was not greater among the inmates of the Asylum who were attacked by this disease, than it was among an equal number who suffered under similar attacks out of the Asylum." /7/

took place. The best of the ordinary houses, that nearest the Mansion house, was converted into a nursery, and all the children between the ages of two and twelve, (seventeen in number,) with the necessary house-keepers, and teachers, were established there, by themselves. The other principal dwelling house, previously occupied by Mr. Burt, was also converted into a nursery, and given up to the infants (six in number) with their nurses and house-keepers. This arrangement proved to be very favorable to the comfort and good-breeding of the children, and at the same time, saved the main household of the Association from much noise and confusion. The women serving as attendants of the children for short periods only, and in rotation, (except in cases of special taste and qualification,) found the business not a burden, but a pleasure. By systematic, but kindly discipline, in connection with religious instruction, good order was easily established in the household of the older children; insomuch that it was affirmed by all witnesses that there was less turbulence and confusion in that family of seventeen, than there had been under previous arrangements in families of only four or five children. The natural apprehensions which arose against the idea of separating infants from their mothers, and breeding them together, vanished before the demonstrations of experience; and it was found to be altogether a more comfortable task to take care of six in the new way, than it had been to wait on one in ordinary circumstances. The novelty and beautiful results of these arrangements for managing children, attracted much attention and admiration from visitors and the community around. The only drawback on the operation was the temporary distress of the mothers in giving up their little ones to the care of others, which made occasion for some melo-dramatic scenes; but the wounds of philo-progenitiveness were soon healed, and the mothers soon learned to value their own freedom and opportunity of education, and the improved condition of their children, more than the luxury of a sickly maternal tenderness. And then the periodical visits of the mothers to the nurseries, and of the children to the Mansion house, were found to be occasions of more genuine pleasure, than could ever be derived from constant personal attendance. Mrs. Mary E. Cragin, a woman who had proved herself, both at Putney and Oneida, specially qualified by nature and attainment, for the care of children, in connection with Mrs. Harriet A. Noyes, had charge of that department, and superintended the above arrangements.

COMMON TABLE.

The meals of the Association, at the Mansion house, were served at one table, extending through the dining-room, and were alike for all, not differing materially in quality from the meals of respectable households in ordinary life. The business of waiting on the table was left open to volunteers, and became a very attractive service, making occasion for lively competition. The culinary department and general domestic economy was under the superintendence of Mrs. Sylvia Hamilton, assisted by the other women in rotation.

THE TENT-ROOM.

It was the wish and intention of the Association, from the beginning, to make the Mansion house its winter quarters, both because larger and more comfortable accommodations than the other houses afforded were needed, and for the sake of the educational and social advantages of consolidation. But as winter drew

near, and the finishing of the house lingered, it became evident that this intention must be abandoned unless some new method of constructing dormitories,
more expeditious than the usual one, could be devised. The original plan was to
make eleven sleeping rooms of the third story, each 14 by 10, for the married
couples and single females. But two difficulties presented themselves. In the first
place, the Association had unexpectedly increased in number till about twenty
married couples, besides eight single females, were to be provided for; and in the
second place, the finishing off of so many rooms in the regular way, would occupy nearly the whole winter. These circumstances suggested a device, which for
its novelty and satisfactory results, deserves to be described. One half of the third
story, i.e. a space of 35 feet by 30, was finished as a single apartment. Within this
apartment twelve tents, (each about 7 feet by 8, large enough for a bed and all
other apparatus necessary to a dormitory,) were erected against the walls of the
room in the form of a hollow square. The tents were made of cotton cloth, supported on upright wooden frames about seven feet high, and open at the top.
The space between the tops of the tents and the ceiling of the room (about 2 feet)
gave free circulation to air and light. The interior of the hollow square, a space
about 18 feet by 14, became a comfortable common sitting-room for the occupants of the tents. One large stove in the center of this sitting-room was found
sufficient to warm the twelve rooms around /8/ it, and two reflectors suspended
in the same apartment gave light enough for all ordinary purposes to the whole.
Thus a space which had been designed for only six bed-rooms, each of which
would have required its separate stove and light, was converted into twelve bed-
rooms, with a spacious sitting-room in the midst, requiring for all only one stove
and two lamps. The cloth for the tents cost about ten dollars, and the labor of
constructing them, and of moving the tenants into them was done by the Association in one day. The most obvious objection to this singular combination of
house and tent is that its accommodations are not favorable to privacy; but the
principles and habits of the Association, being somewhat more gregarious than
usual, made the sacrifice of privacy a small affair in comparison with the advantages of consolidation; and on trial all parties were delighted with the arrangement. 'Christmas eve' was the first evening of the occupation of the tents; and
the Association celebrated the occasion in the sitting-room of the encampment,
with music and sentiment, in the midst of green festoons, and with mirth like
that of the 'feast of tabernacles.' See Neh. 8; and Lev. 23: 40, &c.

The other half of the third story was divided into three small bed-rooms for
pairs, and a long room across the width of the house (35 by 10) for single females.
With these accommodations the main body of the Association found quarters
early in the winter in the Mansion house, leaving only such detachments in the
other houses as were required for taking care of the children.

SHORT DRESSES.

In connection with this new fashion of making rooms it will be appropriate to
allude to one or two other novelties which the Association has fallen into by free-
thinking. Early in the summer, in consequence of some speculations on the subject of women's dress, which will be presented in a subsequent part of this Report, some of the leading women in the Association took the liberty to dress

themselves in short gowns or frocks, with pantaloons, (the fashion of dress common among children,) and the advantages of the change soon became so manifest, that others followed the example, till frocks and pantaloons became the prevailing fashion in the Association. The women say they are far more free and comfortable in this dress than in long gowns; the men think that it improves their looks; and some insist that it is entirely more modest than the common dress.

CHANGE IN HAIR-DRESSING.

Another new fashion broke out among the women in the following manner. The ordinary practice of leaving the hair to grow indefinitely, and laboring upon it by the hour daily, merely for the sake of winding it up into a ball and sticking it on the top or back of the head, had become burdensome and distasteful to several of the women. Indeed there was a general feeling in the Association that any fashion which requires women to devote considerable time to hair-dressing, is a degradation and a nuisance. The idea of wearing the hair short and leaving it to fall around the neck, as young girls often do, occurred frequently, but Paul's theory of the natural propriety of long hair for women (1 Cor. 11) seemed to stand in the way. At length a careful /9/ examination of this theory was instituted, and the discovery was made that Paul's language expressly points out the object for which women should wear long hair, and that object is not ornament, but 'for a covering.' In this light it was immediately manifest that the long hair of women, as it is usually worn, coiled and combed upward to the top of the head, instead of answering to Paul's object of covering, actually exposes the back part of the head, more than the short hair of men. It then occurred also that Phrenology, in pointing to the back of the head and neck as the seat of amativeness, has given a rational basis to Paul's theory of the propriety of women's making their hair a covering. It was evident moreover that the hair is not needed as a covering where the person is covered by the dress. These considerations seemed to establish satisfactorily the natural and scriptural propriety of women's wearing their hair in the simple mode of little girls, 'down in the neck.' Accordingly some of the bolder women cut off their hair, and started the fashion, which soon prevailed throughout the Association, and was generally acknowledged to be an improvement of appearance, as well as a saving of labor.

RELIGIOUS AND SOCIAL EXERCISES.

The meetings of the Association for religious conversation were held, during the first part of the year, at the several houses in rotation, on Sunday afternoon and evening, and on Thursday evening of each week. These meetings were not conducted in the formal way of ordinary religious conferences, but were given up to free and promiscuous conversation, accompanied with occasional songs. Mr. Noyes usually took the lead in the proposal of topics, and sometimes lectured at length. A few persons from the surrounding neighborhood attended occasionally, but no pains were taken to draw in such persons or to operate upon them. Self-improvement and not proselyting, was the object of the meetings, constantly avowed and faithfully adhered to.

After the concentration at the Mansion-house, a gathering in the spacious parlor after supper became a matter of course every evening. The following order of exercises for these gatherings was adopted. At the ringing of the bell all came together, and immediately the roll of the Association was called, not for the purpose of ascertaining the presence or absence of the members, (as all were free in this respect,) but in order to give each member an opportunity and invitation to present any reflections, expressions of experience, proposals in relation to business, exhortations, or any other matter of general interest that might be on the mind waiting for vent. This method of proceeding, (suggested by the practice in Congress of calling the roll on certain occasions in order to give each member an opportunity of bringing in bills,) generally secured good entertainment for a considerable part of the evening.

After this general exchange, the members dispersed to smaller parties of conversation, or to the pursuit of various studies, according to the inclinations of each. Systematic provision, however, was made for a series of exercises, suitable for occupying that part of the evening which remained after roll-call. Monday evening was devoted to readings in the parlor from the public papers; Tuesday evening to lectures by J. H. Noyes, on the social /10/ theory; Wednesday evening to instructions and exercises in Phonography; Thursday evening to the practice of music; Friday evening to dancing; Saturday evening to readings from Perfectionist publications; Sunday evening to lectures and conversation on the Bible. These exercises, though attendance on them was entirely voluntary, were generally well sustained.

RESULTS OF RELIGIOUS OPERATIONS.

As an index of the power and results of the religious influences circulating in the Association through the meetings and other channels, it may be mentioned that all the adults who entered the Association in an irreligious state, (being brought in by husbands, parents, or friends that were believers,) except one young man who seceded, were converted to a confession and happy experience of union with Christ. There were twelve instances of this kind, and several of them were cases of conversion from a state of fortified self-will and infidelity. Besides these conversions, serious and permanent religious impressions manifested themselves among the older children, and prevailed through the juvenile school.

One instance of the salutary effects of the religious influences of the Association deserves to be specially recorded. Horace Burt, brother of Jonathan Burt, (the leader of the movement at Oneida,) had been, for many years previous to the advent of the Association, hopelessly insane. Twice he had been subjected to the hospital discipline at Worcester, without any substantial benefit; and at the time of the commencement of the Association he was under the guardianship of his brother, with no prospect of being anything but a madman for life. He had intervals of sobriety, but was for the greater part of the time a nuisance to the community around, and at times required violent restraints and the strait-jacket. Very soon after J. H. Noyes went to Oneida, this man yielded to his influence, and ceased his wanderings and crazy freaks. In process of time, as the Association increased in numbers and power, he became interested in its principles and operations, received its doctrines and became soberly and happily religious. He has manifested no symptoms of insanity for more than a year, and is now one of the most steady and valuable members of the Association.

SYSTEM OF CRITICISM.

In the machinery of religious and moral discipline employed by the Association, a system of *mutual criticism* has held a very prominent place, and indeed has been relied on for regulating character and stimulating improvement, more than the meetings or any other means of influence. This system was instituted by the Putney Association during the period of its most rapid advancement in spiritual life. The mode of proceeding was this:—Any person wishing to be criticised, offered himself for this purpose, at a meeting of the Association. His character then became the subject of special scrutiny by all the members of the Association, till the next meeting, when his trial took place. On the presentation of his case, each member in turn was called on to specify as far and as frankly as possible, every thing objectionable in his character and conduct. In this way the person criticised had the advantage /11/ of a many-sided mirror in viewing himself, or perhaps it may be said, was placed in the focus of a spiritual lens composed of all the judgments in the Association. It very rarely happened that any complaint of injustice was made by the subject of the operation, and generally he received his chastening with fortitude, submission, and even gratitude, declaring that he felt himself relieved and purified by the process. Among the various objectionable features of the character under criticism, some one or two of the most prominent would usually elicit censure from the whole circle, and the judgment on these points would thus have the force of a unanimous verdict. Any soreness which might result from the operation was removed at the succeeding meeting by giving the patient a round of commendations. This system of open and kindly criticism, (a sort of reversed substitute for tea-party back-biting in the world,) became so attractive by its manifest good results, that every member of the Putney Association submitted to it in the course of the winter of 1846–7; and to this may be attributed much of the accelerated improvement which marked that period of their history. Instead of offences, abounding love and good works followed the letting loose of judgment.

This system was introduced to some extent at Oneida; but the number of members was so large, and their acquaintance with each other in many cases so limited, that it was found necessary to change the mode of proceeding, in order to make criticism lively and effective. Instead of subjecting volunteers for criticism to the scrutiny of the assembly, the Association appointed four of its most spiritual and discerning judges, to criticise in course all the members. The critics themselves were first criticised by Mr. Noyes, and then gave themselves to their work, from day to day for three weeks, till they had passed judgment on every character in the Association. Their method was first to ascertain as much as possible about the character of the individual about to be criticised, by inquiring among his associates, and then after discussing his character among themselves, to invite him to an interview, plainly tell him his faults, converse with him freely about his whole character, and give him their best advice. The testimony of the members to the good effect of this operation will be found in the latter part of this Report.

RELIGIOUS BELIEF OF THE ASSOCIATION.

The religious views of the Oneida Association are presented at large in various publications issued by the Putney press between the years 1838 and 1846, and especially in a work entitled 'The Berean.' A brief mention only of some of the most important of them will be appropriate in this Report.

The Association, though it has no formal creed, is firmly and unanimously attached to the Bible, as the text-book of the Spirit of truth; to Jesus Christ, the eternal Son of God; to the apostles and primitive church, as the exponents of the everlasting gospel. Its belief is that the second advent of Christ took place at the period of the destruction of Jerusalem; that at that time there was a primary resurrection and judgment in the spiritual world; that the final kingdom of God then began in the heavens; that the manifestation of that kingdom in the visible world is now approaching; that its approach is /12/ ushering in the second and final resurrection and judgment; that a church on earth is now rising to meet the approaching kingdom in the heavens, and to become its duplicate and representative; that inspiration, or open communication with God and the heavens, involving perfect holiness, is the element of connection between the church on earth and the church in the heavens, and the power by which the kingdom of God is to be established and reign in the world.

THEORY OF ORGANIZATION AND GOVERNMENT.

The Oneida Association regards itself as a branch of the kingdom of heaven, the exponent of the principles, and servant of the spiritual will, of that kingdom. It has no written constitution or by-laws—no formal mode of electing officers; no other system of organization or means of government, than those which have been incidentally exhibited in the preceding account of its formation and transactions. In the place of all formulas, it relies on inspiration, working *through* those who approve themselves as agents of God, and *by* such apparatus of instruction and criticism as has been described.

A distinct view of the theory of the organization and government of the kingdom of God, held by the Association, is presented in the following extract from the Spiritual Magazine:—

"The kingdom of God is an absolute monarchy. It is a government not of compact between people and sovereign; not limited by constitutional forms and provisos. God takes the entire responsibility of the State; and the only compact in the case, is the very one-sided one called by the prophet the 'new covenant.' It is summed up in these words:—'I *will* be to them a God and they *shall* be to me a people.' The 'patronage' and appointing power of course remain with the responsible party; and all forms of popular representation are dispensed with.

"So far as there is a true church on earth, it is a frontier department of the kingdom; and will possess the great characteristics of heaven's government, viz., central executive power, and subordination. It will manifest in all its operations perfect unity of design, and true harmonious effort. To secure this, it includes a gradation of authority;—officers, not self-elected, not popularly elected, but appointed by God; whose credentials, if truly received of him, need no secondary influence to secure respect. In fact, the credential of authority through all God's kingdom, from the Supreme himself, down, is not a matter of parchment, or a voice from heaven merely, but the possession of actual ability.—Carlyle's doctrine is true, that '*mights* in this just universe do, in the long run, mean *rights.*' God's appointment to office confers on the individual ABILITY corresponding to his commission; and it is as certain that his ability will make his office recognized by those with whom he has to do, as it is that in a mixture of fluids the heaviest will sink to the bottom. Equivocal pretensions to superiority, based on diplomas of divinity schools, or musty apostolic commissions, and which make submission to the clerical authority a merely nominal, gratuitous thing—a matter of custom,—have no place in Christ's church. On the contrary, in that organic body, as we said before, superiority of every degree is a gift of power from God, which vindicates itself by an irresistible ascendancy over that which is inferior. It is this REALITY of power developed in a medium of love, that finally constitutes the church an organized corporation, well compared to the human body; which causes each member to gravitate toward his true place and office, /13/ bringing the 'different gifts' of the church into the order and symmetry which is visibly expressed in the human form.

"In this construction of the church, the autocratic principle of the kingdom of God is seen throughout. The distribution of gifts—the appointment of 'apostles, prophets, evangelists,' &c.,—is far removed from human dictation; and as these offices are not merely nominal, but the channels of God's will, every Christian finds himself under a despotism extending far beyond any earthly rule. In short, wherever we come in contact with his spiritual government, we find it working with a strength which makes it wholly independent of human volitions. Whether in the direct application of the new covenant to our souls, or in the organization of intermediate agencies of his will, the same despotic purpose is manifest, the same disregard of democratic forms and privileges. The question now arises, What is the effect of this tremendous, irresponsible government, upon individual liberty? can freedom exist under it?

"There are two classes of subjects, who will experience differently the operation of God's spiritual dominion. It is inevitable, in the first stages of intercourse with God, while evil influences still exist in the character, that his will should come into constant collision with those influences, and the wills growing out of them. The inner and better part of our nature is even then free and happy; and it is only the selfish, egotistical part which loves darkness, and seeks its own pleasure at all cost, that experiences the effect of collision with a superior will. The effect, is suffering; a bitter sense of bondage; coercion of the soul. No prison can realize the idea of helpless constraint that the soul experiences, when conscious of a hostile contact with the will of God. Yet even then it is not God's purpose to bring the offending part into bondage, but to destroy it. Every spirit opposed to him, is destined not to slavery, but to destruction. The carnal mind is not to be subdued, but crucified. He will have no drudges about him, no unwilling subjects. He will reign in natures like his own, not as a lawgiver and tyrant, but as a helper. For all others is decreed tribulation, wrath, perdition. The whole process which causes the imperfect believer to feel unpleasantly the force of God's will, is not to take away his liberty, but to make him free,— to free the better part of him from an unnatural, selfish disposition; thereby putting an end to the war which exists in every enlightened person between the spirit and the flesh, which is itself (as described in the 7th of Romans) the very essence of bondage. Then, with one undisturbed principle within, coinciding with the will of God, we have perfect liberty. Not so with the willing adherents of Satan; they find themselves in a completely inverted order—at war with all nature and the constitution of things. God made the universe after the pattern of his own heart, and adapted it to a state of love. The whole machinery of it runs directly across selfishness; and for that reason evil men can never be free.

"We would say to those who consider democratic institutions the palladium of individual liberty, that this very blessing is enjoyed to an infinitely greater degree under the monarchy of God. We believe that only those who have passed the quarantine of judgment and become naturalized citizens of the kingdom of heaven, know what is the glorious sensation of unshackled freedom of will.—The highest experience and most glowing conceptions of liberty in the world, are but meagre shadows of the liberty which we achieve when we become sons of God. Our wills act under the attraction of a superior spirit, it is true. But what creature in the universe does not? There is no such thing for men, and there never can be, as willing independently of the great authors of good and evil. Our advantage consists in having escaped the exclusive dominion of the /14/ evil spirit, which would have entailed on us an eternal war of impossibilities;—in having ended the 'joint occupation' of two hostile influences in ourselves, which is incompatible with any sense of freedom; and in having come under the exclusive attraction of God, the author of all peace, harmony and beauty. All men are in one of these three predicaments; and to all purposes of enjoyment the latter affords us perfect freedom.

"It offers us more. Suppose we have a desire to travel in distant countries. Liberty to do so would simply require that we should have leisure, money, conveyance, &c. But suppose a gentleman, a man exactly after our own heart, and entirely trust-worthy, should come and say to us:—"You wish to travel for purposes of pleasure and improvement. Let me go with you, and take the care and trouble of your journey on myself. I will pay your bills and see to all your affairs. I am familiar with all the countries which you will visit, will be your companion, and so direct your journey that you need do nothing but enjoy and improve yourself." Would not the acceptance of this offer, confer upon us something better than mere individual liberty? True, we give up the direction of our affairs to another; but it is to one perfectly worthy of the trust, and we gain in exchange an exemption from the vexations and dangers of the undertaking. The more care we could thus transfer judiciously, the more liberty we should have, and the more completely would the object of our travels be gained. Precisely like this is the relation between God and his people, in making the tour of the universe. We may suppose that we might go alone; but it would be better to have an intelligent power to direct and forward us, and to find all our purposes backed up by Jehovah himself.

"It is necessary and right that this supreme unity of will should run through every department of creation. It is the gravitation that will finally bring human nature, and every member of it, into the harmony of the starry system; so that each in his orbit shall be necessary to all, and the combined effect shall be worthy of God."

THEORY OF THE RIGHTS OF PROPERTY.
The ideas of the Association in regard to the ownership and distribution of property are briefly these, viz:—

1. That all the systems of property-getting in vogue in the world, are forms of what is vulgarly called the 'grab-game,' i.e. the game in which the prizes are not distributed by any rules of wisdom and justice, but are seized by the strongest and craftiest; and that the laws of the world simply give rules, more or less civilized, for the conduct of this game.

2. That the whole system thus defined is based on the false assumption that the lands and goods of the world, previously to their possession by man, have no owner, and rightfully become the property of any one who first gets possession; which assumption denies the original title of the Creator, excludes him from his right of distribution, and makes the "grab-game," in one form or other, inevitable.

3. That God the Creator has the first and firmest title to all property whatsoever; that he therefore has the right of distribution; that no way of escape from the miseries of the 'grab-game' will ever be found, till *his* title and right of distribution are practically acknowledged; that in the approaching reign of inspiration, he will assert his ownership, be acknowledged and installed as distributor, and thus the reign of coveteousness, competition and violence, will come to an end. /15/

4. That God never so makes over property to man, as to divest himself of his

own title; and of course that man can never in reality have absolute and exclusive ownership of lands, goods, or even of himself, or his productions, but only subordinate joint-ownership with God.

5. That in the kingdom of God every loyal citizen is subordinate joint-owner with God of all things. Rev. 21: 7.

6. That the right of individual possession of the specific goods of the universe, under this general joint-ownership, is determined by the arbitrament of God through inspiration, direct or indirect.

7. That there is no other right of property beyond these two; viz., the right of general joint-ownership by unity with God; and the right of possession as determined by inspiration.

8. That the right of possession, in the case of articles directly consumed in the use, is necessarily equivalent to exclusive ownership, but in all other cases is only the right of beneficial use, subject to the principle of rotation, and to the distributive rights of God.

It will be seen from this statement of principles, that the Oneida Association cannot properly be said to stand on any ordinary platform of communism. Their doctrine is that of community, not merely or chiefly with each other, but with God; and for the security of individual rights they look, not to constitutions or compacts with each other, but to the wisdom and goodness of the Spirit of truth, which is above all. The idea of their system, stated in its simplest form, is that all believers constitute the family of God; that all valuables, whether persons or things, are family property; and that all the labors of the family are directed, judged and rewarded in the distribution of enjoyments by the Father.

Perhaps the best encomium on these principles may be deduced from the fact that the Association, under the influence of them, lived in entire harmony in relation to property-interests throughout the year, and met with no difficulty in respect to the distribution of possessions and privileges.

No accounts were kept between the members and the Association, or between the several members; and there was no more occasion for them than there is between man and wife, or than there was between the several members of the happy family which gathered around the apostles on the day of Pentecost. The Association believes that in the kingdom of heaven 'every man will be rewarded according to his works' with far greater exactness than is done in the kingdoms of this world; but it does not believe that money is the currency in which rewards are to be distributed and accounts balanced. Its idea is that love is the appropriate reward of labor; that in a just spiritual medium, every individual, by the fixed laws of attraction, will draw around him an amount of love exactly proportioned to his intrinsic value and efficiency, and thus that all accounts will be punctually and justly balanced without the complicated and cumbersome machinery of book-keeping.

As to the *legal* titles of land and other property, no special measures were taken to secure the Association from individuals. Those who owned or purchased lands in their own names at the beginning, retained their deeds, and no formal transfer of any property brought in by the members, was made /16/ to the Association. The stock of the company was consolidated by love, and not by law.

The terms of admission so far as property is concerned, were stated in the Register of the Association as follows:

"On the admission of any member, all property belonging to him or her, becomes the property of the Association. A record of the estimated amount will be kept, and in case of the subsequent withdrawal of the member, the Association, according to its practice heretofore, will refund the property or an equivalent amount. This practice however stands on the ground, not of obligation but of expediency and liberality; and the time and manner of refunding must be trusted to the discretion of the Association. While a person remains a member, his subsistence and education in the Association are held to be just equivalents for his labor; and no accounts are kept between him and the Association, and no claim of wages accrues to him in case of subsequent withdrawal."

THEORY OF THE SEXUAL RELATION.

This Report would not be complete without a frank and full exhibition of the theory of the Association in regard to the relation of the sexes. An argument therefore, on this subject, prepared by J. H. Noyes early in the spring of 1848, and adopted by the Association from the beginning, as a declaration of its principles, will here be presented, after a few introductory remarks.

1. The radical principles developed in this argument, were early deduced from the religious system evolved at New Haven in 1834, were avowed in print by J. H. Noyes in 1837, and were discussed from time to time in the publications of the Putney press during nine years.

2. The complete elaboration of these principles was a progressive work, carried on in connection with the long continued growth and education of the Putney Association, and necessitated by severe experience and singular providences, of which an account will be given in a future publication.

3. These principles, though avowed (as before stated) in 1837, were not carried into action in any way by any of the members of the Putney Association till 1846.

4. It is not immodest, in the present exigency, to affirm that the leading members of the Putney Association belonged to the most respectable families in Vermont, had been educated in the best schools of New England morality and refinement, and were by the ordinary standards irreproachable in their conduct, so far as sexual matters are concerned, till they deliberately commenced, in 1846, the experiment of a new state of society, on principles which they had been long maturing and were prepared to defend before the universe.

5. It may also be affirmed without fear of contradiction, that the main body of those who have joined the Association at Oneida, and committed themselves to its principles, are sober, substantial men and women, of good previous character, and position in society.

6. The principles in question, have never been carried into full practical embodiment, either at Putney or Oneida, but have been held by the Association, /17/ as the principles of an ultimate state, toward which society among them is advancing, slowly and carefully, with all due deference to sentiments and relations established by the old order of things.

7. The Association abstains from all proselyting, aggressive operations, pub-

lishing its sexual theory (at this time, as heretofore,) only in self-defense, and at the command of public sentiment.

8. The Association, in respect to practical innovations, limits itself to its own family circle, not invading society around it, and no just or even legal complaint of such invasions can be found at Putney or Oneida.

9. The Association may fairly demand toleration of its theory and experiment of society, on the ground that liberty of conscience is guarantied by the Constitution of the United States, and of the several states, and on the ground that Quakers, Shakers, and other religionists are tolerated in conscientious deviations from the general order of society.

10. The principles to be presented, are not more revolutionary and offensive to popular sentiment, than the speculations of Fourier on the same subject; and are simply parallel in their scope, (not in their nature) with the theory of marriage and propagation, which Robert Dale Owen and Frances Wright propounded some years ago, in the public halls of New York, with great eclat. If infidels may think and speak freely on these 'delicate' subjects, why may not lovers of Christ and the Bible take the same liberty, and be heard without irritation?

11. The ensuing argument professes to be nothing more than an *outline* or *programme* of fundamental principles, and the original intention of the author was to have expanded it largely before publishing it. The proper limits of this Report, however, rather require that it should be condensed. It is especially deficient in the development of the prudential and transitionary principles which govern the Association in practice.

12. The argument cannot be perused with the fullest advantage by any but those who are familiar with the religious theory, of which it is the sequel.

With these remarks we submit the document. /18/

BIBLE ARGUMENT;

DEFINING THE RELATIONS OF THE SEXES IN THE KINGDOM OF HEAVEN.

PROPOSITION I.

The Bible predicts the coming of the kingdom of heaven on earth. Dan. 2: 44. Isa. 25: 6–9.

PROPOSITION II.

The administration of the will of God in his kingdom on earth, will be the same as the administration of his will in heaven. Matt. 6: 10. Eph. 1: 10.

PROPOSITION III.

In heaven God reigns over body, soul, and estate, without interference from human governments; and consequently, the advent of his kingdom on earth will supplant all human governments. Dan. 2: 44. 1 Cor. 15: 24, 25. Isa. 26: 13, 14, and 33: 22.

Note 1.—The religious world has constantly professed to be in expectation of the kingdom of heaven, and especially for the last twenty years. The popular hope of the Millennium, the universal use of the Lord's prayer, and the accumulating fervor of the public mind in relation to the Second Advent, Universal Reform, new theories of Society, &c. &c., are varied manifestations of that expectation.

Note 2.—In the introduction of the kingdom of heaven on earth, the citizens of that kingdom will necessarily be called to positions and duties, different from those of the primitive church. The object in view at the beginning of the Christian dispensation, was not to establish the kingdom of heaven on earth immediately, but to march an isolated church through the world, establish the kingdom in the heavens, and prepare the way for the kingdom on earth by giving the Gentiles the Bible and religious training. It was not the business of the primitive church to supplant the governments of this world. Hence they were directed to submit to the 'powers that be.' But at the end of 'the times of the Gentiles' the church of God will be called to break in pieces 'the powers that be,' and take the place of them. This is necessarily implied in the proof of the third proposition above. (See also Dan. 7: 22, 27.) This difference of positions is a sufficient general answer to those who insist on a literal subjection of the present church to the precepts of the primitive church concerning civil governments and institutions.

Illustration.—An army sent into a foreign territory for military purposes simply, is placed under the rules of martial discipline, which have reference to hostile surroundings and are very restrictive. Such was the case of the primitive church. But an army sent for the purpose of introducing civil institutions and settling in a foreign territory, ought to pass, as soon as it can do so safely, from the restrictions of martial law, to the conditions of permanent civilized life. Such is the position of the church which is called to introduce the kingdom of heaven on earth. /19/

PROPOSITION IV.

The institutions of the kingdom of heaven are of such a nature, that the general disclosure of them in the apostolic age would have been inconsistent with the continuance of the institutions of the world through the times of the Gentiles. They were not therefore, brought out in detail on the surface of the Bible, but were disclosed verbally (more or less) by Paul and others, to the interior part of the church. 1 Cor. 2: 6. 2 Cor. 12: 4. John 16: 12, 13. (Compare John 3: 12.) Heb. 9: 5, in the original. The holy of holies in the temple, which was veiled from all but the high-priest, symbolized heaven. It was necessary that the veil should remain between the world and heaven, till the end of the times of the Gentiles. Then it is to be removed. Rev. 11: 15–19.

Note.—From this proposition it follows, that we cannot reasonably look for a parade of proof texts, specifically sanctioning every change which the kingdom of heaven is to make in the institutions of the world. It is to be assumed that the church which is called to introduce that kingdom, will have the same spiritual understanding which was the key to the unwritten mysteries of the inner sanctuary in Paul's time. It is enough, if the Bible furnishes radical principles on which a spiritual mind can stand and reason firmly concerning things within the veil. The Bible must not be asked to lead us step by step into the holy of holies, but only to point the way, consigning us to the specific guidance of 'the spirit of wisdom and revelation.' Eph. 1: 17.

PROPOSITION V.

In the kingdom of heaven, the institution of marriage which assigns the exclusive possession of one woman to one man, does not exist. Matt. 22: 23–30. 'In the resurrection they neither marry nor are given in marriage.'

Note.—Christ, in the passage referred to, does not exclude the sexual distinction, or sexual intercourse, from the heavenly state, but only the world's method of assigning the sexes to each other, which alone creates the difficulty presented in the question of the Sadducees. The constitutional distinctions and offices of the sexes belong to their original paradisaical state; and there is no proof in the Bible or in reason, that they are ever to be abolished, but abundance of proof to the contrary. 1 Cor 11: 3–11. The saying of Paul that in Christ 'there is neither Jew nor Greek, *neither male nor female*,' &c., simply means that the unity of life which all the members of Christ have in him, overrides all individual distinctions. In the same sense as that in which the apostle excludes distinction of *sexes*, he also virtually excludes distinction of persons; for he adds, 'Ye are all *one* in Christ Jesus.' Yet the several members of Christ, in perfect consistency with their spiritual unity, remain distinct persons; and so the sexes, though one in their innermost life, as members of Christ, yet retain their constitutional distinctions.

PROPOSITION. VI.

In the kingdom of heaven, the intimate union of life and interests, which in the world is limited to pairs, extends through the whole body of believers; i.e. *complex* marriage takes the place of simple. John 17: 21. Christ prayed that all believers might be one, *even as* he and the Father are one. His unity with the Father is defined in the words, *'all mine are thine, and all thine are mine.'* Ver. 10. This perfect community of interests, then, will /20/ be the condition of *all*, when his prayer is answered. The universal unity of the members of Christ, is described in the same terms that are used to describe marriage-unity. Compare 1 Cor. 12: 12–27, with Gen. 2: 24. See also I Cor. 6: 15–17, and Eph. 5: 30–82.

Note.—This proposition does not exclude from the kingdom of heaven special companionships, founded on special affinities of nature and position; it only denies exclusive appropriation.

PROPOSITION VII.

The effects of the effusion of the Holy Spirit on the day of Pentecost, present a practical commentary on Christ's prayer for the unity of believers, and a sample of the tendency of heavenly influences, which fully confirm the foregoing proposition. 'All that believed were together, and had all things common; and sold their possessions and goods, and parted them to all, as every man had need.' 'The multitude of them that believed were of one heart and of one soul; neither said any of them that aught of the things which he possessed was his own; but they had all things common.' Acts 2: 44, 45, and 4: 32. Here is unity like that of the Father and the Son. ('All mine thine, and all thine mine.')

Note 1.—The unity of the day of Pentecost is not to be regarded as temporary and circumstantial. On the contrary, the accommodation to the fashion of the world, which succeeded and overlaid it in the apostolic age, was the transitory state of the church, and Pentecostal community of interests was its final and permanent condition in the heavens. The spirit of heaven manifested its nature and tendency for a moment, and then gave way for a season to the institutions of the world. The seed of heavenly unity fell into the earth, and was buried for a time, but in the harvest at the Second Coming it was reproduced and became the universal and eternal principle of the church.

Note 2.—We admit that the community principle of the day of Pentecost, in its actual operation at that time, extended only to goods and chattels. Yet we affirm that there is no intrinsic difference between property in persons and property in things; and that the same spirit which abolished exclusiveness in regard to money, would abolish, if circumstances allowed full scope to it, exclusiveness in regard to women and children. As we infer that an acid which has corroded the surface of a stone, would consume the whole of it, if allowed a full operation, so we infer from the operation of the spirit of heaven on the day of Pentecost, partial and temporary though it was, that in a continuous and perfect experiment, that spirit would consume all exclusiveness. The reason why a partial and temporary experiment only was exhibited, may be inferred from what has already been said in relation to the difference of times. (See Note 2 to Prop. 3, and Prop. 4.) The world was not ripe for a thorough revolution even in regard to property, and much less in regard to sexual morality. A momentary operation of the community spirit on property exclusiveness was tolerated, but the experiment could go no further without a destructive collision with civil government, which was not according to the design of God at that time.

Note 3.—Paul expressly places property in women and property in goods in the same category, and speaks of them together, as ready to be abolished by the advent of the kingdom of heaven. 'The time,' says he, 'is short; it remaineth that they that have wives, be as though they had none; . . . and they that buy as though they possessed not; . . . for the fashion of this world passeth away.' (1 Cor. 7: 29–31.) On the day of Pentecost, 'they that bought /21/ were as though they possessed not.' The fashion of the world passed away in regard to property, for the time being. It is fair to infer from Paul's language, that the fashion of the world in regard to wives was, in his view, to pass away in the same manner; i.e. that exclusiveness was to be abolished, and free love or complex marriage take its place in the heavenly state into which the church was about entering.

PROPOSITION VIII.

The abolishment of appropriation is involved in the very nature of a true relation to Christ in the gospel. This we prove thus:—The *possessive* feeling which expresses itself by the possessive pronoun *mine,* is the same in essence, when it relates to women, as when it relates to money, or any other property. Amativeness and acquisitiveness are only different channels of one stream. They converge as we trace them to their source. Grammar will help us to ascertain their common centre; for the possessive pronoun *mine,* is derived from the personal pronoun *I;* and so the possessive feeling, whether amative or acquisitive, flows from the personal feeling, i.e. is a branch of egotism. Now egotism is abolished by the gospel relation to Christ. The grand mystery of the gospel is vital union with Christ—the merging of self in his life—the extinguishment of the pronoun *I* at the spiritual centre. Thus Paul says, 'I live, *yet not I;* but Christ liveth in me.' The grand distinction between the Christian and the unbeliever—between heaven and the world—is, that in one reigns the *we-spirit,* and in the other the *I-spirit.* From *I* comes *mine,* and from the *I-spirit* comes exclusive appropriation of money, women, &c. From *we* comes *ours,* and from the *we-spirit* comes universal community of interests.

PROPOSITION IX.

The abolishment of sexual exclusiveness is involved in the love-relation required between all believers by the express injunction of Christ and the apostles, and by the whole tenor of the New Testament. 'The new commandment is, that we love one another,' and that not by pairs, as in the world, but *en masse.* We are required to love one another *fervently,*' (1 Peter 1: 22,) or, as the original might be rendered, *burningly.* The fashion of the world forbids a man and woman who are otherwise appropriated, to love one another burningly—to flow into each other's hearts. But if they obey Christ they must do this; and whoever would allow them to do this, and yet would forbid them (on any other ground than that of present expediency) to express their unity of hearts by bodily unity, would 'strain at a gnat and swallow a camel;' for unity of hearts is as much more important than the bodily expression of it, as a camel is bigger than a gnat.

Note.—The tendency of religious unity to flow into the channel of amativeness, manifests itself in revivals and in all the higher forms of spiritualism. Marriages or illegitimate amours usually follow religious excitements. Almost every spiritual sect has been troubled by amative tendencies. These facts are not to be treated as unaccountable irregularities, but as expressions of a law of human nature. Amativeness is in fact (as will be seen more fully hereafter) the first and most natural channel of religious love. This law must not be despised and ignored, but must be investigated and provided for. This is the object of the present treatise. /22/

PROPOSITION X.

The abolishment of worldly restrictions on sexual intercourse, is involved in the anti-legality of the gospel. It is incompatible with the state of perfected freedom towards which Paul's gospel of 'grace without law' leads, that man should be allowed and required to *love* in all directions, and yet be forbidden to *express* love in its most natural and beautiful form, except in one direction. In fact, Paul says with direct reference to sexual intercourse—'All things are *lawful* for me, but all things are not expedient;' 'all things are lawful for me, but I will not be brought under the power of any;' (1 Cor. 6: 12;) thus placing the restrictions which were necessary in the transition period, on the basis, not of law, but of expediency, and the demands of spiritual freedom, and leaving it fairly to be inferred that in the final state, when hostile surroundings and powers of bondage cease, all restrictions also will cease.

Note.—The philosophy of love and its expressions is this: love, in all its forms, is simply *attraction*, or the tendency of congenial elements to approach and become one. The attraction between the magnet and the steel is a familiar illustration of the nature of love. The only important difference between the two is, that while the attraction of inanimate substances is wholly involuntary, love, or the attraction of life towards life, is modified by the will. Volition can concentrate and quicken congenial elements, and so can increase love; but it cannot create congeniality, and therefore it can only modify, not create, love. So that the essence of love is attraction, whether it is modified by the will or not. This, then, we repeat, is the nature of love in all its forms—as well between God and man, and between man and man, as between man and woman—as well between the highest spheres of spiritual life, as between the lowest sensual elements. Life seeks unity with congenial life, and finds happiness in commingling. Love, while *seeking* unity, is *desire*—in unity, it is *happiness*. The commands of the Bible to love God and his family, and not to love the world, are commands to exercise the will in favoring profitable, i.e. spiritual attractions, and in denying unprofitable, i.e. fleshly attractions. In a perfect state of things, where corrupting attractions have no place, and all susceptibilities are duly subordinated and trained, the denying exercise of the will ceases, and attraction reigns without limitation. In such a state, what is the difference between the love of man towards man, and that of man towards woman? Attraction being the essence of love in both cases, the difference lies in this, that man and woman are so adapted to each other by the differences of their natures, that attraction can attain a more perfect union between them than between man and man, or between woman and woman. Attraction between the magnet and the steel is the same in essence whatever may be the forms of the surfaces presented for contact. If a positive obstruction intervenes, the steel advances to the obstructing substance and there stops. If nothing intervenes, and the tangent ends are plane surfaces, the steel advances to plane contact. If the tangent ends are ball and socket, or mortise and tenon [sic], the steel, seeking by the law of attraction the closest possible unity, advances to interlocked contact. So love, restrained by law and the will, as in the world, is stopped by positive obstructions; love between man and man can only advance to something like plain contact, while love between man and woman can advance to interlocked contact. In other words, love between the different sexes, is peculiar, not in its essential nature, but because they are so constructed with reference to each other, both spiritually and physically, (for the body is an index of the life,) that more intimate unity, and of course more intense happiness in love, is possible between them than between /23/ persons of the same sex. Now in a state of unobstructed love, it is as certain that attraction acting between man and woman, will seek its natural expression in sexual intercourse, as that the magnet and steel will approach each other as near as possible, or as that the attraction between man and man will seek its natural expression in the 'kiss of charity' or the embrace; and legal obstructions are no more compatible with spiritual freedom and rational taste in one case than in the other. It was manifestly the design of God, in creating the sexes, to give love more intense expression than is possible between persons of the same sex; and it is foolish to imagine that he will ever abandon that design by unsexing his children, or impede it by legal restrictions on sexual intercourse, in the heavenly state.

PROPOSITION XI.

The abolishment of the marriage system is involved in Paul's doctrine of the end of ordinances. Marriage is one of the 'ordinances of the worldly sanctuary.' This is proved by the fact that it has no place in the resurrection. (See Proposition 5.) The Roman Catholic church places it among its seven *sacraments*. (See Powers' Catholic Manual, p. 29, & 185.) Paul expressly limits it to life in the flesh. Rom. 7: 2, 3. The assumption, therefore, that believers are dead to the world by the death of Christ, (which authorized the abolishment of Jewish ordinances,) legitimately makes an end of marriage. Col. 2: 20.

Note 1.—Marriage stands on the same basis with the sabbath. Both may be *defended*, on the ground of the sanction of the decalogue, and of their necessity and usefulness. Both may be *assailed*, on the ground of their legality and unprofitableness. Both are 'shadows of good things to come.' As one day in seven is to a perpetual sabbath, so marriage in pairs is to the universal marriage of the church of Christ.

Note 2.—The abolishment of the Jewish ordinances was the 'offense of the cross' in the apostolic age. Gal. 5: 11, & 6: 12. The nullification of circumcision was as revolting and impious to the Jew, as the nullification of marriage can be to the Gentile. Written commandments were as formidably arrayed against the spiritual doctrines of the new church in the one case, as they are in the other. The clash of the moral conscience with the spiritual, was as complete in the one case as it is in the other. God's old orders confronted his new. The apostles had even less warrant in the Old Testament for their attack on the Jewish ritual, than we have in the whole Bible for our attack on marriage. The primitive 'offense of the cross' brought the church into collision with the civil as well as the ecclesiastical authorities, compelled believers to die substantially to the world at the outset, and exposed them to constant persecution and the hazard of literal death. If the spirit of Christ and of the unbelieving world are as hostile to each other now as ever, (which is certainly true,) it is clear that the cross of Christ, must have a development in the dispensation of the fullness of times, as offensive to the Gentile world, as its nullification of the Sinai law was to the Jewish world. Where then shall we look for the present 'offense of the cross?' How shall the gospel of death to the world by the death of Christ, protrude itself in a practical form, as it did in the apostolic age, and attack the central life of the Gentile world? The offense cannot come on the same point as it did in the primitive church; for the special ordinances of Judaism have passed away. The same may be said of the ordinances of

Popery, so far as the most important part of the religious world is concerned. The nullification of the ordinances of the popular Protestant sects, cannot be a full 'offense of the
cross' corresponding /24/ to the primitive offense; first, because the *ecclesiastical* authority of those sects is feeble, divided, and clashing; and secondly, because they have no *civil*
authority; so that emancipation from the ordinances of any one of them is only a partial
collision with the ecclesiastical world, and no collision with the civil world. Whereas the
primitive offence of the cross, was a full collision with the highest authorities both ecclesiastical and civil. Where then shall the death-blow of the flesh fall on the Gentile world?
We answer—on marriage. That is a civil as well as religious ordinance, performed by cler-
gymen and magistrates, defended by religion and law, common to all sects, and universal in the world. On that point 'the offense of the cross' will be just what it was in the
apostolic age on the ordinances of Judaism.

Note 3.—We admit that Christ and the apostles, with wise reference to the transitionary necessities and hostile surroundings of the church of their time, and to the purpose
of God to give the Gentiles a dispensation of legal discipline, abstained from pushing the
war against worldly institutions to the overthrow of marriage. Yet we insist that they left
on record *principles* which go to the subversion of *all* worldly ordinances, and that the
design of God was and is, that, at the end of the times of the Gentiles, the church should
carry out those principles to their legitimate results.

PROPOSITION XII.

The law of marriage is the same in kind with the Jewish law concerning meats
and drinks and holy days, of which Paul said that they were 'contrary to us, and
were taken out of the way, being nailed to the cross.' Col. 2: 14. The plea in favor
of the worldly system of sexual intercourse, that it is not arbitrary but founded
in nature, will not bear investigation. All experience testifies, (the theory of the
novels to the contrary notwithstanding,) that sexual love is not naturally restricted to pairs. Second marriages are contrary to the one love theory, and yet are often
the happiest marriages. Men and women find universally, (however the fact may
be concealed,) that their susceptibility to love is not burnt out by one honey-
moon, or satisfied by one lover. On the contrary, the secret history of the human
heart will bear out the assertion that it is capable of loving any number of times
and any number of persons, and that the more it loves the more it can love. This
is the law of nature, thrust out of sight, and condemned by common consent,
and yet secretly known to all. There is no occasion to find fault with it. Variety
is, in the nature of things, as beautiful and useful in love as in eating and drinking. The one-love theory is the exponent, not of simple experience in love, but
of the 'green-eyed monster,' jealousy. It is not the loving heart but the greedy
claimant of the loving heart that sets up the popular doctrine that one only can
be truly loved.

Note 1.—It is true, and an important truth, that in a right spiritual medium, the law of
affinity will bring about special pairing; i. e. that each individual will find a mate whose
nature best matches his own, and whom of course he will love most. But this truth, con-
fessedly, is no barrier to friendly relations and common conversation with others; and in
the nature of things, it is no more a barrier to love and sexual intercourse with others.
The fact that a man loves peaches best, is no reason why he should not, on suitable occasions, eat apples, or cherries. Daintiness and poverty of taste are as odious in love as in
any other affection. /25/

Note 2.—There is undoubtedly a law of dualty in love indicated in all nature, and suggested in the creation of the first pair. Indeed this law takes its rise from the constitution

of God himself, who is dual—the Father and the Son—in whose image man was made, male and female, and of whose nature the whole creation is a reflection. But the question is, how does this law operate in such a multiplex body as the church of Christ? Does it exhaust itself on the petty business of joining individual *persons* in pairs, or is its main force directed to the establishment of the great dualty between the whole of one sex and the whole of the other? There is dualty in a dancing party. All that is done in the complex movements of the whole company, may be summed up in this:—Man dances with woman; but this general dualty is consistent with unlimited interchange of personal partnerships. We cannot fairly infer any thing in favor of restricting sexual intercourse to pairs, from the fact that only two persons were created; for we might just as well infer from that fact that conversation and every other mode of intercourse ought to be restricted to pairs. Adam in the garden, had no body to talk with but Eve, but this is no reason why a man should talk with no body but his wife. We maintain, that, in the body of Christ, *universal* unity is the main point; and that the dualty between all men and all women, overrides all inferior dualties. For example, suppose a man, A, is married to a woman, B; and a man C, to a woman, D. Our position is, that in Christ the union of the whole four is first in importance, and the union of the pairs is secondary. We say that it is not enough that A is married to B, making the dual unit A B; and C to D, making the dual unit C D; but that the unit A B ought also to be married to the unit C D, making the quadruple unit A B C D. And we say further, that in the approach and marriage of the pair A B, to the pair C D, it is the dictate of the law of dualty, and the self-evident demand of nature, that the man of each pair should face the woman of the other.

PROPOSITION XIII.

The law of marriage 'worketh wrath.' 1. It provokes to secret adultery, actual or of the heart. 2. It ties together unmatched natures. 3. It sunders matched natures. 4. It gives to sexual appetite only a scanty and monotonous allowance, and so produces the natural vices of poverty, contraction of taste, and stinginess or jealousy. 5. It makes no provision for the sexual appetite at the very time when that appetite is strongest. By the custom of the world, marriage, in the average of cases, takes place at about the age of twenty-four. Whereas puberty commences at the age of fourteen. For ten years, therefore, and that in the very flush of life, the sexual appetite is starved. This law of society bears hardest on females, because they have less opportunity of choosing their time of marriage than men. This discrepancy between the marriage system and nature, is one of the principal sources of the peculiar diseases of women, of prostitution, masturbation, and licentiousness in general.

Note.—The only hopeful scheme of Moral Reform, is one which will bring the sexes together according to the demands of nature. The desire of the sexes is a stream ever running. If it is dammed up, it will break out irregularly and destructively. The only way to make it safe and useful, is to give it a free natural channel. Or to vary the illustration, the attractions of male and female are like positive and negative electricities. In equilibrium, they are quiet. Separate them, and they become turbulent. Prostitution, masturbation, and obscenity in general, are injurious explosions, incident to unnatural separations of the /26/ male and female elements. Reform, in order to he effectual, must base itself on the principle of restoring and preserving equilibrium by free intercourse. Even in the world it is known that the mingling of the sexes to a certain extent, is favorable to purity; and that sexual isolation, as in colleges, monasteries, &c., breeds salacity and obscenity. A system of complex marriage, which shall match the demands of nature, both as to time and variety, will open the prison doors to the victims both of marriage and celibacy; to those in married life who are starved, and those who are oppressed by lust; to those who are tied to uncongenial natures, and to those who are separated from their natural mates;—to those in the unmarried state who are withered by neglect, diseased by unnatural abstinence, or plunged into prostitution and self-pollution, by desires which find no lawful channel.

PROPOSITION XIV.

The kingdom of God on earth is destined to abolish death. 1 Cor. 15: 24–26, Isaiah 25: 8.

PROPOSITION XV.

The abolition of death is to be the *last* triumph of the kingdom; and the subjection of all other powers to Christ, must go before it. 1 Cor. 15: 24–26. Isaiah 33: 22–24.

Note 1.—This proposition can be shown to be rational as well as scriptural. The body cannot be saved from disease and death till Christ has control of the powers which determine the conditions of the body. The powers of law and custom, organizing society, determine the conditions of the body. For instance, the present form of society compels the mass of mankind to drag out life in excessive labor—a condition inconsistent with the welfare of the body. Before Christ can save the body, then, he must 'put down all [present] authority and rule,' and have power to organize society anew. A physician cannot cure diseases generated in a pestilential dungeon, while the patient remains there. The marriage system is a part of the machinery of present society, which seriously affects the conditions of the body, as appears in Proposition 13 and note, and as will appear further hereafter. Christ must, therefore, have control of this department, and arrange sexual conditions according to the genius of his own kingdom, before he can push his conquests to victory over death.

Note 2.—This proposition gives a sufficient answer to those who insist that the resurrection of the body must *go before* the social revolutions which we propose. These revolutions are the very means by which the resurrection power is to be let in upon the world. It might as rationally be said that the snows of winter must not melt till the grass has grown, or that the clods over the dead must not be broken up till the dead have come forth from their graves, as that the institutions of this world must not be abolished till the resurrection of the body is finished. It is true that, as life works legitimately from within outward, the institutions of the world ought not to be broken up till holiness is established in the heart, and moral discipline has advanced to maturity; i. e., till all things are ready for the resurrection of the body. The shell of the chicken ought not to be broken, till the life of the chicken itself is sufficient to make the breach. Yet in the order of nature, the shell bursts before the chicken comes forth; so the breaking up of the fashion of the world precedes the resurrection of the body.

Note 3.—The interests of human nature may be divided into three classes,—those of the soul, of the body, and of the estate. The rulers of this world corresponding to these three classes of interests, are the priests, the doctors and the lawyers. Christ must supplant all these rulers and take their powers into his /27/ hands, before he can give man the redemption of the body. It is not enough that his kingdom should be emancipated from the priests. This may give redemption to the soul; but so long as the body remains in the hands of the doctor, and the estate in the hands of the lawyer, it cannot be said that 'the Lord is our judge, the Lord is our lawgiver, the Lord is our king;' for 'other Lords besides him, have dominion over us;' and it is only when he is our only ruler that sickness and death are to cease. See Isaiah 26:13, 14, and comp. ver. 19; also Isaiah 33: 22, and comp. ver. 24.

PROPOSITION XVI.

The restoration of true relations between the sexes, is a matter second in importance only to the reconciliation of man to God. The distinction of male and female is that which makes man the image of God, i.e. the image of the Father and the Son. Gen. 1: 27. The relation of male and female was the first social relation. Gen. 2: 22. It is therefore the root of all other social relations. The derangement of this relation was the first result of the original breach with God. Gen. 3: 7; comp. 2: 25. Adam and Eve were, at the beginning, in open, fearless, spiritual fellowship, first with God, and secondly, with each other. Their transgression produced two corresponding breaches; viz., first, a breach with God, indicated by their fear of meeting him, and their hiding themselves among the trees of the garden;—and secondly, a breach with each other, indicated by their shame of nakedness, and their hiding themselves from each other by clothing. These were the two great manifestations of original sin—the only manifestations presented to notice in the inspired record of the apostacy. The first thing then to be done, in an attempt to redeem man and reorganize society, is to bring about reconciliation with God; and the second thing is to bring about a true union of the sexes. In other words, religion is the first subject of interest, and sexual morality the second, in the great enterprise of establishing the kingdom of God on earth.

Note 1.—Perfectionists are operating in this order. Their main work, since 1834, has been to develope the religion of the New Covenant, and establish union with God. The second work, in which they are now specially engaged, is the laying the foundation of a new state of society, by developing the true theory of sexual morality.

Note 2.—The functions of the two churches, Jewish and Gentile, correspond to the two breaches to be repaired. It was the special function of the primitive church (which was the interior or soul-church) to break up the worldly *ecclesiastical* system, and establish true religion, thus opening full communication with God. It is the special function of the present or body-church, (availing itself first of the work of the primitive church, by union with it, and a re-development of its theology,) to break up the *social* system of the world, and establish true external order by the reconciliation of the sexes.

Note 3.—We may criticise the system of the Fourierists, thus:—The chain of evils which holds humanity in ruin, has four links, viz:—1st, a breach with God; (Gen. 3: 8;) 2d, a disruption of the sexes, involving a special curse on woman; (Gen. 3: 16;) 3d, the curse of oppressive labor, bearing specially on man; (Gen. 3: 17–19;) 4th, Death. (Gen. 3: 22–24.) These are all inextricably complicated with each other. The true scheme of redemption begins with reconciliation with God, proceeds first to a restoration of true relations between the /28/ sexes, then to a reform of the industrial system and ends with victory over death. Fourierism has no eye to the final victory over death, defers attention to the religious question and the sexual question till some centuries hence, and confines itself to the rectifying of the industrial system. In other words, Fourierism neither begins at the beginning nor looks to the end of the chain, but fastens its whole interest on the third link, neglecting two that precede it, and ignoring that which follows it. The sin-system, the marriage-system, the work-system and the death-system, are all one, and must be abolished together. Holiness, free love, association in labor, and immortality, constitute the chain of redemption, and must come together in their true order.

Note 4.—From what precedes, it is evident that any attempt to revolutionize sexual morality before settlement with God, is out of order. Holiness must go before free love. Perfectionists are not responsible for the proceedings of those who meddle with the sexual question, before they have laid the foundation of true faith and union with God.

PROPOSITION XVII.

Dividing the sexual relation into two branches, the amative and propagative, the amative or love-relation is first in importance, as it is in the order of nature. God made woman because 'he saw it was *not good for man to be alone;*' (Gen. 2: 18;) i.e. for social, not primarily for propagative purposes. Eve was called Adam's 'help-meet.' In the whole of the specific account of the creation of woman, she is regarded as his companion, and her maternal office is not brought into view. Gen. 2: 18–25. Amativeness was necessarily the first social affection developed in the garden of Eden. The second commandment of the eternal law of love—'thou shalt love thy neighbor as thyself'—had amativeness for its first channel; for Eve was at first Adam's only neighbor. Propagation, and the affections connected with it, did not commence their operation during the period of innocence. After the fall, God said to the woman—'I will greatly multiply thy sorrow and thy conception;' from which it is to be inferred that in the original state, conception would have been comparatively infrequent.

Note.—It is true that God made provision for propagation, in the organization of the first pair, and expressed his design that they should multiply. Gen. 1: 28. This opposes the Shaker theory. But it is clear that if innocence had continued, propagation would have been much less frequent than it is now, and would have been altogether secondary to amativeness.

PROPOSITION XVIII.

The amative part of the sexual relation, (separate from the propagative,) is eminently favorable to life. It is not a *source* of life, (as some would make it,) but it is the first and best *distributive* of life. Adam and Eve, in their original state, derived their life from God. Gen. 2: 7. As God is a dual being—the Father and the Son—and man was made in his image, a dual life passed from God to man. Adam was the channel specially of the life of the Father, and Eve of the life of the Son. Amativeness was the natural agency of the distribution and mutual action of these two forms of life. In this primitive position of the sexes, (which is the position of the sexes in Christ,) each reflects upon the other the love of God; each excites and developes the divine action in the other. Thus amativeness is to life, as sunshine to vegetation. /29/

Note 1.—By man's fall from God, he came into a state (like that of the other animals) of dependence on the fruits of the earth for life; i.e. he became 'dust,' and commenced his return to 'dust.' Gen. 3: 19. At the same time the disruption of the sexes took place. So that in the fallen state, both the source and the distribution of life are deranged and carnalized. Yet even in this state, love between the sexes, separate from the curse of propagation, (as in courtship,) developes the highest vigor and beauty of human nature.

Note 2.—The complexity of the human race does not alter the relation of amativeness to life, as defined in the foregoing proposition. If Adam and Eve in their original union with God and with each other, had become complex by propagation, still the life and love of the Father and the Son would have been reflected by the whole of one sex upon the whole of the other. The image of God would have remainêd a dualty, complex, yet retaining the conditions of the original dualty. Amative action between the sexes would have been like the galvanic action between alternate plates of copper and zinc. As the series of plates is extended, the original action, though it remains the same in nature, becomes more and more intense. So the love between the Father and the Son, in the complexity of Christ's body, will be developed with an intensity proportioned to the extent of alternation and conjunction of male and female. Victory over death will be the result of the action of an extensive battery of this kind.

Note 3.—Sexual intercourse, apart from the propagative act, (and it will appear hereafter that the two may be separated,) is the appropriate external expression of amativeness, and is eminently favorable to life. The contact and unity of male and female bodies, developes and distributes the two kinds of life which in equilibrium constitute perfect vitality. Mere reciprocal communication of vital heat is healthful, (Eccles. 4: 11,) and communication between male and female is more perfect than between persons of the same sex. 1 Kings. 1: 1–4. (The science of Animal Magnetism shows what influences one body has on another.) The principle involved in the doctrine of 'laying on of hands,' (which was a fundamental doctrine of the primitive church, and was brought into practice in the communication of spiritual life both to soul and body) is, that not only animal life, but the Spirit of God, passes from one to another by bodily contact. 'The doctrine of baptisms, of the laying on of hands, and of the resurrection of the dead,' follow each other in Paul's list of the first principles of Christ, in scientific order. Heb. 6: 1 The first indicates the source of life; the second indicates the method of distribution; and the third indicates the result. The principle that life passes by bodily contact, is not restricted to the bare action expressed by the term 'laying on of hands.' Paul revived Eutychus, by falling on him and embracing him. Acts 20: 9–12. So Elijah stretched himself upon the child; (1 Kings 17: 21;) and Elisha 'lay upon the child, and put his mouth upon his mouth, and his eyes upon his eyes, and his hands upon his hands, till the flesh of the child waxed warm,' &c. 2 Kings 4: 34. The specific method of bodily contact is not essential to the principle, but may be varied indefinitely. It is safe to affirm that the more intimate and perfect the contact, the greater will be the effect, other things being equal. On this principle, sexual intercourse is in its nature the most perfect method of 'laying on of hands,' and under proper circumstances may be the most powerful external agency of communicating life to the body, and even the Spirit of God to the mind and heart.

Note 4.—We see how foolish they are who think and speak of amativeness and sexual intercourse as contemptible, and in their nature unclean and debasing. Such persons not only dishonor God's creation, but despise that part of human /30/ nature which is the noblest of all except that which communicates with God.—They profane the very sanctuary of the affections—the first and best channel of the life and love of God.

Note 5.—The familiar principle that the abuse of a thing is no discredit to its use, and that the destructiveness of an element, when abused, is the measure of its usefulness, when rightly managed, applies to amativeness and its expression. If amativeness is a fire, which under the devil's administration burns houses, why may it not under God's administration prepare food, warm dwellings, and drive steamboats? If it is Satan's agency of death, why may it not be God's agency of resurrection?

PROPOSITION XIX.

The propagative part of the sexual relation is in its nature the *expensive* department. 1. While amativeness keeps the capital stock of life circulating between two, propagation introduces a third partner. 2. The propagative act, i. e. the emission of the seed, is a drain on the life of the man, and when habitual, produces disease. 3. The infirmities and vital expenses of woman during the long period of pregnancy, waste her constitution. 4. The awful agonies of child-birth heavily tax the life of woman. 5. The cares of the nursing period bear heavily on woman. 6. The cares of both parents, through the period of the childhood of their offspring, are many and burdensome. 7. The labor of man is greatly increased by the necessity of providing for children. A portion of these expenses would undoubtedly have been curtailed if human nature had remained in its original integrity, and will be, when it is restored. But it is still self-evident that the birth of children, viewed either as a vital or a mechanical operation, is in its nature expensive; and the fact that multiplied conception was imposed as a curse, indicates that it was so regarded by the Creator.

Note 1—Amativeness being the profitable part, and propagation the expensive part of the sexual relation, it is evident that a true balance between them is essential to the interests of the vital economy. If expenses exceed income, bankruptcy ensues. After the fall, sin and shame curtailed amativeness, thus diminishing the profitable department; and the curse increased propagation, thus enlarging the expensive department. Death, i.e. vital bankruptcy, is the law of the race in its fallen condition; and it results more from this derangement of the sexual economy, than from any other cause except the disruption from God. It is the expression of the disproportion of amativeness to propagation—or of life to its expenses—each generation dies in giving life to its successor.

Note 2.—The actual proportion of the amative to the propagative, in the world, may probably be estimated fairly by comparing the time of courtship (which is the limit of the novels) with the breeding part of married life; or by comparing the momentary pleasures of ordinary sexual intercourse with the protracted woes of pregnancy, birth, nursing and breeding.

Note 3.—The grand problem which must be resolved before redemption can be carried forward to immortality, is this:—How can the benefits of amativeness be secured and increased, and the expenses of propagation be reduced to such limits as life can afford? The human mind has labored on this problem already. Shakerism is an attempt to solve it. Ann Lee's attention however was confined to the latter half of it—the reduction of expenses; (of which her own sufferings in child-birth gave her a strong sense;) and for the sake of stopping propagation she prohibited the union of the sexes—thus shutting off the profitable as well as the expensive /31/ part of the sexual relation. This is cutting the knot—not untying it.—Robert Dale Owen's 'Moral Physiology' is another attempted solution of the grand problem. He insists that sexual intercourse is of some value by itself, and not merely as a bait to propagation. He proposes therefore to limit propagation, and retain the privilege of sexual intercourse, by the practice of withdrawing previous to the emission of the seed, after Onan's fashion. Gen. 38: 9. This method, it will be observed, is unnatural, filthy, and even more wasteful of life, so far as the man is concerned, than ordinary practice; since it gives more freedom to desire, by shutting off propagative consequences. The same may be said of the French method—the use of sacks. Madame Restell's system of producing abortions, is a still more unnatural and destructive method of limiting propagation, without stopping sexual intercourse. A satisfactory solution of the grand problem, must propose a method that can be shown to be natural, healthy for both sexes, favorable to amativeness, and effectual in its control of propagation. Such a solution will be found in what follows.

PROPOSITION XX.

The amative and propagative functions of the sexual organs are distinct from each other, and may be separated practically. They are confounded in the world, both in the theories of physiologists and in universal practice. The amative function is regarded merely as a bait to the propagative, and is merged in it. The sexual organs are called 'organs of reproduction,' or 'organs of generation,' but not organs of love or organs of union. But if amativeness is, as we have seen, the first and noblest of the social affections, and if the propagative part of the sexual relation was originally secondary, and became paramount by the subversion of order in the fall, we are bound to raise the amative office of the sexual organs into a distinct and paramount function. It is held in the world, that the sexual organs have two distinct functions, viz., the urinary, and the propagative. We affirm that they have *three*—the urinary, the propagative, and the amative; i.e., they are conductors, first of the urine, secondly of the seed, and thirdly of the vital and social magnetism. And the amative is as distinct from the propagative, as the propagative is from the urinary. In fact, strictly speaking, the organs of propagation are physiologically distinct from the organs of union in both sexes. The testicles are the organs of reproduction in the male, and the uterus in the female. These are distinct from the organs of union. The sexual conjunction of male and female no more necessarily involves the discharge of the testicles than of the bladder. The discharge of the seed, instead of being the main act of sexual intercourse properly so called, is really the sequel and termination of it. Sexual intercourse, pure and simple, is the conjunction of the organs of union, and the interchange of magnetic influences, or conversation of spirits, through the medium of that conjunction. The communication from the testicles to the uterus, which constitutes the propagative act, is distinct from, subsequent to, and not necessarily connected with, this intercourse. On the one hand the seminal discharge can be voluntarily withheld in sexual connection; and on the other it can be produced without sexual connection, as it is in masturbation. This latter fact demonstrates that the discharge of the seed and the pleasure connected with it, is not essentially social, since it can be produced in solitude; it is a personal /32/ and not a dual affair. In fact this is evident from a physiological analysis of it. The pleasure of the act is not produced by contact and interchange of life with the female, but by the action of the seminal fluid on certain internal nerves of the male organ. The appetite and that which satisfies it, are both within the man, and of course the pleasure is personal and may be obtained without sexual intercourse. We insist then that the amative function—that which consists in a simple union of persons, making 'of twain one flesh' and giving a medium of magnetic and spiritual interchange,—is a distinct and independent function, as superior to the reproductive as we have shown amativeness to be to propagation.

Note 1.—We may strengthen the argument of the preceding proposition by an analogy. The mouth has three distinct functions, viz., those of breathing, eating and speaking. Two of these, breathing and eating, are purely physical, and these we have in common with the brutes. The third function, that of speaking, is social, and subservient to the intellectual and spiritual. In this we rise above the brutes. They are destitute of it except in a very inferior degree. So the two primary functions of the sexual organs—the urinary and reproductive—are physical, and we have them in common with the brutes. The third, viz. the amative, is social, and subservient to the spiritual. In this we rise above the brutes. They have it only as a bait to the reproductive. As speech, the distinctive glory of man, is the superior function of the mouth, so the office of the sexual organs is their superior function, and that which gives man a position above the brutes.

Note 2.—Here is a method of controlling propagation, that is natural, healthy, favorable to amativeness, and effectual. 1. It is *natural.* The useless expenditure of seed certainly is not natural. God cannot have designed that men should sow seed by the way-side, where they do not expect it to grow, or in the same field where seed has already been sown, and is growing; and yet such is the practice of men in ordinary sexual intercourse. They sow seed habitually where they do not *wish* it to grow. This is wasteful of life, and cannot be natural. So far the Shakers and Grahamites are right. Yet it is equally manifest that the

natural instinct of our nature demands frequent congress of the sexes, not for propagative, but for social and spiritual purposes. It results from these opposite indications, that
simple congress of the sexes, without the propagative crisis, is the order of nature, for the
gratification of ordinary amative instincts; and that the act of propagation should be reserved for its legitimate occasions, when conception is intended. The idea that sexual intercourse, pure and simple, is impossible or difficult, and therefore not natural, is contra-
dicted by the experience, of many. Abstinence from masturbation is impossible or difficult,
where habit made it a second nature; and yet no one will say that habitual masturbation
is natural. So abstinence from the propagative part of sexual intercourse may seem impracticable to depraved natures, and yet be perfectly natural and easy to persons properly
trained to chastity. Our method simply proposes the subordination of the flesh to the spirit,
teaching men to seek principally the elevated spiritual pleasures of sexual intercourse, and
to be content with them in their general intercourse with women, restricting the more sensual part to its proper occasions. This is certainly natural and easy to spiritual men, however difficult it may be to the sensual. 2. Our method is *healthy*. In the first place, it secures woman from the curses of involuntary and undesirable procreation; and secondly,
it stops the drain of life on the part of the man. This cannot be said of Owen's system, or
any other plan for preventing merely the *effects* of the emission /33/ of the seed, and not
the emission itself. 3. Our method is *favorable to amativeness*. Owen can only say of his
method that it does not *much diminish* the pleasure of sexual intercourse, but we can say
of ours that it *vastly increases* that pleasure. Ordinary sexual intercourse (in which the
amative and propagative functions are confounded) is a momentary affair, terminating
in exhaustion and disgust. If it begins in the spirit, it soon ends in the flesh; i.e., the amative, which is spiritual, is drowned in the propagative, which is sensual. The exhaustion
which follows, naturally breeds self-reproach and shame, and this leads to dislike and
concealment of the sexual organs, which contract disagreeable associations from the fact
that they are the instruments of pernicious excess. This undoubtedly is the philosophy of
the origin of shame after the fall. Adam and Eve first sunk the spiritual in the sensual, in
eating the forbidden fruit, and then having lost the true balance of their natures, they sunk
the spiritual in the sensual in their intercourse with each other, by pushing prematurely
beyond the amative to the propagative, and so became ashamed, and began to look with
an evil eye on the instruments of their folly. On the same principle we may account for
the process of 'cooling off' which takes place between lovers, and often ends in indifference and disgust. Exhaustion and self-reproach make the eye evil not only toward the
instruments of excess, but toward the person who tempts to it. In contrast with all this,
lovers who use their sexual organs simply as the servants of their spiritual natures, abstaining from the propagative act, except when propagation is intended, may enjoy the highest bliss of sexual fellowship for any length of time, and from day to day, without satiety
or exhaustion; and thus marriage life may become permanently sweeter than courtship,
or even the honey-moon. 4. Our method of controlling propagation is *effectual*. The habit
of making sexual intercourse a quiet affair, like conversation, restricting the action of the
organs to such limits as are necessary to the avoidance of the sexual crisis, can easily be
established, and then there is no risk of conception with intention.

Note 3.—Ordinary sexual intercourse, i.e. the performance of the propagative act, without the intention of procreation, is properly to be classed with masturbation. The habit
in the former case is less liable to become besotted and ruinous, than in the latter, simply
because a woman is less convenient than the ordinary means of masturbation. It must
be admitted also that the amative affection favorably modifies the sensual act to a greater
extent in sexual commerce than in masturbation. But this is perhaps counterbalanced by
the cruelty of forcing or risking undesired conception, which attends sexual commerce
and does not attend masturbation.

Note 4.—Our theory, which separates the amative from the propagative, not only relieves us of involuntary and undesirable procreation, but opens the way for *scientific* propagation. We are not opposed after the Shaker fashion, or even after Owen's fashion, to the increase of population. We believe that the order to 'multiply' attached to the race in its original integrity, and that propagation, rightly conducted and kept within such limits as life can fairly afford, is the next blessing to sexual love. But we are opposed to *involuntary* procreation. A very large proportion of all children born under the present system, are begotten contrary to the wishes of both parents, and lie nine months in their mother's womb under their mother's curse, or a feeling little better than a curse. Such children cannot be well organized. We are opposed to excessive, and of course oppressive procreation, which is almost universal. We are opposed to *random* procreation, which is unavoidable in the marriage system. But we are in favor of /34/ *intelligent, well-ordered* procreation. The physiologists say that the race cannot be raised from ruin, till propagation is made a matter of science; but they point out no way of making it so. True, propagation is controlled and reduced to a science in the case of valuable domestic brutes; but marriage and fashion forbid any such system among human beings. We believe the time will come when involuntary and random propagation will cease, and when scientific combination will be applied to human generation as freely and successfully as it is to that of other animals. The way will be open for this, when amativeness can have its proper gratification without drawing after it procreation, as a necessary sequence. And at all events we believe that good sense and benevolence will *very soon* sanction and enforce the rule that woman shall bear children only when they choose. They have the principal burdens of breeding to bear, and they, rather than men, should have their choice of time and circumstances, at least till science takes charge of the business.

Note 5.—It may be urged as an objection to our position that propagation is essential to the consummation of love; i.e., that the unity of two exists and expresses itself in the generation of a third. We assent partially to this view, but reply to the objection thus; simple amative action between two, i.e. the interchange of spiritual without physical seed, actually generates a third. The male and female persons A and B, by amative interchange of life, generate a third, namely, the bisexual being A B; i. e., they return to the conditions of Paradise, and become what Adam was before the fall, a male and female unit.—We say that this kind of generation which acts by spiritual impregnation and condensation, consummates love more effectually than generation by physical impregnation and the production of a separate person. A child is born in both cases. In the first it is a child compounded of the two generating spirits. In the second it is a separate physical being. The principle of *consolidation* rules in the first, and the principle of division in the second. We admit however that physical generation under proper circumstances, is a secondary, though not an essential consummation of love.

Note 6.—The separation of the amative from the propagative, places amative sexual intercourse on the same footing with other ordinary forms of intercourse, such as conversation, kissing, shaking hands, embracing, &c.—So long as the amative and propagative are confounded, sexual intercourse carries with it physical consequences which necessarily take it out of the category of mere social acts. If a gentleman under the cover of a mere social call upon a lady, should leave in her apartments a child for her to breed and provide for, he would do a mean wrong. The call might be made without previous negotiation or agreement, but the sequel of the call—the leaving of the child—is a matter so serious that it is to be treated as a business affair, and not be done without good reason and agreement of the parties. But the man who under the cover of social sexual intercourse, commits the propagative act, leaves his child with the woman in a meaner and more oppressive way, than he would if he should leave it full born in her apartments; for he imposes on her not only the task of breeding and providing for it, but the sorrows and pains of pregnancy and child-birth. It is right that law, or at least public opinion, should frown on such proceedings even more than it does; and it is not to be wondered at, that women, to a considerable extent, look upon ordinary sexual intercourse with more dread than pleasure, regarding it as a stab at their life, rather than a joyful act of fellowship. But separate the amative from the propagative—let the act of fellowship stand by itself—and sexual intercourse becomes a purely social affair, the same in kind with other modes of kindly interchange, differing only by its superior intensity /35/ and beauty. Thus the most popular, if not the most serious objection to free love and sexual intercourse is removed. The difficulty so often urged, of knowing to whom children belong in complex marriage, will have no place in a community trained to keep the amative distinct from the propagative. Thus also the only plausible objection to amative intercourse between near relatives, founded on the supposed law of nature that 'breeding in and in' deteriorates offspring, (which law however was not recognized in Adam's family,) is removed; since science may dictate in this case as in all others, in regard to propagation, and yet amativeness may be free.

Note 7.—In society trained in these principles, as propagation will become a science, so amative intercourse will become one of the 'fine arts.' Indeed it will take rank above music, painting, sculpture, &c.; for it combines the charms and benefits of them all. There is as much room for cultivation of taste and skill in this department as in any.

Note 8.—The reformed practice which we propose, will advance civilization and refinement at railroad speed. The self-control, retention of life, and ascent of sensualism which must result from making freedom of love a bounty on the chastening of physical indulgence, will at once raise the race to new vigor and beauty, moral and physical. And the refining effects of sexual love (which are recognized more or less in the world) will be increased a thousand fold, when sexual intercourse becomes a method of ordinary conversation, and each is married to all.

PROPOSITION XXI.

Sexual shame was the consequence of the fall, and is factitious and irrational. (Gen. 2: 25; comp. 3: 7.) Adam and Eve, while innocent, had no shame; little children have none; other animals have none. To be ashamed of the sexual organs, is to be ashamed of God's workmanship. To be ashamed of the sexual organs, is to be ashamed of the most perfect instruments of love and unity. To be ashamed of the sexual organs, is to be ashamed of the agencies which gave us existence. To be ashamed of sexual conjunction, is to be ashamed of the image of the glory of God—the physical symbol of life dwelling in life, which is the mystery of the gospel. John 17: 21, &c.

Note 1.—One of the *sources* of shame is *personal isolation*, which was the consequence of the victory of the flesh over the spirit, which took place when Adam and Eve forsook the counsel of God. Their unity with God and with each other was in their spiritual part. In the physical they were two. When the physical therefore became paramount, as it did when they sought blessing from fruit instead of from God, they became consciously two. Then began evil-eyed surveillance on the one hand, and morbid shrinking on the other. A man is not ashamed of his body before his own eyes, but before the eyes of another. So Adam and Eve were not ashamed so long as they were one; but when they became two, their eyes were opened and they became ashamed. Another source of shame is *sensual excess*, in the fall from amative interchange to propagative expense, producing exhaustion, consciousness of uncontrolled and ruinous passion, and consequent aversion to the instruments of the mischief. This cause acts particularly on the male. (See Proposition 20, Note 2.) Another cause of shame is found in the *woes of untimely and excessive child bearing*, by which the sexual organs and offices contract odious associations. This cause acts particularly on the female. After the sentiment of shame (i. e. the sentiment which prompts to dishonor and to conceal the sexual organs) is generated by these causes, *jealousy* /36/ falls in with it and strengthens it. The greedy lover is naturally a fierce friend of a sentiment which secludes the charms of his mistress from all eyes but his own. And then custom, and finally law, elevates this spawn of corruption into a virtue.

Note 2.—It is true that God, in the Mosaic law and in other ways, has added to the strength of the shame principle, by precepts directed against lewdness. But it must be remembered that all such legislation is predicated on a state of spiritual derangement, and its end is, not to restore the patient, but to prevent him from destructive violence, even at the expense of increasing his internal malady. Shame is a good straight-jacket for crazy amativeness, and as such God has favored it. Adam and Eve first began to make *flimsy aprons* for their nakedness, and God stepped in and made them complete garments. Gen. 3: 7, 21. But he did not thereby approbate the spiritual and moral condition which made garments necessary.

Note 3.—True modesty is a sentiment which springs, not from aversion or indifference to the sexual organs and offices, but from a delicate and reverent appreciation of their value and sacredness. While the shrinking of shame is produced by a feeling that the sexual nature is vile and shameful, the shrinking of modesty is produced by the opposite feeling, that the sexual nature is too holy and glorious to be meddled with lightly. This healthful delicacy is valuable as a preservative, and increases the zest of love. Modesty and shame ought to be sundered, and shame ought to be banished from the company of virtue, though in the world it has stolen the very name of virtue.

Note 4.—Shame is the real source of the impression, which many persist in exalting into a serious theory, that sexual distinction and sexual offices have no place in heaven. Any one who has true modesty, as above defined, would sooner consent to banish singing from heaven, than sexual music. The impression referred to is too self-evidently absurd to be argued with to any great extent, and can be abolished only by abolishing shame from which it originates, and making men and women truly modest. From pure feelings sensible theories will flow. The loathsome loathings of the debauchee in a state of reaction must not make theories of taste and pleasure for the innocent.

Note 5.—The aversion which many have to thought and conversation on the subject we are considering, is like the aversion of the irreligious to thought and conversation about God and eternity. As irreconciliation makes thought about God disagreeable, so the sentiment of shame, whether contracted by debauchery or by education and epidemic spiritual influence, makes thought, and especially new thought and free discussion about sexual matters, disagreeable. Under the influence of that sentiment the mind is evil-eyed and not in condition to reason clearly and see purely. In such cases a spiritual conversion from the spirit of shame to the spirit of true modesty, must go before intellectual emancipation.

Note 6.—That kind of taste which rises from the sentiment of shame, excludes such books as the Bible and Shakespeare from virtuous libraries. (Vide Webster's Bible, Dr. Humphrey's criticisms of Shakspeare, &c.

Note 7.—That kind of moral reform which rises from the sentiment of shame, attempts a hopeless war with nature. Its policy is to prevent pruriency by keeping the mind in ignorance of sexual subjects; whilst nature is constantly thrusting those subjects upon the mind. Whoever would preserve the minds of the young in innocence by keeping them from 'polluting images,' must first of all carry moral reform into the barn-yard and among the flies. /37/

Note 8.—The true way to purify the mind in its amative department, is to let in the light; to elevate sexual love by marrying it to religion; to clear away the vile, debasing associations which usually crowd around the thoughts of the sexual organs and offices, and substitute true and beautiful associations. The union of the child with its mother in nursing, is not base, but lovely and even sacred to the imagination. Sexual intercourse is as much more lovely and sacred, as we have seen amativeness to be superior to propagation. Instead of thinking of our sexual nature in connection with sensuality and vice and woe, it is just as easy, and much truer to God and nature, to associate with it images of the garden of Eden, of the holy of holies, of God and heaven, thoughts of purity and chaste affection, of joy unspeakable and full of glory. The eucharist is a symbol of eating Christ's flesh and drinking his blood; (Luke 22: 19–24;) of a union with him in which we dwell in him and he in us, (John 6: 56,) whereby we become bone of his bone and flesh of his flesh, (Eph. 5: 30,) and he comes into us and sups with us and we with him. Rev.3: 20. Is not this a *marriage* supper? And is not sexual intercourse a more perfect symbol of it than eating bread and drinking wine? With pure hearts and minds, we may approach the sexual union as the truest Lord's supper, as an emblem and also a medium of the noblest worship of God and fellowship with the body of Christ. We may throw around it all the hallowed associations which attach to the festivities and hospitalities of Christmas or Thanksgiving. To sup with each other, is really less sensual than to sup with roast-turkies and chicken-pies. Such thoughts surely are better than the base imaginations of shame which envelope the whole sexual department in filth and darkness, even in the minds of those who would be thought intelligent and refined. The Bible constantly associates ideas of heaven with sexual intercourse. Isaiah 62: 4, 5. Matt. 22: 2–4; 25: 1–12; Rev. 19: 7; 21: 2, 9, &c. The wisest of men expressed his taste in a song of love.

Note 9.—Shame seeks to degrade sexual intercourse by calling it 'sensual and carnal.' We reply, conversation is 'sensual and carnal.' Speech, in itself, is nothing but a wagging of the tongue (a carnal member) on one side, and a consequent vibration of the tympanum and nerves of the ear on the other.—Yet speech is the medium of spiritual blessings and refined interchange. Music is 'sensual and carnal.' Eating and drinking are 'sensual and carnal,' &c.—Things 'sensual and carnal' are not necessarily vile and unprofitable. See Rom. 15: 27, & 1 Cor. 9: 11. By themselves they are of small value; and out of place, i.e. overtopping and abusing the spiritual, they are diabolical; but in their place, as servants of the spiritual, they are of great value. The senses are to the thoughts and affections of the spirit, as chess-men to a chess-game. By themselves, chess-men are trifles; and to play with them as children do, for their own sake, would be frivolous and degrading; but as instruments of the complicated thought and interest of a chess-game, they are noble. It is the ascetic Manichean philosophy, not the Bible, that despises the senses and matter. Of all the pleasures of the senses, sexual intercourse is intrinsically the most spiritual and refined; for it is intercourse of human life with human life; whereas in every other sensual enjoyment, human life has intercourse with inanimate matter, or life inferior to itself. In the same sense as that in which sexual intercourse is 'sensual and carnal,' Peter's 'kiss of charity,' (1 Peter 5: 14,) which Paul calls 'holy', (Rom. 16: 16, & 1 Cor. 16: 20,) and which both apostles enjoined, is sensual and carnal. In the same sense, 'laying on of hands' is 'sensual and carnal,' &c. /38/

PROPOSITION XXII.

The foregoing principles concerning the sexual relation, open the way for Association. 1. They furnish *motives.* They apply to larger partnerships the same attractions as draw and bind together pairs in the worldly partnership of marriage. A community home in which each is married to all, and where love is honored and cultivated, will be as much more attractive than an ordinary home, even in the honey-moon, as the community out-numbers a pair. A motive thus mighty is needed for the Association enterprise.—2. These principles remove the principal *obstructions* in the way of Association. There is plenty of tendency to cross-ing love, and adultery, even in the system of isolated households. Association increases this tendency. Amalgamation of interests, frequency of interview, and companionship in labor, inevitably give activity and intensity to the social attractions in which amativeness is the strongest element. The tendency to extra-matrimonial love will be proportioned to the condensation of interests produced by any given form of Association; i.e., if the ordinary principles of exclusiveness are preserved, Association will be a worse school of temptation to unlawful love than the world is, in proportion to its social advantages. Love, in the exclusive form, has jealousy for its complement; and jealousy brings on strife and division. Association, therefore, if it retains one-love exclusiveness, contains the seeds of dissolution; and those seeds will be hastened to their harvest by the warmth of associate life. An association of states, with custom-house lines around each, is sure to be quarrelsome. The farther states in that situation are apart, and the more their interests are isolated, the better. The only way to prevent smuggling and strife in a confederation of contiguous states, is to abolish custom-house lines from the interior, and declare free trade and free transit, (as in the United States,) collecting revenues and fostering home products by one custom-house line around the whole. This is the policy of our system—'that they *all* [not two and two] may be one.'

Note 1.—The idea that amative magnetism can, by some miraculous agency peculiar to a state of perfection, be made to point only toward one object, (which is the hobby of some,) is very absurd. It is just as conceivable that a man should have an appetite for one apple but not for another equally good by the side of it, as that a man should have amative desire toward one woman, but not toward another equally attractive by the side of her. True, the will, backed by law and custom, may forbid the evolution of appetite into action in one case, and allow it in another; but appetite itself is involuntary, and asks for that which is adapted to it, as indiscriminately in respect to women as to apples. If the sexual organs were so constructed that they would match only in pairs, we might believe that the affections which are connected with them, attract only in pairs. But as things are, it is quite as easy to believe that a man of integral nature and affections, should have no relish for the presence or the conversation of any woman but his wife, as that he should have no appetite for sexual interchange with any other. We say then, if the marriage fashion is to be continued, and amative appetite is to be suppressed in all directions except one, isolation is better than Association, since it makes less parade of forbidden fruit.

Note 2.—The only plausible method of avoiding the stumbling-blocks of the sexual question in Association, besides ours, is the method of the Shakers. Forbid /39/ sexual intercourse altogether, and you attain the same results, so far as shutting off the jealousies and strifes of exclusiveness is concerned, as we attain by making sexual intercourse free. In this matter the Shakers show their shrewdness. But they sacrifice the vitality of society, in securing its peace.

Note 3.—Association, in order to be valuable, must be, not mere juxtaposition, but vital organization—not mere compaction of material, but community of life. Every member must be vitally organized, not only within itself, and into its nearest mate, but into the whole body, and must receive and distribute the common circulation. In a living body, (such as is the body of Christ,) the relation of the arm to the trunk is as intimate and vital, as its relation to the hand, or as the relation of one part of it to another; and the relation of every member to the heart is as complete and essential, as the relation of each to its neighbor. A congeries of loose particles (i.e. individuals) cannot make a living body.

No more can a congeries of loose double particles, (i. e. conjugal pairs.) The individuals and the pairs, as well as all larger combinations, must be knit together organically, and pervaded by one common life. Association of this kind will be to society what regeneration is to individuals—a resurrection from the dead. In the present order of isolation, society is dead. Association (genuine) will be properly named VITAL SOCIETY. Now as egotism in individuals obstructs the circulation of community life, (see Proposition 8,) precisely so, exclusive conjugal love, which is only a double kind of egotism, obstructs community life. Vital society demands the surrender not only of property interests, and conjugal interests, but of life itself, or, if you please, personal identity, to the use of the whole. If this is the 'grave of liberty,' as the Fourierists say, it is the grave of the liberty of selfishness, which has done mischief enough to deserve death—and it is the birth of the liberty of patriotism. The whole gains more than individuals lose. In the place of dead society, we have vital society, and individuals have the liberty of harmony instead of the liberty of war.

PROPOSITION XXIII.

In vital society, strength will be increased, and the necessity of labor diminished, till all work will become sport, as it would have been in the original Eden state. See Gen. 2: 15, comp. 3: 17– 19. Here we come to the field of the Fourierists—the third link of the chain of evil. And here we shall doubtless ultimately avail ourselves of many of the economical and industrial discoveries of Fourier. But as the fundamental principle of our system differs entirely from that of Fourier, (our foundation being his superstructure, and *vice versa*,) and as every system necessarily has its own complement of external arrangements, conformed to its own genius, we will pursue our investigations for the present independently, and with special reference to our peculiar principles. Labor is sport or drudgery, according to the proportion between strength and the work to be done. Work that over-tasks a child, is easy to a man. The amount of work remaining the same, if man's strength were doubled the result would be the same as if the amount of work were diminished one half. To make labor sport, therefore, we must seek, first, increase of strength, and, secondly, diminution of work: or, (as in the former problem relating to the curse on woman,) first, increase of income, and, secondly, diminution of expenses. Vital society secures both of these objects. It increases strength, by placing the individual in a vital organization which is in communication with the source of life, and which distributes and circulates life with the highest activity by the alternation of male and female. In /40/ other words, as vital society is properly a resurrection state, so individuals in vital society will have the vigor of resurrection. The amount of work to be done is correspondingly diminished. The staple necessaries of life are food, raiment, shelter and fuel. The end of all these is the maintenance of vital heat. Liebeg says, and experience demonstrates, that food is fuel; and that the better men are clothed, or the warmer their climate, the less food they need, especially animal food. On the same principle we say, that the more perfectly men are in communication with the source of vital heat, and the more they are enveloped in the genial magnetism of social life, the less food, raiment, shelter and fuel they will need.

Note 1.—As society becomes vital and refined, drawing its best nourishment from love, the grosser kinds of food, and especially animal food, will go out of use. The fruits of *trees* will become the staple eatables. Gen. 2: 16. The largest part of the labor of the world is now spent on the growth of annual plants and animals. Cattle occupy more of the soil at present than men. The cultivation of trees will be better sport than plowing, hoeing corn, digging potatoes, and waiting on cows and pigs.

Note 2.—As society becomes compact and harmonious, its buildings will be compact, and much labor now expended in accommodating egotism and exclusiveness with isolated apartments, will be saved. The removal of the partition between the sexes, will save many a partition to the carpenter. In many other things, as well as buildings, love will save labor. Unity of heart will prefer unity of accommodations as far as it is possible.

PROPOSITION XXIV.

In vital society, labor will become attractive. Loving companionship in labor, and especially the mingling of the sexes, makes labor attractive.—The present division of labor between the sexes separates them entirely. The woman keeps house, and the man labors abroad. Men and women are married only after dark and during bed-time. Instead of this, in vital society men and women will mingle in both of their peculiar departments of work.—It will be economically as well as spiritually profitable, to marry them indoors and out, by day as well as by night. The difference between the anatomical structures of men and women, indicates the difference of their vocations. Men have their largest muscular developments in the upper part of the trunk, about the arms, and thus are best qualified for hand-labor. Women have their largest muscular developments in the lower part of the trunk, about the legs, and thus are best qualified for duties requiring locomotion. Girls outrun boys of the same age. The miraculous dancers are always females. How abusive then are the present arrangements, which confine women to the house! They are adapted by nature, even better than men, to out-door employments and sports—to running, leaping, &c.,—and yet they are excluded from every thing of this kind after childhood. They are not only shut up, but fettered. Gowns operate as shackles, and they are put on that sex which has most talent in the legs! When the partition between the sexes is taken away, and man ceases to make woman a propagative drudge, when love takes the place of shame, and fashion follows nature in dress and business, men and women will mingle in all their employments, as boys and girls mingle in their sports, and then labor will be attractive. /41/

Note 1.—The present dress of women, besides being peculiarly inappropriate to the sex, is immodest. It makes the distinction between the sexes vastly more prominent and obtrusive than nature makes it. In a state of nature the difference between a man and a woman could hardly be distinguished at the distance of five hundred yards; but as men and women dress, their sex is telegraphed as far as they can be seen. Woman's dress is a standing lie. It proclaims that she not a two-legged animal, but something like a churn standing on castors! Such are the absurdities into which the false principle of shame and sexual isolation betray the world.

Note 2.—When the distinction of the sexes is reduced to the bounds of nature and decency, by the removal of the shame partition, and woman becomes what she ought to be, a *female man,* (like the Son in the Godhead,) a dress will be adopted that will be at the same time the most simple and the most beautiful, and it will be the same, or nearly the same, for both sexes. The dress of children—frock and pantaloons—is in good taste, i.e. taste not perverted by the dictates of shame, and it is well adapted to the free motion of both sexes. This, or something like it, will be the uniform of vital society.

Note 3.—We can now see our way to victory over death. Reconciliation with God opens the way for the reconciliation of the sexes. Reconciliation of the sexes emancipates woman, and opens the way for vital society. Vital society increases strength, diminishes work, and makes labor attractive, thus removing the antecedents of death. First we abolish sin, then shame, then the curse on woman of exhausting child-bearing, then the curse on man of exhausting labor, and so we arrive regularly at the tree of life, (as per Gen. 3.)

PROPOSITION XXV.

The will of God is done in heaven, and of course will be done in his kingdom on earth, not merely by general obedience to constitutional principles, but by specific obedience to the administration of his Spirit. The constitution of a nation is one thing, and the living administration of government is another. Ordinary theology directs attention chiefly, and almost exclusively, to the constitutional principles of God's government. (The same may be said of Fourierism, and all schemes of reform based on the development of 'natural laws.') As loyal subjects of God, we must give and call attention to his actual administration; i.e., to his will directly manifested by his Spirit and the agents of his Spirit, viz. his officers and representatives. We must look to God, not only for a Constitution, but for Presidential outlook and counsel; for a cabinet and corps of officers; for national aims and plans; for direction, not only in regard to principles to be carried out, but in regard to time and circumstance in carrying them out. In other words, the men who are called to usher in the kingdom of God, will be guided, not merely by theoretical truth, but by the Spirit of God, and specific manifestations of his will and policy, as were Abraham, Moses, David, Jesus Christ, Paul, &c. This will be called a fanatical principle, because it requires *bona fide* communication with the heavens, and displaces the sanctified maxim that the 'age of miracles is past.' But it is clearly a Bible principle; and we must place it on high, above all others, as the palladium of conservatism in the introduction of the new social order, which we have proposed in the preceding Argument.

Note 1.—The principles of sexual morality which have been presented, are /42/ called incendiary and dangerous; and they are incendiary and dangerous, as fire, steam, gunpowder, &c. are, in unfit hands. We shall endeavor (as we have done) to keep them out of unfit hands; and we hereby notify all, that we neither license or encourage any one to attempt the practice of these incendiary theories, without clear directions from the government in the heavens. No movement in these matters can be made safely, in the way of imitation, or on the mere ground of acquaintance with the theory of the new order of things. Other qualifications besides theoretical knowledge, are requisite for the construction and handling of a locomotive; and much more for the management of such tremendous machinery as that of vital society. Let no man attempt the work, without the charter and manifest patronage of the general government. Of course we cannot prevent children from playing with fire, but we forewarn them that they will burn their fingers.

Note 2.—The first qualification for office in the kingdom of God, and especially for employment in the critical operations of the revolution in sexual matters, manifestly is true spirituality, securing inspiration; and true spirituality cannot be attained without true holiness, i.e. self-crucifixion and the love-devotion described by Paul in 1 Cor. 13: 4–7. The government in heaven will not employ self-seekers; and whoever meddles with the affairs of the inner sanctuary without being employed by the government, will plunge himself in consuming fire. Thus official distinctions and love-rewards, in the kingdom of God, will be bounties on true spirituality and holiness. If a man desires place and emolument, let him first show that he holds 'the mystery of faith in a pure conscience.' 1 Tim. 3: 9. /43/

TESTIMONY OF THE MEMBERS.

The institutions and principles of the Oneida Association have now been presented without reserve. For the sake of exhibiting, in a bird's-eye view, the effects of those institutions and principles, and the actual spirit and condition of the Association, the members will now be placed upon the stand as witnesses for themselves. The ensuing mass of affidavits were elicited in the following manner. At the close of the year covered by this Report, a series of questions was proposed to the Association by J. H. Noyes, at six successive evening meetings. The question proposed at each meeting was answered by the members in writing on the evening succeeding. The answers were written in the intervals of busy occupation, and no one anticipated at the time that they were to be presented to the public; the only object of the exercise being the satisfaction and improvement of the family circle. They constitute, therefore, together, a portrait of the spiritual, intellectual and moral character of the Association, more ingenuous and graphic than could be presented in any labored description.

QUESTION I.—What has been the general effect of your connection with this Association upon your character?

ANSWERS.

JOHN ABBOTT.

The influence of Association has made me mild and gentle, and taught me, in admonishing others, to speak the truth *in love.* I have learned to respect the judgment of others, and to cultivate love and a community spirit. I value less my own independence, and more the good will of others.

JAMES L. BAKER.

The relation which I sustain to this body has rendered my heart and mind more susceptible of improvement than formerly; and this susceptibility increases. I have in a good degree been saved from selfishness and inordinate love of money.

SARAH A. BRADLEY.

I have gained a victory over self-will which I thought impossible when I came to Oneida. I believe that God has given me a permanent victory, and that it will be my greatest delight in future to act in accordance with his will.

LORINDA BURT.

Previous to my connection with this Association I possessed a strong self-will, which made me sometimes choose to suffer any affliction, even death, rather than yield my will to God. Since I became a member of this body I have submitted my will to the will of God, and have had generally a quiet, peaceful state of mind. I find I have new and enlarged views of God, and have learned to think less of myself, and more of the members of Christ's body.

MARY E. CRAGIN.

I have made the most improvement in overcoming effeminacy and false modesty, which was inherent in my nature, and fostered by education. My connection with this body has awakened a general interest in the family of God, which makes it easy and delightful to be spent in their service. I find myself gaining in courage and true independence of character. /44/

LEONARD F. DUNN.

I have been brought, through the influence of this Association, from a restless, discontented state of mind, to a state of peace and quiet. I am conscious of a growing desire for improvement and growth in grace, and an increasing attachment to this body.

FIDELIA A. DUNN.

Since joining this Association, I have surrendered my will to Jesus Christ, and am now in possession of that peace and happiness which this world can neither give nor take away. I have witnessed the same work in others here.

ERASTUS H. HAMILTON.

In early life I was under the influence of a rigid, overbearing will, and often thought I would be careful not to acquire such a character myself. But I found as I grew up to manhood, that I possessed this same characteristic, and often waged fruitless war with it. Since becoming a member of this Association, I am sensible, by the judgment of others and by my own, of having overcome it in a good degree. I am thankful to God for the deep *heart-education* I have received through the community school, and feel that it is sufficient pay for all that I have been called to do.

SUSAN C. HAMILTON.

Since my connection with this Association I have gained an ambition and courage to conquer my faults. I was formerly discouraged when they were pointed out to me, and excused myself on account of my organization. I have learned that my whole nature must be in subordination to the will of God, and have acquired patience in suffering, and a confidence in God that he will work in me, until all that is discordant with the spirit of truth, is destroyed.

ELEAZER L. HATCH.

I find myself improving in confidence toward God and man. I had but little trust in either when I came here, which made me suspicious and jealous; and nothing but the mild, melting love of God could have overcome my distrust. I find that I am seeking a more permanent spiritual basis, and have a desire to become identified with Christ.

FANNY M. LEONARD.

During the six months I have spent here, I have sensibly improved in practically valuing the cultivation of the heart and intellect above every thing else. I have become more spiritual and reflective, and give less attention to outward things which formerly caused distraction. I have also learned to wait on God for inspiration, and have gained a courageous spirit for improvement.

JOHN H. NOYES.

I am sensible of a great enlargement and improvement of my philoprogenitiveness, by which I do not mean particularly my love of children, but my motherly feeling toward believers. I am learning more rapidly than ever before, to sympathize with Paul in those feelings of family affection, which gush forth so abundantly toward the church in all his epistles. Perhaps my spirit has borrowed of the mothers (who have been exercised so much about their children) some of their superfluous philoprogenitiveness. At all events I have come into sympathy with some of their feelings which I am very much pleased with. I find in my heart an unspeakable yearning for the improvement and happiness of every member of this Association, which gives me a clear insight into the feelings which make mothers so anxious to be sure that their little ones have warm clothing and good accommodations. I am not able to shed many tears yet, (which /45/ has always been a great deficiency in my character,) but I feel occasionally favorable symptoms in this respect, and hope under present influences to make ere long all desirable attainments of tenderness.

HARRIET A. NOYES.

Since I came to Oneida I have been cured of the *hypo* [hypochondria]. My spirit has grown strong and courageous. I was formerly very impressible to evil influences; now my spirit is open to good. For years I had an evil eye, that looked on the dark side of every thing, and transformed good into evil. During the past summer, I have been learning to gather good from my circumstances and the evils which surround me. I am not discouraged, as formerly, when my faults are presented to me, but am willing to learn by my mistakes.

SEWALL NEWHOUSE.

Since I have been here, I have learned to be sober-minded. I have found that trifling conversation produces barrenness, and pray that I may henceforth walk soberly and meekly before God and man.

SOPHIA NASH.

Since I came here I have been led to study my own character, and found much that was contrary to the spirit of heaven. Among other things, bashfulness had troubled me. I have been brought to see that it arises from selfishness and egotism. I have learned some lessons in patience and contentment, and am much happier than ever before.

CHARLES OLDS.

Since I came here, my ambition and desire for improvement has increased. My heart is drawn out into sympathy with all the movements of the Association.

HENRY J. SEYMOUR.

I see a very marked increase of strength in my moral and spiritual nature, arising from my connection with this body. One fault which caused me much trouble, was a dreamy imagination, which made me prone to build air-castles, abstracting my mind from every-day affairs. Since my connection with this Association, I find by practical experience, that my imaginings were not after all so visionary, but God is able and willing to do abundantly above all we can ask or think. The effect of community life has been to make my character more active and practical. So far as I can judge, I can say that the passion of amativeness has been brought into complete subjection to the will of God. Taking my character as a whole, I am entirely satisfied that there has been a miraculous change in it for the better since I came here; and am equally well satisfied that this change will go on with increasing rapidity, until all evil is cast out of my spirit and body, and I shall arise into the purity of the resurrection, and be fit society for the primitive church.

TRYPHENA SEYMOUR.

The spirit of Christ which reigns in this Association has given me peace, and a rejoicing, grateful heart. It has been like a refining fire to my whole character. Hidden selfishness has been brought to light and destroyed. I have learned not to seek my own pleasure, but to glorify God in all things. In the place of a discontented spirit which repined at God's dealings with me, I have found one that says 'Thy will be done.'

HARRIET H. SKINNER.

I think I have made a decided improvement in a meek and quiet spirit, since my connection with this Association. I am getting free from the propensity to self reference, and comparison of myself with others—and learning to think soberly /46/ of myself. My capacity of enjoyment is much increased. I am learning to have more and more confidence in the instincts of the law within my heart and the direct guidance of the Spirit, and depend less upon outward instruction.

HIAL M. WATERS.

The change in my character since joining this Association has been general rather than specific. I have been conscious of a steady and genuine improvement. Numerous secret springs of evil have been discovered, which I supposed did not exist. Selfishness has been uprooted, self-will broken, excessive personal feelings overcome, and isolated habits have given place to the habits of Association; and I am fully convinced that no person can remain under the influence of this community without a favorable change of character.

LEANDER WORDEN.

Before joining this body I had a suspicious spirit towards Mr. Noyes, but since I came here I am constrained to say, (as far as I am capable of judging,) that he is led by the spirit of God. I have now perfect confidence in him. I believe God has chosen him and prepared him to lead his people out of bondage into the glorious liberty of the children of God. My confidence has also increased toward all the members of the community, and it is perfectly manifest to me that this people delight to bear one another's burdens.

KEZIAH WORDEN.

Since my connection with this community, I have learned to trust God with regard to the body, of which I have formerly been over-careful. I have been delivered from a complaining spirit that I had, because I was not more intellectual. I feel conscious that the Spirit of truth is searching my heart and inspiring my mind, and teaching me to walk in the Spirit at all times.

QUESTION II.—What has been the special effect of the system of criticism
practised by this Association, upon your character?

ANSWERS.

JONATHAN BURT.

The effect upon me, of the system of criticism practised in this body, has been to bring my mind to decided action, and give me power to expel defects which had long been manifest to myself, but which were too strong for me. It has produced a general refining influence upon my character, by begetting in me a spirit of meekness and humility.

LORINDA BURT.

Criticism has been a stimulant to action with me. It has caused me to search and find the defects in my character, and to take Christ as a Savior from them. It has drawn me nearer to God. My prayer is that I may overcome all defects, and be adorned with a meek and quiet spirit.

SARAH A. BURNHAM.

We read that 'evil men understand not judgment.' I am satisfied that the criticism which I have received was a just one, and that those who applied it were inspired and guided by a spirit of love and faithfulness. The effect has been to increase my desire for a meek and quiet spirit, and for improvement in all that is excellent. /47/

SARAH A. BRADLEY.

When our plan of criticism was first proposed, I held back, thinking it was serious business; but I made no real advance in faith and love till I submitted to the process. I have found that instead of diminishing love, it increased it very much. It seemed to remove a veil that had existed between me and those who criticised me. I feel very much indebted to those who have proved their love and patriotism by faithful criticism. I consider it a mark of love when a person tells me of my faults.

GEORGE CRAGIN.

The effect of criticism upon my character for more than a year past, has been of incalculable value. Circumstances transpired soon after my confession of Christ, that brought me, in a sense, to the judgment, revealing defects and evils in my character that caused me much suffering. After taking up my abode with Mr. Noyes, I invited him to be faithful to me in administering criticism whenever he saw that I needed it. He assured me that he should certainly be faithful to my spiritual welfare. And now, after an experience of nine years, I can bear witness to the untiring constancy of his love. And under God I am indebted more to faithful criticism for what I am, than to any other means. The testimony of scripture on this subject harmonizes perfectly with the principles and experience of this Association:—'Rebuke a wise man and he will love thee.' 'If ye endure chastening, God dealeth with you as with sons.'

MARY E. CRAGIN.

I am much indebted to criticism for improvement of character, and find that I love those best who have been the most faithful to me. I account it one of the greatest means of grace that we have among us. I admire God's wisdom, manifested in first knitting us together, and then putting on the strain of judgement. From what I see of its effects upon character around me, I am constrained to prize it highly. I think it may be compared to the rain which softens and fertilizes the soil, preparing it to receive the good seed of truth.

ERASTUS H. HAMILTON.

Through the whole of my experience since embracing the doctrine of holiness, criticism, or the spirit of judgment has been upon me. And since my connection with this body, although I have not been subject to much personal criticism, yet there has been almost constantly a criticising spirit at work searching out and judging my most secret thoughts and motives. The effect has been to drive me to Christ—to hate and forsake my own life, seeing that it is full of all manner of evil. I see distinctly that the *spirit* of criticism has been a most prominent means of improving my character.

SUSAN C. HAMILTON.

The effect of criticism on me, has stirred up an ambition and energy for improvement, and increased my love and confidence in those I have received it from. And as I think faithful criticism and love go together, I would not forfeit the privilege of receiving it for any consideration.

FANNY M. LEONARD.

I think criticism one of the best means to improve character. Its effect on me has been to cause me to feel thankful that I have been placed in such a school, where I could have my most subtle faults searched out and *told me in love,* and that too by those I love and have perfect confidence in—for we cannot see our own faults, so well as others can see them for us. I am satisfied that such a state of things could not exist among unbelievers, without causing hard feelings, while here it tends to produce love and good fruits. /48/

HARRIET A. NOYES.

About three years after I received the doctrine of holiness, the spirit of judgment commenced its purifying influence on my character. Although I had light to discern my faults, and a disposition to be rid of them, yet for years I had not strength of myself to cast off evil, but depended upon the help of others.—For a long time I never gained any decided victory without a severe criticism from J. H. Noyes. After I had become fully satisfied of its beneficial effects I used to request him to criticise me. For a year past the revelation of my faults has been accompanied or followed by the resurrection power in myself. The effect of the late system of criticism on me, has been to strengthen my general confidence in God, and to confirm my belief that he favors this method of education.

JOHN L. SKINNER.

The effect of the practice of criticising character, which was begun in Putney, and which has been adopted by the Association at Oneida, has been, so far as I can judge from my own experience and observation, very salutary and improving. However painful at the time, we have seen it yielding the peaceable fruits of righteousness to them who have been exercised thereby. I am persuaded that the spirit of wisdom and of judgment has been given of God for this work, and also that it has been performed in the spirit of love. The secrets of many hearts have thus been revealed. Self-examination has been produced among believers, and godly sorrow for faults has wrought a clearing of themselves from those things that were offensive. I am confident moreover, that instead of producing enmity and grudging, the criticisms that have been performed have increased the love and confidence of the members towards each other.

REPORT OF THE CRITICISING COMMITTEE.

We think that the benefits resulting from the communications between the committee and the Association, have been highly *reciprocal*. The study of character has been a looking-glass to the committee, by which they have received considerable criticism gratis; and at the same time they have been edified and comforted by the faith and goodness abundantly manifest. They have prized their position more particularly for the opportunity it gave them to improve their acquaintance with all the members. If they have speculated on the outside with the eye of criticism, within, heart has met heart.

There were three particulars suggested to us in the beginning that we should bear in mind as prominent faults of the Association. 1st, a want of repose,—restlessness; 2d, the spirit of levity—want of earnestness; 3d, a contrary spirit.

We found that one or other of these faults was constitutional in almost every member; they were observable in the manner of receiving criticism. Some appeared to have over anxiety for criticism—a little impatient of the tide of improvement. In others there was a slight disposition to lightness, and unprofitable talk about the subject. Our conversation with some seemed to open the door for the spirit of judgment from God, while the active presence of this spirit in others forestalled much criticism.

We think that the *spirit* of judgment is fast superceding the use of external discipline. A surprising change is observable in respect to *sensitiveness* since the system was commenced in Putney. I think that J. H. N. has found what he used to wish for—a people who will bear criticism.

Among other things, our observations convinced us that the marriage state is a *school of bad manners*—just the reverse of courtship, which it is well understood is a school of good manners. Lovers are assiduous to make themselves attractive, /49/ but after marriage they fall into a neglect of the little courtesies and attention which adorn social intercourse, and their habits between themselves vitiate their manners in general.

QUESTION III.—What has been the effect of the Social Theory of
this Association, upon your character?

ANSWERS.

JOHN ABBOTT.

The doctrine of free love as advocated by Mr. Noyes, is a subject that my mind has dwelt upon and investigated for a number of years. I had become fully satisfied before I joined this Association, that the time would come when the institutions of the world would give place to the direct government of God;— when exclusiveness and selfishness in respect to marriage would not exist. The conclusions I have come to on that subject, have done much to break up the spirit of legality and selfishness in me, and to turn my thoughts to an acquaintance with the laws of God, not only on that subject but on all others. I am sure that the free-love theory has had a great effect in bringing me into love and union with God, and all the family of God, and to cause me to seek to improve my character and make myself attractive. I think our social theory is the cross of Christ, to separate us from the world and from all false fellowships.

LAURA A. ABBOTT.

The effect of our social theory upon my character, has been to enlarge my heart towards God and his children, and to root out selfishness. I feel that it has given me that love which seeketh not her own; and that it is fast restoring me to the vigor of youth.

JONATHAN BURT.

The effect upon my character, of our social theory, as taught by Mr. Noyes in his Bible Argument, has been—1st, to bring to light deep-rooted and subtle traits of selfishness, previously unthought of by myself. 2d, It has brought to light an unsanctified state of my amative passions, discovering to me the true nature of the spirit of lust which worketh to envy, and is ungovernable and restless in its character. 3d. It has revived in my spirit a new and energetic feeling of loathing toward the spirit of selfishness in all its forms. 4th. It has proved to me more effectually than I ever realized before, the impotency of human energy to overcome the above evils. 5th. It has led me to seek and expect the inspiration of God to control the action of the passions and members of my body. 6th. Facts have proved to be in harmony with my faith—Christ has in an enlarged sense manifested himself my life, wisdom, righteousness and strength.

SARAH A. BRADLEY.

If I had no evidence of the truth of the doctrines presented in the Bible Argument, but the change they have produced in my character, I should know they were of God. 'A corrupt tree cannot bring forth good fruit.' Previous to my knowledge of these doctrines, false modesty found a faithful representative in me; but I have turned traitor and mean to do all in my power to annihilate it, and have true modesty take its place. I used to make a distinction between brotherly love and the love which I had for my husband; but I was brought to see that there was but one kind of love in the kingdom of God. I have found that true /50/ love is a great stimulus to improvement. Free love has brought to light defects in my spiritual character which nothing else could—idolatry, exclusiveness, and various other evils. Although the process of destroying selfishness has been an extremely painful one, I am very thankful for the experience I have had. It has brought me very near to God, and I now feel an interest in the happiness of all. I have learned that love is the gift of God.

HENRY W. BURNHAM.

The theory of sexual morality adopted by this Association, while it allows liberty which in the world would lead to licentiousness degrading to both soul and body, here produces the opposite effects; i.e. it invigorates with *life*, soul and body, and refines and exalts the character generally. It is calculated to abolish selfishness in its most subtle and deep-rooted forms, and practically adapted to fulfil the prayer of Christ in respect to the unity of the church, and thus introduce her gradually into the glories of the resurrection. My chief reason for believing this is because its development is invariably attended by the manifest judgment of God.

ABBY S. BURNHAM.

The effect that free love has had upon my character, has been to raise me from a state of exclusiveness and idolatry, to a greater enlargement of heart, and freedom of communication with God and this body. Selfishness is being purged out, and its place supplied with the pure love of God. I feel that I am not my own, but am bought with a price, therefore I am to glorify God with my body and spirit which are his. I see more clearly than ever before the beauty of Christ's prayer, that we all may be *one,* even as he and the Father are one.

SARAH A. BURNHAM.

The social theory, as advocated by Mr. Noyes and this Association, and sustained by the Bible, has had a tendency to enlighten my understanding, and to try, enlarge and purify my heart.

GEORGE CRAGIN.

The social theory of this community is, and has been from the first, associated in my mind with the end of this world, and the beginning of the kingdom of heaven upon earth. The evidence of its truth is as *firmly rooted* and *grounded* in my heart and mind as the gospel of salvation from sin; and my confidence therefore cannot be destroyed in one, without destroying it in the other. Of its effects upon my character I could say much. But in brief, I can say it has greatly enlarged my heart by purging it from exclusiveness—it has tamed and civilized my feelings, purified my thoughts, and elevated into the presence of God and heaven the strongest passion in the social department of my nature. I regard the 'Bible Argument,' so called, as the *social gospel,* second only to the gospel of salvation from sin, and destined to repair the second breach in the fall.

MARY E. CRAGIN.

I think the development of the social theory most favorable to the formation of character. It brings out the hidden things of the heart as nothing else could, by exciting the stronger passions of our nature, and bringing them out where they can be purified. Love without law, yet under the control of the Spirit of God, is a great beautifier of character in every respect, and puts the gilding on life. It is the manifestation of the resurrection power—revivifying soul and body. The best result in my own experience has been, that it has brought me into fellowship and acquaintance with the Father and the Son, more than any thing else ever did—and thereby I know that the doctrine is of God. /51/

ERASTUS H. HAMILTON.

The social theory brought out by Mr. Noyes investigates the strongest passion of humanity—one that by common consent is considered unapproachable—and disposes of the peculiar relations and restraints which surround this passion of amativeness, and which by the world are considered most sacred, in such a manner that the theory must of necessity stand or fall by its *results.* Its practical application to me, with the Spirit of truth which has accompanied it, has had an unmistakably healthy influence through my whole character. It has delivered me from the bondage of an insubordinate amativeness, which has been the torment of my life. It has brought me into a positive purity of feeling, that I am confident could come from no source but God. It has brought me near to God, increased life, been a most active means in causing me to hate my own life and in crucifying selfishness. The effect it has had upon the relation with my wife, has been directly opposite to what the world would expect to be its legitimate results; and for its fruits on this one relation alone, I should feel willing to give my decided testimony of approval.

SUSAN C. HAMILTON.

Since I have become acquainted with the social theory, it has had the effect of destroying selfishness, shame, and false modesty. It has also refined, strengthened, and increased my *respect* for love; and I look upon amativeness not as a low, sensual passion, but (under the influence of God's Spirit) as holy and noble. It has also taught me that there is no enjoyment in love, only when God takes the lead, and that the only way to perpetuate love is to walk in the spirit and learn to wait on him for it. Therefore I think our theory is the greatest safeguard against sensuality.

SYLVIA HAMILTON.

I feel that the social theory is calculated to enlarge the heart and refine the feelings on the one hand, while on the other it brings out selfishness, which will lead us to see that we need the sanctifying influences of God's spirit to cleanse us from it, and from all unrighteousness.

ELEAZER L. HATCH.

Those who are experimentally acquainted with the associate life and principles, need no other proof that it originated in the mind of God. It expands and elevates the heart, roots out and destroys selfishness in its various forms—destroys isolation—unlocks a fountain in the soul unknown before, and leads us to the boundless ocean of God's love.

HANNAH W. HATCH.

When Mr. Noyes' social theory was first presented to me, I was unwilling to believe it, but was soon brought to feel the force of that truth, 'except a man forsake all that he hath, he cannot be my disciple.' I now feel that I have sufficient reason to believe it, from the tendency it has had to disclose and root out selfishness, from which springs jealousy, exclusiveness, &c., and to supply its place with the free, eternal love of God.

STEPHEN R. LEONARD.

The effect of our social theory upon me has been, to greatly quicken my energy for self-improvement and for every good work. It has brought me into more perfect sympathy with the designs of God, and has given force and direction to my whole character. It has opened the fountain of my heart, and increased its capabilities of loving a hundred-fold. It has tried and strengthened my faith, and given me a more vivid consciousness of God's approbation. The /52/ spiritual wisdom and skill displayed in the production of the document called the 'Bible Argument,' is conclusive evidence to me that the writer is in communication with the same God that dictated the Bible. I regard that document as the second volume of the New Testament.

FANNY M. LEONARD.

The effect of the social theory is like fire which purifies and refines. Its effect on my character has been an enlargement of the heart and softening of the spirit. It destroys envyings and jealousies, and draws us out from an isolated egotistical state, into the sunshine of God's free and eternal love—that love which envieth not and seeketh not its own.

JOHN LEONARD.

The effect which the social theory has had upon me, has been, firstly, to develop the selfishness that was in my heart; and secondly, to sever me from the world and its sympathies on that subject—placing my selfishness upon the cross to die, enabling me to rejoice in the good of the whole, and to appreciate the worth of bare salvation.

SEYMOUR W. NASH.

Our social theory is well worthy of its wise and benevolent author, God. A system so perfectly congenial to man's nature could never have originated from any other source. Its first effect on me was the crucifixion of exclusiveness in its strong hold, viz. the marriage relation. Second, a sense of permanent unity with the church of God, of which I had never felt the like before. Third, an enlargement of my whole spiritual nature, more enlarged views of the kingdom of God, its laws and regulations, and a greater clearness of perception and understanding, and flexibility of spirit.

HARRIET A. NOYES.

Our social theory has been like a fire to me bringing to light and destroying selfishness. It has enlarged my heart, and developed in it love that *thinketh no evil, envieth not,* and *seeketh not its own.* It has increased my happiness, my justification, and my acquaintance with God. It is the natural sequence of salvation from sin, and so intimately connected with it, that I have felt if I gave up one, I must give up the other; and God's providence has favored it so manifestly, that if I doubted its truth I must doubt the existence of God.

TRYPHENA SEYMOUR.

When the social principles of this Association were presented to me, I asked, Am I not a Christian unless I adopt these sentiments? The answer in my heart was, 'Unless you yield yourself unreservedly to the care and teaching of Christ, without dictating what shall be the ordinances and institutions of his kingdom, you cannot be saved;' and not till I ceased caviling and heeded the words of Gamaliel—'If this doctrine or this work be of men, it will come to nought,' &c., did I find peace. I then found rest in believing that 'he that doeth the will of God shall know of the doctrine.' I saw that the church of Christ must have a 'stumbling-block and rock of offense' to the world. I am confident these principles, controlled and guided by the Spirit of God, will purge selfishness from the world, and restore man to the original purity and innocence of the garden of Eden. Their effect on me has been to enlarge my heart, give me clearer ideas of God and truth, and to merge selfish interests in the desire for the fulfillment of Christ's prayer for his disciples, that they 'all may be one.'

JOHN L. SKINNER.

The social theory held by this Association, as explained in Mr. Noyes' Bible Argument, has greatly enlarged my heart and mind; and the views which it presents /53/ of the relations of the sexes, and of the character and condition of love in the heavenly state, have done much to break up in me the power of the spirit of legality and routine, and to make room for and strengthen the spirit of universal unity with the members of Christ's body—that unity which will be the fulfillment of his prayer for his followers, 'that they all may be one, even as he and his Father are one.'

HARRIET H. SKINNER.

I think that the *present* results of our social theory give lively promise of all that is described in the following passage from the article in the Berean, headed Condensation of Life:—"By the unity of life to which Christ calls believers, the good elements of an innumerable multitude of characters will be condensed into one, and the perfection of the compound will be transfused through every individual. It is easy to see that the operation will develope magnificent treasures of righteousness and beauty. The spiritual atmosphere in which individuals will grow and ripen, when the life and love of God and of the millions of the human race shall be concentrated in one glowing sphere, will be as different from that of the present order of things, as summer is from winter, or as the years of Palestine are from those of Greenland. 'The desert shall rejoice and blossom as the rose.' Education in its highest and most valuable form, will be a natural growth. As plants, which in northern regions require hot-beds and tedious cultivation, under the sun of the tropics grow spontaneously, so intellectual, moral and physical life, under the sunshine of divine and human love, will spring up with a rapidity, and bring forth fruit in an abundance which will put to shame the tillage of all our present schools for mind and body. I think we are realizing the splendid idea of *vital society* or organic union. I conceive of common society as vapid and lifeless. It is like inorganic matter, while ours is like animate nature, in which there is a heart-spring, circulation, growth and infinite change. I think that community of the affections gives play to all the noble and generous sentiments— brings out all the qualities of charity; while marriage-exclusiveness covers selfishness and littleness which we should despise in respect to other things. I should withhold honor where honor is due, if I did not say that free love had improved my character very much.

KEZIAH WORDEN.

With regard to the social theory, I can say in the spirit of truth and soberness, that I have seen great beauty and celestial purity in it, and I am sure that nothing but omnipotence could create such blissful, soul expanding and mind-elevating realities. That they were created for man's happiness in a state of purity I have no doubt. As we lost that state in Adam, I believe we shall find it in Christ.

QUESTION IV.—What has been the effect of the principles of
this Association upon your industrial character?

ANSWERS.

LAURA A. ABBOTT.

In regard to industry, it has been delightful to me to see the contrast in my feelings. When I was in the world, I was working for myself, and selfish purposes,
and was constantly in the 7th of Romans. I am happy to say that I can perform
twice as much work here as I ever did in my own family, without tiring. Instead
of selfishness, I have the spirit and love of God to prompt me to labor for him
and his people. /54/

JONATHAN BURT.

Since my connection with this Association my ambition for activity has greatly
increased. The impression constantly sustains me that I am working for those I
love as I love myself. To labor for the friends of God has a stimulus in it far exceeding anything I had previously known. The pleasant faces and buoyant spirits I see around me, have contributed to a large extent to remove the fatigue and
feeling of drudgery usually attendant upon what is called labor. I find that I can
endure more fatigue than formerly.

ABRAM L. BURT.

Since my connection with this body I have felt that I was at work for the interests of God's kingdom, which has given me an ambition for labor which I never
had before. It used to be very repulsive for me to do anything like *work;* but with
the motives I have before me now, I find a total change in my feelings, and am
willing to do all that is set before me.

HENRY W. BURNHAM.

The growing effect of Association upon my character in relation to the industrial department, so far as I can judge, has been to overcome a love of ease and a
desire of freedom from responsibility, and to establish habits of energy, promptitude and faithfulness, both mental and physical.

SARAH A. BURNHAM.

The effect of Association on me has been to increase the spirit of true industry
and activity, and to diminish worldliness and selfishness. I find my individual
interests are being swallowed up in the general interests of the body.

SARAH A. BRADLEY.

The experience I have had in Association in regard to labor has effected a very
favorable change in my character. Before living in Association I wanted to do
every thing alone, and was rather particular about what I did. I now find it much
pleasanter to work in large companies, and I can change from one kind of work
to another without any trouble. I take more pleasure and interest in work now
than when I lived by myself. I used to think if I had stronger motives for laboring I could enter into it with more enthusiasm. The idea that was brought out
in one of our meetings, that all we did was undermining the world's selfish system, is sufficient to inspire any one with courage.

JAMES L. BAKER.

Previous to my connection with this Association, I worked for money, but found labor up-hill work—the pain far outweighing the pleasure. I have now an infinitely higher motive to action in doing all that I do for the glory of God, and find work unattended with exhaustion. I love to labor for God and those whom he loves. I believe this motive will inspire a man or woman as no other motive can, with the spirit of industry.

GEORGE CRAGIN.

My own experience goes to prove that the motives to industry and activity of mind, as well as body, are a hundred-fold stronger in community life than they are in the world. I may say—by how much *truth, heaven,* and *heaven's love,* are greater, purer, and lovelier than *selfishness,* by so much are community life and motives preferable to isolated habits.

SYLVIA HAMILTON.

Association has not diminished my habits of industry and economy. My desire is to improve the talent that God has given me for the benefit of his church, and I wish to serve in the way that I can be the most useful. /55/

ERASTUS H. HAMILTON.

I feel disposed to be as active in business, if not more so, than when I was in the world. Business is now a part of my religion. My heart is in it. A vigor and elasticity of body and mind, a feeling of satisfaction in accomplishing, go with me in labor, which I never felt under the world's system. No matter what engages me, I feel that my calling is honorable. I am thankful that I am in circumstances where body and soul can work together and all things can be done unto the Lord. Objects high and noble as heaven rouse our ambition—the responsibility of our position excites us to industry, while love and attraction sweeten labor and make it sport.

ALBERT KINSLEY.

The effect of living in Association has been to make labor easy and pleasant. I am satisfied that the spirit of love and purity existing in this body is beneficial to health, and gives activity to labor. I find it is a powerful stimulus to labor to do it to the Lord and his church instead of self. I think this community a poor place for any one who wishes to indulge in a spirit of laziness.

STEPHEN R. LEONARD.

I have lived in Association for six years, and have found by abundant experience the stimulus to labor to be far greater and much more effectual than in the world. I have been a faithful servant to work in the world, but selfishness and the money-motive were not sufficient to keep me from getting entirely sick of the whole system. From the commencement of my associate life, the influences that make labor attractive and invigorating to soul and to body have been steadily increasing, until now I solemnly aver, that I would rather work hard almost night and day with such associates as surround me, than to return to the worldly system, and work for my 'roast beef and eight dollars per day.'

DANIEL P. NASH.

I have been acquainted with this Association from its beginning, and have seen with interest the effect it has had on individual character. I have frequently heard individuals say, 'I can perform twice as much work since I have lived in Association as I could while living in the world.' I have done more work the past year than in any year since I was 18 years old.

HARRIET A. NOYES.

I was educated in the most systematic method of working which worldly wisdom could invent. Rules, routine and economy, governed my business habits. The effect of living in Association at Putney, was to break up these habits, and the desire to have my own way. My love of order and economy became subordinate to the love of harmony with others of different tastes and habits. My house-work was placed secondary to the publishment of the truth and my own education. As long as I worked from the force of habit, I was distressed; but when my motive was changed to that of serving God's children, I worked comfortably. At Oneida my employment has chiefly been sport. I have taken pleasure in conquering difficulties—in doing things which once would have appeared impossible for me.

JOHN H. NOYES.

I am not very well qualified to judge by experience of the comparative merits of the two industrial systems, having never labored under the stimulus of the money-motive in my life. But I am satisfied from all my experience under God's training, and especially from what I have seen and felt during the last year, that perfect community of interests and perfect freedom in respect to labor, are not only compatible with, but essential to the best development of industrial energy and enterprise. /56/

HIAL M. WATERS

One prominent objection of the world against Association is, that it destroys the motive to labor, by removing the pressure of necessity; but my observation and experience in this body contradicts this assertion. I find that love, confidence and esteem, are a far stronger stimulus than money or necessity. The thought that we are laboring for those who are dear to us, inspires us with new energy, and makes work sport. Public sentiment in the body makes labor honorable; drones cannot live here. I think we present to the world a true system of attractive labor.

CHARLES OLDS.

As far as my experience goes, I can testify that the industrial system in this body is calculated to stimulate to greater ambition and love for labor, than the influence of selfishness and necessity. Love is the motive power here which incites me to labor, and it is a strong stimulus. I rejoice much that I am in a community where each one delights to do his neighbor good.

JAMES. W. PERKINS.

Since I became a member of this body, I have changed my motives for labor. I can labor for Jesus Christ in undermining the devil's kingdom with considerable zeal. I find the law of love makes it pleasant to me to serve others.

QUESTION V.—What has been the effect of the influences of
this Association upon your health?

ANSWERS.

JOHN ABBOTT.

Previous to my joining this Association I was very sensitive about the suffering
of the flesh—and found I had more life in it than I was aware of, which I discovered while undergoing a painful disease last summer and fall. I found my attention drawn away from exercising faith in God, and brought into sympathy with
my disease to an extent which rendered my spirit weak and powerless. By the help
of the Association, and Mr. Noyes' writings, I was enabled to turn my thoughts
from my disease to God, and refuse sympathy with the part afflicted. In this way
I got a healthy, joyful spirit, which held my flesh in a state of subjection and
quietness and enabled me to hold sweet communion with God, while my flesh
was suffering severely. I know that my life in the flesh has to a great extent been
crucified, and a foundation laid for true health of body.—I have a strong desire
for the full redemption of the body, which state I believe will be attained by following the spirit of this Association.

LAURA A. ABBOTT.

I have been for many years afflicted with sick-headache, but since my connection with this Association I have gained the victory over it, and my health has
much improved.

HENRY W. BURNHAM.

Previous to my connection with this Association, I labored under a disease of
the kidneys which unfitted me for labor, and which physicians' prescriptions had
failed to cure. Within two years this difficulty has been gradually leaving me, so
that now I consider myself a well man, physically able to do any thing; which
results I ascribe to the power of life received by communication with this Association. /57/

ABBY S. BURNHAM.

I have been troubled with sick headache as often as once in two or three weeks
ever since my remembrance until since my connection with this Association.
Since that union was formed I have gained an important victory over it.

JONATHAN BURT.

During the last year I have experienced a steady and rapid improvement of health,
and strength of body—so that at present I feel, to a large extent, the vigor of my
youth. The change from an enfeebled condition of body, to my present condition, I attribute to the spiritual influences with which I am surrounded.

HORACE BURT.

I think living in Association has been beneficial to my health. From a state of
trouble and anxiety of mind, I have been brought to a state of peace;—from a
wandering, restless and unsettled state, to a steady state of composure and rest.
My bodily health is also much improved.

GEORGE CRAGIN.

The effect of Association upon my health has been rather progressive than sudden. Previous to my connection with the Putney Association my health was miserable. As a last resort, before making a confession of Christ, I adopted what was called the 'Graham system,' and for two years walked in all the ordinances of Grahamism blameless. But notwithstanding my strict attention to the subject of eating and drinking, the gospel found me a cadaverous looking object. From that time to the present, I have been gradually overcoming physical weakness. If feelings are allowed to testify in this case, I should say that I am ten years younger than I was nine years ago, when I found salvation from sin. One of the greatest means employed in gaining victories over disease, has been a firm, unwavering *faith* in Christ as the physician of the body as well as the soul; and I may add, the next best means is, a steady purpose to attend to whatever the interests of Christ's kingdom demand, without excusing myself on the ground of ill health.

MARY E. CRAGIN.

Since I joined the Oneida Association I have gained in strength and vigor, and found myself able to 'endure hardness.' I find the resurrection power steadily but surely triumphant over the weakness of the flesh. I find the promise verified in my case from time to time, that 'my youth shall be renewed like the eagles', and fully believe the atmosphere of Association to be the best of all safeguards against disease and death.

ERASTUS H. HAMILTON.

Since I joined this Association I am sensible of possessing more vigor, and freedom from former ailments and lassitude. I was formerly subject to asthma, but since I became identified with the doctrine of Association at Genoa in 1847, have been almost entirely free from it. I am sensible that there is a life amongst us which is steadily driving disease before it.

SUSAN C. HAMILTON.

When I first Joined the Association I was not far from being an invalid. I had a tedious fit of sickness which ended in ague and fever, and left me with an inflammation of the liver which was considered chronic. I almost despaired at times of being delivered from a pain in my side, and general weakness. But now my health is good; the swelling in my side has disappeared, and I sometimes feel as though I had been raised from the dead; and I am satisfied that it is the power of God's life in this Association that has done it. /58/

ELEAZER L. HATCH.

Since my connection with the Association there has been a very decided improvement in my health. For some years previous I suffered with weak lungs, accompanied with cough and general debility, which made me unfit to labor more than two thirds of the time. I had some hesitation in coming here on that account, but I found an atmosphere here that seemed to infuse new life and vigor into my system, rendering recourse to the 'sovereign balms' I formerly used quite unnecessary. I find that the buoyancy which I feel is not so much owing to the circumstances that surround me as to the spirit and power of God working from the inner man outward.

HANNAH W. HATCH.

Since 1840 I have been afflicted with various diseases, and resorted to medicines, but found nothing which affected a permanent cure. After I became interested in the doctrine of holiness, my mind was turned towards Christ as my physician; but I had not sufficient faith to throw myself upon him as the Savior of the body, until I became acquainted with, and joined this Association. Since that time I have perceived a gradual restoration to health and strength which I have not enjoyed for ten years. I cannot attribute this recovery to any thing but the power of God manifest in this body.

FANNY M. LEONARD.

Since my connection with this Association in July, my health has materially improved. Previous to my coming here my health was poor, but ever since my arrival the healthy spiritual atmosphere with which I am surrounded has had a beneficial effect upon me. I attribute my recovery to the condensation of life in the Association.

JOHN H. NOYES.

The contentions with opposers which attended the beginning of the Association last winter, renewed the throat disease which disabled me some years ago; and the cares and labors of the spring and summer gradually reduced my general health, till at length in the latter part of the fall I found it necessary to stop preaching and throw off care. No very decided change for the better ensued till the early part of December, when I was blessed for two or three days with a most painful boil in the corner of my mouth, attended with a baptism of hell-fire on my whole body. This interesting season was given up to meditation on the principles of resurrection-health, to prayer and to fasting, i.e. unavoidable abstinence not only from food, but from all conceivable creature comforts. The result was a strong and effectual reaction of my spirit against the disorders of my body, which impelled me to stir up the whole Association against disease and death, and so brought on a revolution which has restored me to more than my former strength of life and lungs. So I have had a victory at Oneida quite similar to that which I had at Putney in the fall of '46. The enthusiasm and love generated by Association, has thus in my case twice baffled the approaches of consumption; and I expect with more confidence than ever, that these mighty influences will ere long bring forth the life-cholera, before whose march disease shall vanish and death shall die.

HARRIET A. NOYES.

Association has been the means of increasing the vigor of my life wonderfully. It manifests itself to me by endurance of active exercise without fatigue, as well as in repulsing disease. I have been growing young for two or three years, and am looking for death to be swallowed up of life. /59/

SARAH B. NASH.

Since I came into sympathy with this Association, I have been conscious of a gradual yet constant improvement of my health, which before was very feeble.

From my childhood I have been subject to severe attacks of headache, but I have gained the ascendancy over it.

QUESTION VI.—What evidence have you that the power and kingdom of God are present in this Association?

ANSWERS.

JOHN ABBOTT.

The strongest proof to me that God is at the head of this Association, is an *internal* evidence—the Spirit of God bearing witness in my spirit, that we are built on the foundation of Christ and the apostles. The fruits of the Association are such as might be expected according to the testimony of all good men; namely, *faith, confidence, love* and *harmony* with each other, which cannot be found in any other institution. The success that has attended all our movements in temporal things, and the power which brings all who come among us to acknowledge Christ as their Savior, is proof that God is with us. The improvement of character, the intelligence, honesty and sincerity of the members composing this community, are evidence to me that God would not suffer us to be deceived.

JANE ABBOTT.

My belief that the power of God is with this community, arises from seeing his goodness in giving them the victory in all their movements, and from the *joy* and *peace* I have had since I confessed Christ.

JONATHAN BURT.

One of the standing evidences that the power of God is here, is seen in the clearness and rationality with which its members perceive *truth,* going beyond any thing which has appeared since the days of the primitive church. Connected with this, is the truth that the members of this body are spiritual plants which for years past have been enlarging and putting forth leaves, answering to the sayings of Christ concerning his Second Coming,—'When ye shall see all these things, know that summer is nigh.' We also have a unity of interests in all respects, distributing justice to all alike by the power of love, without any of the rules of law. There is a spirit here which repels disease without the aid of medicine. The old testify that they are growing younger; and the spirit of peace reigns. Our enemies are in many instances converted into friends, by the power which reigns among us.

JAMES L. BAKER.

The evidences of God's power are manifest among us in saving from sin, and perfecting the whole character. I have seen too much of God's power in healing the sick and casting out devils, to doubt that many of the signs spoken of in Mark 16: 17, follow us. The fact too that so many can live together in peace and harmony, with different tastes and habits, is evidence that God is with us.

HENRY W. BURNHAM.

By comparing the spirit and purposes of this body with those of Christ and Paul in the primitive church, as exhibited in the New Testament, it will he seen that they harmonize;—that is to say, the preparatory process of discipline and /60/

deep judgment which this body is manifestly passing through, is in perfect keeping with God's method of dealing with his people in Bible times. The experience that has been brought out relative to the health of the body, and the actual, substantial improvement of the whole man, make it certain that God is amongst us, raising from the dead and purifying to himself a peculiar people.

SARAH A. BURNHAM.

I fully believe that God reigns here in the power of his judgment and resurrection. I am conscious of its effects upon my own heart and character. I have also seen changes in others that nothing else could effect. The faithfulness, love and unity manifest here—in short every move that is made—confirm me in the belief that the kingdom of God is being established in this world.

GEORGE CRAGIN.

The evidence to my own mind that this Association is God's work, is found in the *fact* that it is undergoing a process of refinement, through the operation of judgment and crucifixion of the old man, and a resurrection of the new. Another evidence, and a very manifest one, may be found in the harmony and correspondence between the whole tenor of scripture, bearing on the prophecies and promises of the final establishment of the kingdom of heaven on earth, and the principles and deeds upon which this Association is founded. The great central idea of the Bible, and that which overtops all others, is the unity of the church of Christ. The promise is, 'that in the fullness of times,' 'there will be a gathering together in one, all things in Christ, both which are in heaven and which are on earth, even in him.' This scripture, together with many parallel passages, harmonize perfectly with the leading features of this Association. The aspirations for unity with the primitive church—the ambition for improvement, and the miraculous transformation of character, in answer to the desires and prayers of the body, are facts that go to show very conclusively that all things on earth and in heaven are being gathered into one.

MARY E. CRAGIN.

I find internal evidence that the power of God is present here, from feeling its positive effects on my body and spirit. Many times I discover that God has used me to do his will, without my being aware of it at the time, taking possession of my desires and tastes and will, and bending them to his purposes. I see also the same results brought about in the Association generally—the same power producing subordination, zeal for improvement, an appreciation of the value of criticism, and a desire to do the will of God, which offers the flesh to death. I see private tastes in all things submitting themselves to the general interests—and selfishness giving place to love. The fact that unbelievers who come among us from time to time, find an influence which they cannot resist, is a strong proof to me that God is here. And last, though not least, the happy faces which I see all around me, bespeak the presence of the Spirit of God.

SARAH A. BRADLEY.

The fact that no evil or selfish spirit can enter here without being detected, proves to me that God is here. I have been astonished sometimes to see the power of God bring to light the hidden things of my heart. Natural defects of the most stubborn kind have been overcome, and I find myself in another world. What but the power of God could break such iron wills and subdue such unsanctified natures?

SOPHIA DUNN.

The evidences I have of the power of God in this Association, are satisfactory to myself beyond a doubt. When I became convinced that God had commenced /61/ his kingdom on earth, I felt that all I had belonged to him, to assist in establishing it. The providences of God in favoring the movements I made in joining this Association, were numerous, as well as the strength I had given me from God to endure hardships and the fires of persecution that came upon me. Since I came here, the conversion of my children, and the criticism I have received on my own character, are evidences of God's power in this body.

JULIA S. DUNN.

When I came here I was an infidel; and I feel that nothing but the power of God in this Association could have brought me to a confession of Christ.

LEONARD F. DUNN.

The question as to God's presence in this Association was settled in my mind before joining it, by the evidence I saw of the attachment of the members to each other—the good luck that attended the efforts of the Association, and the happiness of its members. Since joining, I have had no reason to change my mind, only that I have partaken in some degree, of the attachment, good luck and happiness of the Association, by giving up all into the hands of God. The nearer I get to God, the nearer I find myself to this body; which is a convincing proof to me 'that we are that happy people whose God is the Lord.'

ERASTUS H. HAMILTON.

A community school under the care of God, would produce the following fruits, namely:—'love joy, peace, long-suffering, goodness,' &c. That these fruits are being produced, and abound among us, is evident to me from my own experience and observation, and from abundant testimony relative to each other, and *personal testimony* such as was given in answer to the last question. We have had visitors from time to time who have testified without exception (unbelievers as well as believers) that we were a peaceful, harmonious, happy, family.

Righteousness rules here. This is an unmistakable fact, with every member. It seems to me that to the reflecting, intelligent mind, *seeing* and *believing* that such is our condition, is the best possible proof that we are indeed a people whose God is the Lord. The universal testimony of the world is, that man is a selfish being, and that the idea of living in community, is a perfect humbug. The whole history of the world coincides with this position. That *we* are an example right in the face of all this, can only be ascribed to the omnipotent power of God.

CHARLES L. HAMILTON.

I am satisfied that this Association is under the guidance of God, because none but God's people can live together in such peace and happiness. I know that I was not happy until I confessed Christ and became one with this body. And I know that selfish and worldly persons could not come here and mingle with this Association, any more than we can mix oil and water together.

LOIS F. KNOWLES.

There are many evidences manifest to my mind that God is with us. The following are some of them. 1st. The power that is daily manifested among us in sub-
duing self-will and bringing it into subjection to the power of truth. 'Is not my
word as a fire, saith the Lord, and like a hammer that breaketh the rock in pieces?'
2d. The power of love that is being developed among us. 'God is love, and he that
dwelleth in love, dwelleth in God and God in him.' 3d. The rapid change of character that is going on among us, in translating us from the kingdom of darkness
into the kingdom of God. Old things are passing away, and all things are becoming new. 4th. The change that has taken place in my own character, I am well
persuaded that nothing less than omnipotent power could effect. /62/

SARAH KINSLEY.

There are many evidences to me of the power of God in this Association.—Some
of them are these:—that selfishness cannot live here; that inspiration and good
luck mark all our movements; that 'charity which suffereth long and is kind,
envieth not,' &c., is manifested here. Another evidence is, that the commandments of God are not grievous to us, especially the one which requires us to 'love
one another.'

STEPHEN R. LEONARD.

My reasons in brief for believing that we are that happy people whose God is the
Lord, are—1st, The gospel we have received comes to us through one who has
manifestly (to me) approved himself as a *minister of God,* according to Paul's
standard in 2 Cor. 6: 4–10, viz: 'In much patience, in afflictions,' &c. 2d. I think
it is evident that our Association, as a body, is characterized by the same traits
described above. 3d. It is plain to see that the difference between 'the works of
the flesh' and the 'fruits of the spirit,' as specified in the 5th chapter of Galatians,
is just the distinction between our Association and the unbelieving world around
us. According to this standard we contrast with the world in the following particulars:—'Now the works of the flesh are manifest, which are these—adultery,
fornication, uncleanness, lasciviousness, idolatry, witchcraft, hatred, variance,
emulations, wrath, strife, seditions, heresies, envyings, murders, drunkenness,
revelings, and such like. But the fruit of the Spirit is *love, joy, peace, long-suffering, gentleness, goodness, faith, meekness, temperance:* against such there is no law.'
4th. Christ's test of discipleship will apply to this Association, but not to the world,
or to the religious sects about us:—'Hereby shall all men know that ye are my
disciples, *if ye have love one to another.'* 5th. The whole policy of our Association
from its commencement—at swords points as it has been with the policy of the
world on every question that has arisen—evinces by its success the presence of
wisdom and power that can be attributed to God only. 6th. The confessions, of
the Association as the representative of the kingdom of God on earth, and of its
leader as a minister of Christ, would, if they were not true, be blasphemy of the
most damnable kind, fitted to insure the speedy judgment of heaven upon us.
But instead of this, even unbelief is led to query whether God may not be with
us, and to exclaim—'Can a man [or an Association] that is a *sinner* do these
things?'

FANNY M. LEONARD.

It is very evident to me that God has been with us ever since the Association was first formed in Putney. The evidence I have had from time to time in my own experience for several years, and in the experience of others, has oftentimes served to convince me that we were the people of God, and that the eyes of the Lord were over us. The fruits of the Spirit are manifest among us. The harmony and oneness of spirit that prevail in this body, together with the judgment of character that is going on continually, is also conclusive evidence to me that God is with us.

SEYMOUR W. NASH

My first ground (and that upon which all others are based) for believing this to be a school under the care of God, is the testimony of God's Spirit within my own heart. The next ground is the universal diffusion and manifestation of pure unselfish love and unity through the body. Another is the uniform and marked manifestation of God's care over this body in managing its external matters generally. /63/

OTIS H. MILLER.

The evidence of God's presence and power in this Association, I think can be easily shown to all who have a single eye to the truth. No people have ever lived together before, for any great length of time, in entire community of interests, without law. The association of the Shakers is little more than joint stock of property and labor. They lock up the passions, and trust themselves to be governed, not by grace, but by walls, and rigid rules. Whereas here, the passions are unlocked, and reliance is placed on the Spirit of God and truth, to tame and civilize them. The success that we have met with is a proof to me that we are governed and led by inspiration. In my own case, I have found that selfishness and the manifold evils which the world engenders, have been brought to light.—I find I have now a more loving and peaceful heart, and am ready to do the will of God in all things; which I attribute to the power of God in this Association.

HARRIET A. NOYES.

I see evidences almost every day of the power of God working in this body. One is the spirit of judgment which is bringing to light the defects in the characters of all. The *strength* and *wisdom* by which these defects are overcome, I believe to be superhuman also. The *order* and *harmony* of this work of transforming character—the bearing one's experience has on another, the ability to *admonish* one another, and the *subordination* of one to another which is leavening the body, are proofs of God's power. The *unity* existing among us, I consider the work of God. And then the *strength of life to overcome disease,* which has been manifested here, I think is from God.

SARAH B. NASH.

There are many reasons to my mind for believing that the kingdom of God is set up here. Health and character are renewed—stubborn wills are broken—haughty looks are brought low, and confessions of Christ are made daily. These facts, together with the love and unity which I have felt with this body, all tend

to satisfy me that God is setting up his kingdom here. Nothing short of his power could keep so many hearts together.

SOPHIA NASH.

The evidences I think are numerous, that the power of God rules in this Association. Love seems to be the prevailing element. In my own case, I feel nothing
but the Spirit of God, which is manifest here, could have wrought so effectually
on my mind in turning me from the darkness which reigned within, to see the
light which gives great joy and peace. There is that here which is like a two-edged
sword; and it is a discerner of the thoughts and intents of the heart.

EVELIZA NEWHOUSE.

I can bear witness to the power of God in this Association, manifested in healing us from sickness, and in bringing hidden things to light. I have been conscious
of a refining process going on in my spirit ever since I became acquainted with
this body.

JAMES W. PERKINS.

In looking over the history of the world, its past and present condition, I should
say that the world is ripe for Association. There have been a great many attempts
made to form or organize society anew, which have nearly all failed. I believe that
this Association will stand and prosper, because I believe it is the work of God,
and that it is the stone spoken of by Daniel, which is destined to fill the whole
earth; for I discern a spirit here that prizes the truth and light more than any thing
else. /64/

JOHN L. SKINNER.

My principal reasons for believing that this Association is under the special care
and guidance of God, are these: 1st. All evidence I have (and it is very weighty
and convincing) in favor of the visible head of this Association, J. H. Noyes, as
the one chosen of God to develope in this age the primitive gospel of holiness,
and to bring in the 'dispensation of the fullness of times,' is so much evidence
that the Association, as it has been gathered chiefly by his influence, is under
God's special care. 2d. All the proofs I have had that the *Putney* Association was
gathered and guided by God, are so many proofs that *this* Association is also
under his care and guidance; since this Association includes that of Putney, or
in other words, the Putney Association is here re-established and enlarged. 3d.
The spiritual power which has been manifest in the Association, both here and
at Putney, producing great, beneficial changes of character, subjecting the will
to truth, overcoming selfishness, &c., is convincing proof to me that God is with
us, and reigning over us. I may here include the effects produced on my own
character, and the consciousness I have that God has led me, and that he has
established his reign in my heart. 4th. The manifest providential leadings and
interpositions of God, in bringing this Association together from various parts,
and in overcoming the obstacles and difficulties that stood in the way of our
progress, are strong proofs of God's care over us. 5th. My confidence in the up-
rightness of heart, the mental intelligence and love of truth, which characterize
the members of this body—a confidence founded on personal acquaintance—
greatly strengthens my persuasion that they are not following a delusion, but that

they are in truth, what they profess to be, the people of God, and that he therefore rules and guides them.

HARRIET H. SKINNER.

When I look *abroad* for evidence that this is a manifestation of the kingdom of
God, I see plain enough, as we have heard it said, that God has been at work this
1800 years, grading the road and laying the rails for just such a locomotive as he
is building here—the world is all ready for just such a religion, just such a social
theory, and just such external arrangements as we are carrying out.

Within the Association, the impossible combinations or paradoxes which exist here, always strike me as evidence of a superhuman power at the center, and
that power omnipotent, wise and holy. First, the combination of *purity* with *license;* of *good behavior* with *liberty.* We have modesty without shame—order
without rule—business character without worldliness. Second, the combination
of *love* with *faithful criticism.* Third, the combination of *spirituality* with the *pleasures of the senses,* or *religion* and *amusements.* We have going at the same time,
the most cruel mortification of the flesh, and the highest cultivation of all our
natural instincts and tastes. For instance—cutting off the hair is the repulsive
ceremonial by which a nun seals her renunciation of the world; but we mix it in
with what the world would consider a life of free pleasure.

In my own heart I know that the God of the Bible is here. The same Spirit is
here that inspired Paul and James and John to write their epistles. Their writings continually witness to the living word which is searching the thoughts and
intents of my heart.

HENRY J. SEYMOUR.

One great evidence to me that God is our teacher, and lawgiver and guide, is an
instinct similar to that which perceives warmth, strength and happiness by communion with some power separate from itself. If God is not with us, why do our
hearts burn within us when our thoughts and desires are directed towards /65/
him? Another evidence that God in an especial manner superintends this Association, is to be found in the peculiar system of education which is to be found
here. That system of education which the world adopts is defective, inasmuch
as it cultivates one part of our nature at the expense of the other. The fact that
our system provides for every department of our nature, is proof to me that God
is its founder.

TRYPHENA SEYMOUR.

My belief that God's peculiar care is over this Association is very strong, and is
founded on the evidence which I have that the fruits of the Spirit are being
brought forth here. 'A corrupt tree cannot bring forth good fruit.'

HIAL M. WATERS.

I joined this Association with the belief that it was the will of God that his children should combine their efforts for the establishment of a better state of things,
and that his blessing would follow; and I can say that I have not been disappointed. Universal success has attended our efforts. God has seemed to direct us in a
peculiar manner. We have not had to strain our credulity in order to believe that
superior wisdom is directing us. But the great reason that presents itself to my

mind, is, that we bear fruit in accordance with the requisition of the Bible. I see evidence that we are fulfilling the prayer of Christ, that we all may be one.

KEZIAH WORDEN.

I find abundant proof that God is the author of this Association, in the evidence I have that all who are under its influence are governed by love. All are willing to be taught; and we have the promise that the willing and obedient shall eat the good of the land.

CHARLES OLDS.

In looking at my past experience, and at the history of this Association from the commencement of its operations in Putney, I see many evidences of God's care and protection over them. One evidence that they are the people of God, is their reverence for God's word. He has promised to dwell with them who believe his word. Another evidence is—that no man or body of men could have preached or written, and practically carried out their principles, as this Association has done, unless they were in communication with the power of God.

ALBERT KINSLEY.

As to the evidence that the kingdom of God has come, and is with us, I think much may be found in the daily experience of the members of this Association. The power to overcome sickness, to conquer bad habits and evils both in mind and body, and the spirit of judgment to bring out and destroy evil—together with the confidence and harmony that prevails in every heart, are sufficient evidence to me that God is with us.

JANE A. KINSLEY.

There are many evidences to my mind that the power of God reigns in this Association. The rapid improvement in the character of its members, the love and union that prevails, and the witness of the Spirit in my own heart, are sufficient to keep me from ever doubting this truth.

JOHN H. NOYES.

I know that the same God who quickened my spirit and opened my understanding in 1831 and 1834, is still with me, and is with this Association. If I am asked how I know that God to be the true God? I answer, it is certainly the God of the Bible; for it has led me constantly and above all things to prize and /66/ search the Bible. It is certainly the God of all righteousness; for it has constrained me to seek for myself and proclaim to the world perfect holiness. It is certainly the God of all power; for it has given me a succession of victories over all principalities and powers. It is certainly the God of all consolation, love, and joy; for these have abounded to me from the beginning, and abound more and more in this Association. My heart and mind ask for no proof that the God of the Bible—the God of all righteousness, power, consolation, love, and joy, is the true God. I have seen the glorious works of this God in the affairs of this Association more distinctly than in all my past course. His manifest providences have encompassed us and buoyed us up in the midst of a raging ocean of enmities and uncertainties. His power over heart and character has been manifested in unsearchable abundance. The testimonies which have been given in concerning the physical and spiritual improvement of the members, constitute a huge pile of proof that

God is with us. He is manifestly leading us rapidly and victoriously into a position at war with the kingdoms of this world, and at the same time, those kingdoms are being dashed in pieces. I believe therefore that this Association is the germ of the kingdom of God;—and as the past foretells the future, I expect without wavering, the steady, irresistible advances of this Association to the conquest of the world.

THE END.

Index

GEORGE WALLINGFORD NOYES (1870–1941), a nephew of Oneida Community founder John Humphrey Noyes, was born as part of the community's "stirpiculture" or eugenics experiment and grew up during the final decade of the community's existence and its subsequent transition into a joint-stock company. He became a member of the board of directors, and then the treasurer and vice president, of the Oneida silverware company that developed after the community's breakup in 1881. Dedicated to the religious ideals of John Humphrey Noyes, George Wallingford Noyes spent the last decades of his life in semiretirement, preserving the documents and writing the history of the Oneida Community. He published two documentary volumes on John Humphrey Noyes: *The Religious Experience of John Humphrey Noyes, Founder of the Oneida Community* (1923) and *John Humphrey Noyes: The Putney Community* (1931).

LAWRENCE FOSTER is professor of American history at Georgia Institute of Technology in Atlanta and past president of the Communal Studies Association. A former Woodrow Wilson, Ford Foundation, National Endowment for the Humanities, and Fulbright fellow, he has written extensively on American social and religious history. His first book, *Religion and Sexuality* (1981), analyzes the introduction of new patterns of marriage, family life, and sex roles in the celibate Shaker, "free love" Oneida, and polygamous Mormon communities in nineteenth-century America. *Women, Family, and Utopia* (1991) further explores the impact these three alternative communal systems had on the lives of women and the implications such experimentation may have for reorganizing relations between the sexes today.

Composed in 10.5/13 Minion
with Minion display
by Jim Proefrock
at the University of Illinois Press
Designed by Paula Newcomb
Manufactured by Thomson-Shore, Inc.

University of Illinois Press
1325 South Oak Street
Champaign, IL 61820-6903
www.press.uillinois.edu